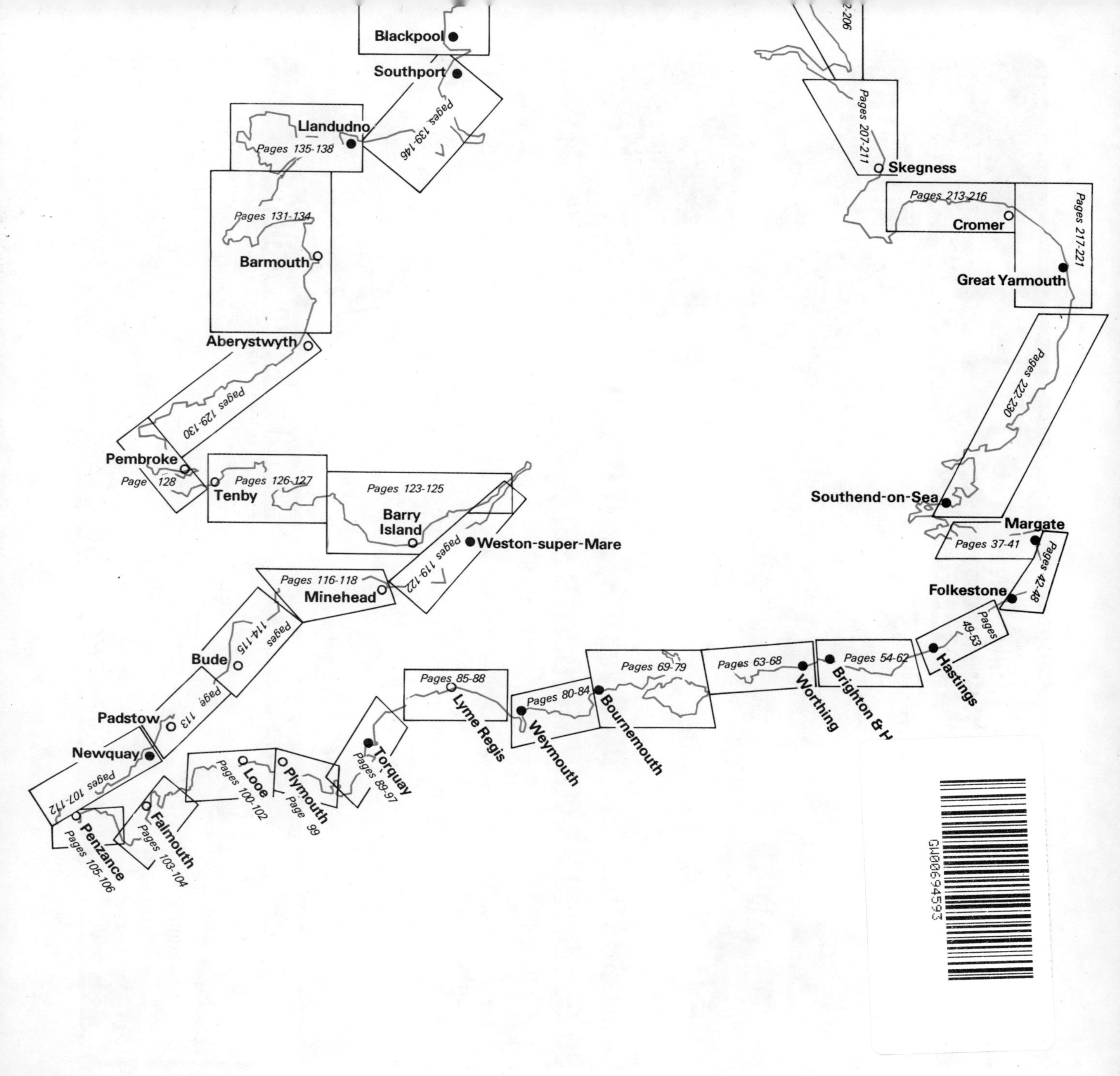
Blackpool
Southport
Pages 139-146
Llandudno
Pages 135-138
Pages 131-134
Barmouth
Aberystwyth
Pages 129-130
Pembroke
Page 128
Pages 126-127
Tenby
Pages 123-125
Barry
Island
Weston-super-Mare
Pages 119-122
Pages 116-118
Minehead
Pages
114-115
Bude
Page 113
Padstow
Newquay
Pages 107-112
Penzance
Pages 105-106
Falmouth
Pages 103-104
Looe
Pages 100-102
Plymouth
Page 99
Torquay
Pages 89-97
Pages 85-88
Lyme Regis
Pages 80-84
Weymouth
Bournemouth
Pages 69-79
Pages 63-68
Worthing
Pages 54-62
Pages
49-53
Hastings
Folkestone
Pages 42-48
Margate
Pages 37-41
Southend-on-Sea
Pages 222-230
Great Yarmouth
Pages 217-221
Cromer
Pages 213-216
Skegness
Pages 207-211

AROUND BRITAIN'S SEASIDE

Abbreviations and Symbols

- ★ Star-rated establishment
- ☆ White star
- ✕ Restaurant
- Ⓐ Approved hotel
- ♣ Country house hotel
- **GH** Guesthouse
- **SC** Self-catering establishment
- ☎ Telephone

Abréviations et symboles

- ★ Établissement à étoile(s)
- ☆ Étoile blanche
- ✕ Restaurant
- Ⓐ Hotel agrée
- ♣ Château-Hôtel
- **GH** Pension
- **SC** Établissement où cuisine non fournie
- ☎ Téléphone

Abkürzungen und Zeichen

- ★ Etablissement mit Stern(e)
- ☆ Weisser Stern
- ✕ Restaurant
- Ⓐ Genehmigtes Hotel
- ♣ Landhaushotel
- **GH** Pension
- **SC** Etablissement mit Selbstverpflegung
- ☎ Telefon

Afkortingen en tekens

- ★ Etablissement met ster(ren)
- ☆ Witte ster
- ✕ Restaurant
- Ⓐ Goedgekeurd Hotel
- ♣ Landelijk gesitueerd hotel
- **GH** Pension
- **SC** Etablissement met zelf-voorziening
- ☎ Telefoon

Key to hotel and restaurant classifications

Signs All AA-appointed hotels and classified restaurants are entitled to display the familiar yellow and black sign. Hotels are denoted by star classifications and restaurants by crossed knives and forks.

Hotels Hotels are classified by stars; each classification reflects the provision of facilities and services rather than comparative merit. The range of menus, service and hours of service are appropriate to the classification, although some hotels often satisfy several of the requirements of a classification higher than that awarded.

★ Good hotels and inns, generally of small scale and with modest facilities and furnishings, frequently run by the proprietor himself. All bedrooms with hot and cold water; adequate bath and lavatory arrangements; main meals with a choice of dishes served to residents; menus for residents and meal facilities for non-residents may be limited, especially at week-ends.

★★ Hotels offering a higher standard of accommodation, more baths and perhaps a few private bathrooms/showers; lavatories on all floors; wider choice of meals (but these may be restricted, especially to non-residents).

★★★ Well appointed hotels with more spacious accommodation and at least 40% of the bedrooms with private bathrooms/showers; full meal facilities for residents every day of the week but at week-ends service to non-residents may be restricted.

★★★★ Exceptionally well appointed hotels offering a high standard of comfort and cooking with 80% of the bedrooms providing private bathrooms/showers. At week-ends meal service to non-residents may be restricted.

★★★★★ Luxury hotels, offering very high standard of accommodation, service and comfort. All bedrooms have private bathrooms/showers.

Ⓐ Denotes approved hotels which do not conform to the minimum classification requirements in respect of porterage, reception facilities, and choice of dishes; facilities for non-residents often limited.

White stars ☆ Denotes purpose built hotels, some motels, motor hotels, motor inns, posthouses and similar establishments which conform to the major requirements for black star classification. In some cases, porterage, room service, and lounge accommodation may be rather restricted. This is offset by the provision of studio type bedrooms, all with either private bath and/or shower, more parking space, and extended meal hours. It is emphasised that white stars are an indication of a type of hotel only.

Country house ♣ Denotes hotels set in secluded rural surroundings having many of the characteristics of a country house. Reception and service facilities may be of a more informal nature than in conventional hotels of similar classification.

Disabled persons Members with any form of disability should notify proprietors so that appropriate arrangements can be made to minimise difficulties, particularly in the event of an emergency.

Town Plans legend

- AA Recommended route
- Other roads
- Restricted roads (Access only/ Buses only)
- Traffic roundabout
- One-way street
- Parking zone
- Official car park (open air) — P
- Parking available on payment (open air) — P
- Multi-storey car park — G
- Convenience — C
- Convenience with facilities for the disabled — C ♿
- Tourist Information Centre — i
- Pedestrians only
- Shopping area
- Parks and open spaces
- AA Service Centre — AA
- AA Road Service Centre — AA 83
- Church/Cathedral — + ✝
- City Walls
- Post Office — *HPO/GPO/PO*
- Public buildings and places of interest — ⑩ *(appears in text next to grid square as (10))*
- Accommodation/Restaurants — ⑩ *(appears in text next to grid square letter as 10)*
- Grid square letter

CONTENTS

Cover photograph: *Swanage, Dorset by courtesy of the BTA Photographic Library*

Gazetteer: *Publications Research Unit*

Editor: *Gail Harada*

Designer: *Gerry McElroy* assisted by: *Nick Belshaw and Neil Roebuck*

Advertising: *Peter Whitworth Tel Basingstoke* 20123

Town Plans produced by the Cartographic & Research Department of the Automobile Association.

Produced by the Publications Division of the Automobile Association, Fanum House, Basingstoke, Hants RG21 2EA.

Phototypeset by: *Vantage Photosetting Co Ltd, Southampton, Hants*

Printed and bound in Great Britain by: *Wm Clowes and Sons, Beccles*

ISBN 0 86145 004 3 © The Automobile Association 1979 55783

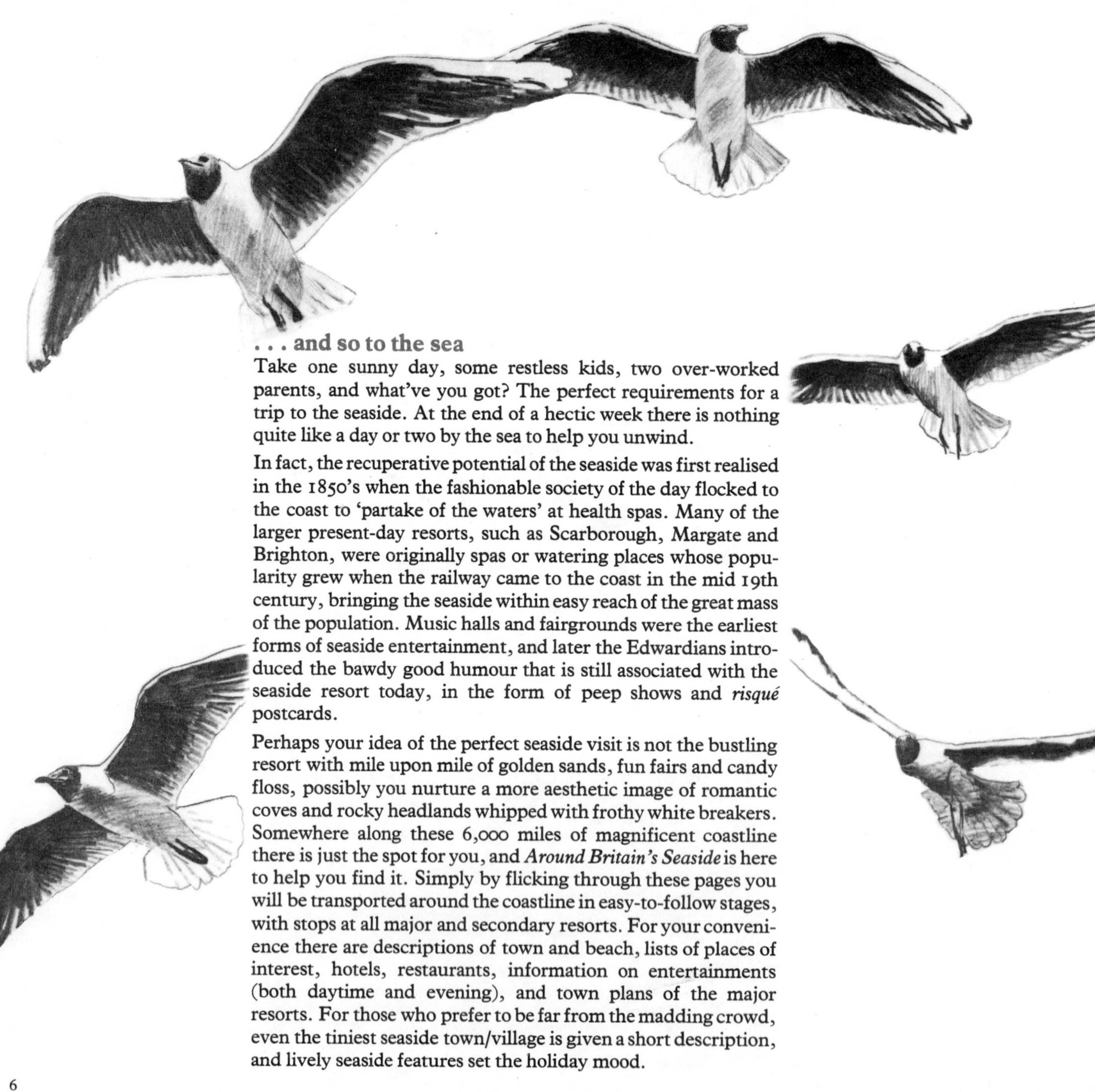

. . . and so to the sea

Take one sunny day, some restless kids, two over-worked parents, and what've you got? The perfect requirements for a trip to the seaside. At the end of a hectic week there is nothing quite like a day or two by the sea to help you unwind.

In fact, the recuperative potential of the seaside was first realised in the 1850's when the fashionable society of the day flocked to the coast to 'partake of the waters' at health spas. Many of the larger present-day resorts, such as Scarborough, Margate and Brighton, were originally spas or watering places whose popularity grew when the railway came to the coast in the mid 19th century, bringing the seaside within easy reach of the great mass of the population. Music halls and fairgrounds were the earliest forms of seaside entertainment, and later the Edwardians introduced the bawdy good humour that is still associated with the seaside resort today, in the form of peep shows and *risqué* postcards.

Perhaps your idea of the perfect seaside visit is not the bustling resort with mile upon mile of golden sands, fun fairs and candy floss, possibly you nurture a more aesthetic image of romantic coves and rocky headlands whipped with frothy white breakers. Somewhere along these 6,000 miles of magnificent coastline there is just the spot for you, and *Around Britain's Seaside* is here to help you find it. Simply by flicking through these pages you will be transported around the coastline in easy-to-follow stages, with stops at all major and secondary resorts. For your convenience there are descriptions of town and beach, lists of places of interest, hotels, restaurants, information on entertainments (both daytime and evening), and town plans of the major resorts. For those who prefer to be far from the madding crowd, even the tiniest seaside town/village is given a short description, and lively seaside features set the holiday mood.

I do like to be beside the seaside . . .

Becos I like looking for reflektchens, in the sea and diging In the Sand and I lik having tea at the beech and going into the sea.

Kate Wilson Age 5½

because I like to have ice-creems and I like to go in the sea and Pick up Shells. I Wonder if oneday I Will Pick up a Shell With a creecher in it.

Sarah Francis Age 6

Who doesn't like to be beside the seaside? Who doesn't love the first glimpse of sun sparkling on bright blue-green waves, a salt tang in the air? Shops bulge with brightly-coloured buckets and spades, shrimping nets and vulgar postcards, sand shoes and funny hats, pink lettered rock and china souvenirs.

Seagulls scream and dip above the beach and promenade, funfair and pier. Down on the sands, striped deckchairs cluster in family groups. Children shriek in rapture at the ever-popular antics of Punch, beg for a bounce on the trampoline, ride on the woolly, sturdy donkeys, or carefully pat sand into buckets to build yellow moated fortresses. Farther off by the soaring white cliffs boys slither and slip over seaweed strewn rocks, peer into mysterious pools, poke crabs into action and shade their eyes to see ships far out at sea. With rolled-up trousers, sandals in hand, day-trippers from the gleaming coaches paddle at the sea's edge, feeling the sand between their toes, watching the swimmers in multi-coloured costumes bobbing in the waves, laughing and splashing. Teenagers in miniscule bikinis carefully turn and toast themselves to the strains of Radio 1. Families stroll far out to sea along the pier to watch the patient fisherman hunched expectantly over their rods. Along the promenade money is lost and won in a thousand ways in the amusement arcades, and children delight in ice-cream parlours or sample sweet rock in a hundred shapes. Who doesn't love the seaside?

Kid's stuff – traditional

SPACEWALK

Children

2
3

Down on the Beach

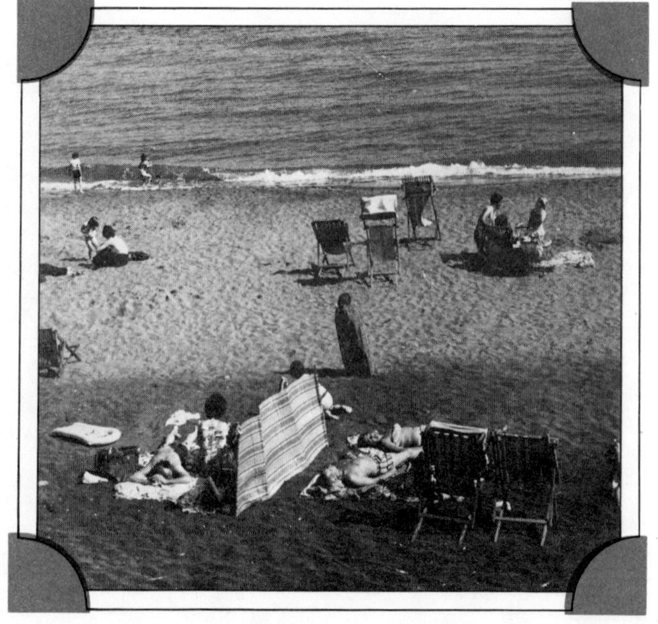

All the Fun of the Fair

The first seaside fair was opened at Skegness in 1936. Today fine examples of large fairgrounds can be found at Blackpool, Margate, Morecambe and Great Yarmouth. Traditional attractions include the roller coaster (also known as the 'scenic railway' or 'big dipper'); the merry-go-round (traditionally with horses galloping abreast, now with a variety of animals); the dodgems; the helter-skelter (with its modern versions, the astra and mountain glides) and the water splash.

The merry-go-round is the oldest fairground ride; the first example was depicted in a Byzantine carving 1500 years ago.

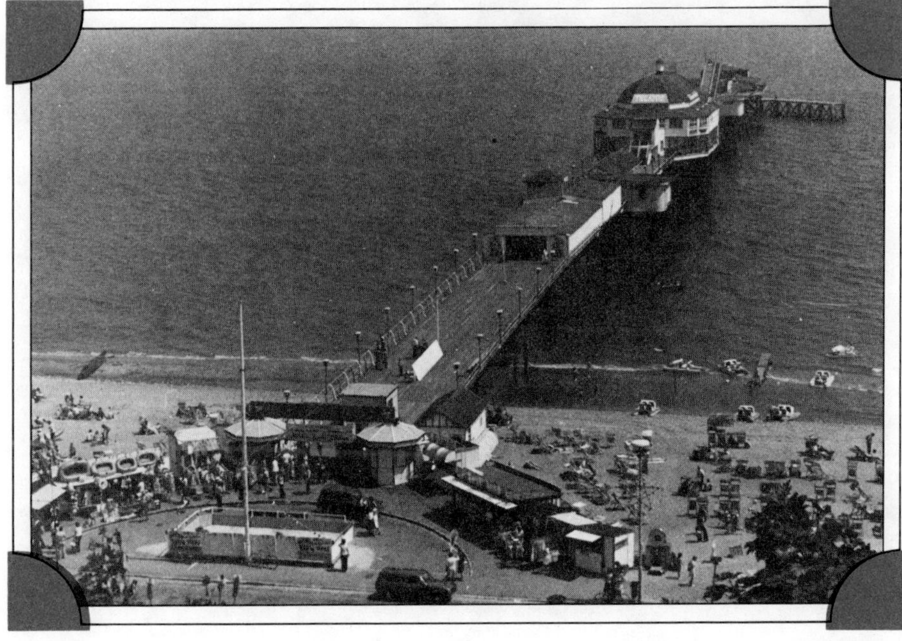

Piers

Marching out to sea with a lattice-work of iron girders, supporting amusement arcades and cafés, deckchairs and fishermen, bandstands and pavilions, kiosks and domes, Britain's piers are a unique ingredient of a seaside holiday. Most of the piers date back to Queen Victoria's reign. Many have been damaged by storms, fire and wear and tear, but all have been loved by generations. Originally mere platforms for promenaders to take a daring stroll out to sea, and a landing stage for steamers, they soon began to support a growing number of vaguely oriental domes. By the end of Queen Victoria's reign no self-respecting holiday resort was without one.

Notable examples can be found at Brighton, Hastings, Clacton and Southend (the longest pier in the world).

Perpetual motion – the story of Britain's coastline

As surely as the earth is moving round, Britain's coastline is constantly changing. Rock-pools and shingle ridges seem to have moved; cliffs and rocks show new features; and points on the land seem closer to the sea. All this is the result of erosion by the sea. The waves hurl tons of sand and fragmented rock against the land, grinding its weakest points and leaving its harder rocks exposed. Apart from the occasional landslips or other inroads of the sea, destruction of the coast is so gradual that it goes almost unnoticed. It can only really be appreciated by historical comparisons. For example, Old Dunwich used to be a busy port on the East Anglian coast until the 17th and 18th centuries when it was washed away. Likewise, Seaton and Ravenspur on the North East coast and Old Winchelsea and Brighthelmstone, the forerunner of Brighton in the south, have all been destroyed along with the countryside around them.

The sea's destructiveness is aided by that of the weather. Alternately heated and cooled by changes in temperature, the surface of the cliffs expands and contracts and its loosened fragments fall away. The wind pelts the rocks with grit like a sand blast. Rain and sea water penetrate into the crevices, and when water freezes in winter it expands irresistibly. So both below and above tide level, the face of the cliff is slowly worn away. The Chines in the Isle of Wight are examples of this cliff type, where short streams descend to the shore through ravine-like cuttings in the rocks. The austere grandeur of Blackgang Chine, the gentler scrub-covered contours of Luccombe Chine and the deep gorge-like Shanklin Chine are further examples of this dramatic 'sea sculpture'.

Despite this erosion however, more land is gained than lost. For instance, the cliffs of Dover are receding in parts by 15in per year. Simultaneously, land is increasing naturally through the raising up of coasts or the silting up of flat shorelands, and is being reclaimed by man, who builds sea defences and drains marshes. However, a single storm can undo the work of several years of patient building; a natural bank that has built up over a period of five years can disappear overnight as the sea reclaims what the land has so laboriously won.

Since the recession of the last Ice Age, the area of the world's crust released from the weight of ice has been slowly rising. This movement is so slow that it can be measured only over millions of years. The effect of this, and other movements of the earth's crust, has been to tilt our continent back and forth. There is clear evidence that areas have risen out of the sea. In places on the Scottish coast two, or even three, of these raised beaches are situated one above the other, at heights of from 25 to 100ft above high tide. Equally clear is the fact that parts of the coast have sunk bodily, so that what was once dry land is now covered by the waves. St Michael's Mount, near Penzance, has a Cornish name which means 'the ancient rock in the midst of the woods' – it is now an island connected with the shore only at low tide.

Composite shorelines

Where different types of rock lie side by side, the sea erodes them unequally, producing a varied coastline. The softer rocks yield quickly, forming bays, coves and inlets separated by headlands formed of the most resistant substances. Where the softer rocks underlie the hard, their destruction may produce a landslip such as those west of Lyme Regis, at the Warren near Folkestone and the Isle of Wight Undercliff, between Ventnor and St Catherine's Point.

At Lulworth Cove, Dorset, the limestone has been widely breached, and the destruction of the clay has resulted in a circular inlet of great beauty. To the west the limestone has been reduced to a line of offshore reefs, the clay has gone completely, and the sea is now attacking the chalk. Further along the coast a resistant mass of limestone, formerly continuous with that of Purbeck, remains as the Isle of Portland.

The formation of a beach

Beaches are formed when the shallow waters are slowed down as they approach the shore by friction from the sea floor. This action causes the materials carried by the once fast-flowing waters to drop and form a platform or either shingle or sand, mingled with fragments of sea shells. Some beaches extend unbroken for miles, but most feature in bays and inlets which help to check the water's flow. The opposite action takes place around the headlands where the movement of water is so swift that, far from depositing loose material, it actually sweeps it away. The larger fragments, however, are too heavy for the waves to move and these meet the brunt of the sea's attack and protect the land. The relentless waves jostle these large rock masses, blunting their angles and smoothing their surfaces until they eventually become pebbles. These, in turn, are washed away and the sea attacks the coast anew.

Variations in sand

North of the chalk-belt in the Isle of Wight are found a variety of more recent clays and sands. These variations, caused in many cases by their mixture with different minerals, are found very close to Alum Bay and give rise to 'coloured sands' of more than 20 shades, from chocolate-brown to strawberry pink.

Other areas which display this phenomenon are Goodrington Sands, near Paignton where pink sands darken to deep red where the waves wash over them, and at Maidencomb where the sands are also deep red. Torridon, near Lochinver in Scotland can also boast red and sea-jade green sands.

North of the Bay of Laig on the Isle of Eigg there are beautiful white sands that 'sing' when walked on. Their whistling sound is caused by the rounded grains of quartz rubbing together.

Sport on the waves

Water-skiing Water-skiing began in this country in the early sixties but its popularity was well-established in the sunnier climes of California and the French Riviera in the 1920's.

A suitable stretch of water is required for water-skiing, one that is far away from swimmers and other sea users, as the noise and speed of a motor boat can be annoying and dangerous. Practised in the right area, this is a sport which gives pleasure to participant and spectator alike.

The action of water-skiing is dependent upon the skier reaching enough speed for his skis to support his weight, usually around 25mph with a minimum of 18mph. The *standard twin ski* is made of resin-bonded laminated plywood, and is about 5ft 6in wide. It has a squared off rear and the front end curls upwards. This is a popular ski with beginners as it is best at slow speed and does not react well at high speeds. The thinner *slalom ski* is less stable but more suited to fast speed; the design is slimmer towards the front and curled at both ends. The slalom is one of the most spectacular feats; carried out, usually in competitions, on a single or 'mono'-ski and the skier must weave from side to side to clear small buoys that are laid out at set intervals. As the skier turns, a plume of spray rises up to 20ft behind his ski, and his shoulder seems to brush the water. At times the skier can reach a speed of 15mph faster than the boat. *Jumping skis* are never more than one inch thick, and are very strong and pliable enough to take the full impact when the skier hits the water. Skiing on bare feet is the ultimate skill; it takes a great deal of strength and can be carried out only on glassy water at more than 36mph.

The most difficult part of learning to ski is the getting started. This may require several attempts and the assistance of an instructor, but once the knack is acquired it is never forgotten.

Step 1 Holding onto the tow rope, wade waist deep into the water and crouch so that the tips of the skis just break the surface, about 6in apart. The help of someone to steady the skis is invaluable at this stage. Nod when ready.

Step 2 The boat pulls slowly away, taking up the slack, then accelerates hard as the tow rope tightens. Keep the arms straight and lean back against the pull of the boat.

Step 3 As the skis begin to surface, stay in the crouching position to gain confidence; then slowly straighten the knees. Bend the knees to recover balance and to absorb bumps. if the rope slackens, drop down to the crouching position until the slack is taken up again by the towing boat. Do not bring the arms back to the chest or you will fall backwards.

Step 4 *Signals* Clear communication between driver and skier is essential at all times. A good driver signals to the skier when he is about to turn so that the skier is not left with slack rope. One arm raised above the head means stay with the boat. An arm raised and quickly let fall means let go of tow-rope.

★ ★ ★

Those who are planning a holiday by the sea, and wish to learn how to water-ski should contact the British Water Ski Federation, 70 Brompton Road, London SW3 1EG. They are the governing body of the sport in the UK, whose aim it is to 'encourage and administer family, club and competitive water-skiing based on a code of water safety which ensures harmony with other water users.' They will supply the name and address of the nearest club providing equipment, basic instruction and encouragement to the novice skier.

Go faster

slow down

speed correct

turn right

return to base

cut engine

Step 1

Step 2

Surfing The large ocean rollers that sweep the coastline of North Cornwall, Devon and parts of Wales offer the ideal conditions on which to practice this exhilarating and relatively new sport. The excitement is in riding these huge waves as they curl over, break and rush towards the shore at around 35mph.

Body surfing is the simplest method of surfing. Without the aid of a board, the body-surfer waits until the wave is close behind, then takes a deep breath as the crest almost reaches him. He pushes off hard with his legs, keeping his body straight and his arms drawn back to his sides. If the timing is correct, the surfer travels forward on the face of the wave until it expires.

Belly-boarding is the conventional surfing technique. The rider simply pushes the board forward as the wave begins to break. Lying on the board with his weight to the rear and the front of the board slightly raised, he is propelled shorewards by the impetus of the wave. Some experienced surfers paddle with their hands to give them more speed but beginners are advised to keep their hands on the board. When more confidence is gained the surfer can try riding the wave by kneeling on the board with the knees slightly apart. Highly-skilled surfers stand on their Malibu boards, adjusting their balance in response to the movement of the board. The ultimate thrill is to loop inside the tunnel of a breaking wave.

Beginners can hire surf boards at most beaches where surfing is an established sport or alternatively, a simple model can be made from plywood to a measurement of about 4ft long and 12in wide. For better grip, the surface should be polished with paraffin wax. The Malibu surf board was developed by Hawaiian princes and it became popular in Australia and California, before coming to this country in the 1960's. This sophisticated model is pod-shaped, measuring 5ft 9in to 7ft long, 20in wide and about 3in deep, with a flexible dagger-like keel at the rear end. Made of glass-reinforced plastic, and extremely lightweight, it can be home-built, or bought for around £60. Using this type of board makes for a far more exciting style of surfing, but it is also more dangerous. At some beaches, such as Newquay, Malibu boards have to be registered and insured for third-party risks.

Step 3

Step 4

'There are about 1,000 drowning accidents annually in the UK.'

Amid the cheerful bustle of the average seaside resort these disturbing statistics are only too easy to forget. But **everyone** must consider the safety aspect of a day at the seaside; not least the 'townies' among us who only venture to these sandy shores once or twice a year. For those people especially, here are a few 'musts' for seaside safety.

On the beach

Always observe the noticeboards and safety flags. Know the flag code and remember it:

Red	unsafe to bathe. Do not enter the water.
Red & Yellow	patrolled bathing areas; with life-saving facilities provided by patrols of lifeguards.
White & Blue	divers' flag: divers down, boat owners keep well clear of this area.
Black & White	surfing area: set aside for surf or malibu board riding.

Protect your feet at all times. Due to the thoughtless actions of others our seashore is often littered with broken bottles, rusty tin cans and similar hazardous objects.

Should you see someone in the water who seems to be in trouble, quick thinking and fast action are imperative. Remember the rules and apply them to the situation; either:

a REACH with a stick, scarf or anything in sight
b THROW – if there is no lifebuoy use something that floats like a tyre or plastic ball
c WADE – test the depth with a long stick as you go

All of those are quicker than to:

d ROW – if there is a boat to hand.

Alert the lifeguard immediately, if there is one, or dial 999 and ask for the coastguard.

In the water Being able to swim well is a primary requirement for seaside safety. It is vital that children learn to swim at an early age and that they are taught to observe the safety rules. Children who cannot swim must be watched constantly and should never be allowed to go in beyond waist depth. Never swim out with the current; it might prove impossible to get back. Likewise, it is dangerous to swim around rocks or headland where the main tidal stream travels at about 2½mph. In an emergency, if caught in a strong current, swim calmly across it diagonally. Never swim against the current and always use a slow long stroke, such as breast stroke, to preserve your energy. Try to keep calm at all costs – panic rather than the original situation, can prove fatal. To signal help raise one arm and move it from side to side.

Hypothermia is a severe state of chilling which occurs when the body temperature drops to below 35°C from the normal 37°C. This can happen as a result of a bathing accident, but parents should keep a close watch on children who are very susceptible to the chilling effects of cold conditions. At the first sign or mention of coldness get your child out of the water, dry him well and dress him quickly in warm clothing. Never take alcohol before entering the water as this causes heat loss and impairs judgement.

Boating If, when boating, you find yourself unexpectedly in the water, get out and back into your craft if you possibly can. If you cannot get out of the water, do not panic; reduce your movements to a minimum to conserve body heat (movement causes cold water to circulate between your body and your clothing). Always stay with your boat, unless it is being swept into a dangerous situation. Shout and signal for help raising one arm. Lifejackets should always be worn when boating; it is advisable to wear your lifejacket in a swimming pool first to test just how much support it provides. Those which rely on inflation should be checked for leaks by blowing them up three or four times a year.

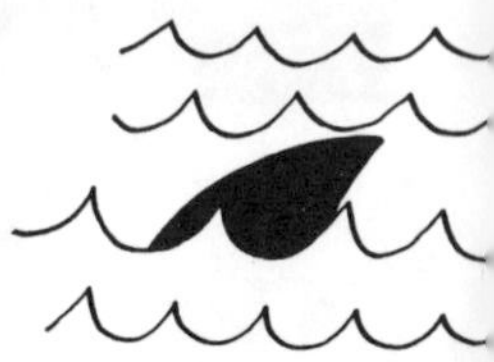

Needless to say these are only the very basic instructions for water safety. Any serious sailor should take a proper course of training at a centre run by the local education authority, or by the Sports Council or by one of the commercial sailing schools approved by the Royal Yachting Association. For further advice and booklets contact *The Royal Society for the Prevention of Accidents, Cannon House, The Priory, Queensway, Birmingham B4 6BS, tel 021–233 2461.*

SEASIDE ENTERTAINMENT

by
Jerry Dawson

Holidays by the sea have, for well over a century, been successively therapeutic, then fashionable, then desirable, until today when they are now a sheer necessity and have become an institutional part of the British way of life.

In the early days, it quite naturally followed that where the 'ladies and gentlemen' gathered to 'take the waters', enjoy the ozone, and generally relax from the everyday chores . . . so entertainers began to appear, to add further enjoyment to their seaside sojourn.

Punch and Judy: picture courtesy of The Museum of London

History is fairly vague as to the manner and form of the earliest seaside entertainment, but it is safe to assume that strolling minstrels and players first appeared on the beaches. Later they transferred to those 'modern marvels of engineering' – the piers. Firstly appearing outdoors, then under a canvas awning for the artistes, which was later extended to protect the audience too. So the seaside theatre was born! But the alfresco entertainer remained, and even continued well into this century. I have many (and happy) personal recollections of my extreme youth (in the 'twenties) when itinerant musicians, singers and dancers were regularly to be seen performing in the streets – or even in the gardens of boarding houses – in Blackpool, Morecambe and Rhyl, where I was taken on family holidays. These performances were usually at mealtimes (when vistors were all back in their 'digs'), and were inevitably followed by the passing round of a hat, usually by a bedraggled clown, a tatty-looking Chaplinesque comedian, or perhaps a slightly incapacitated and therefore more heart-tugging member of the company.

Even today, some of their successors are still plying their trade as beach performers, despite the changes that the modern theatre and cinema, radio, television, clubs and pubs, have brought to bear in 20th-century entertainment. For on seashores at several of the big resorts around the British Isles, children still laugh, wonder and even cry a little at the antics of the Punch and Judy men, or the ventriloquist with his dummy, perched high atop a step-ladder.

But nostalgic as it may be, all this really belongs to the past. For towards the end of the last century, sophistication began to creep into entertainment generally, and theatres sprang up all over the country. This included the then well-established seaside resorts which were soon in the forefront of the theatrical scene. In some resorts, it was the Corporation that was first into the business of entertaining the town's visitors. In others, it was left to private enterprise – of which there was no lack! The latter, led by men of vision and courage – a product of the industrial revolution – were willing to back their ideas with hard cash. Thus, such foresighted projects as the Winter Gardens complex (100 years old in July 1978) and in the 1890s, the sensational Tower (inspired by the Eiffel Tower in Paris) with its aquarium, circus ring and ballroom, appeared on the Blackpool scene.

'Holidays in general are basically a release from conformity' says **Bernard Crabtree,** of the Blackpool Tower Company, now a subsidiary of the mighty EMI Leisure group.

'Consequently, seaside visitors are far more ready, even anxious, to indulge in entertainment, than in their home towns, and so the theatre continues to thrive in the resorts, at least in the holiday season. And, strange though it may seem, there has been little change in the basic format of summer shows since the end-of-pier concert party gave way to the bigger and better stage productions.'

'The thirty-year span between the wars was the hey-day of the theatre, and back in the 1930s such showbiz giants as Charles B Cochran and Andre Charlot set a pattern – the effects of which are still with us!'

'Immediately prior to World War Two, the Opera House, Blackpool, was staging spectacular shows with star comedians and singers, dancers speciality acts and wondrous stage effects – just as it does today, and which are repeated at resorts all over the British Isles.'

'Despite the fact that present-day producers enjoy the benefits of more exciting materials for dress, props, stage drapes and backcloths, superior lighting and amplification equipment, also cinematic tricks to deploy, and in many cases, bigger and better orchestras – basically the big-time seaside holiday shows serve to pay tribute to the genius and inventiveness of the theatre mogul of forty or more years ago.'

★ ★ ★

The other side of the seaside coin is the south-eastern resort of **Eastbourne** where the Borough Council and not private enterprise, is responsible for the town's chief holiday entertainment venues. And if your impression of Eastbourne (as opposed to the Brightons and Blackpools of this world) is one of elderly retired, ex-army colonels and /or dowagers, then be prepared to change your views. For it is, as far as entertainment is concerned, a go-ahead, lively resort. Says the Borough's Director of Tourism and Entertainment, **Peter Bedford:**

'My experience, first at Blackpool, then at Margate, before settling at Eastbourne eleven years ago, prompts me to express the decided opinion that it is essential for local authorities to take a leading part

Hippodrome Circus, Great Yarmouth

Scarborough at night

Illuminated Pleasure Beach, Great Yarmouth

in the provision of entertainment – particularly at seaside resorts. Apart from resorts where the big-time moguls of show business are in command, most holiday towns, without Council assistance, could only present 'live' entertainment at the very peak of the season – such are the effects of ever-spiralling costs. That the Council's policy is successful at Eastbourne is evidenced by the fact that it is the only town in Britain with less than 75,000 inhabitants that can sustain two 'live' theatres throughout the year.'

Eastbourne offers no less than five Council-owned entertainment establishments – three of them providing top-name stars in summer season shows. In the winter two remain open with a mixed programme of concert appearances by top popular artistes, at the Congress Theatre which also stages a Christmas pantomime, and at the Royal Hippodrome which caters for the slightly more serious lovers of the arts with opera, ballet and musical concerts.

You will notice that neither of the two entertainment executives quoted make any mention of that 'other' type of relaxation, popular at both seaside and in the big towns, cities and even villages – bingo.

Whilst bingo has not over-run seaside theatres to the same extent as it has those in the inland towns, its addicts still demand facilities on the coast whether that coast be north, south, east or west! And so long as that demand exists – so it will be met by the scores of individual operators who flock to the seaside every summer to fill the needs of holidaymakers. Apart from the north-west and the south coast, probably one of their happiest hunting-grounds is the east coast with its large resorts such as Margate, Great Yarmouth (which now vies with Blackpool as the entertainment centre of the British coast), Bridlington and Scarborough in the forefront. Again, most of the theatre entertainment in these resorts is provided by a combination of local council and private enterprise, a pattern which is repeated in still another cluster of resorts on the North Wales coast.

This beautiful region is, of course unique in the grandeur of its natural scenery but it also offers to its family visitors beaches, buckets, spades – and summer shows. Llandudno leads the way with three theatres, a ballroom, late-night cabaret establishments, and the quaint, nostalgic open-air theatre in Happy Valley at the foot of the Great Orme which presents fun for all, twice daily.

Here, too, the Council takes a hand in the entertainment scene as it does in neighbouring Prestatyn and Rhyl, where variety, in its literal sense, is the order of the day, ensuring the whole family evening enjoyment as well as sunny days on the beach.

One person who would like to see increased showbiz activity on the south coast of Wales is comedian **Stan Stennett** who for the 1978 summer season took over the 650-seater Caesar's Palace cinema in Porthcawl and converted it into a theatre.

'It is now a beautiful theatre, suitable for presenting 'live' shows, and/or cinema,' says Stan. 'We have built a pukka stage, dressing-rooms and orchestra pit. As for me – not only did I produce and appear in the show – I also handled the theatre publicity, supervised the box-office, actually taking money myself, and on occasion, even operated the film-projector!'

As with Wales, Scotland is inclined to attract lovers of the great outdoors rather than the sand castle and showbiz types. Despite a distinct falling-off in the number of shows to be seen at some of the resorts, there are still a few – usually with a Scottish flavour as one would expect, and featuring homegrown stars of comedy and song.

Generally speaking, despite bingo and slot machines, and the outdoor pursuits such as golf and racing, it is still that one word 'Stars' that attracts thousands of holidaymakers to the big resorts. The big names of television and record is one of the few things that can drag Mr and Mrs Britain from the comfort of their armchairs, or the delights of a seaside stroll; names such as the Bachelors, Norman Vaughan, John Inman and **Ken Dodd** . . .

'There is a vast difference between seaside audiences and those which one meets during the rest of the year in the clubs and at pantomimes,' says the 'Nut from Knotty Ash' – that zany Liverpool comedian who has made the art of inciting laughter into what is almost an exact science.

'They are on holiday – they have cast aside most of their worries for the duration of their one- or two-week break, and they are usually quite happy to applaud and laugh for as long as one might care to remain up there on the stage. For one thing – they don't have to go to work the next day – and that's enough to make anyone feel happy and charitable! But there is, inevitably, just one snag. That's the weather! Make no mistake, holiday audiences like any other, are affected by the weather. Especially if they have walked a quarter-mile down a wind-swept pier in the pouring rain! Believe me, it can be very unnerving to see the steam rising from an audience – and to realise that one's opening gag hasn't received quite its natural response. This is when entertainers – especially comics – have to buckle down and work even harder to get the audience on their side and to help them forget their discomfort.'

Wellington Pier Pavilion, Great Yarmouth

Ken Dodd: picture by courtesy of Syndication International Ltd

Cabaret at the Knightstone Theatre, Weston-super-Mare

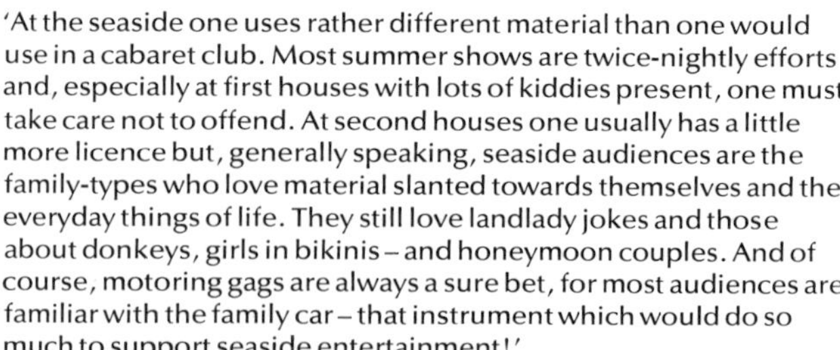

'At the seaside one uses rather different material than one would use in a cabaret club. Most summer shows are twice-nightly efforts and, especially at first houses with lots of kiddies present, one must take care not to offend. At second houses one usually has a little more licence but, generally speaking, seaside audiences are the family-types who love material slanted towards themselves and the everyday things of life. They still love landlady jokes and those about donkeys, girls in bikinis – and honeymoon couples. And of course, motoring gags are always a sure bet, for most audiences are familiar with the family car – that instrument which would do so much to support seaside entertainment!'

'My present hobby-horse is "Bring back 'live' entertainment!" I firmly believe that people can be tempted from their TV sets – at the very least in the summer. I don't much care where they go for their entertainment, be it clubs, theatres, bingo, wrestling or what-have-you, providing that the entertainment is 'live'. Motorways have provided fast travel to the coast but the snag is that they have also provided fast travel home again, eliminating the necessity for a long or short stay in a resort.'

'How tickled I ham to to think that your family might just stay that little bit longer next time, and see a 'live' show – have *you* ever been tickled at a 'live' show Missus?'

★ ★ ★

Little Theatre, Rhyl

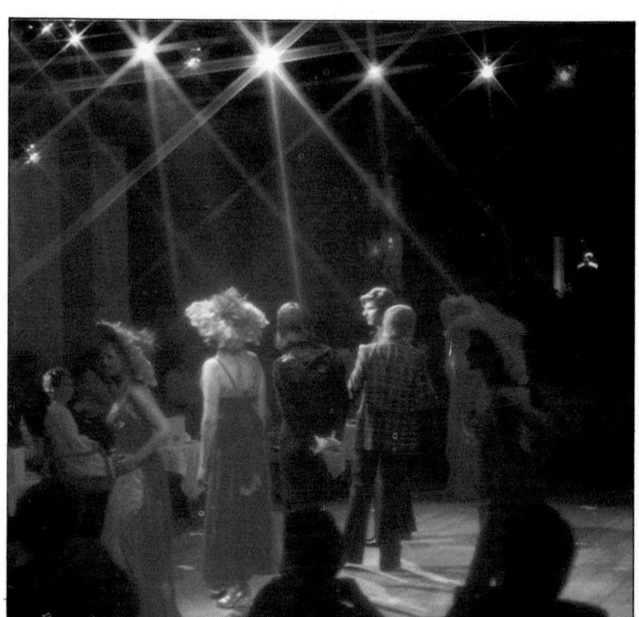

Palace Hotel, Weston-super-Mare

'I've always enjoyed appearing in summer-season shows' says the "tall one with glasses" from TV's favourite comedy duo **Morecambe and Wise.**

'But I'll never forget our first attempt to get into a seaside show. Ernie and I were trying everything we knew to fix a season in a concert party in Newquay, but they turned us down – we just weren't good enough. Mind you, we were in very good company – they also turned down Bruce Forsyth! These days we just don't do summer-season shows but we've done our share in the past, including no less than ten seasons at Blackpool, playing most of the leading theatres there except the Opera House where we have since appeared in concerts. Our first Blackpool season (at Central Pier) springs readily to mind – it lasted from Easter to the end of the autumn illuminations! Twenty-six weeks in all! Just imagine a struggling variety act playing twenty-six weeks at one theatre – and at the seaside too! For us it was manna from heaven. But we always enjoyed ourselves at the seaside – the audiences, in holiday mood, were always very receptive, except after a very hot day! Those who came to first house were completely exhausted – too whacked to either laugh or applaud. And by the time the second-house patrons arrived, the humidity in the theatre made it more like a Turkish bath! Of course, the weather matters a lot to the theatre management, who are concerned solely with filling seats.'

'I remember one summer on a dull but very hot and humid day. We were in the theatre during the afternoon when the manager complained that the heat would most likely keep people away that evening. "Yes", we chorused. "We could just do with a nice downpour of rain about five o'clock". "No – no – no", screamed the manager. "We don't want rain – what we need is a strong cold wind . . .!" In the middle of August!'

★ ★ ★

Morecambe & Wise: pictures by courtesy of Syndication International Ltd

Showtime at Scarborough

Derek Batey

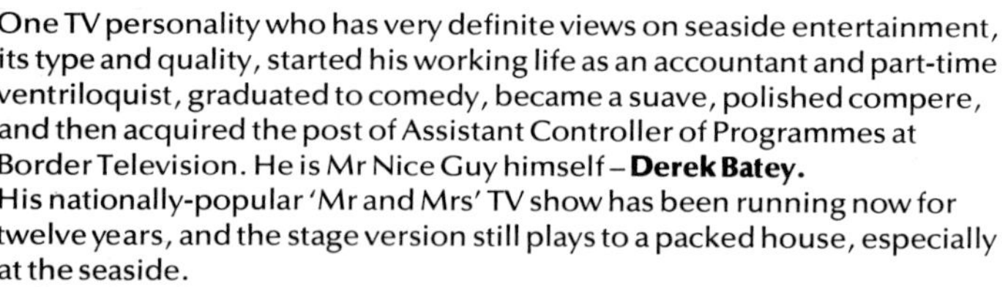

One TV personality who has very definite views on seaside entertainment, its type and quality, started his working life as an accountant and part-time ventriloquist, graduated to comedy, became a suave, polished compere, and then acquired the post of Assistant Controller of Programmes at Border Television. He is Mr Nice Guy himself – **Derek Batey.**

His nationally-popular 'Mr and Mrs' TV show has been running now for twelve years, and the stage version still plays to a packed house, especially at the seaside.

> 'I have loved the theatre for as long as I can remember,' says Derek 'and I always feel that (even more so in those days), when people have made an occasion of a night show with ladies in their long dresses and carrying a box of chocolates, I too should make just that little extra effort. I feel it incumbent on me to take particular care of what type of show I give them, and I have a particular philosophy too, about seaside shows.'
>
> 'It is my firm opinion that the theatre is just as much a holiday amenity as deck chairs, buses, parks, bathing and boating pools, and local authorities ought to invest in good-type theatres and shows. For my part (at the seaside or elsewhere) I offer a family show. Apart from the "Mr and Mrs" competition (for which the participants are democratically chosen *by* the audience, *from* the audience), I give them comedy, a children's spot, a lot of happy participation plus two or three variety acts and nothing at all offensive – they seem to enjoy it!'

★ ★ ★

This brings us to that unique type of holiday-for-the-masses, the holiday camp. Throughout the British Isles there must be literally hundreds of these camps, and the 'big boys', dealing as they do with thousands of holidaymakers per week, must get closer to public tastes and demands than most individual seaside caterers. An executive of Pontins, controlling nineteen establishments in the North and a number in Europe, says,

Oddicombe Beach, Torbay

Babbacombe Model Village, Torquay

'In recent years there have been noticeable changes in campers' tastes. For years we operated two theatres with full-scale shows featuring top-quality artistes. Not now! One has been converted into a children's theatre, the other to a cabaret club and bar. Two shows per night is the pattern; the first show for families, the second one for adults. This is a reflection of the changes in taste that have taken place over the past five years. What is also very noticeable is the fact that (especially in the North) campers are demanding much more sophistication in their entertainment.

At the ten establishments, spread nationwide, operated by Butlins, they find that their formula of a resident stage revue, plus star-spangled Sunday and late-night variety concerts is still meeting campers' requirements. Both of the big 'uns also feature bands of all types, including pop groups, for dancing. So – never let it be said that the providers of seaside entertainment are not aware of the tastes and demands of their potential customers. In fact, they rely on their foresight and the holidaymakers' appreciation for their existence.

Holiday Fun at Clacton

Many people think that the various rock pools, left behind by the ebbing tide, harbour nothing more than the odd shore crab and a few limpets and mussels. How wrong they are! On close inspection, after a cautious approach, a miniature world of fantastic sea creatures will be revealed to the patient onlooker. The photographs shown overleaf were taken in pools around our coast and offer a fine example of what one can expect to find in *any* rock pool.

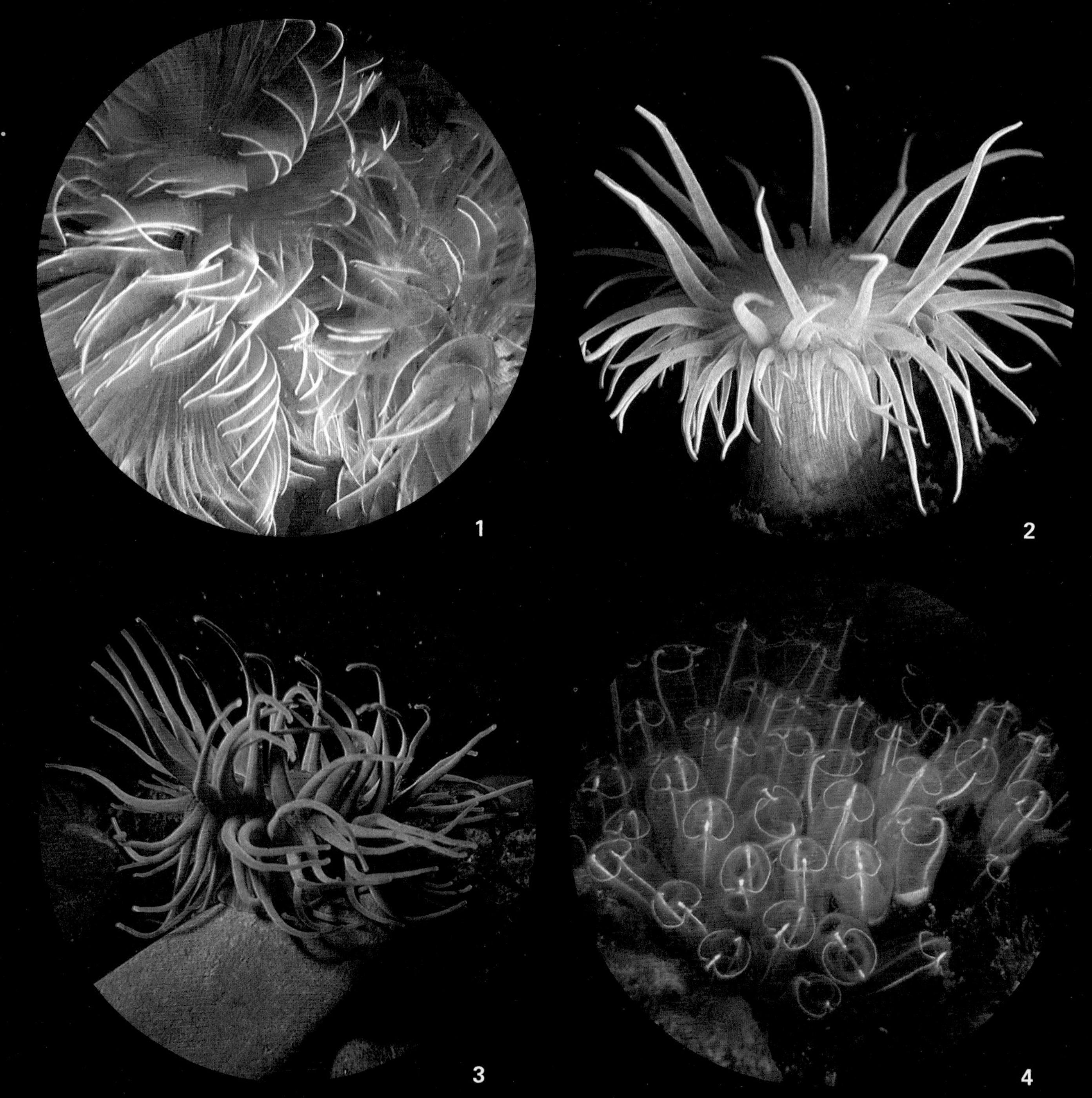

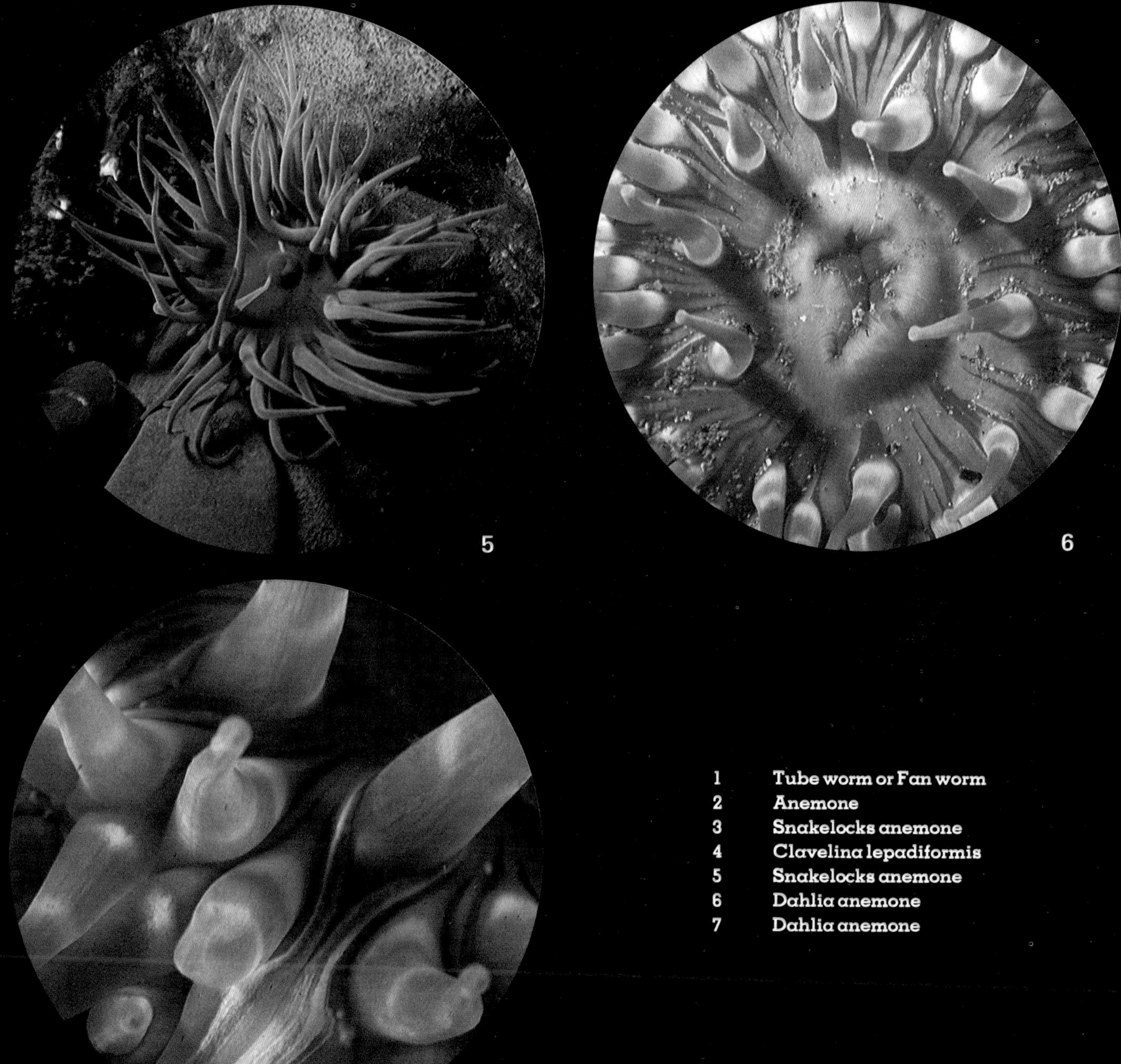

1 Tube worm or Fan worm
2 Anemone
3 Snakelocks anemone
4 Clavelina lepadiformis
5 Snakelocks anemone
6 Dahlia anemone
7 Dahlia anemone

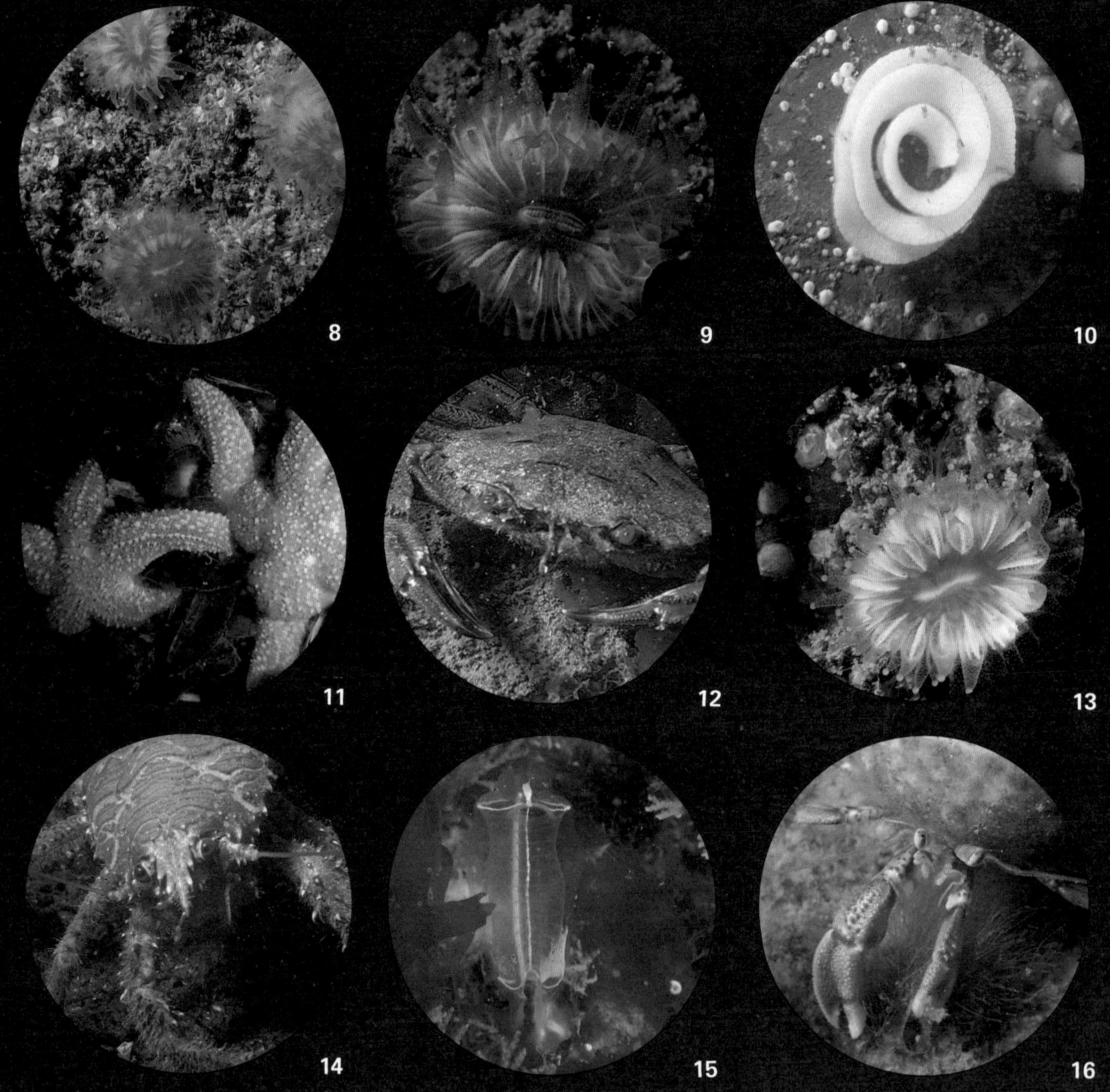
8
9
10
11
12
13
14
15
16

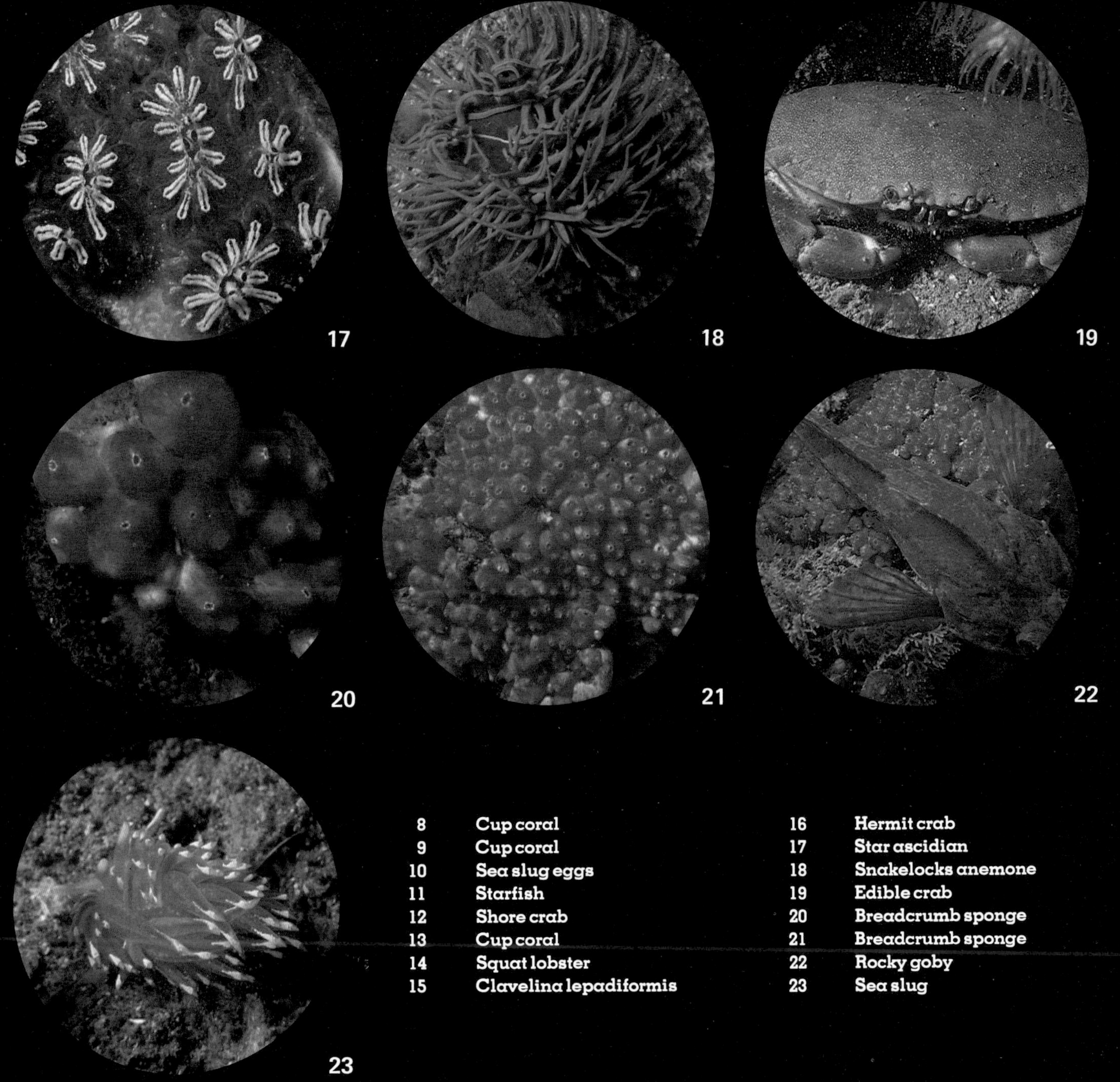

8	Cup coral	16	Hermit crab
9	Cup coral	17	Star ascidian
10	Sea slug eggs	18	Snakelocks anemone
11	Starfish	19	Edible crab
12	Shore crab	20	Breadcrumb sponge
13	Cup coral	21	Breadcrumb sponge
14	Squat lobster	22	Rocky goby
15	Clavelina lepadiformis	23	Sea slug

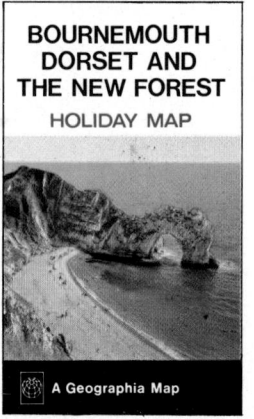

Keeping busy on the beach

When the bliss of lazing in the sun begins to pall, there are hundreds of beach activities to keep everyone amused and interested. Here are a few ideas:

Beach Games

Sand building. Hours of fun can be had with sand and water, by everyone from Grandad to the tiniest toddler. A bucket and spade are the only 'tools' required and the resulting masterpiece depends much upon the skill and imagination of the builder. Castles piled high with sand pies are a rather worn-out standard. So why not try something different:

canals – intricate waterway systems can be built in two ways. If a stream runs across the beach this can be dammed and filled with sand at various places to make channels. Water can also be obtained by digging deep channels into damp sand and the water that seeps into these channels can then be formed into canals.

sand structures – on a sandy beach with lots of space it is fun to make an object that can actually be played in. Outlines of ships, submarines, aircraft or motor cars are drawn in the sand and wells and ledges are made within the outline to form decks, holds, seats or instrument panels.

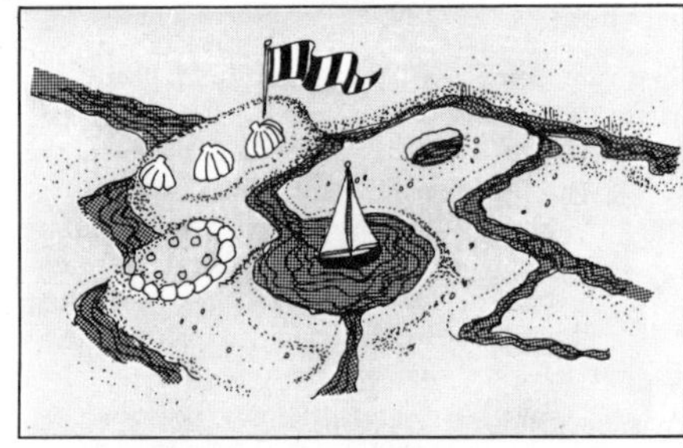

marble tracks – a game of marbles becomes something much more exciting on a complex sand track. The base of the track is a huge mound of firm sand into which is carved an ingenious runway with embankments, hairpin bends, flyovers and tunnels. Empty tin cans make excellent tunnels, but always make sure the edges are clean and not ragged.

Fun with bat and ball

Clock golf – In this game the numbers one to twelve are drawn in a circle to represent the face of a clock. In the centre of the circle a hole is dug and a bucket is placed inside mouth upwards. The object of the exercise is to get a 'hole in one' by batting a small ball from number one into the bucket. If the first person fails then the next in line takes a turn; if he succeeds he moves to two. The first person to reach twelve o'clock is the winner.

French bowls – This is a beach variation of the French game of *boule*. Firstly a small ball is thrown along the beach then each player stands at a marked distance from the small ball and throws two larger balls each. The winner is the person whose ball is nearest the target and points may also be given to the second and third nearest shots.

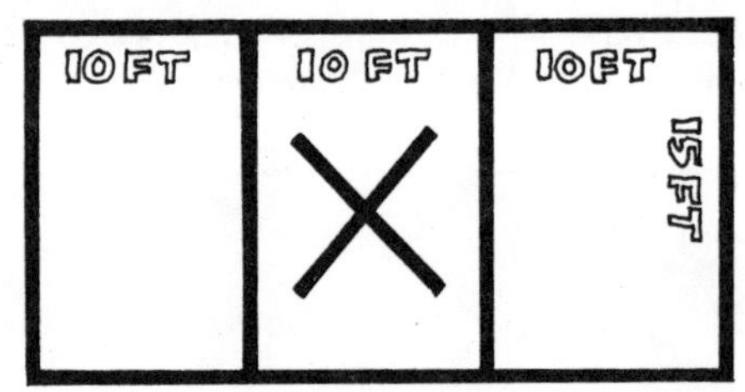

Beach tennis – This game needs a court of three equal rectangles which can be drawn in the sand to form one large oblong. There should be two teams (Almost any number can play). The teams face each other from either end of the oblong and pat a large beach ball to each other across the centre court. Points are lost when the ball falls outside the oblong or into the centre court. The table tennis system of scoring can be used for this game.

Endless enjoyment can be had with a beach *treasure hunt*. The basic idea is to give a list of objects to each participant and the first one to return to base with an example of each object is the winner. Items should be of the type that can be found easily on the beach *eg* a seagull's feather, a shell, red pebble etc. For older participants the list can vary to include some more unusual, and therefore difficult-to-find objects. A time limit can also be introduced.

More serious beach pursuits can prove very interesting and often quite rewarding.

Beachcombing

There are many pleasurable, valuable or just plain edible items to be found on our beaches; fishermen's floats, pieces of timber, ships' cargoes, messages in bottles or coins – the variety of 'booty' is endless. However, if you want to make a real 'find' you must know the times of high and low tide – and possess a keen eye.

Apart from the many unexpected items that are washed ashore daily, there are other more likely finds such as shells, semi-precious stones, fossils, sea creatures, flowering plants and seaweed that can be found with varying regularity on most beaches.

Sea shells

There are some 600 species of shellfish around Britain's coast and their discarded shells found on the shore can be easily identified by even the newest beachcomber if some study is done beforehand. Shell collecting is a fascinating hobby and one that can be put to some practical use: many houses in coastal towns and villages have their walls and gardens decorated with beautiful shells laid out in attractive patterns, and artists give collages a new dimension with these ornate objects.

A selection of the more common shells:
Common limpet – (2in) lives attached to rocks.
Tower or Auger shell – (1½in) shell often found in large numbers.
Common whelk – (2¾in) Right-handed spiral, Left-handed spiral (unusual).
Razor shell – (4in).
Cockle – (1½in).
Mussel – (2½in) found on rocks and piers.
Edible oyster – (1½in) this most famous of all molluscs lives in estuaries just off shore.
Great scallop – this is the shell of a delicious edible delicacy often fished commercially from natural beds.

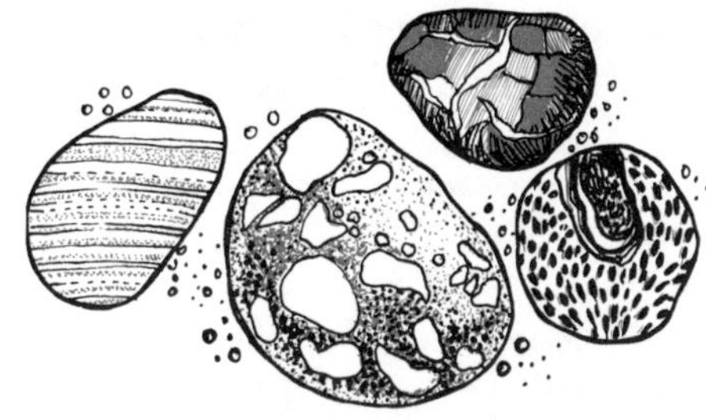

Pebbles and semi-precious stones

Almost all types of rock will form pebbles. Most have a frosted surface film which is only seen when the pebbles are dry. Their appearance can be improved with a coat of clear varnish or the softer pebbles can be polished smooth with some carborundum powder on a piece of plate glass. Valued specimens can be treated by a professional tumble stone-polisher. The resulting 'gems' can be used in jewellery making or as ornamental paperweights – a treasured keepsake of a happy holiday.

On the Yorkshire coast there are deposits of shale which yield small lumps of pure coal called jet, a material once highly prized for jewellery, that has been used by craftsmen since the Bronze Age. In Victorian England, Whitby was the recognised centre for the industry. The raw jet is black only after it has been polished or broken. It is easily identified by rubbing with emery paper – if brown scratch lines appear, then it is jet.

Another equally beautiful semi-precious stone is amber, found on the shores of the East Coast, mainly in Norfolk and Suffolk. Amber comes in two forms; cloudy and an almost clear 'ice colour', and as it is often tangled with seaweed, it is quite easy to miss. Other notable stones include quartzite which occurs on Highland beaches and in South Devon and Dorset; kidney stones, created when calcium carbonate impregnated the clays, found in the Weymouth area and limestone fossil (coral) which is located on beaches backed by limestone cliffs, especially Tenby, Barry and the Gower Peninsula. The Lizard in Cornwall is renowned for its green and red serpentine, which is ornamentally cut and polished locally, as is the Portsoy variety from Banffshire.

Quartz is widely distributed – semi-precious stones include the clear, colourless rock crystal, purple amethyst, cloudy brown Cairngorm, yellow citrine and pink Rose quartz. The extremely hard chalcedony is also fairly widespread and types include the translucent red cornelian, opaque red or brown jasper, and banded onyx and agate.

Minerals, rocks and fossils

Most sea cliffs harbour a host of minerals, rocks and fossils that have taken nearly 3,000 million years to evolve. Due to the natural coastal erosion many of these interesting specimens have been dislodged and some can be identified quite easily. If you're lucky you may come across some of the following on your fossil hunt:

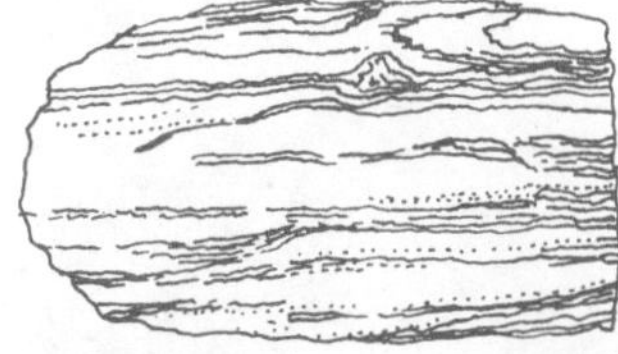

fossil wood: fragments of tree roots and trunks which have been converted to mineral matter but still retain their original structure. Such a fossil forest was discovered in the cliffs at Lulworth Cove, Dorset. This particular forest thrived about 140 million years ago.

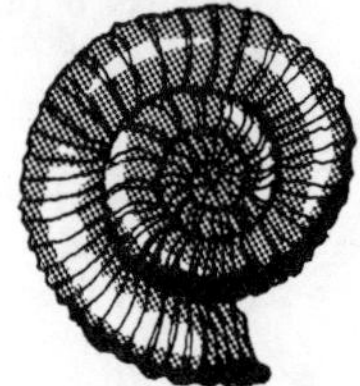

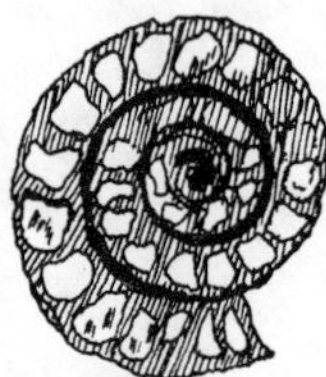

ammonites: these are fossil shells of extinct marine animals related to the octopus and are common in rocks 180 to 70 million years old. Mostly found near Whitby, they are also present in cliffs between Lyme Regis and Portland Bill. Of the same age, are Belemnite Guards, bullet-like objects which, when broken across, reveal a structure of radiating calcite crystals. The Guards formed part of the bodies of extinct animals resembling squids.

brachiopods: otherwise known as 'lamp-shells', are relatively scarce today but were the commonest type of shell-fish 160 to 70 million years ago. Examples can occasionally be found in red chalk areas, such as Hunstanton or Chesil Beach near Weymouth.

fossil sponges: these sponges were living on the floor of the Chalk Sea 60 million years ago and were preserved when flint was deposited in and around them. These sponges may look like any other flint pebbles on Brighton beach but if they are split open they reveal the original sponge.

The living rock-pool

Rocky shores are the richest in animal species, due largely to the seaweeds which flourish on rocks and provide shelter for other forms of life. The pools among the rocks are microcosms of the seashore, supporting plants and creatures which cannot survive in the areas alternately exposed and covered by the sea. It is also a dangerous world, however. What appears to be a beautiful underwater flower, for instance, may be a sea-anemone waiting with tentacles tipped with fatal poison. Sea-anemones belong to the animal group *coelenterata*, one of the most common type of rock-pool life. All of its family members have bodies consisting of a jelly-like sac with a mouth surrounded by tentacles armed with stinging cells. One type is the sea fir, colonies of which attach themselves to rocks in pools. Their brightly-coloured stalks wait to capture unwitting victims and paralyse them.

Jellyfish are often washed into pools by the tide. If stranded on the seashore they not only die but dry up from the effects of sun and wind. Pools are also inhabited by creatures able to come and go as they please, such as crabs. Others, the smaller crustaceans, such as prawns and small fish, may become cut off by the tide. By several visits to the same pool, one can learn to distinguish the resident inhabitants from tidal visitors.

The living beach

For those interested in flora and fauna, the seashore is the habitat of many fascinating creatures and plants, some of which can be easily collected and examined.

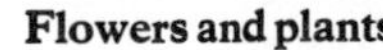

Flowers and plants

Many species not found inland grow on the shore. Here, the sand is continuously shifted by wind and waves, and plants must withstand spasmodic burial and exposure of the roots as the sand is dragged away. They must also survive inundations of sea water and summer drought. Included in this hardy group would be the sea sandwort, a creeping foreshore plant with deep roots and fleshy leaves; the sea rocket, an annual whose seeds are dispersed by the sea; and the yellow-horned poppy; sea holly; sea lavender; marram grass and the sea spurge.

Seaweeds

Gathered by man for centuries, seaweed proved most popular with the Victorians who lovingly collected and preserved it in albums. The most common types on British shores are the hardy brown varieties – rubbery, flat strands growing from a stem. Beneath these strands, which retain droplets of water after the tide has exposed them, many other tiny lifeforms find a refuge. The smaller and more delicate red and green seaweeds are usually found in the rock-pools at low tide.

Sea birds

A great variety of sea birds can be seen around Britian's cliffs because man has generally left them alone to breed. Gannets, for instance, nest in colonies off the Dyfed coastline in Wales, on St Kilda in the Outer Hebrides and in the Scilly Isles, where herring gulls and shags are also regular visitors. Guillemots and razorbills are familiar sights off North Devon and the Pembrokeshire coast, whereas fulmars and puffins congregate at Flamborough Head and in the Farne Islands off the Northumberland coast. These are a small selection of the birds that grace our shores at some time:

terns, kittiwakes, cormorants, eiders and plovers.

Read all about it

A bibliography of seaside-related subjects

Bird and animal life

Campbell B – The Oxford Book of Birds
Clark A M – Starfishes
Eales N B – Life in Mud and Sand
Fisher J & Lockley R M – Sea Birds
Hollom P A D – The Popular Handbook of British Birds
Norman D – The Oxford Book of Invertebrates
Witherby H F – The Handbook of British Birds

Shells, rocks and fossils

Casanova R – Fossil Collecting
Dance S P – Seashells
Ellis C – The Pebbles on the Beach
Forsyth W S – Common British Seashells
Francis J G – Beach Rambles in Search of Seaside Pebbles and Crystals
Ritchie C I A – Carving Shells and Cameos and other Marine Products
Street P – Shell Life on the Sea Shore

Flowers and plant life

Brightman F H – Coastal Vegetation
Chapman V J – Flowers of the Coast
Masefield G B – The Oxford Book of Food Plants
Newton L – A Handbook of British Seaweeds
Nicholson B E, Ary S & Gregory M – The Oxford Book of Wild Flowers

Miscellaneous

Bennett J & Yonge C M – Collins' Pocket Guide to the Sea Shore
Countryside Commission – The Coastal Heritage
Evans I O – Observer's Book of Sea & Seashore
Soper T – Shell Book of Beachcombing
Vevers H G – The British Seashore

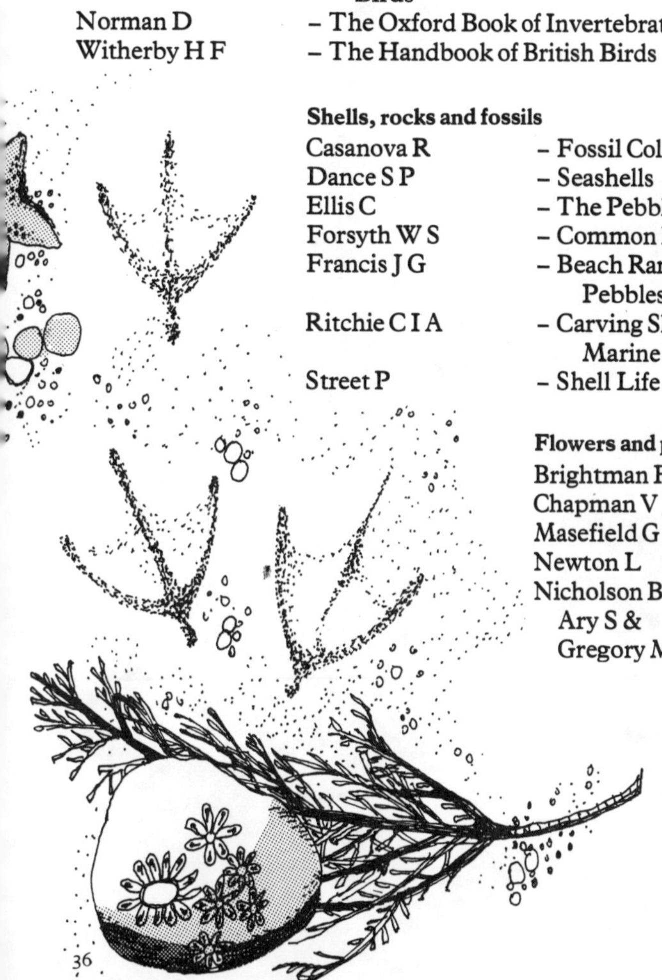

Sheerness
The largest town on the Isle of Sheppey, noted for its dockyard which was established in the 17th century. Sheerness was a naval base until 1960 but the docks are now used mainly by commercial vessels and a vehicle and passenger ferry which serves the Dutch port of Flushing.

The town's most memorable naval connection is the fact that Nelson's body was brought here on the *Victory*, following his death at Trafalgar. Sheerness has a sand and shingle beach backed by a mile-long promenade. Bathing near the River Swale estuary should be avoided. There is an open-air swimming pool and the town offers a variety of amusement, entertainment and sporting facilities.

Minster-in-Sheppey
This old established village stands on a hilltop above a muddy, stoney beach which is noted for an abundance of cockles and fossils. Twin churches, both retaining their medieval structure, are Minster's main feature and the village offers fine views of the surrounding countryside.

Leysdown
A small town which has been developed as a holiday centre over the last forty years and now attracts large numbers of visitors each year. There is a sand and shingle beach, a fairground and several amusement arcades.

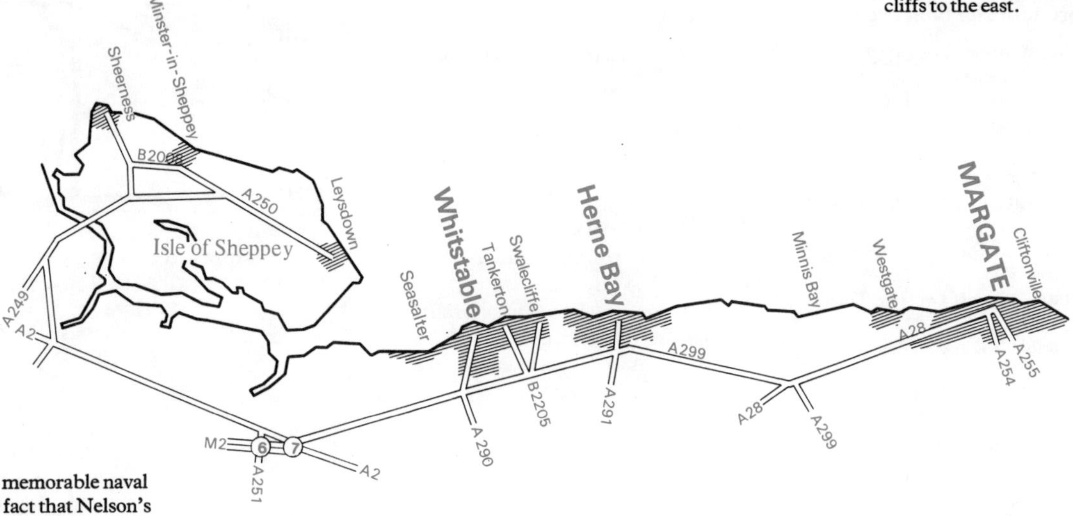

Seasalter
This small resort was once an important salt-making centre but is now best known for the high quality of its cockles. It has a shingle beach where swimming is safest at high-tide. A number of Roman relics were discovered in the bay some years ago. The headquarters of Seasalter Sailing Club are located near the beach.

Whitstable *see page 38*

Tankerton
Tankerton is almost an extension of neighbouring Whitstable. It is a peaceful resort with a sand and shingle beach which is safe for bathing.

Swalecliffe
This ancient village received a mention in the Doomsday Book. Today it is a small holiday and residential centre with a natural beach backed by grasslands where many interesting rock-pools are uncovered at low-tide.

Herne Bay *see page 39*

Minnis Bay
A pleasant little resort serving the inland town of Birchington with a long, sandy, rock-strewn beach, which is flat and safe for swimming. The long promenade, backed by several grassy areas containing a putting green, gives way to high chalk cliffs to the east.

Westgate *see Margate*

MARGATE *see page 40*

Cliftonville *see Margate*

WHITSTABLE

Whitstable is a largely unspoiled resort where the amenities of a modern town stand side by side with cottages, inns and sail-lofts which date back to the last century when the town was associated with oyster fishing. The shingle beach, banked between wooden groynes, gives way to muddy sand at low-tide and is safe for swimming. Whitstable's main beach lies to the east, towards Tankerton, where an unusual mile-long shingle spit, known as 'The Street', juts out to sea providing an interesting low-tide walk.

The town is an ideal yachting centre for both the beginner and the experienced sailor and various national and international yachting events are held there throughout the year. Trips with local fishermen can be arranged and a number of well-preserved local footpaths offer excellent opportunities for rambling.

A 'Blessing of the Waters' ceremony takes place each July, and a regatta and the town Carnival are usually held in August.

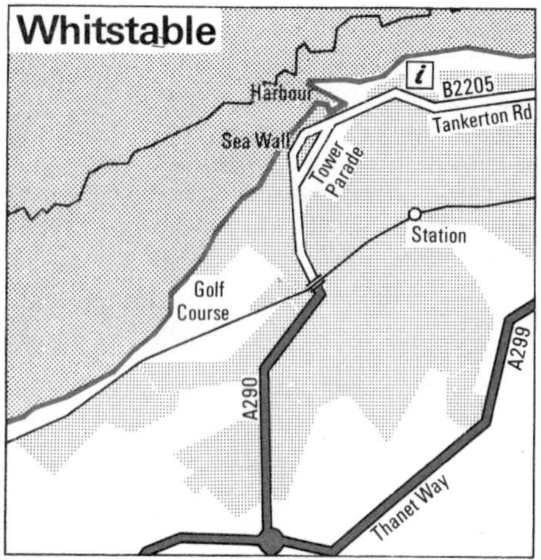

Recreation and Sports

Castle Grounds – Bowls
Marine Parade – Tennis
Seasalter Golf Club Collingwood Rd ☎*272020*
West Beach – Putting, swimming pool, tennis
Whitstable Bowl (Ten-pin) Tower Pde ☎*274661*
Whitstable Yacht Club Sea Wall ☎*272343*

Cinema

Oxford Cinema Oxford St ☎272736

Tourist Information Centre

Division Office Tankerton Rd ☎*272233*

Accommodation

The following establishments are recommended by the AA. Further information may be obtained from the Tourist Information Office.

★★ **Marine** Marine Pde, Tankerton (1m E) ☎*272672*

Restaurants

XX **Giovanni's** 49–51 Canterbury Rd ☎*273034*
XX **Windmill** Borstal Hill ☎*272866*

An ideal yachting centre

A quiet, seaside town which has developed into a pleasant residential area whilst retaining the essential ingredients for a family holiday. The beach is mainly composed of pebbles but sand and rock-pools are uncovered at low-tide and, at certain times during the summer, a shallow natural paddling pool appears on the beach about half a mile from the shore which is ideal for small children. Bathing is generally safe and Herne Bay is a favourite spot for shrimping, especially around the rock-pools. The area to the west of Hampton Pier is set aside for water-skiing, boat trips are available and the town is a popular centre for angling and sailing. The main pier was recently damaged by winter storms and is no longer entirely safe, although the Pier Pavilion Leisure Centre is still in operation. Numerous sailing events take place during the summer, attracting enthusiasts from all over the South East and Herne Bay Carnival is held in August.

To the east lies Bishopstone Glen, a secluded spot suitable for picnics or sunbathing. Beyond lies Reculver where the twin towers of a Norman church mark the spot where a Roman fort and a 7th-century church once stood. The site was formerly a quarter of a mile inland but erosion has brought the sea close under the walls. The towers were restored during the 19th century to serve as a landmark for Thames Estuary Shipping. Inland, the village of Herne retains an unspoiled charm and is overlooked by an 18th-century windmill which may be visited at certain times. The village stages the popular Cripplecraft Fête each year.

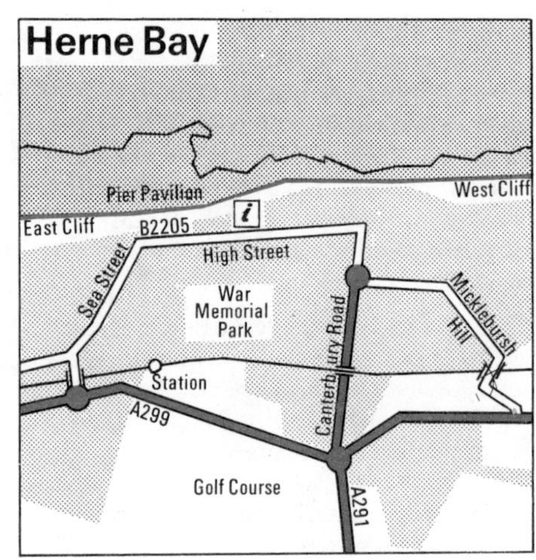

Recreation and Sports

Hampton – Amusements, boating pool
Herne Bay Golf Club Eddington ☎3964
Herne Bay Sailing Club The Downs ☎5650
Memorial Park – Boating, bowls, tennis
Pier Pavilion Leisure Centre ☎66921 – Bar, most indoor sports, spectator gallery
Seafront – Bandstand, crazy-golf, rides, trampolines

Cinema

Classic 4 Avenue Rd ☎4930

Theatre

Kings Hall East Cliff ☎4188

Places of Interest

Museum Herne Bay Library, High St ☎4896

Tourist Information

[i] **Tourist Information Office** 1 Richmond St ☎66031

Accommodation

The following establishments are recommended by the AA. Further information may be obtained from the Tourist Information Office.

★★ **St George** Western Espl ☎3776
GH **Beauvalle** 92 Central Pde ☎5330
GH **Northdown Hotel** 14 Cecil Park ☎2051

Relaxing by the sea

MARGATE

Long before the town began to develop into a holiday resort Margate was used extensively as a base for smugglers who concealed their contraband in spacious caves which can still be visited during the summer in lower Cliftonville. The area was fortified, in common with the surrounding coastline, during the Napoleonic Wars and it was not long afterwards that Margate, or 'Bartholomew Fair by the Sea', as it was then known, gained publicity when the first bathing machines were operated from its sands. During the 19th century the town blossomed into one of the most popular resorts in Kent, particularly beloved by Londoners, crowds of whom would arrive on what was known as the 'Saturday Boat' to spend the weekend beside the sea.

Today the harbour shelters a flotilla of small boats and is the starting point for speedboat and fishing trips and the visitor to Margate is presented with wide, sandy beaches scattered with outcrops of rock, where safe bathing can be enjoyed, except when red flags are displayed. The central beach area, Marine Sands, backed by a conglomeration of shops, cafés and amusement arcades, offers beach huts, deck chairs and windbreaks for hire and can become very crowded in the height of the summer. On the opposite side of the promenade lies the entrance to Dreamland, Margate's famous 20-acre amusement park, a complex containing bars, cinemas, a gymnasium and squash courts in addition to the expected roller coaster, ghost train, dodgems, candy floss and fairground music. The pier, badly damaged during recent winter storms, is being dismantled and may be rebuilt in the near future.

Those who prefer quieter, less commercialised beaches will find equally good sands to the east at Cliftonville or to the west at Westbrook or Westgate where there are opportunities for pleasant walks along the cliffs which extend as far as Minnis Bay.

Fêtes and events are held in the area throughout the summer and Margate's colourful Carnival takes place each August.

Recreation and Sports

D	**Cliftonville Bowling Centre (Ten-pin)** Ethelbert Cres, Cliftonville ☎ *Thanet 28632*
H	**Dane Park** – Bowls, tennis
F	**Dreamland Amusement Park** ☎ *Thanet 27011*
E/F	**Hartsdown Park** – Approach golf, indoor swimming pool, tennis
C	**Lido** Cliftonville – Amusements, children's pool and play area, crazy-golf
F	**Marine Terrace** – Putting, outdoor swimming pool
E	**Royal Esplanade** Westbrook – Bowls, putting, tennis
	Tivoli Park Hartsdown Rd – Margate FC – Southern League (adjoining Hartsdown Park)
	Westgate and Birchington Golf Club Canterbury Rd (A28), Westgate ☎ *Thanet 31115*

Cabaret/Dancing

F	**Bali Hai Bar** Marine Ter ☎ *Thanet 27011*
D	**Bowlers Arms** Ethelbert Cres ☎ *Thanet 28632*
F	**El Toro Bar, Galleon Bar and Mad Hatters** Dreamland Amusement Park ☎ *Thanet 27011*
C	**Hades** The Lido, Cliftonville ☎ *Thanet 23456* (June – Sep)

Cinemas

F	**Dreamland Twin Cinemas** Dreamland Park ☎ *Thanet 27011*
F	**Plaza** High St ☎ *Thanet 20058*

Theatres

C	**Lido Theatre** Cliftonville ☎ *Thanet 23456*
D	**Oval** Cliftonville ☎ *Thanet 22880*
C	**Winter Gardens** Fort Cres ☎ *Thanet 21348*

Places of Interest

C	**Margate Caves** Northdown Rd, Cliftonville ☎ *Thanet 20139*
G(1)	**Shell Grotto** Grotto Hill ☎ *Thanet 20008* An 18th-century Grotto displaying shell-studded walls
	Salmestone Grange 1m S of town centre off Shottendane Rd (B2049) ☎ *Thanet 21136* A restored 12th-century building owned by St Augustine's Abbey, Canterbury
C(2)	**Tudor House** King St ☎ *Thanet 25511 ext 353* Early 16th-century building, the oldest in Margate, now open as a museum.

Tourist Information

	Teletourist Daily Information Service ☎ *Thanet 291540*
[i] F	**Tourist Information Centre** Marine Ter ☎ *Thanet 20241*
	Sports and Recreation Information ☎ *Thanet 25511*

Accommodation

The establishments listed below are a selection of AA-recommended accommodation located in the area covered by the Town Plan. Further information may be found in AA publications or obtained from the Tourist Information Centre.

1GH	**Charnwood** 20 Canterbury Rd ☎ *Thanet 24158*
2GH	**Lancelot** 39 Edgar Rd, Cliftonville ☎ *Thanet 22944*
3SC	**Mr & Mrs Mather** 39 Princes Ave, Cliftonville, Margate, Kent CT9 2NT
4GH	**Tyrella Private Hotel** 19 Canterbury Rd ☎ *Thanet 22746*
★★	**Walpole Bay** Fifth Ave, Cliftonville ☎ *Thanet 21703* (off plan)
★	**Ye Olde Charles Inn** Northdown Rd, Cliftonville ☎ *Thanet 21817* (off plan)

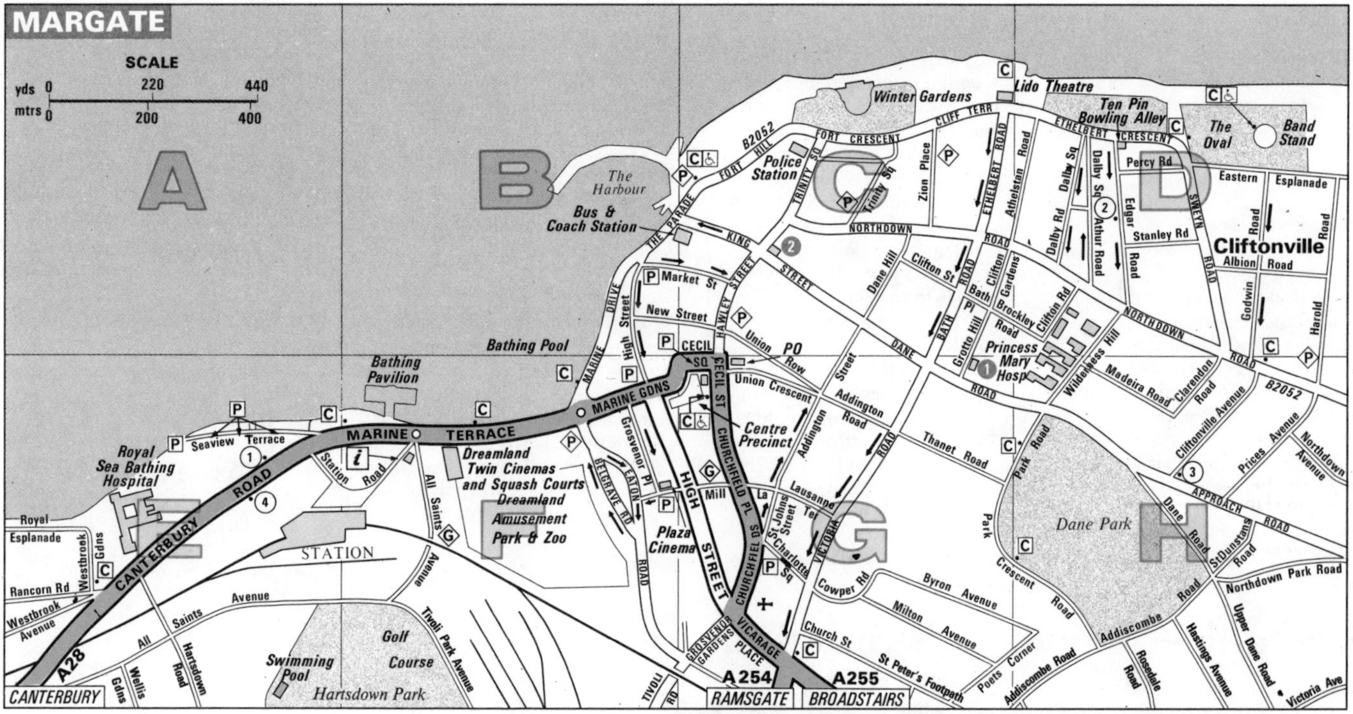

MARGATE

SCALE
yds 0 220 440
mtrs 0 200 400

WEATHER CHART	Av hours of Sunshine in month	Hottest Av daily Temp °C
April	182	9
May	223	12
June	236	15
July	220	17
August	205	17
September	161	16

Joss Bay

Kingsgate Bay
The stretch of sandy beach at Kingsgate Bay is reached by steps from the cliffs above. Outcrops of rock along the beach contain pools when the tide is low.

Broadstairs *see page 43*

Ramsgate *see page 44*

Sandwich Bay
A toll road gives access to this wide, sandy beach recommended for both swimming and fishing. The town, which gave its name to the bay, was once one of the Cinque Ports until the silting up of the river made this use impracticable. Such was the extent of the build-up of sand that Sandwich now lies 1½ miles inland.

Deal *see page 45*

Walmer
Here stands Walmer Castle, built by Henry VIII to protect a coastline susceptible to invasion. In 1730 it was transformed from a fortress into the official residence of the Lords Warden of the Cinque Ports. It is still used for this purpose, the present holder of the title being Sir Robert Menzies. The Duke of Wellington was a former Lord Warden and a museum devoted to the Iron Duke is housed in the castle.

Kingsdown
Once a small fishing village, Kingsdown is now a residential area, some of its houses enjoying a fine cliff-top position with extensive views over the Straights of Dover. The shelving shingle beach gives way in the south to a military firing range.

St Margaret's Bay
This sheltered bay is often used by cross-Channel swimmers who set out from its shingle, sand and rocky beach. Swimming at low-tide, however, is not recommended. A 90-foot high obelisk on Leathercote Point commemorates the Dover Patrol who, during the war, kept mine-free shipping lanes open to the Channel ports.

Dover
While more than a million tourists pass through Dover each year, earning it the reputation of the busiest international passenger port in the world, many more come to visit the historic town. Dover has some of the most important Roman remains in the country with its Pharos (lighthouse) standing next to the castle and the remarkable, recently excavated Roman Painted House. The impressive Norman castle stands in a commanding position over the famous white cliffs. For the sporting enthusiast there is a good sports complex, and four golf courses exist in the area. Naturally enough marine activities also thrive here, such as angling, sailing and power boat racing. Regular regattas are held in the area during the summer.

FOLKESTONE *see page 46*

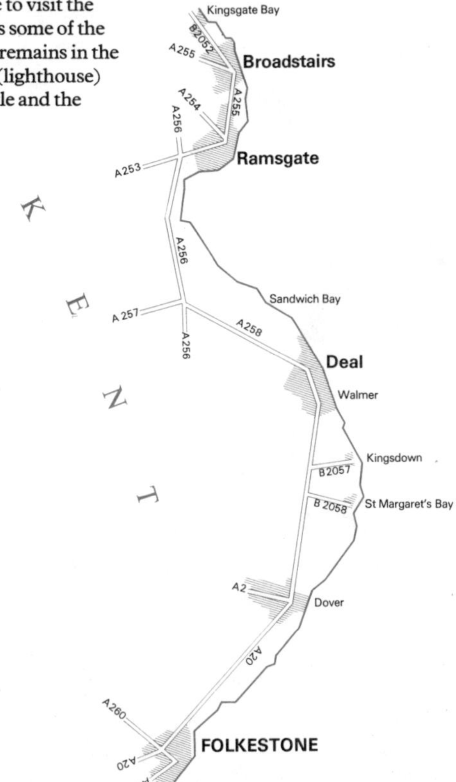

BROADSTAIRS

A 16th-century port which became a fashionable resort during the Regency era and continued its development under Victorian patronage. A notable visitor during the latter period was Charles Dickens who worked on *David Copperfield* and *Nicholas Nickleby* while staying at Bleak House, then known as Fort House, which stands on the cliffs above the harbour. Below Bleak House lies the oldest surviving part of the town – a maze of twisting streets full of quaint inns – which lends itself admirably to the annual Dickens Festival when the local people dress up as characters from his novels, parade through the town and perform plays and readings. Bleak House and the Dickens House Museum, the original model for the house of Betsy Trotwood in *David Copperfield*, are both open to the public.

There are several sandy bays on the surrounding shoreline and the main beach is at Viking Bay, sheltered by a 16th-century jetty, where donkey rides and children's amusements are available. Lifeguards are on duty in Viking Bay when a blue flag is displayed and can reach the neighbouring bays by boat if required.

Broadstairs is a popular centre for dinghy sailing and there are ample opportunities for sea fishing or freshwater angling on the nearby River Stour.

In addition to the Dickens Festival, seasonal events include fishing festivals, a Horse Show and Gymkhana, a Carnival and Water Gala and a Music Festival.

To the north towards Kingsgate stands North Foreland Lighthouse which has guided shipping around the notorious Goodwin Sands since 1636. The lighthouse is also an important radio beacon for aircraft crossing the Channel towards England and is open to the public during the summer.

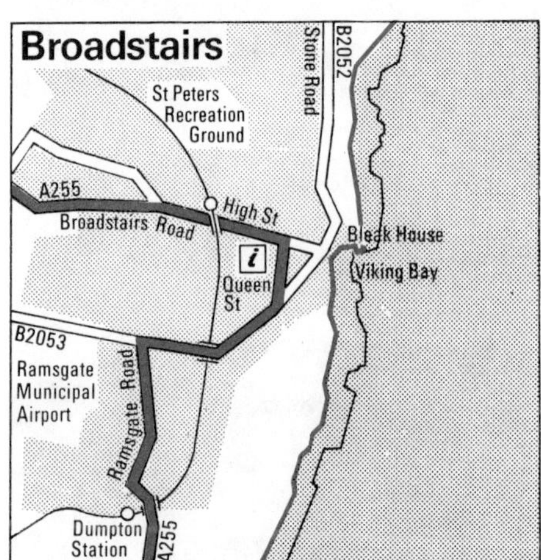

Recreation and Sports

Broadstairs Sailing Club Harbour St ☎ *Thanet61373*
Grand Pool Promenade – Outdoor heated swimming pool
Memorial Recreation Ground Lawn Rd ☎ *Thanet61283* – Bowls, children's playground and supervised Holiday Play Scheme, putting, tennis
North Foreland Golf Club Convent Rd, Kingsgate ☎ *Thanet62140*
St Peters Recreation Ground Callis Court Rd ☎ *Thanet61499* – Tennis

Theatre

Pavilion on the Sands Promenade ☎ *Thanet64682*

Places of Interest

Bleak House Fort Rd ☎ *Thanet62224*
Dickens House Museum Victoria Pde ☎ *Thanet62853*
North Foreland Lighthouse North Foreland Rd (B2052)

Tourist Information

Broadstairs Harbour ☎ *Thanet61879*
Teletourist Daily Information Service ☎ *Thanet291540*
Tourist Information Office Pierremont Pk ☎ *Thanet68399*

Accommodation

The following establishments are recommended by the AA. Further information may be obtained from the Tourist Information Office.

★★★	**Castle Keep** ☎ *Thanet65222*
★★	**Castlemore** Western Esplanade ☎ *Thanet61566*
★★	**Fayreness** Marine Dr, Kingsgate ☎ *Thanet61103*
★★	**Royal Albion** Albion St ☎ *Thanet62116*
★	**Dutch House** North Foreland Rd ☎ *Thanet62824*
AP	**Curzon** 26 Granville Rd ☎ *Thanet63227*
AP	**Warwick** 16 Granville Rd ☎ *Thanet62246*
GH	**Bay Tree Hotel** 12 Eastern Esplanade ☎ *Thanet61327*
GH	**Corner Ways** 49–51 Westcliff Rd ☎ *Thanet61612*
GH	**Denmead Hotel** 13 Granville Rd ☎ *62580*
GH	**Empress Hotel** 9 Seapoint Rd ☎ *Thanet64726*
GH	**Kingsmead Hotel** Eastern Esplanade ☎ *Thanet61694*
GH	**St Augustine's Private Hotel** 19 Granville Rd ☎ *65017*
GH	**Seapoint Private Hotel** 76 Westcliff Rd ☎ *Thanet62269*

RAMSGATE

Ever since the 18th century, when the present harbour was constructed, Ramsgate has been an important seafaring town. It was the embarkation point for the Duke of Wellington's troops en route for the Continent and, more than a century later, received thousands of survivors from Dunkirk, a fact commemorated by the Dunkirk Window in St George's Church. Today the harbour is used extensively by ships bringing imported cars into the country and the International Yacht Marina offers a haven for smaller sea-going craft. Nevertheless Ramsgate has retained the appearance of an old-fashioned port with its chandlers, repair yards, fishing boats and Regency and Victorian harbour surroundings.

For all its commercial maritime connections Ramsgate is a thriving family holiday resort offering a varied programme of entertainment and sandy beaches which are quite safe for swimming, provided the harbour walls are avoided. Lifeguards and safety boats patrol the shoreline during the summer. There is a Children's Corner on the main beach, to the east of the harbour, containing rides and swings. Beach chalets are available for hire on West Cliff Sands, and there are plentiful amusements along the length of the promenade. Annual events include the town Carnival, the London-Ramsgate-Calais-London Power Boat Race, Thanet Sailing Week and various fêtes during July and August.

To the south-west lies Pegwell Bay which contains the International Hoverport where visitors may book a day trip to Calais or watch the cross-Channel comings and goings from the public viewing platform. On the cliffs above stands a Viking Ship which crossed the sea from Denmark in 1949 to commemorate the landing of the Chieftains Hengist and Horsa in the 5th century. St Augustines Cross at nearby Ebbsfleet marks the spot where the saint set foot on English soil over one hundred years later.

Recreation and Sports

King George VI Park East Cliff – Pitch and putt
Montefiore Avenue Dumpton – Bowls, tennis
Pleasurama Marina Esplanade ☎ *Thanet52382* Amusement Park, bars, disco, night club
St Augustines Golf Club Ebbsfleet ☎ *Thanet821346*
Ramsgate Greyhound Stadium Dumpton Pk ☎ *Thanet53333*
Ramsgate Football Club Southwood Rd ☎ *Thanet51636*
Warre Recreation Ground Newington Rd ☎ *Thanet53754* – Indoor heated swimming pool
Westcliff Royal Esplanade – Boating, bowls, mini-golf, putting

Cabaret/Dancing

Club Tiberius (Casino), Harbour Pde ☎ *585678*
Papa Doc's Marina Esplanade ☎ *52383*

Cinemas

Classic King St ☎ *Thanet51081*
Kings Market Pl ☎ *Thanet52524*

Theatre

Granville Theatre Victoria Pde ☎ *Thanet51750*

Places of Interest

International Hoverport Pegwell Bay ☎ *Thanet54761/55555*
Model Village St Augustines Rd ☎ *Thanet52543*
Museum Public Library, Guildford Lawn ☎ *Thanet53532*

Tourist Information

Harbour Authorities ☎ *Thanet52277*
Teletourist Daily Information Service ☎ *Thanet291540*
Tourist Information Office Queen St ☎ *Thanet51086*

Accommodation

The following establishments are recommended by the AA. Further information may be obtained from the Tourist Information Office.

★★	**Court Stairs Hotel and Country Club** Pegwell Rd, Westcliff ☎ *Thanet51850*
★★	**San Clu** East Cliff Prom ☎ *Thanet52345*
★★	**Savoy** Grange Rd ☎ *Thanet52637*
GH	**Abbeygail** 17 Penshurst Rd ☎ *Thanet54154*
GH	**Sylvan Hotel** 160–162 High St ☎ *Thanet53026*
GH	**Westcliff** 9 Grange Rd ☎ *Thanet56872*

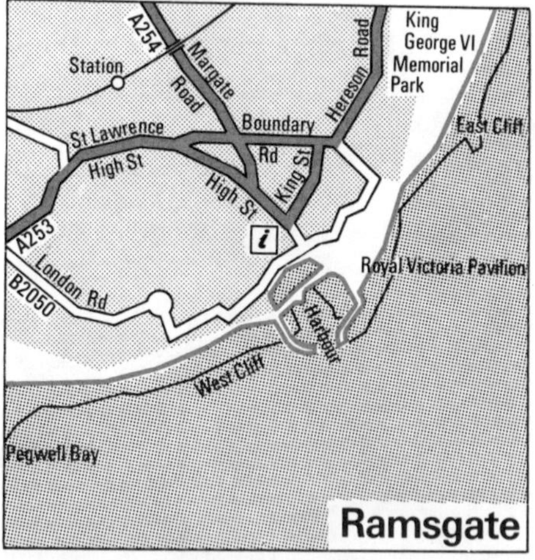

Inner harbour

Deal, the landing place of Julius Caesar in 55 BC, became an important maritime town around the middle of the 16th century when Henry VIII established Deal, Walmer and Sandown Castles as a protection against invaders and thereafter benefited from an increase of trade as vessels were prevented from using the old Cinque port of Sandwich by the silting up of Sandwich Haven. Deal continued to thrive as a Channel port and was used as a naval base during the years of war which followed. The town has now become a popular holiday resort, but retains much of its former character and the oldest area, around Middle Street, which contains a number of 18th-century cottages in narrow streets leading to the seafront, has been declared a Conservation Area. The old Time Ball Tower on the promenade, which now houses the Information Office, was used to semaphore messages to London during the Napoleonic Wars and, until 1927, the black ball on its rooftop was lowered by an electrical current direct from Greenwich Observatory at 1pm each day to give the correct time to passing shipping.

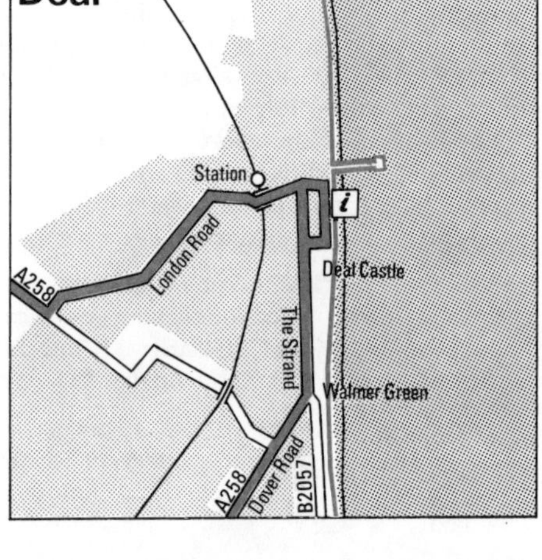

The present-day resort offers the visitor a shelving, shingle beach which is ideal for fishing but swimmers, particularly children, should remain close to the shore. Lifeguards patrol certain stretches of the beach regularly and a red flag is displayed when bathing is considered unsafe. Amusements and places of entertainment are plentiful and the Royal Marines, whose School of Music is situated in the local barracks, stage displays and concerts and usually play an active part in civic ceremonies. Deal has a Maritime Museum, and the castle, built in the pattern of a Tudor Rose, is open to the public.

Inland, to the north, lies the town of Sandwich which has many ancient buildings and is separated from the coast by three famous golf courses, and the ruined Richborough Castle, dating from Roman times.

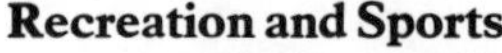

Recreation and Sports

Deal Bowling Club The Pavilion, Mill Rd ☎*4701*
Deal Town FC Charles Sports Ground, Mill Rd ☎*5623*
Royal Cinque Ports Golf Club ☎*4007*
Walmer Green ☎*5029* – Mini-golf, outdoor draughts, paddling pool
Walmer and Kingsdown Golf Club Kingsdown ☎*3256*

Cinemas

Classic Queen St ☎*4479*
Royal King St ☎*4393*

Theatres

Astor Theatre Stanhope Rd ☎*4931*
The Quarterdeck 37 Beach St ☎*4629*

Places of Interest

Deal Castle Marine Rd
Maritime and Local History Museum 22 St Georges Rd, ☎*4869*
Walmer Castle Kingsdown Rd, Walmer
Walmer Norman Manor House Church St, Walmer

Tourist Information

Tourist Information Office Time Ball Tower, Seafront ☎*61161* Ext263

Accommodation

The following establishments are recommended by the AA. Further information may be obtained from the Tourist Information Centre.

GH **Pension Castle Lea** 2 Gladstone Rd ☎*2718*
GH **Winthorpe Private Hotel** Kingsdown Rd, Walmer ☎*5788*

Lifeguard patrol

FOLKESTONE

Perched on chalk cliffs above extensive sandy beaches, Folkestone presents the visitor with a clean, elegant picture of a flourishing seaside resort whilst retaining its position as one of the country's major cross-Channel ports. Lawns and flowerbeds line the walks along the broad cliff-top promenade, known as The Leas, which extends for more than a mile, and winding paths, bordered with alpine plants, descend the wooded slopes to the shore some 200ft below. The Leas has no shops or kiosks although it has a bandstand where concerts are staged during the summer. The cliffs provide a fine view of Channel shipping and the French coast is visible on clear days. A 19th-century water-driven lift, one of the few of its kind in the country, connects the cliffs with Marine Gardens and the beach below.

Folkestone's two beaches, one sand, one shingle, lie on either side of the harbour. There is safe bathing for all, provided the harbour entrance is avoided. Further pleasant beaches are to be found beyond the East Cliff Gardens below the rugged, wooded areas of The Warren and Little Switzerland which abound in wild flowers.

The town's maritime past lives on in the harbour area where narrow cobbled streets and buildings from another age contrast with the modern ferries which carry passengers to France and Belgium. If a visit to the busy harbour whets your appetite for travel, day trips may be arranged.

Folkestone offers the holidaymaker a varied programme of amusements, sports and entertainment and seasonal events include Cricket Week, Folklore Festivals, Horse Shows and Carnivals.

H **AA Port Service Centre** Folkestone Harbour ☎*58111*

Recreation and Sports

J(1) **Bandstand** The Leas

Cheriton Road Sports Ground (off A2034) – Bowls, cricket, tennis

H **East Cliff** Wear Bay Rd – Bowls, mini-golf, tennis

A(2) **Folkestone Sports Centre** Radnor Park Ave ☎*58222* – Most indoor sports including skiing

Folkestone Race Course Westenhanger ☎*Hythe66407* (6m W off A20)

Folkestone Town FC Cheriton Rd ☎*51374* (off A2034) – Southern League

J/K(3) **Lower Sandgate Rd** ☎*54488* – Swimming pool

K **Marine Gardens** – Mini-golf

J **Marine Walk** – Amusements, boating, swimming pool

B **Radnor Park** – Bowls, tennis

K **Rotunda** Marine Pde ☎*53461* – Amusements

Sene Valley Golf Club Blackhouse Hill ☎*Hythe66726* (3m W off A20)

Cabaret/Dancing

C **Oliver's La Clique** 32 Dover Rd ☎*59437*

C **Sundowner Club** 28 Dover Rd ☎*58385*

Cinema

G **Curzon** George Ln ☎*53335*

Theatres

J(4) **Leas Cliff Hall** ☎*53193*

K(5) **Leas Pavilion** ☎*52466*

K(6) **Marine Pavilion** ☎*53708*

Places of Interest

I(7) **Folkestone Art Centre** New Metropole, The Leas ☎*55070*

G(8) **Museum and Art Gallery** Grace Hill ☎*57583*

Spade House Radnor Cliff Cres, Sandgate ☎*38311* (off Lower Sandgate Rd)

Tourist Information

G **Official Information Centre** Pedestrian Precinct, Sandgate Rd ☎*53840* (Summer only)

[i]G **Tourist Information Office** Harbour St ☎*58594*

Accommodation

The establishments listed below are a selection of AA-recommended accommodation and restaurants located in the area covered by the Town Plan. Further information may be found in AA publications or obtained from the Official Information Centre.

1GH **Argos Private Hotel** 6 Marine Ter ☎*54309*

2GH **Arundel Hotel** 3 Clifton Rd ☎*52442*

3GH **Beaumont Private Hotel** 5 Marine Ter ☎*52740*

4GH **Belmonte Private Hotel** 30 Castle Hill Av ☎*54470*

5★★★★ **Burlington** Earls Av ☎*55301*

6GH **Claremont Private Hotel** 20–22 Claremont Rd ☎*54897*

7★★★ **Clifton** The Leas ☎*53191*

8✕ **Emilio's Portofino** 124a Sandgate Rd ☎*55866*

9★★★ **Garden House** Sandgate Rd ☎*52278*

10Ⓟ **Greystones** Clifton Cres ☎*54090*

11GH **Guest House** 74–76 Dover Rd ☎*55313*

12✕✕ **Hop Kweng** Majestic House, Sandgate Rd ☎*56532*

13GH **Horseshore Private Hotel** 29 Westbourne Gdns ☎*52184*

14GH **Michaels** 35 Tontine St ☎*55961*

15✕ **Nicolas L'Escargot** 3 Trinity Cres ☎*53864*

16GH **Pier Hotel** 1 Marine Cres ☎*54444*

17GH **Shannan Private Hotel** 59–61 Cheriton Rd ☎*52138*

18✕✕ **La Tavernetta** Leaside Court ☎*54955*

19GH **Wearbay** 25 Wear Bay Cres ☎*52586*

20★ **Westbourne** 7–8 Westbourne Gdns ☎*55045*

21GH **Westward Ho! Private Hotel**, 13 Clifton Cres ☎*52663*

22★★ **Windsor** Langhorne Gdns ☎*51348*

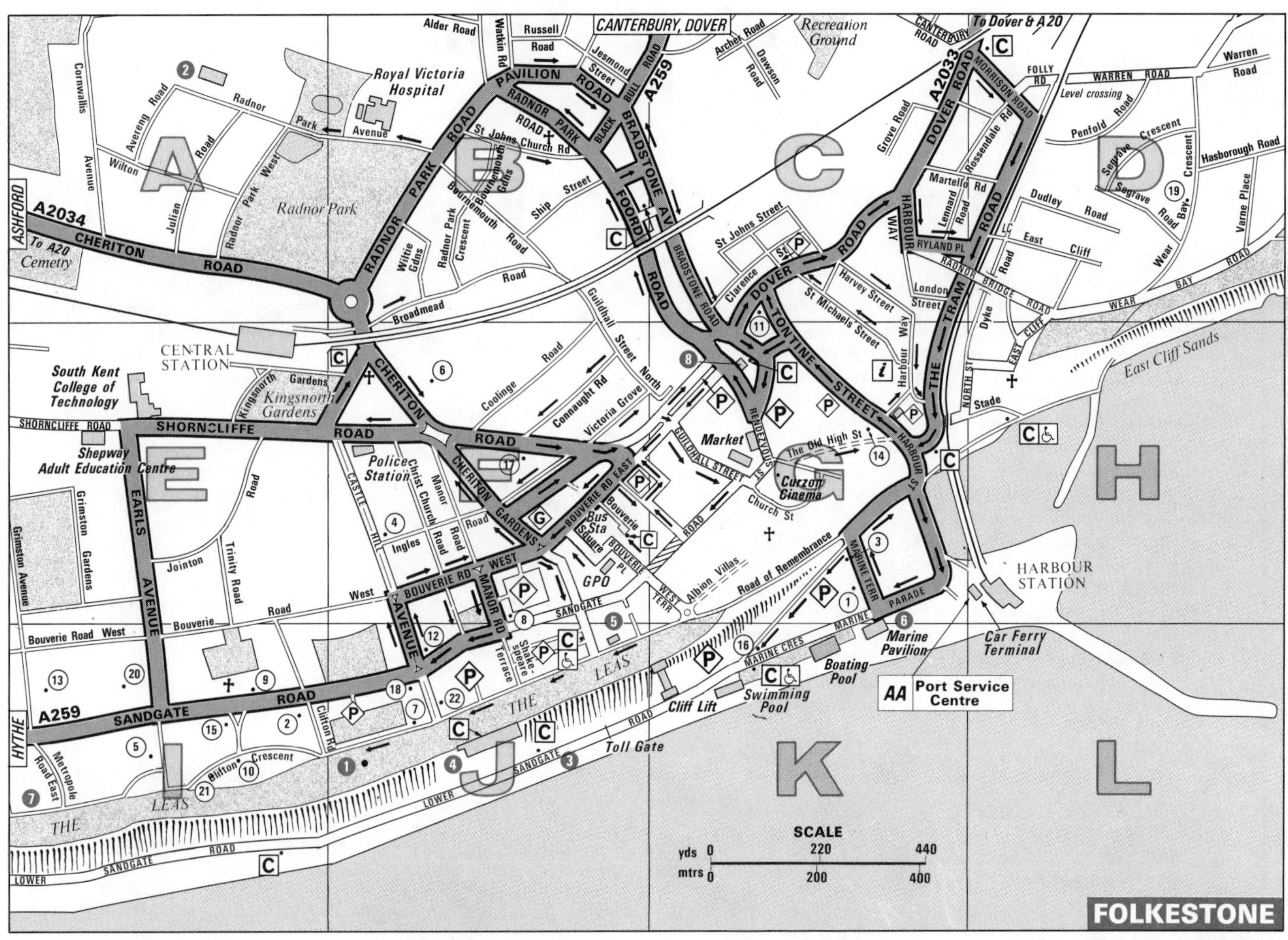
FOLKESTONE
CANTERBURY, DOVER
To Dover & A20
ASHFORD
A2034
CHERITON ROAD
To A20 Cemetry
HYTHE
A259
SANDGATE ROAD
Royal Victoria Hospital
Radnor Park
Recreation Ground
CENTRAL STATION
South Kent College of Technology
Kingsnorth Gardens
Shepway Adult Education Centre
Police Station
Market
Curzon Cinema
GPO
Bus Sta
HARBOUR STATION
Car Ferry Terminal
Marine Pavilion
Boating Pool
Swimming Pool
Cliff Lift
Toll Gate
AA Port Service Centre
East Cliff Sands
Level crossing
SCALE
yds 0 220 440
mtrs 0 200 400

FOLKESTONE and the Shepway holiday towns

Folkestone, Hythe, Dymchurch, St Mary's Bay, New Romney and Lydd on the South Kent Coast are among the best known holiday towns in Kent. They provide a wide range of holiday accommodation (hotels, guest-houses and self-catering), events and entertainments. Many delightful and fascinating day or half-day excursions to the beautiful surrounding **Garden of England** countryside are available. Or for a holiday with a difference, what about a no-passport day excursion to France? Breakfast in England, lunch in France and back again in time for dinner.

Entertainments include an excellent summer show at the Marine Pavilion, Folkestone, a wide range of concerts and events at the Leas Cliff Hall, Folkestone and repertory at the Leas Pavilion Theatre, Folkestone.
Many specialised festivals are held each year including Folkestone Carnival (August), Day of Steam, Sellindge (June) and Lydd Club Day (July). On alternate years the well-known Venetian Fête — a floating tableau — takes place in Hythe (August 1978, 1980, etc) and the International Folklore Festival in Folkestone (June 1979, 1981, etc).

Local places to visit include the 270-acre Wildlife Sanctuary, restored gardens and mansions at Port Lympne, the smallest public (steam) railway in the world — one third actual size — which runs from Hythe to Dungeness, castles at Lympne and Saltwood and a splendid Arts Centre at Folkestone. In addition to these, the district embraces excellent sporting facilities, a wide range of town and country walks, excellent beaches and the well-known Leas Promenade in Folkestone.

Further afield but still within easy touring distance is Canterbury (with its Cathedral and fascinating heritage), Dover (now a modern cross-Channel port — but still with its imposing Castle), Rye (pottery plus an olde-worlde charm) and, of course, Boulogne (in La Belle France) with its splendid old walled town, pavement cafes and restaurants.

Free literature is available from Dept AA1, Information Centre, Civic Centre, Folkestone, Kent CT20 2QY.

Tel (0303) 57388

Sandgate
A toll road, running through attractive Mediterranean-type pine woods, links Sandgate to Folkestone. Sandgate has a shingle beach and entertainment is provided by the Folkestone and Hythe Operatic and Dramatic Society who stage procuctions at the Little Theatre.

Hythe *see page 50*

St Mary's Bay
A small holiday centre with a long sandy beach divided by wooden groynes. Launching facilities may be used on payment of a small charge.

Littlestone-on-Sea
This quiet resort has a sandy beach which is safe for swimming apart from some areas near the concrete war-time pontoons which are marked as dangerous by red flags. Littlestone has a small shopping centre, a children's playground and golfing and putting facilities. Beach chalets are available for hire.

Greatstone-on-Sea
There is a long, peaceful sandy beach here, overlooked by bungalows and a holiday camp.

Lydd-on-Sea
A sandy beach, backed by a shingle bank lies on the shore overlooked by a row of bungalows. Swimming is safe. To the west is the ancient town of Lydd with many old buildings and a parish church known as the 'Cathedral of Romney Marsh'. Lydd Airport, the main air-car ferry link with the Continent, is open to the public.

Camber
A modern, coastal village with a broad sandy beach backed by dunes. Children may find the deep ridges in the sand hazardous when the tide is coming in.

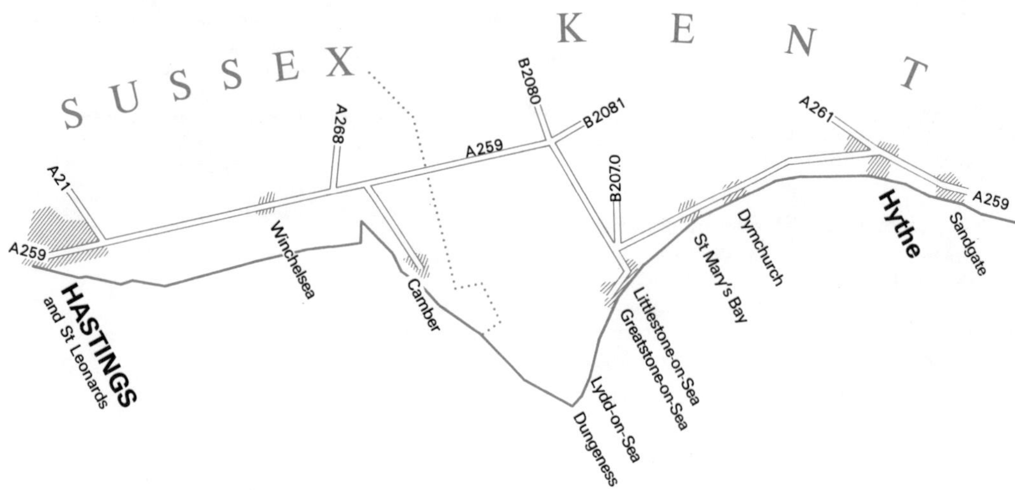

Dymchurch
This small, popular resort has a long, sandy beach which is one of the safest in the vicinity. An amusement centre, cafés, restaurants and parking facilities are all located close to the beach and a restored Martello tower is open to the public during the summer. Dymchurch was immortalised by Russell Thorndike in his *Dr Syn* novels and a *Syn Day* is held in the town each year when the exploits of the Doctor and his band of smugglers are enacted.

Dungeness
A desolate promontory containing a sancuary run by the Royal Society for the Protection of Birds. Two lighthouses, one of them with extremely modern equipment, are open to the public as is the Dungeness Nuclear Power Station. Swimming is generally very dangerous from the shingle foreshore and the famous Dungeness lifeboat is always ready for launching. The Romney, Hythe and Dymchurch Light Railway ends its 14-mile run here.

Winchelsea
The town, once the busiest of the Cinque Ports, now stands two miles inland. It has many ancient buildings and a museum illustrating the history of the Cinque Ports. Winchelsea Beach, which is mainly composed of shingle, provides safe bathing but care should be taken to avoid sunken debris and mud holes.

HASTINGS AND ST LEONARDS *see page 52*

HYTHE

The history of Hythe can be traced back to at least the 8th century and by the middle of the 12th century it had been proclaimed one of the Cinque Ports whose obligation it was to provide ships and men for the King's service and protect the Channel coast, in return for various privileges and tax exemptions. In fact, Hythe holds the oldest Cinque Ports charter in existence. Today Hythe is a peaceful, unspoiled resort with most of its modern development centred around Prince's Parade on the seafront whilst the remainder of the town has altered little since the days when Martello towers were built to guard against Napoleon's invasion. The beach is a mixture of sand and shingle and provides safe bathing and good fishing and the promenades are remarkably free from commercial enterprises. The Hythe Royal Military Canal, originally built as part of the coastal defences during the Napoleonic wars, is now mainly a pleasure boating area with craft of all kinds available for hire. Its tree-lined banks are ideal for summer walks and, every two years, a colourful water carnival, known as the Vevetian Fête, is held on its waters. Parts of Hythe parish church date from 1090 and the building contains an unusual ossuary, or charnel house, where thousands of medieval bones are stored.

The Romney, Hythe and Dymchurch Light Railway, the world's smallest public railway, begins its 14-mile journey from Hythe. The 15-inch track runs parallel to the coastline, about one mile inland, as far as Dungeness and has provided a regular service during the spring and summer since its opening in 1927. There is an engine shed at New Romney Station and exhibitions are sometimes held there.

The countryside around Hythe offers some pleasant areas for rambling and nearby Saltwood Castle, from which the murderers of St Thomas-à-Beckett set out on their bloody errand, is open to the public during the spring and summer. Lympne Castle, dating mainly from the 15th century, is also open to the public and the neighbouring Port Lympne Wildlife Sanctuary and Gardens contains a wide variety of animals, including bears, leopards, monkeys, tigers and wolves, within the grounds of an imposing Dutch Colonial-style mansion.

Recreation and Sports

Hythe Bowling Club Ladies Walk ☎*66356*
Hythe Cricket Club The Grove ☎*66356*–Cricket, putting
Hythe Imperial Golf Club Princes Parade ☎*60659*–9 holes.
Hythe Swimming Pool South Rd ☎*69177*
Recreation Ground South Rd–Tennis
Royal Military Canal–Boating
Sene Valley Golf Club Blackhouse Hill ☎*66726*
Vogue Bingo and Social Club Prospect Rd ☎*66292*

Cinema

Classic Prospect Rd ☎*66292*

Places of Interest

Lympne Castle (4m NW off B2067) ☎*67571*
Port Lympne Wildlife Sanctuary and Gardens (5½m NW off B2067) ☎*60618/9*
Saltwood Castle (1m N off Grange Rd) ☎*67190*

Tourist Information

Chamber of Commerce High St ☎*68024*

Accommodation

The following establishments are recommended by the AA. Further information may be obtained from the Tourist Information Office.

★★★★ **Imperial** Princes Pde ☎*67441*
★★★ **Stade Court** West Pde ☎*68263*
★★ **Seabrook** Seabrook (2m E A259) ☎*67279*
★ **Swan** High St ☎*66236*

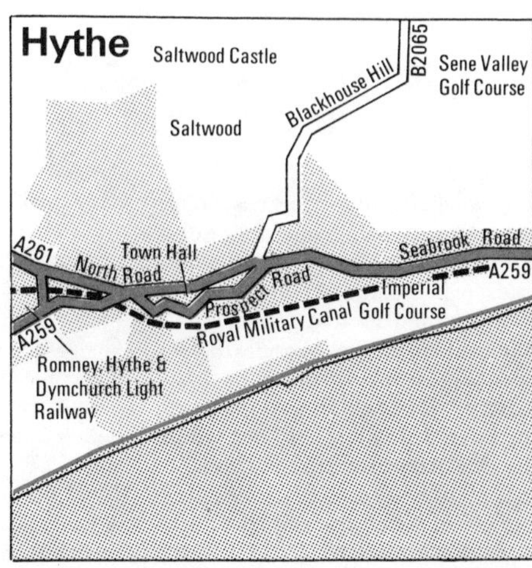

HASTINGS & ST LEONARDS

The Battle of Hastings, perhaps the best remembered event in British history, actually took place some six miles inland at a spot then known as Senlac, but since renamed Battle, where the abbey founded by William the Conqueror now stands. Nevertheless, the Duke of Normandy, according to legend, ate his first meal on English soil from a stone slab which is preserved on Hastings seafront, near the pier, and the ruins of the castle he established in 1068, to protect the coast against further invasion, still stand on the cliffs above the town. Hastings was later nominated as one of the original Cinque Ports and gradually became a centre for the fishing industry and although the town has now merged with neighbouring St Leonards to become one of the most popular resorts on the South Coast its connections with this trade are still in evidence. Fishing vessels may be seen beached on the eastern shore which is backed by the oldest part of the town, an interesting maze of narrow streets containing many ancient inns, a collection of 'net houses' over which fishing nets were once hung to dry and a Fisherman's Museum, housed in what was once a fisherman's church.

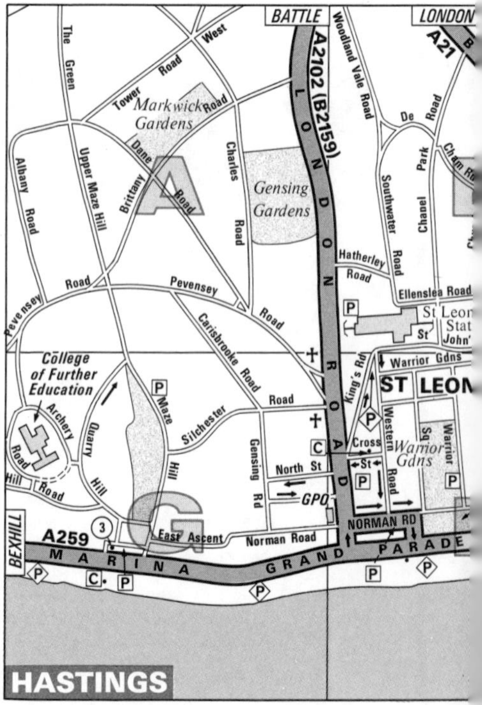

The main resort area lies to the west of the old town where two-tiered promenades overlook wide beaches mainly composed of shingle, although sand is exposed at low-tide when numerous rock-pools are revealed between the groynes. Bathing is generally safe and lifeguards patrol the beaches during the summer months. Pony rides are available and there are 'sea-floats' for hire. Ample amusement facilities adjoin the seafront and Hastings provides the visitor with entertainment ranging from orchestral concerts to professional wrestling. There are several museums and the Town Hall contains a 243ft embroidery, made at the Royal School of Needlework to commemorate the 900th anniversary of the Battle of Hastings, which recalls 81 events in British history since 1066. St Clements Caves, formerly used by local smugglers, are open to the public and dances held in this unusual setting on summer evenings. The town stages two carnivals and a Town Criers' Championship annually.

Hastings Country Park, to the east of the town, covers over 520 acres encompassing cliff-top walks, nature trails, picnic areas and the well-known beauty spot of Ecclesbourne Glen.

Recreation and Sports

D(1)	**Alexandra Park**–Aviary, bandstand, boating, bowls, children's playground, putting, tennis
L	**East Hill**–Pitch and putt
A	**Gensing Gardens**–Children's playground
	Hastings Country Park–Covers 4 miles of clifftop E of East Hill
D	**Hastings Central Cricket Ground** Priory Meadow ☎*424546*
I	**Hastings Model Village** White Rock Gardens ☎*427861*
K	**Hastings Motor Boat and Yacht Club** Rock-a-Nore ☎*429779*
	Hastings Municipal Golf Course Beauport Park ☎*52977*–3m NW off A2100
I	**Hastings Pier**–Amusements, Cash Bingo
	Hastings United FC Pilot Field ☎*43718*–Southern League–1½m N off Elphinstone Rd
I	**Indoor Bowls Centre** Falaise Rd ☎*435504*
K	**De Luxe Entertainment Centre** George St ☎*437373*–Amusement Arcade
L	**Playland** Fishmarket–Amusement Park
K	**The Stade**–Boating lake, miniature railway
H	**Warrior Gardens**–Bandstand, putting
	West Marina Gardens St Leonards–Bowls, putting–Off A259
I	**White Rock Baths** ☎*436549*–Indoor swimming pool, sauna, solarium
I	**White Rock Gardens**–Bowls, putting, tennis

Cinemas

J	**Classic** Queens Rd ☎*420517*
J	**Orion** Cambridge Rd ☎*436457*

Dancing

D(1)	**Alexandra Park**–Outdoor
I	**Falaise Hall** White Rock Gardens ☎*423975*
I	**Hastings Pier** 49 Priory St ☎*441824*
E	**St Clements Caves** West Hill ☎*422964*
G	**Sun Lounge** Grand Pde ☎*437277*

Theatres

F	**Stables Theatre** High St ☎*423221*
I(2)	**Triodrome** Hastings Pier ☎*436607*–Children's entertainment
I(3)	**White Rock Pavilion** White Rock ☎*424912*

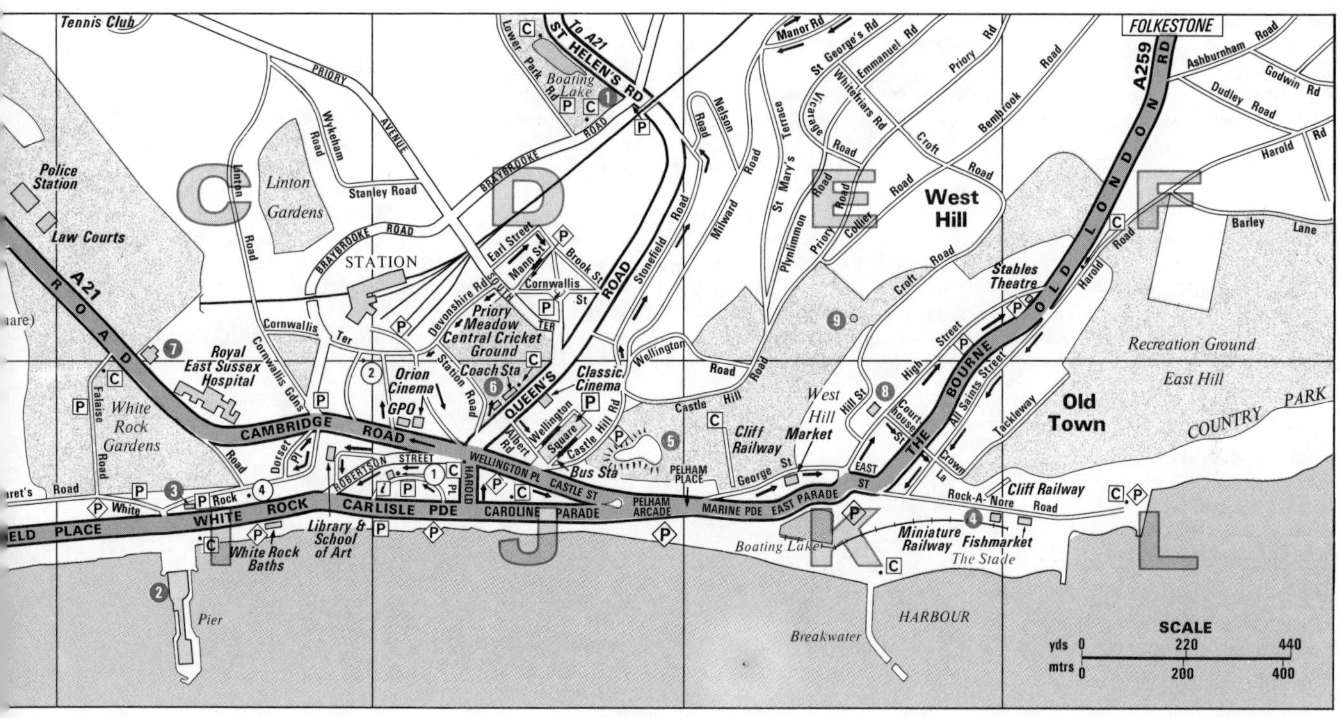

Places of Interest

K(4)	**Fisherman's Museum** Rock-a-Nore
J(5)	**Hastings Castle** Castle Hill
J(6)	**Hastings Embroidery Exhibition** Town Hall, Queens Rd
C(7)	**Hastings Museum and Art Gallery** Cambridge Rd ☎*435952*
K(8)	**Museum of Local History** Old Town Hall, High St ☎*425855*
E(9)	**St Clements' Caves** West Hill ☎*422964*

Tourist Information

[i] J	**Information Centre** 4 Robertson Ter ☎*424242*

Accommodation

The establishments listed below are a selection of AA-recommended accommodation located in the area covered by the Town Plan. Further information may be found in AA publications or obtained from the Information Centre.

1GH	**Burlington Hotel** 2 Robertson Ter ☎*429656*
2GH	**Harbour Lights** 20 Cambridge Gdns ☎*423424*
3★★	**Royal Victoria** Marina, St Leonards-on-Sea ☎*433300*
4★	**Yelton** White Rock ☎*422240*

WEATHER CHART	Av hours of Sunshine in month	Hottest Av daily Temp °C
April	177	9
May	222	12
June	238	15
July	215	17
August	202	17
September	160	15

Bexhill-on-Sea *see page 55*

Cooden Beach
A shingle beach lies below a cliff-top residential area, accessible by means of steps. Sand and outcrops of rock are exposed at low-tide.

Normans Bay
The majority of historians now agree that this bay was the spot where William the Conqueror landed with his troops in 1066 prior to defeating Harold in the Battle of Hastings. The shingle beach is reached via a level crossing.

Pevensey Bay
A medieval seaport where the Normans established a castle on the site of a Roman fort. Pevensey Bay was the scene of a violent battle in 1088 when the Conqueror's eldest son, Robert, unsuccessfully attempted to invade England and overthrow the rule of his brother, William Rufus. Modern Pevensey Bay is a popular resort. The shingle beach, divided by groynes, gives way to sand at low-tide and bathing is generally safe. The village of Pevensey has some ancient buildings and the ruins of the castle stand one mile inland.

EASTBOURNE *see page 56*

Beachy Head
This well-known viewpoint rises to over 500 feet providing the many sightseers who visit it during the summer with a coastal panorama stretching from Dungeness in the east to the Isle of Wight in the west. There is extensive parking and police patrol the cliff top during the season. The lighthouse below emits a beam visible up to 16 miles from the shore.

Seaford *see page 59*

Newhaven
The busy harbour is the focal point of this town, serving freighters and fishing boats as well as the cross-Channel car and passenger ferries to Dieppe. A car park overlooks the harbour and to the west lies a shelving shingle beach which is not recommended for swimming. Newhaven offers good sporting facilities and the local sailing club organises regular weekend races during the summer.

Peacehaven
This area was scheduled for development into a resort but the transformation never actually took place. A shingle beach with low-tide rock-pools lies below steep cliffs. There is a golf course and a monument on the cliff top marks the spot where the Greenwich meridian leaves England.

Rottingdean
A small village nestling in a valley between chalk cliffs with a shingle beach. There is an outdoor swimming pool. Rudyard Kipling once lived in the house beside the church which now contains the Grange Museum and Art Gallery.

BRIGHTON AND HOVE *see page 60*

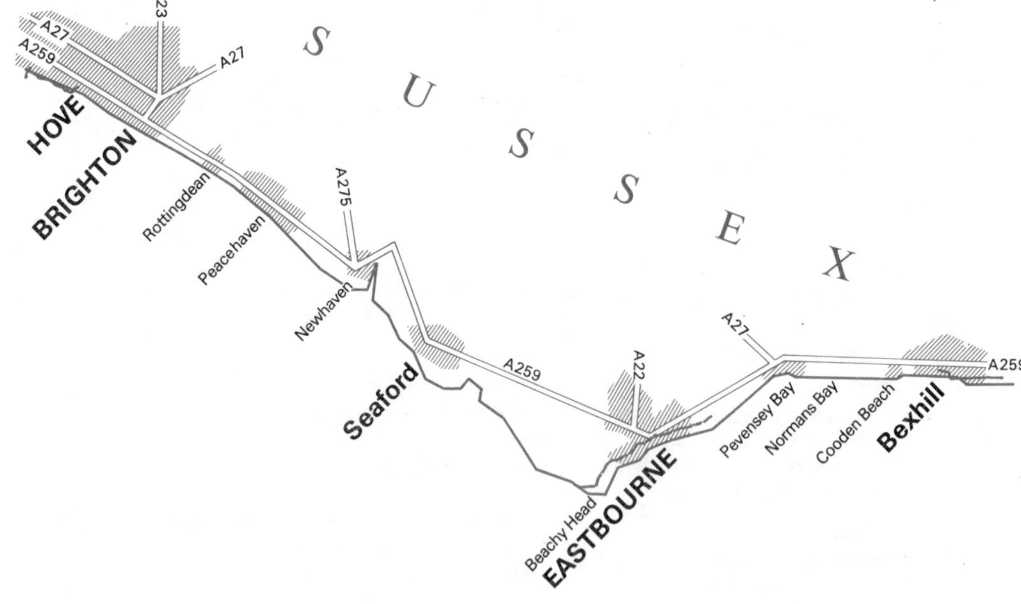

BEXHILL

A quiet peaceful town ideally suited to family holidays. The beach is a mixture of sand and shingle and is generally safe for bathing, apart from some mud-holes which are marked by red flags. Beach cabins are available for hire.

The beach is overlooked by the De La Warr Pavilion, the first seafront entertainment complex to be built in this country. This imposing structure, completed in 1935, contains sun terraces, a bar, a restaurant and cafeteria, a ballroom, a theatre and a concert hall where leading entertainers appear during the summer. Children's shows and antique fairs etc are also held there. Bexhill is an angling and sailing centre and sub-aqua enthusiasts will find a number of submerged wrecks of vessels and aircraft around the coast.

The town itself has good shopping facilities and is mainly residential. St Peters Church is of Saxon origin and contains some interesting carvings. There is a museum of local archaeology and natural history in Egerton Park and The Bexhill Manor Costume Museum contains a display of costumes, toys and dolls.

Galley Hill, to the east of the town, provides fine views of the surrounding countryside. At low-tide the remains of a forest can be seen, part of the 'land bridge' which joined Britain to the Continent 10,000 years ago.

Recreation and Sports

Egerton Park – Bowls, open-air swimming pool, putting, tennis
Little Common Recreation Ground – Cricket, football, tennis
Polegrove Recreation Ground – Bowls, cricket, football, rugby
Sidley Recreation Ground – Bowls

Cinema

The Curzon Leisure Centre Western Rd ☎*210078*

Theatre

De la Warr Pavilion Theatre ☎*212022*

Places of Interest

Bexhill-on-Sea Museum Egerton Park ☎*211769*
Manor Barn Old Town ☎*212023* A 12th-century manor house and period costume museum.

Tourist Information

Tourist Information Office De La Warr Pavilion Marina ☎*212023*

Accommodation

The following establishments are recommended by the AA. Further information may be obtained from the Tourist Information Office.

★★	**Granville** Sea Rd ☎*215437*
★	**Southlands Court** Hastings Rd ☎*210628*
GH	**Alexandra Hotel** 2 Middlesex Rd ☎*210202*
GH	**Dunselma Private Hotel** 25 Marina ☎*212988*
GH	**Victoria Hotel** 1 Middlesex Rd ☎*210382*
SC	**Quebec Close** For bookings: Mrs H Cummings, 171 Cooden Dr, Bexhill-on-Sea ☎*Cooden 2999*

EASTBOURNE

Eastbourne became recognised as a fashionable 'watering place' after George III's children spent a holiday there in the late 18th century and was developed by Victorian landowners into the present-day elegant resort, famous for its landscaped gardens and seafront floral displays. Eastbourne lies at the foot of the South Downs in the shelter of Beachy Head which effectively disperses a good deal of bad weather before it reaches the town thus assisting the resort to achieve an enviable sunshine record each year. The beaches are backed by shingle but extensive sands are uncovered at low-tide and bathing is normally safe although red flags are displayed when weather conditions render swimming dangerous. Beach huts and sea-floats are available for hire and motor and speedboats trips operate from the beach and pier. Although the seafront is relatively clear of kiosks and shops there are ample amusement facilities near the beach, notably in the area around The Redoubt, a relic of the Napoleonic Wars coastal fortifications, where an aquarium and the Treasure Island Play Centre, containing a large-scale model of a galleon set amid attractive paddling pools, are to be found. Eastbourne offers a comprehensive programme of entertainments including concerts, drama, shows and dancing and local events include carnivals, regattas, International Tennis Championships in Devonshire Park, County Cricket at the Saffrons and speedway at Arlington Stadium.

There is a Napoleonic Museum in the Wish Tower, a converted Martello Tower, and a National Lifeboat Museum is to be found in the same area on the western seafront. The older part of the town contains the ancient Lamb Inn which has a vaulted crypt, dating from the 13th century, and the Towner Art Gallery, housed in a Georgian mansion surrounded by pleasant gardens.

Places of interest within easy reach of Eastbourne are Beachy Head with its impressive views, 13th-century Michelham Priory, Polegate with its restored windmill and milling museum and Alfriston, one of the most picturesque villages in Southern England, with its timbered buildings and 13th-century church known as the 'cathedral of the Downs'.

Recreation and Sports

	Arlington Stadium The Hyde ☎*Hailsham 841642* – Speedway
R	**Devonshire Park** ☎*29942* – Tennis, squash
	Downs Golf Club East Dean Rd ☎*20827* NW off East Dean Rd A259
M	**Eastbourne Bowling Club** 3 Saffrons Rd ☎*24340*
D	**Eastbourne Leisure Pool** Royal Pde – Indoor pools & diving pit, bar, restaurant
O	**Eastbourne Pier** ☎*22889* – Amusements, fishing
	Eastbourne Rugby Football Club Park Ave, Hampden Park ☎*53076*
K	**Eastbourne Sailing Club** Splash Point, The Redoubt ☎*22217*
	Eastbourne Town FC The Saffrons, Compton Place Rd ☎*37932* – Athenian League
H	**Eastbourne United FC** The Oval, Princes Park ☎*764825* – Athenian League
	Gildredge Park – Bowls
	Hampden Park – Bowls, putting, tennis
	Helen Garden – Bowls, putting
	Manor Gardens – Tennis
	Motcombe Gardens – Bowls
	Princes Park – Bowls, pitch and putt
K	**Redoubt** – Bowls, putting, tennis, Treasure Island Play Centre
	Royal Eastbourne Golf Club Paradise Dr ☎*29738* W of The Saffrons
M	**The Saffrons** Saffrons Rd ☎*24328* – Club and County Cricket
K	**Sovereign Sailing Club** Royal Pde ☎*20715*
	Willingdon Golf Club Southdown Rd ☎*638728*

Cinemas

N	**ABC** Pevensey Rd ☎*23612*
N	**Curzon** Langney Rd ☎*31441*
N	**Tivoli** 111 Seaside Rd ☎*21031*

Dancing

O	**Dixieland Showbar** Eastbourne Pier
R(1)	**Winter Gardens** Compton St ☎*25252*

Theatres

R(1)	**Congress Theatre** Devonshire Park ☎*36363*
R(1)	**Devonshire Park Theatre** 8 Compton St ☎*21121*
N	**Royal Hippodrome** Seaside Rd ☎*24336*
R(1)	**Winter Gardens** Compton St ☎*25252*

Places of Interest

R(2)	**Coastal Defence Museum** The Wish Tower, King Edward's Pde ☎*35809*
K	**Eastbourne Circular Redoubt** Royal Pde, ☎*33952* – Aquarium, exhibition centre
	Lamb Inn High St, Old Town
R(3)	**Royal National Lifeboat Museum** King Edward's Pde ☎*30717*
	Towner Art Gallery Borough Ln, Old Town ☎*21635*

Tourist Information

ℹN	**Information Centre** 3 Cornfield Ter ☎*27474*
ℹN	**Information Centre** Terminus Rd Precinct
ℹN	**Information Centre** Lower Prom, (Summer only) ☎*27474*

Accommodation

The establishments listed below are a selection of AA-recommended accommodation and restaurants located in the area covered by the Town Plan. Further information may be found in AA publications or obtained from the local Tourist Information Offices.

1GH	**Aberfoyle Hotel** 83 Royal Pde ☎*22161*
2GH	**Alfriston Hotel** Lushington Rd ☎*25640*
3★★★	**Burlington** Grand Pde ☎*22724*
4★★★★	**Cavendish** Grand Pde ☎*27401*

5GH	**Cavendish** 1 Cavendish Pl ☎*24284*
6GH	**Le Chalet** 7 Marine Pde ☎*20029*
7★★★	**Chatsworth** Grand Pde ☎*30327*
8GH	**Chesleigh Hotel** 4 Marine Pde ☎*20722*
9GH	**Courtlands Hotel** 68 Royal Pde ☎*21068*
10GH	**Edelweiss** 10 Elms Ave ☎*32071*
11GH	**Edmar** 30 Hyde Gdns ☎*33024*
12GH	**Elmscroft Private Hotel** 53 Jevington Gdns ☎*21263*
13★★	**Farrar's** 3–5 Wilmington Gdns ☎*23737*
14★★★★★	**Grand** King Edward's Pde ☎*22611*
15★★★	**Imperial** Devonshire Pl ☎*20525*
16★★	**Langham** Royal Pde ☎*31451*
17★★★	**Lansdowne** King Edward's Pde ☎*25174*
18★	**Latham House** Howard Sq ☎*20985*
19GH	**Little Crookham** 16 Southcliffe Ave ☎*34160*
20GH	**Lynwood Hotel** Jevington Gdns ☎*23982*
21★★★	**Mansion** Grand Pde ☎*27411*
22★	**Oban** King Edward's Pde ☎*31581*
23★★★	**Princes** Lascelles Ter ☎*22056*
24★★★★	**Queens** Marine Pde ☎*22822*
25★★★	**Sandhurst** Grand Pde ☎*27868*
26★	**San Remo** Royal Pde ☎*21831*
27✕✕	**Summer Palace** Park Gates, Chiswick Pl ☎*33056*
28★★	**Sussex** Cornfield Ter ☎*27681*
29GH	**Traquair Private Hotel** 25 Hyde Gdns ☎*25198*
30★★★	**Wish Tower** King Edward's Pde ☎*22676*

WEATHER CHART	Av hours of Sunshine in month	Hottest Av daily Temp °C
April	191	9
May	235	12
June	255	15
July	236	17
August	217	17
September	168	16

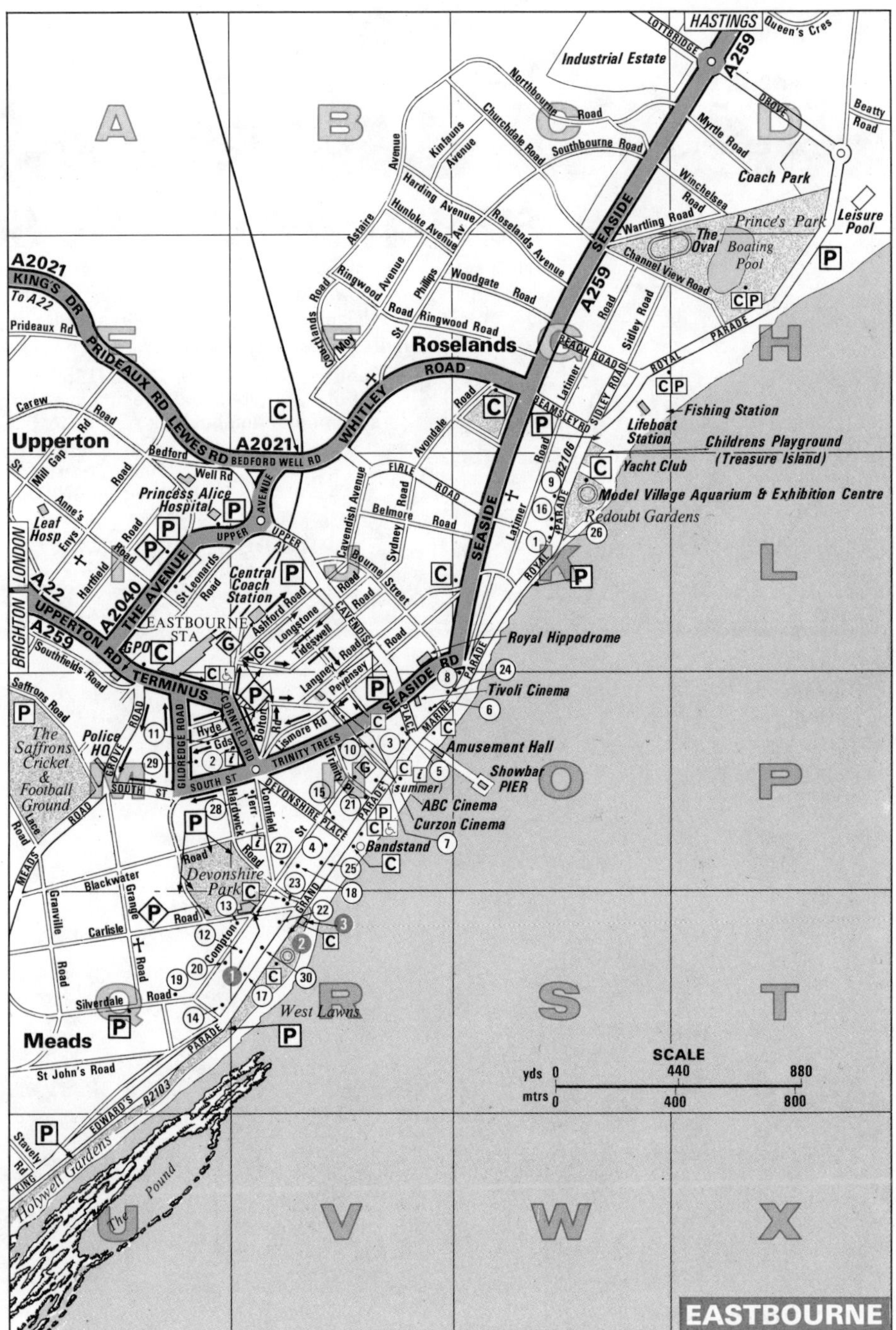

The famous Brighton Pavilion

SEAFORD

Seaford was a flourishing port in medieval times but its maritime connections were virtually destroyed in the late 16th century when a violent storm caused the River Ouse to burst its banks, diverting its course to the west where Newhaven stands today. Modern Seaford, a small, quiet resort, popular mainly because of its lack of traditional seaside amenities, has now achieved a world-wide reputation as an educational centre having no less than seven boarding schools within its boundaries.

The shingle beach, divided by wooden groynes, has a rather steep slope and is backed by a wide promenade and a large recreation ground in a grassy hollow.

An extensive renovation scheme is being carried out on the Martello tower which stands at the eastern end of the beach to restore many of the original features and return the building to public use. A total of 74 of these towers were built between Seaford and Folkestone as a precaution against invasion by Napoleon in the early 19th century. Brick-built, with a gun mounted on a revolving platform on top, they were about 30ft high and 25ft thick.

Seaford Head, 282 feet above sea level, is surmounted by the earthworks of a prehistoric camp and provides panoramic views into Sussex and Hampshire. To the east the Seven Sisters cliffs span the coastline, eventually merging with the towering Beachy Head.

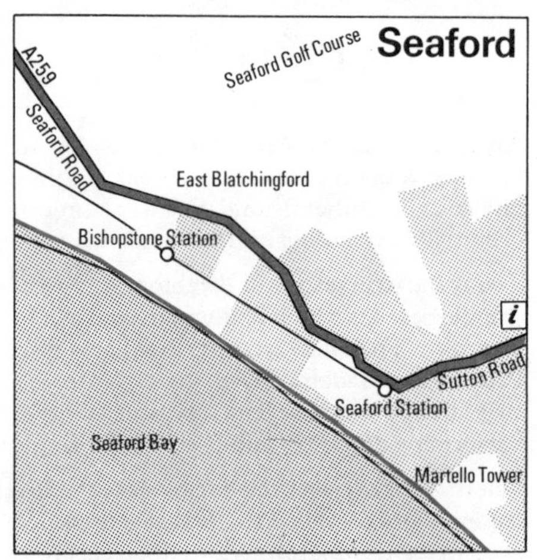

Restaurant

✕ **Masthead** 5 High St ☎*896135*

Recreation and Sports

Crouch Gardens – Bowls, football, playground, putting, tennis

The Downs Sutton Rd – Children's swimming pool and pleasure ground

Newhaven and Seaford Sailing Club The Buckle ☎*890077*

Salts Recreation Ground – Cricket, hockey, mini-golf, paddling pool and play area, putting, tennis

Seaford Golf Club Blatchington ☎*892597*

Seaford Head Golf Course Southdown Rd ☎*890139*

Cinema

Ritz Dane Rd ☎*892988*

Tourist Information

Council Offices The Downs, Sutton Rd ☎*892224*

Accommodation

The following establishments are recommended by the AA. Further information may be obtained from the Tourist Information Centre.

☆☆ **Newhaven Mercury Motor Inn** (on A259) ☎*891055*

GH **Clearview Hotel** 36–38 Claremont Rd ☎*890138*

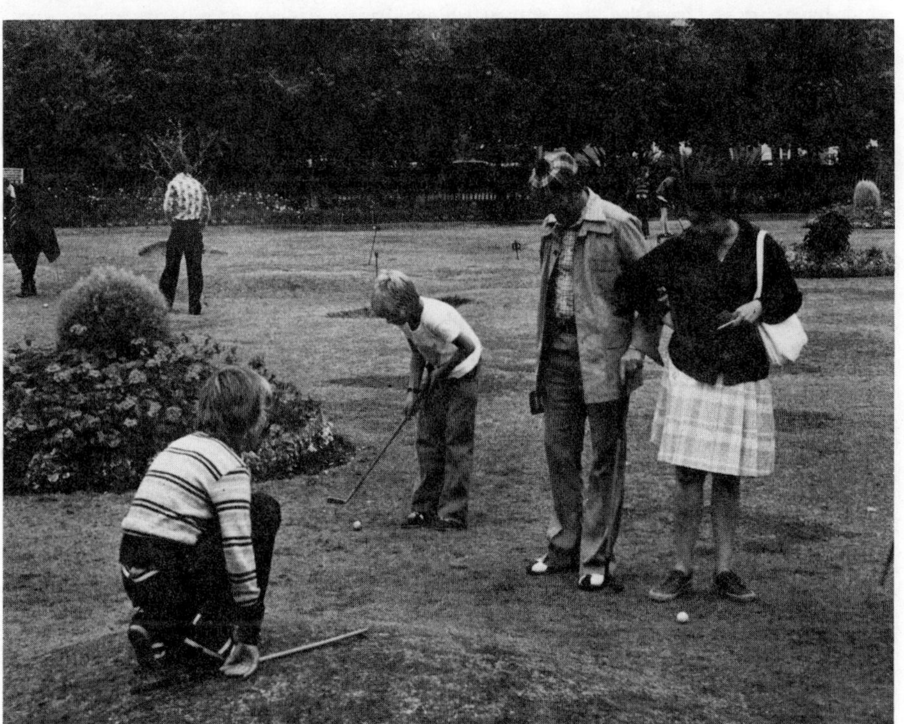

Fun on the putting green

BRIGHTON & HOVE

Around the middle of the 18th century Dr Richard Russell produced a thesis on the health-giving properties of sea water, singling out for special praise the waters around the little village of Brighthelmstone. From that time onwards the village flourished as a resort, eventually expanding into fashionable Brighton under the patronage of the Prince Regent.

Today the twin resorts of Brighton and Hove lie side by side on the South Coast overlooking shingle beaches which give way to sand at low-tide and extend for several miles in each direction. The sands around Hove Lagoon are generally less crowded than those around the Palace Pier. Madeira Drive, the well-known seafront finishing point for the London to Brighton Veteran Car Run, contains a large Aquarium with fish, penguins, seals, and performing dolphins, and Peter Pan's Playground and Funfair.

One of the most celebrated features of the Brighton seafront is the Royal Pavilion, commissioned by the Prince Regent in the late 18th century and finally completed in its present exotic Moghul style by John Nash, who designed London's Regents Park, in 1822. The interior is open to the public, furnished with the original fittings, and a Regency Exhibition is held there each summer. In fact, the town itself has a distinct Regency flavour, its long crescent-shaped terraces of tall, cream-coloured houses providing the visitor with a vision of 'Belgravia beside the sea'. The area known as the Lanes contains many buildings which have survived from the 17th-century fishing village and is noted for its maze of narrow brick-paved alleys containing antique shops, boutiques, cafés and pubs. There is also a Continental-style shopping precinct complete with what is said to be Britain's first café-pub.

The first phase of a new yacht marina is now complete and is the largest in Europe with a capacity for over 2,000 vessels. The complex is scheduled to accommodate an hotel, leisure centre and flats. The Marina is best reached by Volks Electric Railway, first opened in 1883, which runs from the Palace Pier to the Marina entrance.

Entertainment facilities are the finest in the south. Brighton has an abundance of cinemas and concert halls and the Theatre Royal stages pre-London release plays. The Brighton Festival attracts international artists from all spheres of the entertainment world to take part in a feast of drama and music each May.

J **AA Service Centre**

Recreation and Sports

Black Rock Open-Air Swinning Pool ☎*681861*
Brighton and Hove Albion FC Goldstone Ground, Hove ☎*739535* – League Division II
Brighton and Hove Golf Club Dyke Rd ☎*556482*
Brighton and Hove Stadium Nevill Rd, Hove ☎*731028* – Greyhound racing
Brighton Race Ground ☎*603580*
J **Brighton Sailing Club** 109 Kings Road Arches ☎*21802*
East Brighton Golf Club Rodean Rd ☎*603989*
King Alfred Sports Centre Kingsway, Hove ☎*734422* – Most indoor sports, pool, sauna, ten-pin bowling. Also bar, children's playground, restaurant
G **North Road Swimming Baths** ☎*682519* – Indoor pool
Peter Pan's Playground Madeira Dr – Children's entertainment, funfair, swings, etc
D **Queens Park** – Bowls, children's playground, tennis
A **St Anns Well Gardens** – Bowls, Children's playground, putting, tennis
I **Seafront** (Regency Sq) – Boating and paddling pools, putting
F **Sussex Sports Centre** 11 Queens St – Ice skating

Cabaret/Dancing

J **Kingswest Centre** West St ☎*25895*
I **Mardi-Gras Club** 34 Regency Sq ☎*23996*
J **New Zorba's Taverna** 75a West St ☎*24381*
L **Salonika Taverna** 14 Madeira Dr ☎*604462*
J **Sherry's Showbar** 7a Middle St ☎*21628*
F **Sloopys** 11 Dyke Rd ☎*24144*

Cinemas

K **ABC** East St ☎*27010*
F **Brighton Film Theatre** 64 North St ☎*29563*
E **Classic** Western Rd, Hove ☎*29414*
E **Embassy** Western Rd, Hove ☎*735124*
J **Odeon Film Centre** Kingswest Centre, West St ☎*23317*

Theatres

J **Brighton Centre** ☎*202881*
G(3) **Dome** Church St ☎*682127*
Gardner Centre University of Sussex, Falmer ☎*685861*
G **Pavilion Theatre** ☎*682046*
G **Theatre Royal** New Rd ☎*28488*

Places of Interest

K(1) **Aquarium and Dolphinarium** Marine Pde ☎*604233*
A(5) **Booth Museum of Natural History** Dyke Rd ☎*552586*
Brighton and Hove Engineerium – Permanent Steam Exhibition, Nevill Rd, Hove ☎*559583*
J(2) **Dolls in Wonderland Museum** Kings Rd ☎*27147*
K(4) **Louis Tussauds Waxworks** Grand Junction Pde ☎*26811*
K(6) **The Lanes**
K(7) **Marlborough House** Old Steine ☎*23755* – Designed by Robert Adam in 1786 and now houses the Tourist Information Centre
G(8) **Museum, Art Gallery and Library** Church St ☎*603005*
G(9) **Royal Pavilion** ☎*603005*
L(13) **Volks Electric Railway** Madeira Dr ☎*681061*

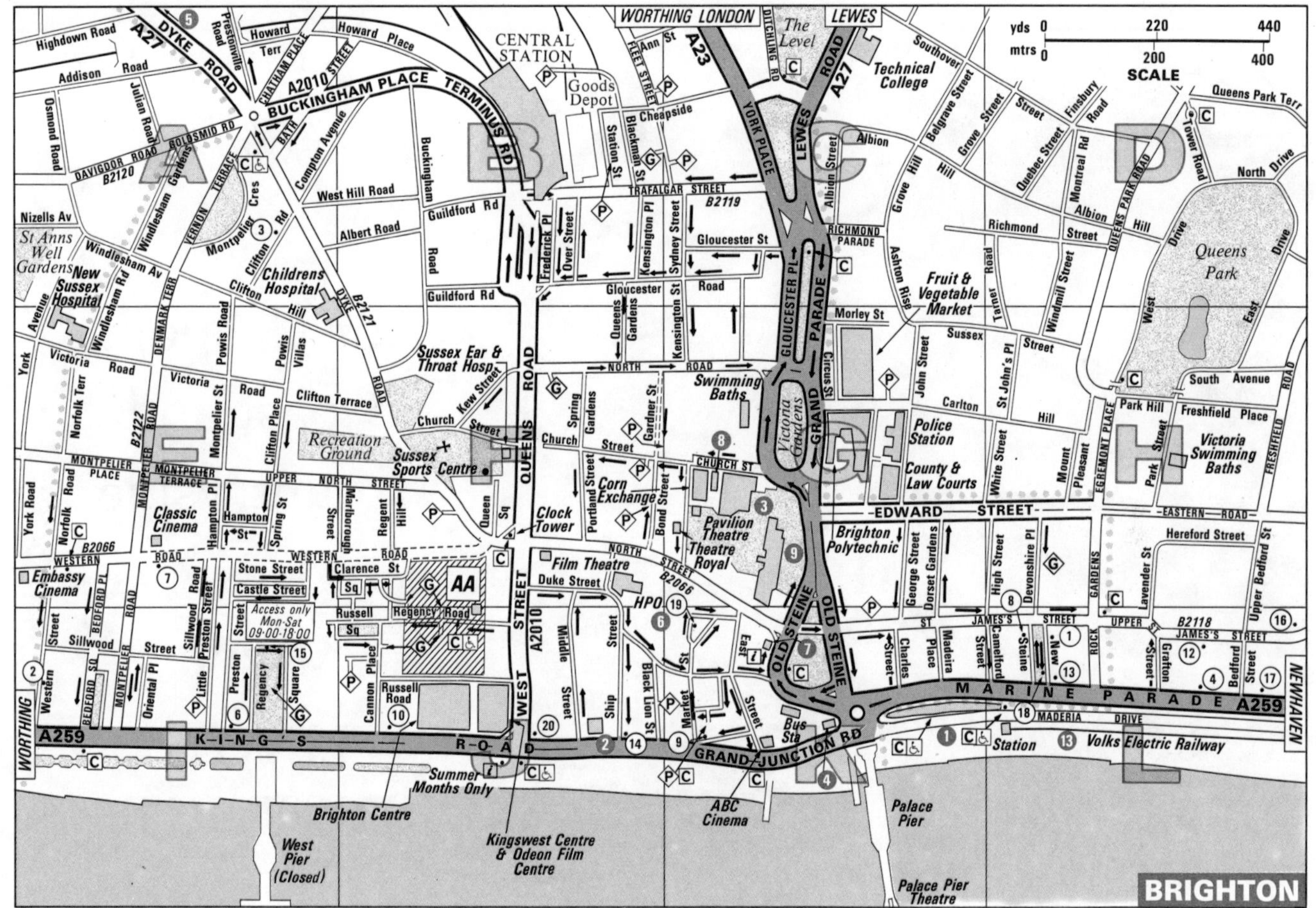

Tourist Information

ⓘJ	**Seafront Tourist Information Centre** (summer only) ☎*26450*
ⓘK	**Tourist Information Centre** Marlborough House, 54 Old Steine ☎*23755*
	Tourist Information Centre Town Hall, Church Rd, Hove ☎*775400*

Accommodation

The establishments listed below are a selection of AA-recommended accommodation and restaurants located in the area covered by the Town Plan. Further information may be found in AA publications or obtained from the Tourist Information Centres.

1GH	**Ascott House** 21 New Steine ☎*688085*
2✕	**Christopher's** 24 Western St ☎*775048*
3SC	**18 Clifton Road** for bookings: Holiday Lettings Office, The Refrectory, University of Sussex, Falmer, Brighton, E Sussex BN1 9QU ☎*606755 ext376*
4GH	**Crest Hotel** 70 Marine Pde ☎*689606*
6★★	**Curzon** Cavendish Pl ☎*25788*
7GH	**Dolce Vita** 106A Western Rd ☎*737200*
8GH	**Ellesmere** 8 New Steine ☎*607812*
9✕✕	**French Connection** 11 Little East St ☎*24454*
10★★★★	**Grand** Kings Rd ☎*26301*
12GH	**Marina** 8 Charlotte St ☎*605349*
13GH	**Melford Hall** ☎*681435*
14★★★	**Old Ship** Kings Rd ☎*29001*
15GH	**Regency Hotel** 28 Regency Sq ☎*202690*
16GH	**Rowland House** 21 St George Ter ☎*603639*
17★★★★	**Royal Crescent** 100 Marine Pde ☎*606311*
18GH	**Twenty Three** 23 New Steine ☎*684212*
19✕✕	**Wheeler's Oyster Room** 17 Market St ☎*25135*
20✕✕✕	**Wheeler's Sheridan Tavern** 83 West St ☎*28372*

Shoreham-by-Sea
This busy seaport lies at the mouth of the River Adur where the sand and shingle beach is separated from the town by a bend in the course of the river. It is safe for bathing, with the exception of the area around the Adur estuary where currents are dangerous. The Marlipins Museum, housed in a 12th-century building, contains a selection of maritime and local exhibits.

Lancing
A beach of sand, backed by shingle is accessible on foot from the car park on Beach Green. Once two small villages, North and South Lancing have now combined to form a growing residential area, increasingly popular with visitors. Standing on a hill behind the town, Lancing College is well known for its impressive Chapel which is open to the public.

WORTHING *see page 64*

Goring-by-Sea
Worthing's western suburb has a sandy beach, backed by shingle behind which is a low grassy hill. Bathing is safe.

Angmering-on-Sea
Angmering was once a smuggler's village. Today its sand and shingle beach is overlooked by a housing estate. Bathing is safe. A little way inland are Stone Age flint mines, Iron Age earthworks and an excavated Roman Villa.

Littlehampton *see page 66*

Middleton-on-Sea
This small resort is very popular with its many visitors who can enjoy safe bathing from its sand and shingle beach.

Felpham
This is a residential resort where the beach and promenade are accessible on foot.

Bognor Regis *see page 67*

Selsey
Its somewhat exposed position on the headland of Selsey Bill makes swimming dangerous in this area. Selsey's eastern beach, which is mainly shingle, provides good opportunities for fishing and there is an amusement arcade and parking facilities.

East Wittering
A long, safe, sandy beach here is reduced to shingle at high-tide. On the shore, which is only accessible on foot, bathing huts, deck chairs etc are available for hire.

West Wittering
Once a fishing village, West Wittering is now a small residential resort. The beach, accessible via a toll road, is sandy with shingle along the high-water mark. Bathing is generally safe, but the entrance to Chichester harbour, with its currents and busy yachting activities should be avoided.

Hayling Island *see page 68*

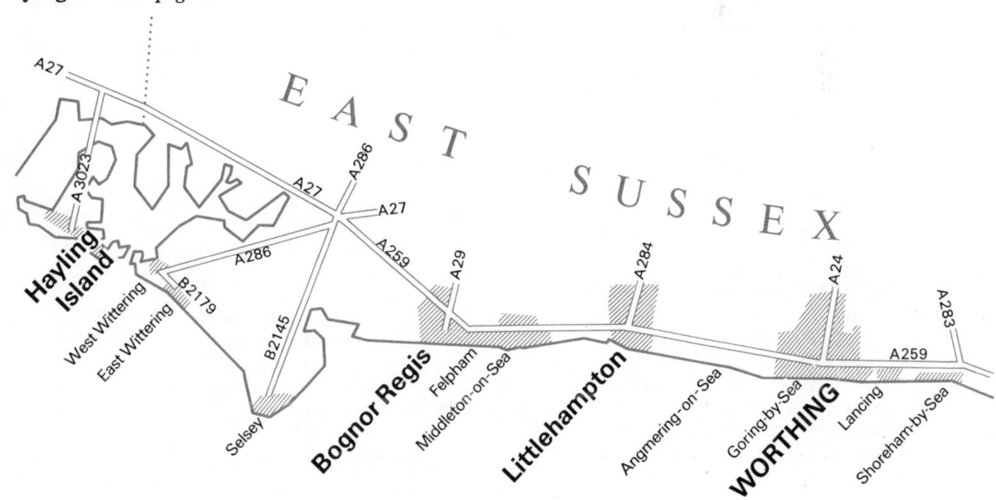

WORTHING

A peaceful fishing village which became popular as a holiday centre after George III's daughter, Princess Amelia, stayed there in 1798. Smuggling was still rife during this period and in 1832 visitors were afforded the added attraction of witnessing a running battle between a local gang and excisemen. Worthing has since evolved into a pleasant mixture of residential town and seaside resort, its remaining Georgian and Victorian buildings merging tastefully with the surrounding modern development, and is a popular haven for the retired settler in addition to the seasonal visitor.

The gently sloping beach, backed by a broad expanse of shingle, provides safe bathing, although care should be taken near the eastern extremity where derelict war-time defences are submerged at high-tide. There are plentiful amusement facilities on and around the seafront, notably the Brooklands Pleasure Park at East Worthing which contains an eight-acre boating lake, playgrounds and a miniature railway which encircles the entire park. A miniature railway also operates on the pier. Worthing's programme of summer entertainments includes concerts, dances, films, plays and variety shows and national and international bowls championships are held annually in Beach House Park.

Worthing is renowned for its 100 or so acres of ornamental parks and gardens such as Steyne Gardens of the seafront and nearby Beach House Park where modern sports and refreshment facilities are to be found in a pleasant woodland setting.
Worthing Museum and Art Gallery has many items of local interest, collections of historical costumes and exhibitions of arts and crafts, while at West Tarring, on the northern outskirts, a group of three late 15th-century buildings, known as the Thomas-à-Beckett cottages, have been restored and now house a folk museum.

Recreation and Sports

F	**Beach House Grounds** – Boating, mini-golf, Peter Pan's Playground, roller-skating
C	**Beach House Park** – Bowls, tennis
C	**Brooklands Pleasure Park** East Worthing – Adventure playground, boating, miniature railway, pitch and putt, putting
F	**Denton Gardens** – Putting, tennis
	Field Place Durrington – Bowls, putting, table-tennis, tennis
	Hill Barn Golf Course ☎ *204788* (N off A24)
B	**Homefield Park** – Tennis
	Marine Gardens West Pde – Bowls, putting
	Sports Centre Shaftsbury Ave ☎ *502237* (W off A259)
E	**Worthing Bowl** Agusta Pl, Marine Pde ☎ *30835* – Ten-pin bowling
A	**Worthing FC** Woodside Rd ☎ *39575* – Athenian League
	Worthing Golf Club Links Rd, ☎ *60801* (N off A24)
E	**Worthing Pier** – Amusements
	Worthing RFC Castle Rd, Tarring ☎ *66140*
D/E	**Worthing Sailing and Motor Club** Marine Pde ☎ *32733*

Cinemas

E	**The Dome** Marine Pde ☎ *200461*
E	**Odeon** Liverpool Gdns ☎ *35016*

Dancing

B(1)	**Assembly Hall** Stoke Abbot Rd ☎ *33399*
A	**Wet Paint Disco** 13 Pavilion Rd ☎ *207716*

Theatres

B(1)	**Assembly Hall** Stoke Abbot Rd ☎ *33399*
B	**Connaught Theatre** Union Pl ☎ *35333*
E(2)	**Pavilion** Marine Pde ☎ *202221* (Closing for repairs Apr 1979)

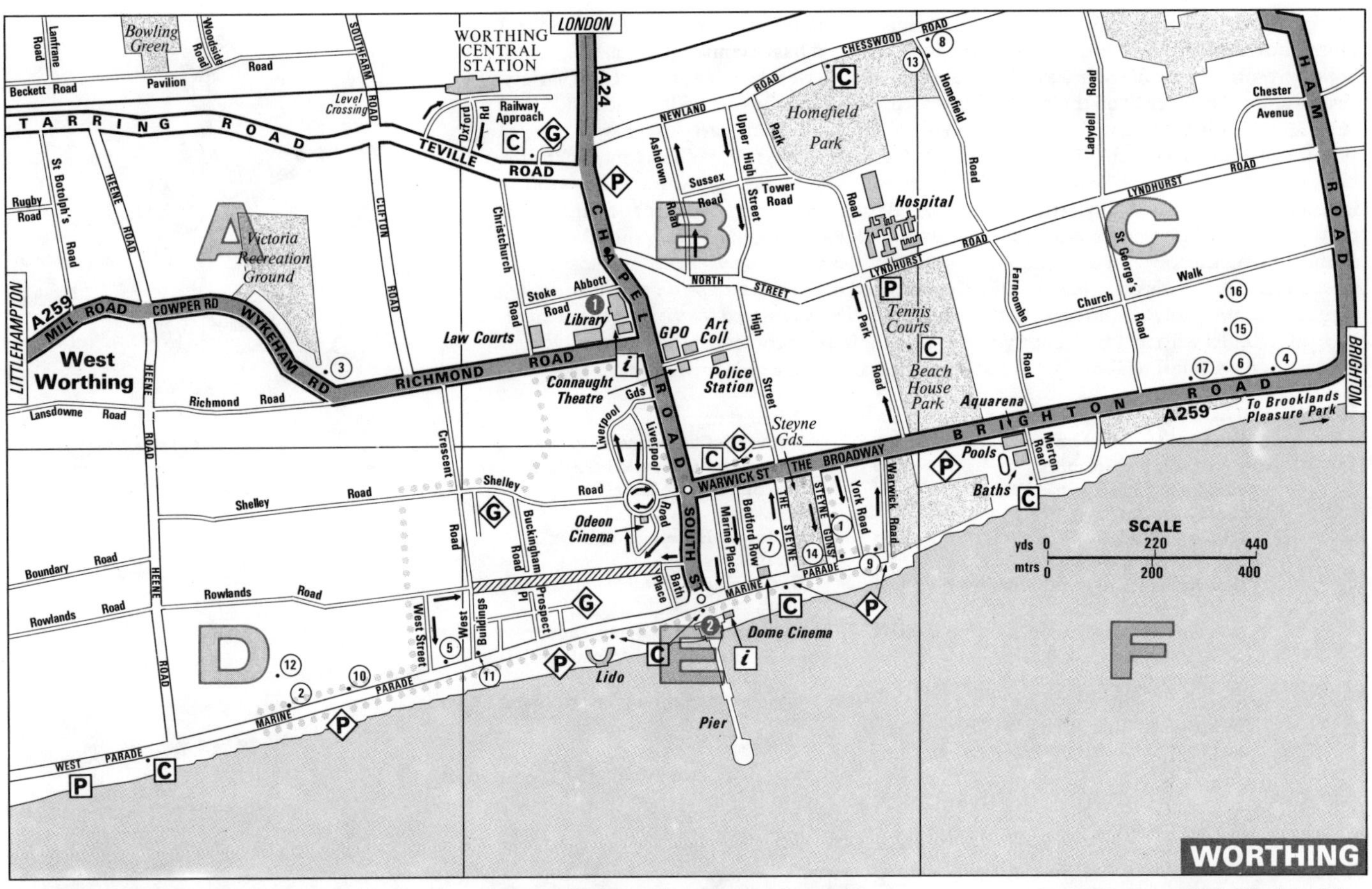

Places of Interest

B — **Museum and Art Gallery** Chapel Rd ☎204226
Parsonage Row Cottages High St, West Tarring ☎36385

Tourist Information

[i]E — **Tourist Information Centre** Marine Pde ☎35934

[i]B — **Tourist Information Office** Chapel Rd ☎204226

Accommodation

The establishments listed below are a selection of AA-recommended accommodation and restaurants located in the area covered by the Town Plan. Further information may be found in AA publications or obtained from the Tourist Information Centres.

1★★	**Ardington** Steyne Gdns ☎30451
2★★★	**Beach** Marine Pde ☎34001
3★★	**Beechwood** Park Cres, Wykeham Rd ☎32872
4GH	**Belmont Private Hotel** 211 Brighton Rd ☎202678
5★★★	**Berkeley** Marine Pde ☎31122
6GH	**Burcott** 6 Windsor Rd ☎35163
7★★★	**Chatsworth** The Steyne ☎36103
8SC	**The Chesswood** 56 Homefield Rd, for bookings: Miss B F Green, Chesswood End, 4 Chesswood Rd, Worthing W Sussex BN11 2AD ☎36027
9★★★	**Eardley** Marine Pde ☎34444
10★★	**Kingsway** Marine Pde ☎37542
11XX	**Parade Wine Lodge** Marine Pde ☎33825
12XX	**Paragon Continental** 9–10 Brunswick Rd ☎33367
13GH	**Wansfell Hotel** 49 Chesswood Rd ☎30612
14★★★	**Warnes** Marine Pde ☎35222
15GH	**Williton** 10 Windsor Rd ☎37974
16GH	**Windsor House** 16–18 Windsor Rd ☎39655
17GH	**Wolsey Hotel** 179–181 Brighton Rd ☎36149

LITTLEHAMPTON

During the 11th century the town was the principal port for travellers between England and Normandy and for the importation of Caen stone. Today it has become a popular, family holiday resort and the harbour, which divides the east and west beaches, is used by a variety of vessels and pleasure craft on their way to the Marina. The beaches are wide, sandy and generally safe for bathing with the exception of the area around the harbour where it is prohibited. The east beach offers bathing floats for hire and has trampolines for the children but west of the Arun the beach remains unspoiled with vast grassy dunes and golden sand and is generally less crowded. Boat trips up the River Arun operate from the pier and a miniature railway operates between the seafront and Mewsbrook Park which has a boating lake. There are facilities in the town for all types of sporting activities including yacht racing most weekends. The town's maritime traditions are recalled in the local museum which also contains paintings of local interest. Littlehampton is ideally situated for visiting the ancient town of Arundel with its 11th-century castle, now the hereditary seat of the Duke of Norfolk, or Peter Scott's Wildlife Trust, set in a 60-acre water meadow a mile further north.

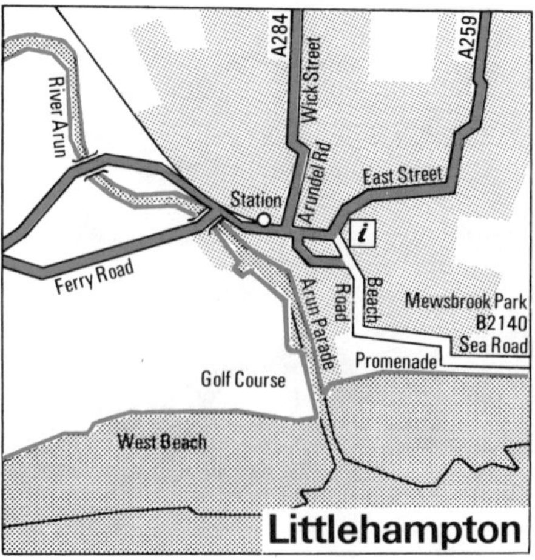

Recreation and Sports

Arun Parade – Amusement Park, Fun Fair, Oyster Pond (canoes)
Arun Yacht Club Riverside West ☎*6016*
Maltavers Garden – Tennis
Mewsbrook Park – Boating
Promenade – Donkey rides, mini-golf, putting, tennis
Littlehampton Golf Club Club House, 170 Rope Walk ☎*7170*
Littlehampton Sailing Club & Motor Club 90/91 South Ter ☎*5545*
The 6,18 Golf Club 38 Hillview Cres, East Preston ☎*Rustington 70394*

Cinema

Palladium Church St

Theatre

Windmill Complex Sea Front ☎*21106*

Places of Interest

Museum 12 River Rd ☎*5149*

Tourist Information

Information Bureau Council Offices, Church St ☎*6133*

Accommodation

The following establishments are recommended by the AA. Further information may be obtained from the Tourist Information Office.

★★★	**Beach** ☎*7277*
★★	**Stetson** St Catherines Rd ☎*6081*
GH	**Arun Hotel** 42 New Rd ☎*21206*
GH	**Braemar Private Hotel** Sea Front ☎*5487*
GH	**Burbridge Hotel** 93 South Ter ☎*21606*
GH	**Harley House Hotel** St Catherines Rd ☎*5851*
GH	**Regency Hotel** 85 South Ter ☎*7707*
SC	Mr J A Sinclair, **The Canadian Village** Rope Walk ☎*3816*

Happy families on the beach

A former medieval fishing village which developed into the compact, popular resort of Bognor around the turn of the 18th century. It was one of Queen Victoria's favourite resorts and gained the title Regis in 1929 after George V convalesced in the town. Today Bognor Regis offers the visitor over a mile of seafront and a gently sloping sandy beach which provides safe bathing, although the rocks at the western end are best avoided. Young holidaymakers are well catered for by the provision of special play areas, organised beach sports and a Punch and Judy Show on the promenade, and adult entertainment takes the form of concerts, seasonal shows, band concerts and wrestling at the Esplanade Theatre and outdoor dancing and Folk Dance displays in the beautiful setting of Hotham Park. Seasonal events include Fishing Festivals, Horse and Flower Shows, bowls and tennis championships and Bognor Cricket Week.

Places of interest include Hotham Park House, the 18th-century Dome House, used as a holiday home by Princess Charlotte, and the 18th-century Ice House, an example of early refrigeration methods, all built by Sir Richard Hotham, the founder of Bognor.

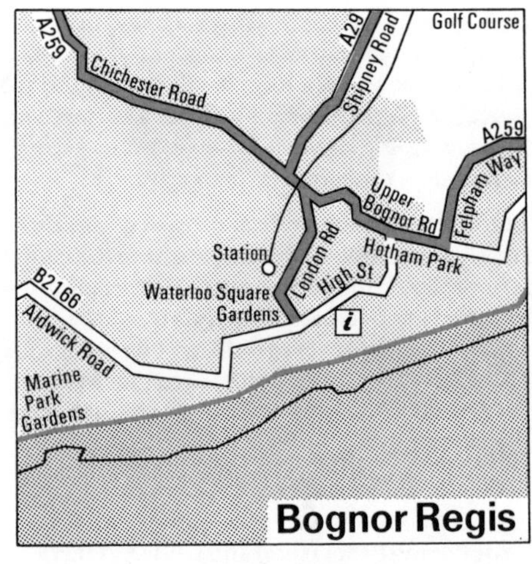

Recreation and Sports

Arun Leisure Centre – Most indoor sports
Blakes Road – Putting, tennis
Bognor Regis Golf Club Downview Rd ☎*5867*
Bognor Regis Yacht Club Esplanade ☎*5735*
Hotham Park – Bandstand, boating, children's playground, crazy-golf, miniature Go-Karts, miniature railway, putting, tennis, zoo
Marine Park Gardens – Putting
Seafront – Motor and rowing boats and pedalos for hire
Swansea Gardens – Bowls, tennis
Waterloo Square Gardens – Bowls, crazy-golf, model yachting pool

Cinema

Picturedrome Opposite the railway station ☎*23138*

Theatre

Esplanade Theatre Aldwick Rd ☎*21902*

Places of Interest

Dome House Upper Bognor Rd
The Ice House London Rd
Blake's Cottage Felpham

Tourist Information

Tourist Information Centre Belmont St ☎*23140*

Accommodation

The following establishments are recommended by the AA. Further information may be obtained from the Tourist Information Office.

★★	**Clarehaven** Wessex Ave ☎*23265*
★★	**Royal** Esplanade ☎*4665*
★	**Black Mill House** Princess Ave ☎*21945*
★	**Victoria** Aldwick Rd ☎*22335*
GH	**Homestead Private Hotel** 90 Aldwick Rd ☎*23443*
GH	**Lansdowne Hotel** 55–57 West St ☎*5552*
GH	**Lyndhurst Private Hotel** 3 Selsey Ave ☎*22308*
SC	**No 33. Glamis Street** For bookings: Mrs E R Karon, 88 Westminster Dr, Aldwick Park ☎*27479*

HAYLING ISLAND

This roughly triangular-shaped island lies between Langstone and Chichester harbours and is joined to the mainland at Langstone by a road bridge. There is little of historical interest although the site of a Roman villa was found at Stoke and there is an interesting 12th-century church in North Hayling Village. The northern area of the island is a peaceful mixture of fields, winding lanes and villages while the main beach and the three-mile-long seafront are to be found on the southern extremity.

The Central Beachlands, an area of grassy dunes lying between the coast road and the shore, is largely uncommercialised apart from the central area, near the bus station, which contains a funfair, cafés and restaurants. Further east, towards Sandy Point, amusement arcades, bingo halls and shops cluster thickly around the seafront road. This is the most popular beach area where large expanses of sand are uncovered at low-tide and swimming is normally safe, although both harbour entrances should be avoided. Evening entertainment takes the form of dances etc, organised by local social clubs but there is a cinema at nearby Havant.

National and international sailing events take place around the Hayling Island Sailing Club at Sandy Point, providing a colourful spectacle for holidaymakers on the beaches. Langstone Harbour contains water ski-ing areas and its mud-flats attract large numbers of migrating birds during the autumn and winter. A ferry operates across the harbour mouth linking South Hayling with Eastney.

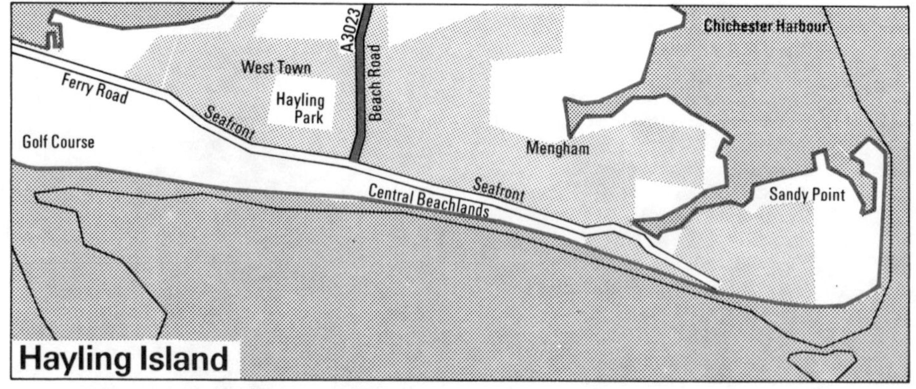

Recreation and Sports

The Central Beachlands – Amusement park
Hayling Golf Club Ferry Rd, West Town ☎*3712*
Hayling Island Sailing Club Sandy Point ☎*3768*
Hayling Park – Bowls, children's playground, putting, tennis
Mengham Rythe Sailing Club Marine Walk, Salterns Ln ☎*3337*
Sandy Point – Amusement arcades
Sealands – Putting
Western Beachlands – Mini-golf, putting

Places of Interest

Hayling Billy Inn – Hayling Billy Railway Engine
North Hayling Village – St Peter's Church (12th century)
South Hayling – St Mary's Church (Early English), Manor House (1777)
Stoke – Site of Roman building
Tournerbury – Bird sanctuary and heronry

Accommodation

The following establishments are recommended by the AA. Further information may be obtained from the local council.

☆☆☆☆	**Havant Post House** Northney Rd ☎*Havant5011*
★★	**Newtown House** Manor Rd ☎*4071*
GH	**Avenue** 5 Wheatlands Ave ☎*3121*
GH	**Dolphin Court Hotel** 37 St Leonard's Ave ☎*2910*

PORTSMOUTH AND SOUTHSEA *see page 70*

Ryde *see page 74*

Bembridge
A small resort in wooded surroundings. It is a boating and yachting centre and swimming is normally safe. An 18th-century windmill, preserved by the National Trust, is open to the public during the summer.

Sandown *see page 75*

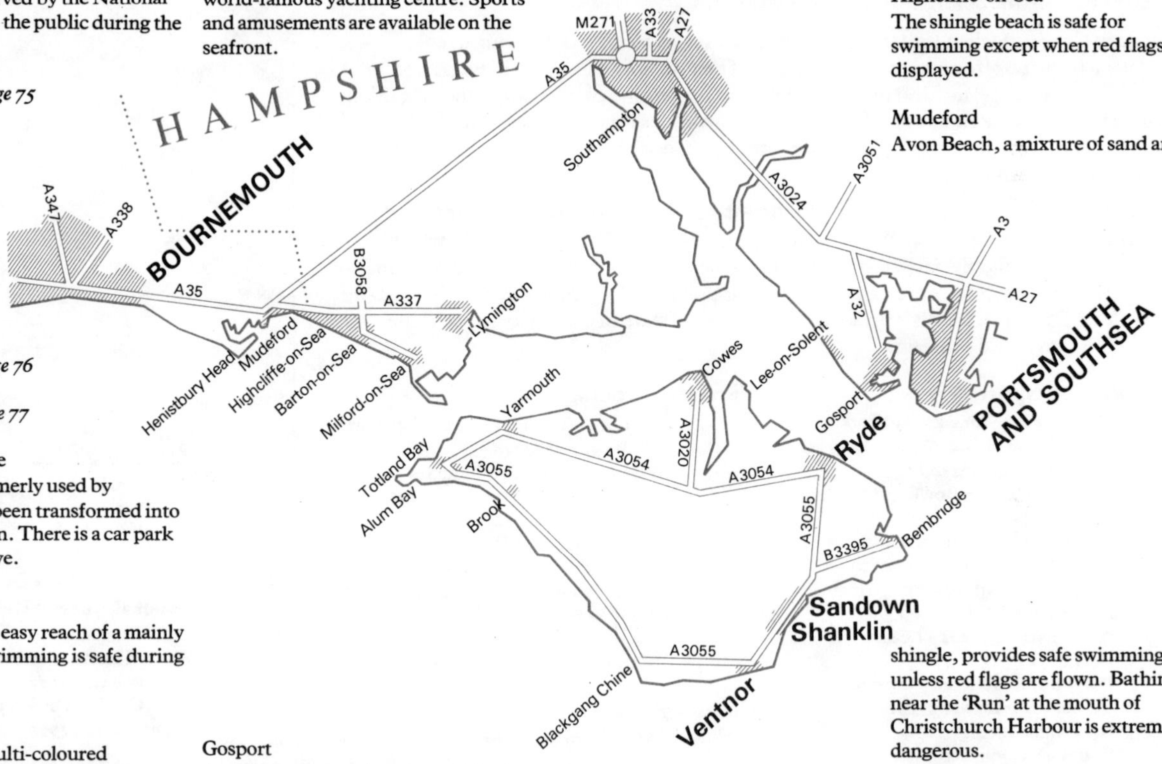

Shanklin *see page 76*

Ventnor *see page 77*

Blackgang Chine
This ravine, formerly used by smugglers, has been transformed into a pleasure garden. There is a car park on the cliffs above.

Brook
A hamlet within easy reach of a mainly sandy beach. Swimming is safe during calm weather.

Alum Bay
Noted for the multi-coloured sandstone which adorns the cliffs. A chair-lift connects the beach with the cliff top. Swimming is dangerous due to strong tides.

Totland Bay
A good sand and shingle beach, sheltered by cliffs. Amusements and car parking are available.

Yarmouth
An ancient market town and port now well known for its ferry terminal and as a yachting centre. There is a sand and shingle beach but strong tides around the harbour entrance make it generally unsuitable for swimming.

Cowes
The Isle of Wight's main port and a world-famous yachting centre. Sports and amusements are available on the seafront.

Gosport
A well-known naval town noted for its submarine base and containing the facilities for amusement and entertainment normally associated with a holiday centre.

Lee-on-Solent
A popular resort with a shingle beach giving way to sand at low-tide. Bathing is safe and there is an open-air swimming pool on the seafront.

Southampton
Britain's foremost passenger port, Southampton contains many interesting areas and was a popular resort until the beginning of the last century. It has swimming pools, parks, museums and a small zoo.

Lymington
A yachting centre and ferry terminal which retains a quiet attraction despite the fact that it lies on one of the busiest minor waterways in the area.

Milford-on-Sea
The steep pebble beach is somewhat exposed and swimming can be dangerous during rough weather.

Barton-on-Sea
A pebble and shingle beach is suitable for swimming in good weather. There is a car park on the cliffs above.

Highcliffe-on-Sea
The shingle beach is safe for swimming except when red flags are displayed.

Mudeford
Avon Beach, a mixture of sand and shingle, provides safe swimming unless red flags are flown. Bathing near the 'Run' at the mouth of Christchurch Harbour is extremely dangerous.

Hengistbury Head
Most of this area, containing sandy beaches, lagoons, saltings and footpaths, is a nature reserve with a bird observation station. Bathing is generally safe.

BOURNEMOUTH *see page 78*

SOUTHSEA & PORTSMOUTH

There has been a harbour here since Roman times and Portsmouth has played an important part in English naval history since the 14th century, while Southsea, to the east, a mainly residential area, retains the peaceful atmosphere of a holiday resort.

Southsea's two piers extend over a sand and shingle beach which is suitable for bathing, provided the harbour mouth is avoided. Sun-huts are available for hire along the length of the esplanade and the Lumps Fort area, near the South Parade Pier, contains a canoe lake, model village, sports facilities and a rose garden. The western seafront is flanked by Southsea Common with its castle, established during the reign of Henry VIII, which now houses a military and naval museum. The Common extends to the Clarence Pier which has the largest amusement park on the South Coast near its entrance.

The modern Concert Hall in Portsmouth's Guildhall stages concerts appealing to every musical taste from 'pop' to classical and the Kings Theatre, Southsea, provides a varied programme of drama and musical productions, often presenting plays prior to their London opening. There is a wide choice of cinemas and opportunities for playing or watching most sports. The Skatepark on Southsea Common is the most modern skateboarding and roller skating centre in the south.

Portsmouth's historic past has left the city with a wealth of interesting areas. Although much of the town was destroyed during World War II bombing raids, Old Portsmouth, which occupies the area around the ferry terminal, retains the cobbled streets, lanes and buildings of a bygone age. Perhaps the most famous naval monument is HMS Victory, Nelson's Flagship at the battle of Trafalgar, which is preserved in its original state in the dockyard near the Portsmouth Royal Naval Museum.

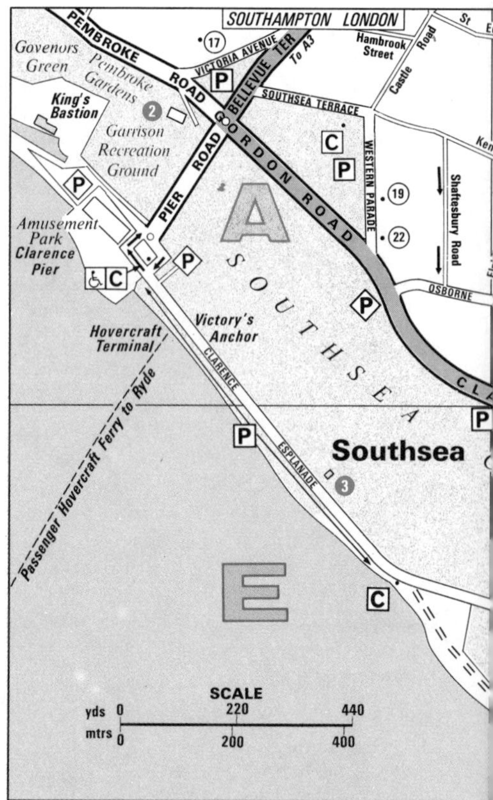

Recreation and Sports

A **Clarence Pier Amusement Park**

Great Salterns Golf Course Eastern Rd ☎ *Portsmouth64549*

Humber Ten-Pin Bowling Arundel St ☎ *Portsmouth20505*

G/H **Lumps Fort** – Boating, bowls, mini-golf, model village, putting, tennis

A **Pembroke Gardens** – Bowls, tennis

Portsmouth FC Fratton Pk ☎ *Portsmouth731204* – League Division IV

Portsmouth Stadium Target Rd, Tipner ☎ *Portsmouth63231* – Greyhound racing

F **Southsea Common** – Bowls, children's corner, putting, tennis

F **Southsea Skatepark** Southsea Common ☎ *Portsmouth25005*

Victoria Park Swimming Pool Anglesea Rd ☎ *Portsmouth23822* – Indoor pool

G **Wimbledon Park Sports Centre** Taswell Rd, Southsea ☎ *Portsmouth25075* – Most indoor sports

Cabaret/Dancing

Granny's Tricorn Centre, Marketway ☎ *Portsmouth24728*

G **Pleasurama Entertainments Complex** South Pde, Southsea ☎ *Portsmouth31070*

F **Some Place Else** Palmerston Rd, Southsea ☎ *Portsmouth750352*

G **South Parade Pier** Southsea ☎ *Portsmouth732283*

Tricorn Club Tricorn Centre, Marketway ☎ *Portsmouth24728*

Cinemas

ABC Commercial Rd ☎ *Portsmouth23538*

C **Odeon** Festing Rd, Southsea ☎ *Portsmouth32163*

Odeon London Rd ☎ *Portsmouth61539*

Palace Guildhall Wk, Southsea ☎ *Portsmouth25029*

Tatler Fratton Rd ☎ *Portsmouth22933*

Theatres

Guildhall Concert Hall ☎ *Portsmouth24355*

B **Kings Theatre** Albert Rd, Southsea ☎ *Portsmouth28282*

F **Rock Garden Pavilion** Southsea ☎ *Portsmouth21992*

Places of Interest

Buckingham House High St – The Duke of Buckingham was murdered here in 1628

City Museum and Art Gallery Museum Rd ☎ *Portsmouth811527*

G(1) **Cumberland House Museum** Eastern Pde, Southsea ☎ *Portsmouth732654*

Dickens Birthplace Museum Old Commercial Rd ☎ *Portsmouth26155*

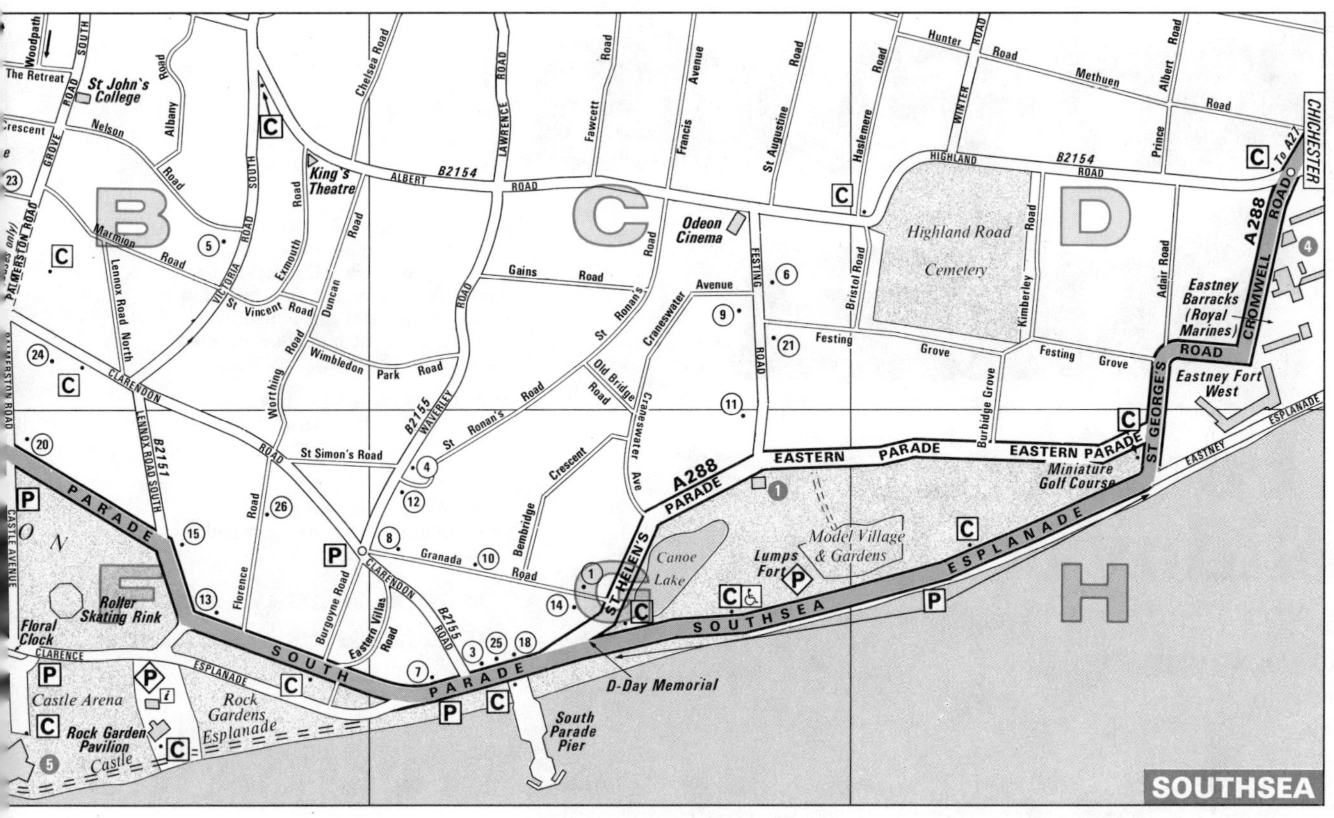

	Eastney Pumping Station and Gas Engine House Henderson Rd
	HMS Victory and Portsmouth Royal Naval Museum The Hard
A(2)	**Lord Nelson Statue**
E(3)	**Naval Memorial**
	Portchester Castle W off A27
	Round Tower and Point Battery Broad St – An old tower dating back to 1417
D(4)	**Royal Marines Museum** Eastney Barracks
F(5)	**Southsea Castle Museum** Castle Esplanade
	Square Tower Broad St – Dates from the time of Henry VIII and is surmounted by a bust of Charles I.

Tourist Information

🛈F	**Tourist Information Centre** Castle Bldgs, Clarence Esplanade ☎Portsmouth26722

Accommodation

The establishments listed below are a selection of AA-recommended accommodation and restaurants located in the area covered by the Town Plan. Further information may be found in AA publications or obtained from the Tourist Information Centre.

1GH	**Averano** 65 Granada Rd ☎*Portsmouth20079*
2✕	**Bamboo House** 110–114 Palmerston Rd ☎*Portsmouth22100*
3★★	**Berkeley** South Pde ☎*Portsmouth735059*
4GH	**Birchwood** 44 Waverley Rd ☎*Portsmouth811337*
5GH	**Elms** 48 Victoria Rd South, Southsea ☎*Portsmouth23924*
6GH	**Embell** 31 Festing Rd ☎*Portsmouth25678*
7★	**Garden** South Pde ☎*Portsmouth732376*
8GH	**Grosvenor Court Hotel** 37 Granada Rd ☎*Portsmouth21653*
9GH	**Homeleigh** 42–44 Festing Gv ☎*Portsmouth23706*
10GH	**Jesamine** 57 Granada Rd ☎*Portsmouth734388*
11GH	**Lyndhurst** 8 Festing Gv ☎*Portsmouth735239*

Portsmouth 
Southsea

For those great holiday reflections.

Savour the glories of *Portsmouth* — a city full of history and antiquities, and 'Home' of HMS Victory. Have fun in *Southsea*, Hampshire's largest and most go-ahead resort — for fun, sun and a bustling sea-shore. Enjoy them *together* for those great holiday reflections.

The colourful guide tells more. For your copy and useful street map, send 30p postal order or cheque to:

Room AA79
Tourist Information Centre,
Castle Buildings, Clarence Esplanade,
Southsea, Hampshire PO5 3PE.

where holidays begin and memories never fade.

Portsmouth & Southsea

A 'Golden Rail' Resort

Links with the Continent

Three car ferry services now operating — to Cherbourg, St. Malo, Le Havre and the Channel Islands — from Britain's newest ferry port.

12★★ **Mayville** Waverley Rd *☎Portsmouth732461*

13✕✕ **Murrays** 27A South Pde *☎Portsmouth732322*

14★★ **Ocean** St Helens Pde *☎Portsmouth734233*

16★★★ **Pendragon** Clarence Pde, Southsea *☎Portsmouth23201*

17★★★ **Portsmouth Centre** Pembroke Rd *☎Portsmouth27651*

18★★★ **Royal Beach** South Pde, Southsea *☎Portsmouth731281*

19GH **Ryde View** 9 Western Pde *☎Portsmouth20865*

20★★ **Saville** Clarence Pde *☎Portsmouth27032*

21GH **Salisbury Hotel** 57–59 Festing Rd *☎Portsmouth23606*

22GH **Somerset Private Hotel** 16 Western Pde *☎Portsmouth22495*

23GH **Tudor Court Hotel** 1 Queens Gv *☎Portsmouth20174*

24GH **Upper Mount House** The Vale, Clarendon Rd *☎Portsmouth20456*

25★ **Vermont** South Pde *☎Portsmouth733348*

26Ⓖ **Wairoa** 2 Florence Rd *☎Portsmouth732282*

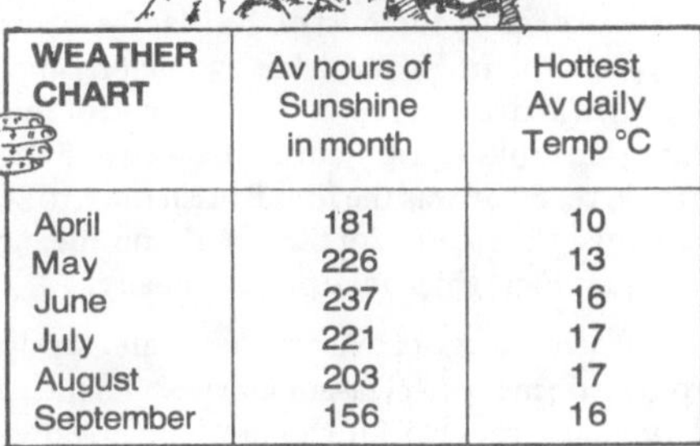

WEATHER CHART	Av hours of Sunshine in month	Hottest Av daily Temp °C
April	181	10
May	226	13
June	237	16
July	221	17
August	203	17
September	156	16

RYDE

Ryde's hillside setting overlooking Spithead provides fine views of the naval and commercial maritime traffic which uses the busy Solent. It has developed over the years from two insignificant hamlets to become a popular holiday resort where colourful seafront gardens back the sandy beach which slopes gently towards the sea and is safe for swimmers. It is also the point of entry for most of the island's visitors. The passenger ferry from Portsmouth docks at the head of the Pier which is 2305ft long and was opened in 1814. The hovercraft from Southsea arrives nearby at the shore end of the pier. Many of the town's Regency and Victorian buildings remain unchanged and the Town Hall and the Colonnade are particularly attractive. Ryde was the first British town to stage a Carnival and its colourful mile-long parade is still a feature of the town's summer attractions. There are also regattas and an Antiques Fair which take place annually.

The nearby village of Seaview has a safe, sandy beach and the toll road which follows the coast from Ryde makes a pleasant journey. To the west of Ryde is Fishbourne, terminal for the Portsmouth car ferry and home of the Royal Victoria Yacht Club who hold regattas during July and August each year.

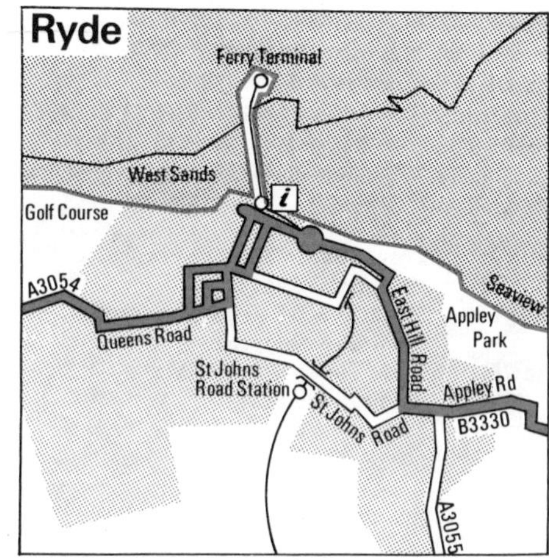

Recreation and Sports

Appley Park – Golf, tennis
Esplanade – Amusements, bandstand, boating lake, bowls, putting, swimming pools (heated)
Puckpool Park – Aquarium, aviary, bowls, children's playground, putting, tennis
Ryde Airport – Go-karts, indoor bowls (winter)
Ryde Golf Club Spencer Rd ☎*62088*
Ryde Lawn Tennis & Croquet Club Play St Ln ☎*62095*
Ryde Mead Lawn Tennis Club Church Ln ☎*65817*
Seaview Yacht Club ☎*Seaview3118/3268*
Sports Club Ryde Rd, Seaview ☎*Seaview3108* – Badminton, sauna, squash, tennis
Town Hall – Wrestling
Vectis Boating & Fishing Club Club House, Ryde

Cinemas

Commodore 1, 2 and 3 Star St ☎*64930*

Theatre

Pavilion Esplanade ☎*63465*

Places of Interest

Flamingo Park Bird Sanctuary Oakhill Rd, Springvale, Seaview ☎*Seaview2153*
Isle of Wight Steam Railway Havenstreet ☎ *Wootton Bridge882204*

Tourist Information

Tourist Information Centre Western Gdns, Esplanade ☎*62905*

Accommodation

The following establishments are recommended by the AA. Further information may be obtained from the Tourist Information Office.

★★ **Yelf's** Union St ☎*64062*
GH **Dorset Hotel** Dover St ☎*64327*
SC **Appley Rise House** Appley Rise. For bookings: Mrs J Rose, Treetops, Morton Rd, Brading, Isle of Wight. ☎*Brading241* (day) *Brading426* (evening)
SC **Eastfield House** For bookings: Dorset Hotel, 31 Dover St ☎*64327*
SC **Elm Court** Great Preston Rd. For bookings: Mrs A J Fiander, 4 Westfield Pk, Spencer Rd, Ryde ☎*66322*
SC Mrs M Hines, **Solent House**, Playstreet Ln ☎*64133*

Busy Ryde streets

Its sheltered position on Sandown Bay, protected by the headlands of Dunnose to the south and Culver Cliff to the north, puts Sandown high up in the British sunshine ratings. This, together with its wide sweep of safe, sandy beach, has developed the town over the last hundred years into the popular resort it is today. For the walking enthusiast there is a coast path leading over Culver Cliff where a column stands in memory of Charles Anderson Pelham, first Earl of Yarborough. In the opposite direction, another path climbs the cliffs, passing through the Battery Gardens with its ancient remains of Sandown Fort. Both walks give fine views over the town and the bay. Sandown has two Carnivals, one at Easter and the other during the summer season, and there is also a regatta.

The neighbouring town of Lake, half a mile to the south, is a more secluded resort and several interesting areas lie within a relatively short distance. Brading, its roots in Roman times, was once a harbour village 'moved' from the sea by land reclamation. It has stocks, a whipping post and a bull-bating ring, none of which, thankfully, are still in use. Alverstone is a delightful village with the remains of an old mill.

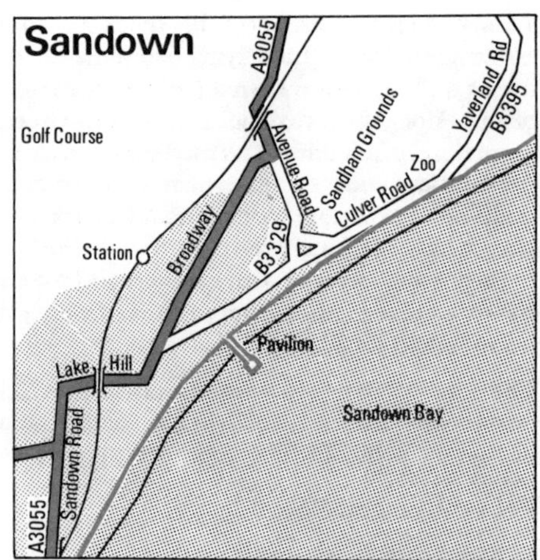

Note: The telephone numbers quoted below are liable to change in the near future.

Recreation and Sports

Culver Parade – Approach-golf, beach huts, bowls, canoe lake, playground, putting, tennis
Ferncliff Gardens – Crazy-golf
Lake Cliff – Putting
Pier – Amusements, angling
Sandham Grounds – Approach-golf, bowls, playground, putting, tennis
Sandown/Shanklin Golf Club ☎ *3217*

Cinema

Queens Albert Rd (summer only) ☎ *3478*

Theatre

Sandown Pavilion The Pier ☎ *2295*

Places of Interest

Arreton Manor Arreton ☎ *Arreton255*
Museum of Isle of Wight Geology Sandown Branch Library, High St ☎ *4344*
Lilliput Museum of Dolls High St, Brading ☎ *Brading231*
Morton Manor ☎ *Brading322*
Nunwell House and Park Brading ☎ *Winchester3374*
Osborn-Smith's Wax Museum High St, Brading ☎ *Brading286*
Robin Hill Country Park and Zoological Park Robin Hill ☎ *Arreton430*
Roman Villa Yarbridge, Brading ☎ *Ryde65852*

Tourist Information

Tourist Information Centre Esplanade ☎ *3886*

Accommodation

The following establishments are recommended by the AA. Further information may be obtained from the Tourist Information Office.

★★★	**Broadway Park** Melville St ☎ *2007*
★★★	**Melville Hall** ☎ *3794*
★★	**Royal Cliff** Beachfield Rd ☎ *2138*
★	**Rose Bank** 6 High St ☎ *3854*
GH	**Chester Lodge Hotel** Beachfield Rd ☎ *2773*
GH	**Cliff House Hotel** Cliff Rd ☎ *3656*
GH	**Rostrevor Private Hotel** 96 Sandown Rd ☎ *2775*
GH	**Trevallyn** 32 Broadway ☎ *2373*
SC	**Bedford House** 2B Heath Gdns, Lake. For bookings: Mrs M V Weeks, 21 Heath Rd, Lake, Sandown ☎ *3613*
SC	**Downsview Chalet Site** Perowne Way, off The Fairway ☎ *4513*

SHANKLIN

This split-level resort invariably holds the United Kingdom sunshine record with its esplanade and beach area lying below the town in the shelter of Dunnose Head. An electric lift, as well as paths and a road, connects the town to the sandy beach and safe swimming below. Along the top of the cliffs is Keats Green, so named in memory of the poet who spent some time in Shanklin. The modern town with its hotels and shopping centre is contrasted at the southern end by what remains of the original village, a picturesque collection of thatched buildings and cottage gardens and the attractive old Crab Inn. Constant erosion by a small stream has cut through the cliffs to form the beautiful chasm of Shanklin Chine where the rocks are now covered with greenery and the stream falls rather than flows. Paths have been constructed for visitors to enjoy this attractive gorge which is illuminated at night. Shanklin's Carnival and Regatta take place annually.

The nearby village of Luccombe also has its Chine, wilder than Shanklin's, but attractive in its own way, which leads down to Luccombe Bay and its smugglers caves. Godshill is a pretty, picture-book inland village, probably one of the most visited on the island.

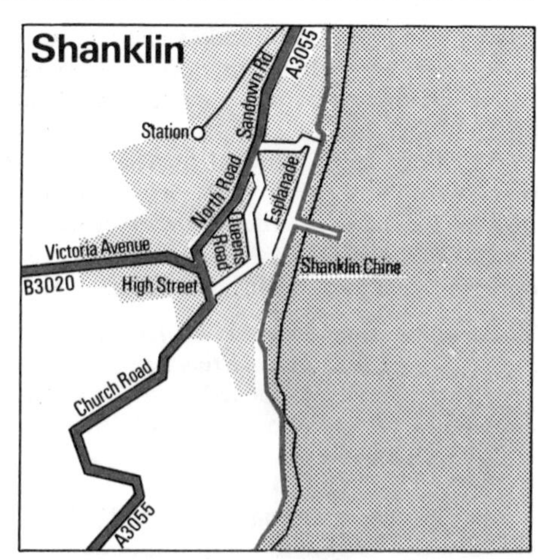

Recreation and Sports

Big Mead – Playground
Esplanade – Beach huts, putting, surfing
Hyde Sports Ground – Putting, tennis
Oaklyn Gardens – Playground
Pier – Amusements, angling
Rylstone Park – Bandstand, gardens, putting
Shankling Bowling Club Pavilion, Brooke Rd ☎*3777*
Shanklin Cricket Club Westhill ☎*2807*
Shanklin & Sandown Golf Club ☎*Sandown3217*

Cinema

Regal High St ☎*2272*

Theatre

Shanklin Theatre Prospect Rd ☎*2739*

Places of Interest

Model Village Old Vicarage Gdns, Godshill
Motor Museum Cliff Tops Hotel ☎*3262*
Natural History Collection Godshill

Tourist Information

Tourist Information Centre High St ☎*2942*

Accommodation

The following establishments are recommended by the AA. Further information may be obtained from the Tourist Information Office.

★★★	**Cliff Tops** ☎*3262*
★★★	**Shanklin** Eastmount Rd ☎*2286*
★★	**Luccombe Hall** ☎*2719*
★★	**Melbourne Ardenlea** Queens Rd ☎*2283*
GH	**Berry Brow Hotel** Pophal Rd ☎*2825*
GH	**Culham Private Hotel** 31 Landguard Manor Rd ☎*2880*
GH	**Cumberland Private Hotel** 26 Arthur's Hill ☎*3000*
GH	**Fernbank** Highfield Rd ☎*2790*
GH	**Langthorne Private Hotel** 3 Witbank Gdns ☎*2980*
GH	**Meyrick Cliffs** Esplanade ☎*2691*
GH	**Ocean View Hotel** 38 The Esplanade ☎*2602*
GH	**Overstrand Private Hotel** Howard Rd ☎*2100*
GH	**Roseglen** 12 Palmerston Rd ☎*3164*
SC	**71 Landguard Road** For bookings: Mrs I M Evans, West View, 69 Landguard Rd ☎*3876*
SC	**Lower Hyde Leisure Park** Lower Hyde Rd ☎*2865*
SC	**19 St John's Road** For bookings: Mrs I M Evans, West View, 69 Landguard Rd, Shanklin ☎*3876*
SC	Mrs D Fassotte, **Sansonnet** 56 Westhill Rd ☎*4155*

A resort with a distinctly Continental appearance, Ventnor was developed following a commendation of its healthy climate by Sir James Clarke in 1829. Situated on the lower slopes of St Boniface Down, its houses form terraces around streets which zig-zag up the hillside. The nature of the terrain has prevented a great deal of new development, thus preserving the Victorian character of the most southerly town on the island. The beach, sandy, safe for swimming and sprinkled with rock-pools, is backed by attractive gardens and cliff-top walks where palm trees and semi-tropical shrubs thrive. A hillside stream tumbles down the rocks emerging beside an unusual paddling pool with a scale model of the Isle of Wight as its central feature. Extending some six miles to the west of Ventnor is the Undercliff, a strip of rough ground created by landslides and changing still as sea, streams and the elements continually erode the clay-based soil. Ventnor has a Folk Dance and Music Festival in May or June each year and a Carnival in August.

The nearby village of Bonchurch, with its large village pond, was popular during the 19th century with many famous writers and poets.

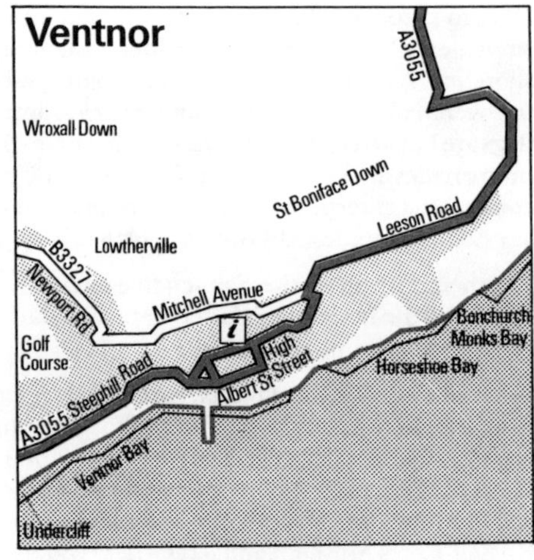

Recreation and Sports

Botanic Gardens – Adventure playground
Esplanade – Beach huts, canoe lake, crazy-golf, playground, paddling pool, roller skating, swing boats, trampolines
Pier – Amusements, angling
Mitchell Avenue – Bowls
St Boniface Road – Putting, tennis
Ventnor Golf Club Steephill Down Rd ☎*853326*
Western Cliffs – Putting

Cinema

Rex Church St ☎*852400* (summer only)

Theatre

Winter Garden ☎*852465*

Places of Interest

Appuldurcombe House Wroxall ☎*852484*
Museum to the History of Smuggling Botanic Gardens ☎*853677*
St Catherine's Lighthouse St Catherine's Point ☎*Niton284*
Tropical Bird Park Old Park, St Lawrence ☎*852583*
Yafford Water Mill Farm Park Shorwell ☎*Brightstone740610*
Ventnor Botanic Garden

Tourist Information

Tourist Information Centre 34 High St ☎*853625*

Accommodation

The following establishments are recommended by the AA. Further information may be obtained from the Tourist Information Office.

★★★ **Royal** Belgrave Rd ☎*852186*
★★ **Metropole** Seafront ☎*852181*
★★ **Ventnor Towers** Madeira Rd ☎*852277*
★ **Madeira Hall** Trinity Rd ☎*852624*
(ap) **Lake** Bonchurch (1m E) ☎*852613*
GH **Channel View Hotel** Hambrough Rd ☎*852230*
GH **Collingtree** Bellevue Rd ☎*852322*
GH **Kings Bay Hotel** Kings Bay Rd ☎*852815*
GH **Macrocarpa Hotel** Mitchell Ave ☎*852428*
GH **Picardie Hotel** The Esplanade ☎*852647*
GH **Richmond Private Hotel** The Esplanade ☎*852496*
GH **Under Rock Hotel** Shore Rd, Bonchurch ☎*852714*
SC **Ashcliffe Holiday Flats** The Pitts, Bonchurch. For bookings: Sandford Park Caravans Ltd, Holton Heath, Poole, Dorset ☎*Lytchett Minster2513*
SC Mrs M A Johnson, **Beresford** Spring Hill ☎*853782* (day); *853332* (evening)
SC Mrs Y E Fassotte, **La Falaise** Undercliffe Dr, St Lawrence ☎*853440*
SC Mrs L Watson, **Hawthorne** St Boniface Rd ☎*853302*
SC Mrs M R Jones, **Hillslea House** Bath Rd ☎*852259*
SC Mr N Hanley, **King's Bay Hotel** Kings Bay Rd ☎*852815*
SC **Punch Bowl Chalets Co Ltd** King's Bay Rd. For bookings: Mrs R Jones, Rose Cottage, Whitwell ☎*Niton730109*
SC Mrs A S Philpott, **Ravenscourt Holiday Bungalows** Ocean View Rd ☎*852555*
SC **Smugglers Cottage** 10 South St. For bookings: Mrs J Wearing, South Bank Park Ave, Ventnor ☎*852138*
SC **Westfield Holiday Centre** Shore Rd, Bonchurch ☎*852268*

BOURNEMOUTH

Prior to 1810 the valley in which Bournemouth lies was a desolate common, much favoured by smugglers. Today the town provides the holidaymaker with some seven miles of mainly sandy shoreline, lying in the shelter of 100ft cliffs. Wooded valleys or chines dissect the cliff face and the overall picture is one of colour and cleanliness. Swimming is generally safe, although red flags are hoisted at certain times when the weather makes conditions unsuitable. The promenades are kept free of traffic during the summer months and are surprisingly free of commercial enterprises, although the pier and the surrounding areas provide the usual amusement arcades, children's pools and playgrounds.

Bournemouth offers the visitor a fine selection of entertainment ranging from variety shows to opera and the Ice Rink and Pier Approach Baths stage an Ice Show and an Aqua Show respectively during the summer.

Bournemouth's vista of parks, gardens and Victorian buildings may all be viewed in comfort from the open top deck of a Yellow Sunshine Bus or the more energetic may cover the same ground on a hired bicycle. Bournemouth is one of the best shopping centres on the South Coast offering branches of most well-known stores, boutiques and a number of attractive enclosed arcades. The town's Victorian associations are recalled by the contents of the Russell-Cotes Museum and Art Gallery which include mementos of Sir Henry Irving and a freshwater aquarium. The Rothesay Museum, near the pier, contains a collection of early Italian prints, marine exhibits and a unique British Typewriter Museum. The Big Four Railway Museum has a large collection of locomotive nameplates and a working model railway.

Christchurch with its Norman cathedral, ruined castle and Tucktonia Amusement Park, which contains 'The Best of Britain in Miniature', an exhibition of models of Tower Bridge, Westminster etc is only a few miles away and other touring areas include the New Forest, the many attractions of Beaulieu and Longleat House and Safari Park.

E	**AA Service Centre** Fanum House, 3 Wimbourne Rd ☎*25751*

Recreation and Sports

	Boscombe Chine Gardens – Mini-golf, paddling pool
	Boscombe Cliff Bowling Club Woodland Ave, Boscombe ☎*427810*
	Bournemouth & Boscombe AFC Dean Court Ground ☎*35381*
H	**Bournemouth Pier** – Amusements
C	**Dean Park Sports Ground** Cavendish Rd ☎*20946* – County Cricket
G	**Durley Chine** – Crazy-golf
	Kings Park – Athletics, bowls, children's playground, cricket, football, tennis
F	**Knyveton Gardens** – Bowls, tennis
H(1)	**Lower Gardens** – Aviary, mini-golf, table-tennis
A	**Meyrick Park** – Bowls, cricket, football, hockey, squash, tennis
	Meyrick Park Golf Course ☎*20871*
	Queens Park Golf Course ☎*36198*
	Shelley Park Boscombe – Bowls, putting, tennis
	Stokewood Road Baths ☎*529658* – Indoor swimming pool
E	**Upper Pleasure Gardens** – Outdoor draughts, putting, table-tennis, tennis
	West Hants Lawn Tennis Club Roslin Rd South ☎*519455* – International Tennis Championships
	Woodland Walk Boscombe – Bowls

Cabaret/Dancing

	Aquitaine Disco 25 Townsville Rd, Moordown ☎*511120*
D	**Cuddles** 20 The Triangle ☎*28931*
E	**Fernandos** Terrace Rd ☎*20026*
	Kaleidoscope 61 Curzon Rd ☎*38681*
F	**Silvers** 205 Old Christchurch Rd ☎*293497*
	Tiffanys 507 Christchurch Rd ☎*36238*
D	**Winstons** 28 Poole Rd ☎*762385*

Cinemas

E	**ABC** Westover Rd ☎*28433*
	Continental Wimbourne Rd ☎*59779*
H	**Galaxy** Westover Rd ☎*23277*
H	**Gaumont** Westover Rd ☎*22402*
	Grand Poole Rd ☎*763118*
E	**Tatler** Albert Rd ☎*21391*

Theatres

E(3)	**Ice Rink** Westover Rd ☎*22611*
H(4)	**Pavilion** ☎*25861*
H(2)	**Pier Approach Baths** ☎*24393*
H	**Pier Theatre** ☎*20250*
H	**Playhouse** Westover Rd ☎*23275*
H(5)	**Winter Gardens** ☎*26446*

Places of Interest

E(7)	**Big Four Railway Museum** Dalkeith Hall, Old Christchurch Rd ☎*29349*
	Christchurch Castle and Norman House
F(6)F	**Municipal College and Library**
	Red House Museum and Art Gallery Quay Rd, Christchurch ☎*Christchurch2860*
H(8)	**Rothesay Museum** 8 Bath Rd ☎*21009*
I(9)	**Russell-Cotes Art Gallery and Museum** ☎*21009*
	Tucktonia Stour Rd, Christchurch ☎*Christchurch2710*

Tourist Information

ℹE(10)	**Tourist Information Centre** Westover Rd ☎*291715*

Accommodation

The establishments listed below are a selection of AA-recommended accommodation located in the area covered by the Town Plan. Further information may be found in AA publications or obtained from the Tourist Information Centre.

1★★★★	**Anglo Swiss** Gervis Rd, East Cliff ☎*24794*
2★★★	**Burley Court** Bath Rd ☎*22824*
3★★★★★	**Carlton** East Cliff ☎*22011*
4★★	**Durley Hall** Durley Chine Rd ☎*766886*
5★★★	**Durlston Court** Gervis Rd, East Cliff ☎*291488*
6★★★	**Embassy** Meyrick Rd ☎*20751*

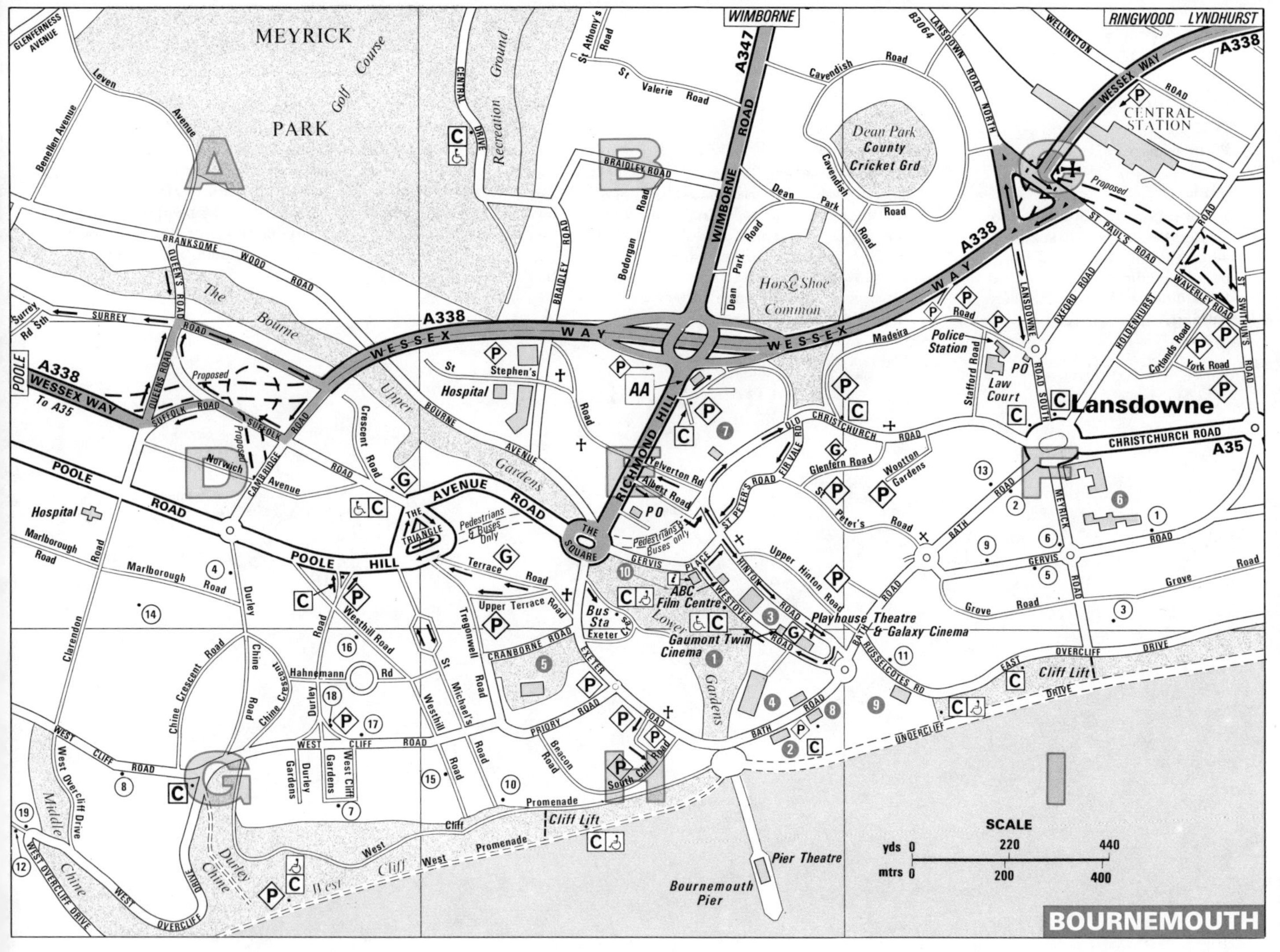

7SC **Eyeworth Lawn** West Cliff Gardens, Bournemouth, Dorset BH2 5HL ☎*22228*

8SC **Gayhurst Superior Holiday Flats** Mr Adey, 44A West Cliff Rd, Bournemouth, Dorset BH4 8BB ☎*764488*

9GH **Gervis Court Hotel** 38 Gervis Rd ☎*26871*

10★★★★ **Highcliff** West Cliff ☎*27702*

11★★★★ **Marsham Court** Russelcotes Rd, East Cliff ☎*22111*

12SC Mr J V McCabe, **Midchines** 14 McKinley Rd, Bournemouth ☎*522685*

13★★★ **Pavilion** Bath Rd ☎*291266*

14SC **3 Portarlington Road** West Cliff for bookings Mr & Mrs F R Peverelle, White Wings, 14 Mornish Rd, Branksome Park, Bournemouth ☎*762149*

15★★★ **Savoy** West Cliff, West Hill Rd ☎*20357*

16★★ **Tralee** West Hill Rd, West Cliff ☎*26246*

17★★★ **Wessex** West Cliff Rd ☎*21911*

18SC **Wessex Court** Durley Rd, Bournemouth ☎*21911*

19SC **White Wings** 25 McKinley Rd, West Cliff. For bookings: Mr & Mrs F R Peverelle, White Wings, 4 Mornish Rd, Branksome Park, Bournemouth, Dorset ☎*762149*

Sandbanks *see Poole*

Poole *see page 81*

Studland
The wide sweep of Studland Bay shelters behind Handfast Point, where the Old Harry Rocks are popular landmarks, and beneath Ballard Down. Some of the safest bathing in the south can be enjoyed from its two miles of white sands which are heaped into large dunes behind the flat beach. At the southern end of the bay rock-pools are exposed at low-tide. From the large car park just outside the village, an attractive leafy lane leads down to the beach. There is a Nature Reserve at Studland Heath and a Nature Trail begins close to Knoll House Hotel. The Dorset Coast Path follows the line of the bay.

Swanage *see page 84*

Kimmeridge Bay
Reached via a toll road from Kimmeridge village, this is a secluded bay with a car park and toilet facilities on the cliff-top. The shingle beach is backed by crumbling cliffs which contain a wealth of fossils and the sea barely covers the rocky ledges jutting out from the beach. Swimming is not recommended, but the fascinating rock-pools provide some consolation.

Lulworth Cove
One of the most popular beauty spots on the South Coast and consequently often very crowded in summer. The high cliffs form a natural harbour around a rocky, shingle beach where swimming is generally safe. There is a cliff-top car park which also gives access to a neighbouring bay where Durdle Door, a huge limestone arch, juts into the sea.

Osmington Mills
A steep cliff path leads down to the pebble and stone beach below. Rock-pools are exposed at low-tide and the area is noted for its freshly caught lobsters and crabs. A white horse is cut into the chalk hills nearby.

WEYMOUTH *see page 82*

Portland
This rugged, bleak peninsula is, in fact, eight square miles of solid rock, the famous Portland Stone so well loved by architects for centuries. Quarrying is still very much in evidence. The northern end of the island is built up with houses rising in steps and terraces on the steep hillside, the naval base clustered around the harbour and the stark building of the former prison, once one of the most dreaded in the country. The Portland Museum at Wakeham is housed in Avices Cottage which has Thomas Hardy connections. At the southern tip, Portland Bill, with its lighthouse is a favourite, though windswept, viewpoint. Swimming is dangerous all around Portland, with exceedingly strong currents and fierce seas. There is excellent fishing in the harbour and in Weymouth Bay where some record catches have been recorded. Sailing is also popular.

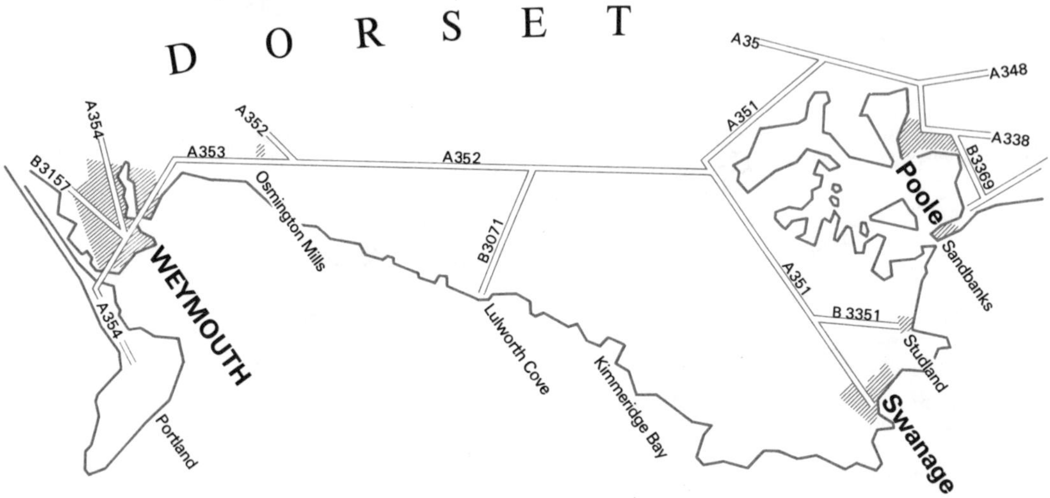

Poole became a prominent port during the 15th century when the channel serving neighbouring Wareham became impossible to navigate and has grown into a popular holiday resort encircled by heathland and pinewoods. Most of the town's activities are centred around the almost land-locked natural harbour which has retained much of its 18th-century atmosphere despite the presence of a modern shopping complex.

Poole's main beach is the mile-long peninsula of Sandbanks where gently sloping golden sands, backed by dunes, provide safe bathing for all. Beach floats and children's amusements are available here and further inland Poole Park offers 50 acres of pleasure grounds containing a boating lake, miniature railway and a zoo. Most sporting activities are catered for within the town and the Poole Arts Centre provides holidaymakers and residents with a wide programme of entertainment. The Town Cellars, on the quayside, now house a maritime museum and Poole Aquarium and the famous Poole Pottery where guided tours may be arranged are also to be found in this area. A vehicle and passenger ferry runs from Sandbanks to Shell Bay on the Isle of Purbeck and a motor boat service covers a similar route. Brownsea Island, a National Trust property, lies within Poole Harbour. It contains a restored castle and a nature reserve and may be visited by motorboat. It was here that Lord Baden-Powell held his first scout camp in 1907.

Places of interest include Compton Acres – a collection of seven beautifully landscaped gardens overlooking Poole Harbour, Merley Tropical Bird Garden, and Upton Park with its nature trails and picnic areas.

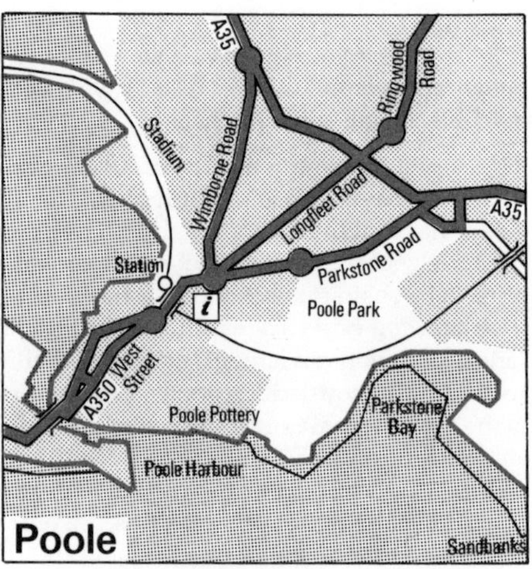

Recreation and Sports

Broadstone Golf Club 27 Lower Golf Links Rd ☎ *Broadstone 693363*
Cobbs Quay Yacht Club Hamworthy ☎ *3690*
The Dolphin Swimming Pool Kingland Rd ☎ *77217* – Indoor pool
East Dorset Sailing Club 37 Pearce Ave ☎ *Parkstone 740609*
Lilliput Sailing Club Sandbanks Rd ☎ *Parkstone 740317*
Parkstone Golf Club ☎ *Canford Cliffs 708025*
Parkstone Yacht Club Pearce Ave ☎ *Parkstone 743610*
Poole Harbour Yacht Club and Marina Salterns Way ☎ *Canford Cliffs 700262*
Poole Park – Band concerts, boating lake, bowls, crazy-golf, cricket, hockey, miniature railway, tennis, zoo
Poole Quay – Amusements
Poole Sports Centre Arndale Centre ☎ *5922* – Most indoor sports
Poole Stadium Wimborne Rd ☎ *3020* – Greyhound racing and speedway
Poole Town FC The Stadium, Wimborne Rd ☎ *4747* – Southern League
Poole Yacht Club New Quay Rd, Hamworthy ☎ *2687*
Royal Motor Yacht Club Panorama Rd ☎ *Canford Cliffs 707227*

Theatre

Poole Arts Centre Kingland Rd ☎ *70521* – Incorporating cinema and concert hall

Places of Interest

Brownsea Island Poole Harbour
Byngley House Market St ☎ *70830*
Compton Acres Gardens Canford Cliffs Rd ☎ *Canford Cliffs 708036*
Maritime Museum The Quay ☎ *3939*
Merley Tropical Bird Gardens Merley ☎ *Wimborne 883790*
Poole Aquarium The Quay ☎ *86712*
Poole Guildhall Museum Market St ☎ *5323*
Poole Pottery Ltd The Quay ☎ *3866*
Rock and Gem Centre The Quay ☎ *77650*
Scalpens Court High St ☎ *6066* – Museum of local history
Upton Country Park – Children's play areas, nature trails

Tourist Information

Tourist Information Centre Civic Centre ☎ *5151*
Tourist Information Centre Arndale Centre ☎ *3322*

Accommodation

The following establishments are recommended by the AA. Further information may be obtained from the Tourist Information Centre.

★★★ **Dolphin** High St ☎ *3612*
★★★ **Sandbanks** 15 Banks Rd, Sandbanks ☎ *707377*
★★ **Harbour Heights** 73 Haven Rd, Sandbanks ☎ *707272*
GH **Norfolk Lodge** 1 Flaghead Rd, Canford Cliffs ☎ *708614*

Restaurants

XX **Grovefield Hotel** Pinewood Rd, Branksome Park ☎ *766798*
XX **Warehouse** The Quay ☎ *77238*

WEYMOUTH

There has been a port here since Roman times but Weymouth owes its development to two English monarchs, Henry VIII who established a naval base there and George III who enhanced its reputation as a resort by becoming the first reigning king to use a bathing machine during one of his visits.

The present harbour is used by cargo vessels and is the main embarkation point for the Channel Islands. A regular car ferry service also operates between Weymouth and Cherbourg. To the north of the harbour typically Georgian buildings and floral gardens overlook the sheltered, gently sloping beach which provides safe swimming in most conditions. Beach huts, deck chairs, canoes and 'fun-floats' are available for hire and children's amusements such as swing-boats, trampolines and a Punch and Judy show are permanent fixtures on the sands. Weymouth is famous for sand-modelling and the resident expert regularly produces some extremely artistic creations. Boat trips run from the beach and from the harbour. There is an amusement area near the pier and a funfair a short distance inland while Radipole Lake, an extension of the harbour, in addition to being a well-known breeding ground for swans, has facilities for boating, putting and tennis. There is a summer Carnival and sailing events take place throughout the year. The Museum of Local History traces the development of Weymouth and neighbouring Portland and two 17th-century cottages in Trinity Street have been restored and converted into a single dwelling which is open to the public.

Weymouth lies in the heart of Thomas Hardy country, featuring in his novels as *Budmouth*. Hardy was born near Dorchester and the County Museum there contains his manuscript for *The Mayor of Casterbridge*. West of Weymouth, on the far side of Portland lies Chesil Beach, an extensive natural pebble ridge some 20ft high, enclosing a salt-water lake, and Abbotsbury Swannery, the largest of its kind in England, originally established to provide birds for the table of the nearby Benedictine monastery.

Recreation and Sports

B	**Greenhill Gardens** – Bowls, putting, tennis
	Lodmoor Car Park – Go-karts, model village – N off A353
C	**Melcombe Regis Gardens** – Bowls, putting
C	**Radipole Lake** – Amusements, boating
A/C	**Radipole Park Drive Gardens** – Go-karts, putting, tennis
C	**Westham Coach Park** – Chipperfields Amusement Park
E	**Weymouth FC** The Recreation Ground ☎*5558* – Southern League
D	**Weymouth Pier** – Amusements, deck games
	Weymouth Sailing Club Nothe Pde, ☎*5481*
	Weymouth Sports Ground Redlands ☎*Upwey2400* – Cricket
E	**Weymouth Swimming Pool** Knightsdale Rd ☎*74373*
	Weymouth Town Golf Course Links Rd ☎*4994*

Cinema

C	**Classic** Gloucester St ☎*5847*

Dancing

F	**Pavilion Ballroom** ☎*6732*

Theatre

F	**Pavilion Theatre** ☎*3225*

Places of Interest

C(1)	**Museum of Local History** Westham Rd ☎*74246*

Tourist Information

[i]C	**Information Centre** Esplanade ☎*5747*

Accommodation

The establishments listed below are a selection of AA-recommended accommodation and restaurants located in the area covered by the Town Plan. Further information may be found in AA publications or obtained from the Information Centre.

1	**Bay View** 35 The Esplanade ☎*2083*
2SC	**Glen Court** Glendinning Ave ☎*2886*
3★★	**Gloucester** 84 The Esplanade ☎*6404*
4★★	**Golden Lion** St Edmonds St ☎*6778*
5★★★	**Ingleton** Greenhill ☎*5804*
6SC	Mr & Mrs Grove, **Ing Ravan Holiday Flats**, 10 Carlton Road North, Weymouth, Dorset DT4 7PX ☎*6271*
7GH	**Kenora** 5 Stavordale Rd ☎*71215*
8★★	**Kingswood** Rodwell Rd ☎*4926*
9SC	Mr & Mrs P R S Allen, **Panda Holiday Flats**, 12 Grosvenor Rd, Weymouth, Dorset DT4 7QL ☎*73817*
10★★	**Prince Regent** 139 The Esplanade ☎*71313*
11✕	**Pullingers** Pier Bandstand ☎*2021*
12SC	**Regent Holiday Flats** 2 Westbourne Rd. For bookings: D & L Archibald, 30 Greenhill, Weymouth, Dorset DT4 7SG ☎*6987*
13★★	**Rembrandt** 12 Dorchester Rd ☎*6253*
14★★	**Rex** 29 The Esplanade ☎*73485*
15GH	**Rosedene** 1 Carlton Rd North ☎*4021*
16✕	**Sea Cow Bistro** Custom House Quay ☎*3524*
17✕	**Spinacker** Custom House Quay ☎*2767*
18SC	Mr & Mrs D G Rees, **Stavordale Holiday Flats**, 6 Stavordale Rd, Weymouth, Dorset DT4 0AB ☎*6060*
19★★	**Streamside** 29 Preston Rd ☎*Preston833121*

WEATHER CHART	Av hours of Sunshine in month	Hottest Av daily Temp °C
April	191	9
May	228	12
June	237	15
July	226	16
August	207	16
September	156	15

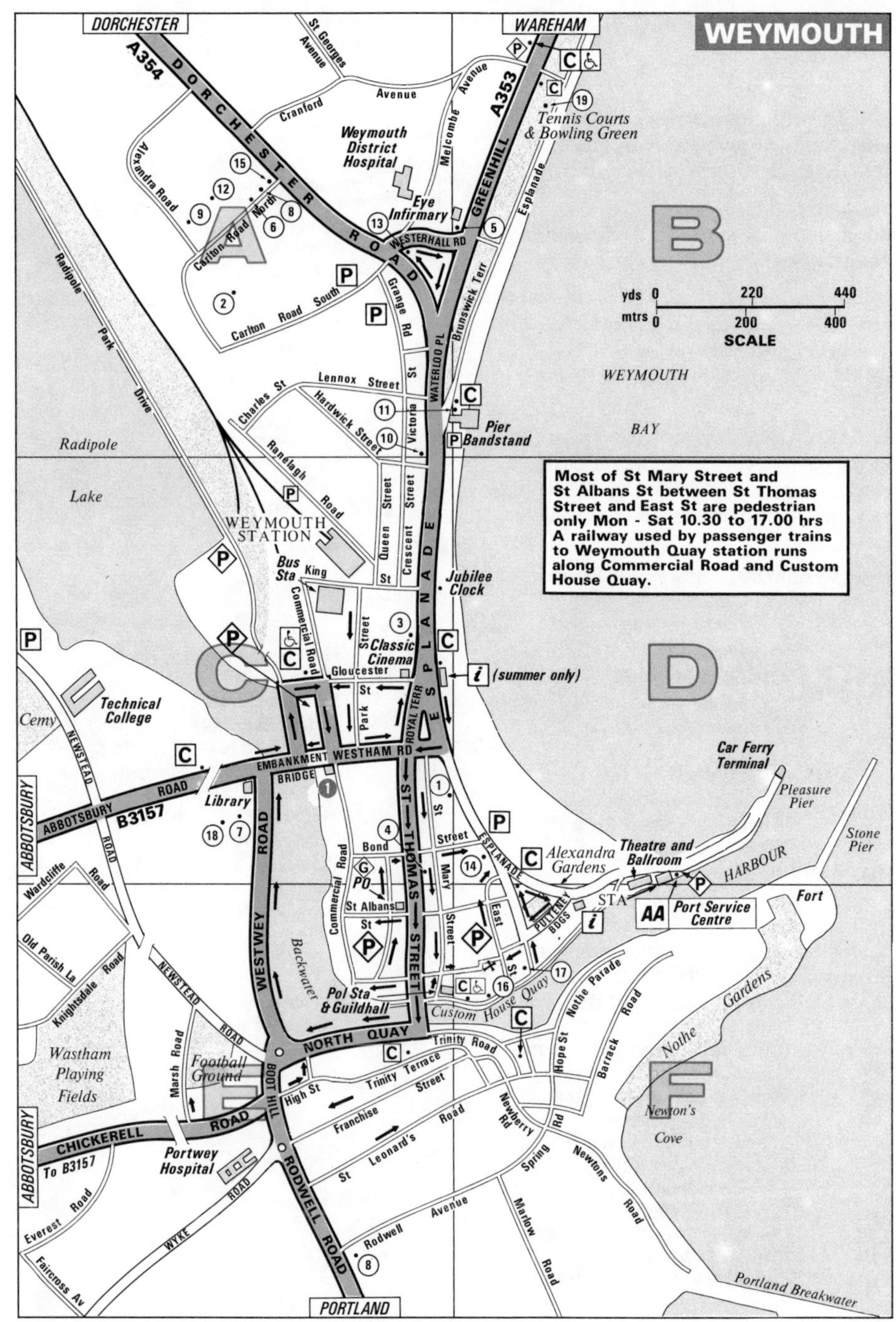
WEYMOUTH
DORCHESTER
WAREHAM
PORTLAND
A354 DORCHESTER ROAD
A353 GREENHILL
Weymouth District Hospital
Eye Infirmary
Tennis Courts & Bowling Green
Esplanade
WEYMOUTH BAY
Radipole Lake
Radipole Park Drive
WEYMOUTH STATION
Pier Bandstand
Jubilee Clock
Classic Cinema
(summer only)
Technical College
Library
ABBOTSBURY ROAD B3157
Car Ferry Terminal
Pleasure Pier
Stone Pier
Theatre and Ballroom
Alexandra Gardens
HARBOUR
Fort
Port Service Centre
Pol Sta & Guildhall
Backwater
Custom House Quay
NORTH QUAY
WESTWEY ROAD
ST THOMAS STREET
Nothe Gardens
Newton's Cove
Portland Breakwater
Wastham Playing Fields
Football Ground
Portwey Hospital
CHICKERELL ROAD
To B3157
RODWELL ROAD
SCALE
yds 0 220 440
mtrs 0 200 400
Most of St Mary Street and St Albans St between St Thomas Street and East St are pedestrian only Mon - Sat 10.30 to 17.00 hrs
A railway used by passenger trains to Weymouth Quay station runs along Commercial Road and Custom House Quay.

SWANAGE

A former Anglo-Saxon port and, in later centuries, used for shipping Purbeck Marble quarried in the nearby hills, Swanage lies in a sheltered bay with gently sloping golden sands and clear shallow water. Bathing is generally safe but the chalk cliffs to the north can be dangerous.

There are facilities for launching pleasure craft and amenities for most sports. Rowing, motorboats and pedal-craft are available for hire from the beach or quay.

Swanage is a picturesque town with some old buildings although the Parish Church, near the old Millpond, was mainly rebuilt in the 19th century. Local industry and art are featured in the Tithe Barn Museum and the façade of the 19th-century town hall was once part of Mercer's Hall in London. The Wellington Clock tower was also removed from London in 1867.

Standing in Durlston Country Park to the south of the town is the famous stone 'Great Globe', weighing 40 tons, with its wealth of information on the planets, earth, sun, moon and the stars, Anvil Point Lighthouse, built at the beginning of the 19th century and the Tilly Whim Caves (closed to the public). There are excellent views from the footpaths along the cliffs, which are a natural habitat for numerous sea birds.

For the railway enthusiast there is the old Station with its miniature railway and historic engines.

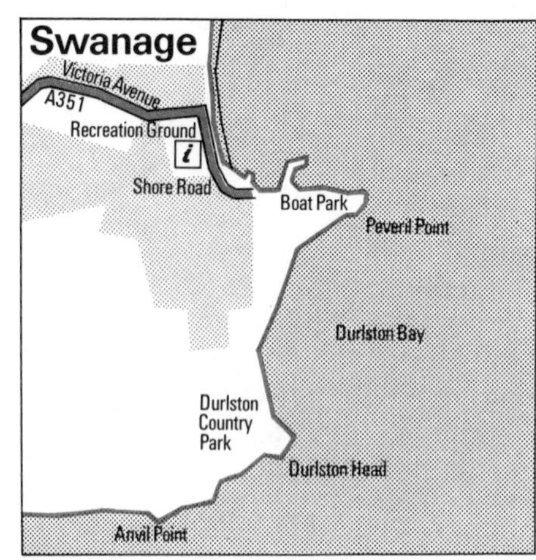

Recreation and Sports

Beach Gardens De Moulham Rd – Bowls, putting, tennis
Broad Road – Mini-golf
Days Park – Children's play area
Isle of Purbeck Golf Club ☎ *Studland 210*
King George's Playing Fields – Children's play area, go-karts
Municipal Boat Park Peveril Point ☎ *3636* – Launching facilities and parking
Parish Slipway The Square – Launching (no parking)
Recreation Ground Sea Front – Children's play area, crazy-golf, miniature railway, model boating pool, putting, trampolines
Swanage Sailing Club The Pier ☎ *2987*

Cinema/Theatre

Mowlem Theatre The Parade ☎ *2239*

Places of Interest

Durlston Country Park
Mill Pond
Parish Church of St Mary the Virgin
Peveril Point
Tithe Barn Museum
Town Hall
Wellington Clock Tower

Tourist Information

Tourist Information Centre The White House, Shore Rd ☎ *2885*

Accommodation

The following establishments are recommended by the AA. Further information may be obtained from the Tourist Information Office.

★★★	**Corrie** De Moulham Rd ☎ *3104*
★★★	**Grosvenor** ☎ *2292*
★★	**Cliff Top** 8 Burlington Rd ☎ *2091*
★★	**Grand** Burlington Rd ☎ *3353*
★★	**Pines** Burlington Rd ☎ *2166*
★★	**Ship** The Square ☎ *2078*
★	**Suncliffe** 1 Burlington Rd ☎ *3299*
Ⓐ	**Malverns** Park Rd ☎ *2575*
Ⓐ	**Saxmundham** Burlington Rd ☎ *2870*
GH	**Boyne Hotel** Cliff Ave ☎ *2939*
GH	**Byways** 5 Ulwell Rd ☎ *2322*
GH	**Eversden** Victoria Rd ☎ *3276*
GH	**Golden Sands** 10 Ulwell Rd ☎ *2093*
GH	**Havenhurst Hotel** 3 Cranbourne Rd ☎ *4224*
GH	**Ingleston Hotel** 2 Victoria Rd ☎ *2391*
GH	**Oxford Hotel** 3 & 5 Park Rd ☎ *2247*
GH	**Tower Lodge** 17 Ulwell Rd ☎ *2887*
GH	**Westbury Hotel** 6 Rempstone Rd ☎ *2345*
SC	Mr & Mrs Fowler, **Alexander Court** Grosvenor Rd ☎ *4606*
SC	**Waverley** Park Rd. For bookings: Mr & Mrs Fowler, Alexander Court, Grosvenor Rd ☎ *4606*

Burton Bradstock
A coastal village, popular with holidaymakers, which has a steep pebble and shingle beach. The surrounding cliffs abound in colourful masses of wild flowers during the spring and summer.

West Bay
Pleasure craft and commercial vessels use the small harbour at the mouths of the Rivers Brit and Asker. The shingle beach shelves steeply and swimming is not recommended when the sea is rough. Boats are available for hire. To the north lies the ancient town of Bridport, well known for the manufacture of fishermen's equipment. Bridport has sports and entertainment facilities and a museum containing a section devoted to fishing implements.

Golden Cap
The highest cliff in southern England rising to over 600ft. Its name relates to the golden glow which its sandstone reflects when bathed in the rays of a setting or rising sun. The cliff top is accessible on foot.

Charmouth
A quiet, unspoilt resort with a secluded sand and shingle beach which is generally safe for swimming. The surrounding cliffs are renowned for an abundance of fossils and an ichthyosaurus was found here in the 19th century. Charles II was hidden in the Queen's Arms at Charmouth after the Battle of Worcester in 1651.

Lyme Regis *see page 86*

Dowlands Cliffs
A wide chasm, caused by a landslide in the 19th century, now forms part of the Axmouth-Lyme Regis Undercliff National Nature Reserve which covers a five-mile stretch of coastline and contains many species of plant and animal life. Visitors must keep to the path at all times.

Seaton *see page 87*

Beer
Here the chalk cliffs end giving way to the deep red of the coastline to the west. Beer is a quiet fishing village with a pebbly beach where many rock-pools are to be found at low-tide. Boats are available for hire. Modelrama, an exhibition of model railways with a narrow gauge railway, pleasure park and putting green, stands on the hillside behind the village. A mile from the village lie the ancient quarries which have supplied the material for many local buildings. The quarries have been constantly in use since Roman times.

Branscombe
A long, lonely pebble beach, backe by grassland and a stream. The area is owned by the National Trust and its natural charm is carefully preserved. There are a number of attractive thatched cottages in the village.

Sidmouth *see page 88*

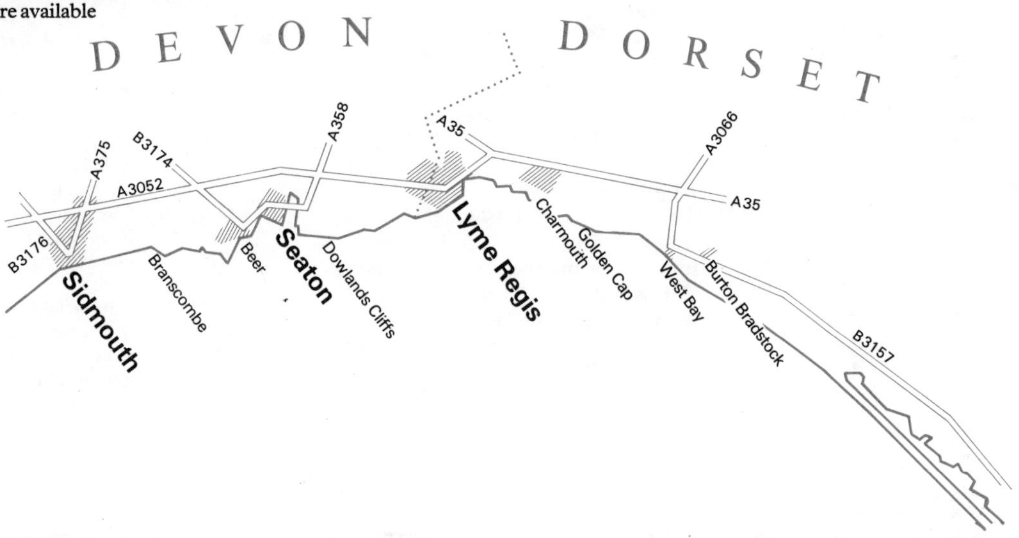

LYME REGIS

A small holiday resort full of character and history situated right on the Devon – Dorset border. Originally a cloth town and naval base, Lyme Regis was once an important trading port. Possibly the most well-known event in its history was the landing by the Duke of Monmouth in 1685 at the start of his ill-fated rebellion against James II.

Its declining fortunes were revived during the 18th century as a result of its discovery as a watering place by the fashionable gentry of Bath, and even though its history as a resort extends over two hundred years, the town has not been over-commercialised and retains much of its original atmosphere.

The Cobb is the name given to the town's harbour whose origins date back a thousand years. Today it is filled with fishing boats, yachts and pleasure craft. To the west of the Cobb is the predominantly pebble Monmouth Beach, but to the east lie the golden sands of the main beaches extending towards Cobb Gate. Swimming is safe in the immediate area of the town but dangerous from the more exposed, and in places steeply shelving, pebble beaches elsewhere along the coast.

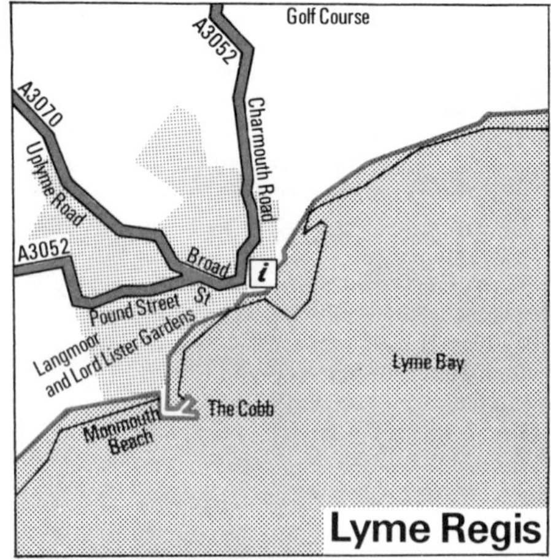

Recreation and Sports

Langmoor Gardens – Putting
Lord Lister Gardens – Mini-golf
Marine Parade – Performances by local bands every Sunday during season
Monmouth Beach – Bowls

Cinema

Regent Broad St ☎*2053*

Theatre

Marine Theatre ☎*2394*

Places of Interest

Philpot Museum Bridge St ☎*3127*

Tourist Information

Tourist Information Office The Guildhall, Bridge St ☎*2138*

Accommodation

The following establishments are recommended by the AA. Further information may be obtained from the Tourist Information Office.

★★★	**Alexandra** Pound St ☎*3229*
★★★	**High Cliff** Sidmouth Rd ☎*2300*
★★	**Bay** Marine Pde ☎*2059*
★★	**Beuna Vista** Pound St ☎*2494*
★★	**Mariners** Silver St ☎*2753*
★★	**Royal Lion** Broad St ☎*2768*
★★	**St Michaels** Pound St ☎*2503*
★★	**Three Cups** ☎*2732*
★	**Stile House** ☎*2052*
★	**Tudor House** Church St ☎*2472*
GH	**Coverdale** Woodmead Rd ☎*2882*
GH	**Kersbrook** Pound Rd ☎*2596*
GH	**Old Monmouth Hotel** Church St ☎*2456*
GH	**Rotherfield** View Rd ☎*2811*
GH	**White House** 47 Silver St ☎*3420*
SC	Mr & Mrs L D Clarke, **Coram Tower** Pound Rd ☎*2012*
SC	L D Clarke, **Coram Tower** Pound Rd ☎*2012*

The harbour filled with pleasure craft

A small, unspoiled resort situated near the mouth of the River Axe. The beach is mainly composed of shingle and its slope renders it hazardous for non-swimmers. The safest bathing area is Seaton Hole on the western shore where some sand and several rock-pools are exposed at low-tide. It is possible to walk along the cliffs from this point to neighbouring Beer where boats of all types are available for hire from the beach. Visitors with sailing dinghies may obtain temporary membership of the Axe Yacht Club in Seaton.

Shows, concerts and discos are held throughout the summer at the modernised town hall, regular band concerts are held in the Festival Gardens and Seaton stages an Arts and Drama Festival each year.

An unusual feature is the well-known Seaton and District Electric Tramway which extends for several miles alongside the River Axe connecting the town with Colyford and Cloyton.

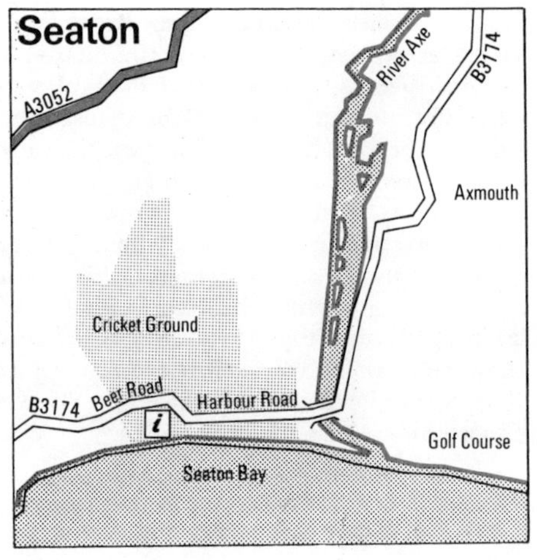

Recreation and Sports

Axe Cliff Golf Club ☎*20499*
Axe Yacht Club Esplanade
Beer Road – Bowls, tennis
Seaton Cricket and Lawn Tennis Club Court Ln, Cloyford Rd ☎*20445*

Theatre

Seaton Town Hall Fore St

Places of Interest

Seaton and District Electric Tramway Harbour Rd ☎*21702* (Depot)

Tourist Information

Tourist Information Centre The Esplanade ☎*21660* (mid-May to Sep30) ☎*21345* (Oct–mid-May)

Accommodation

The following establishments are recommended by the AA. Further information may be obtained from the Tourist Information Office.

★★ **Bay** East Walk ☎*20073*
★ **Pole Arms** Fore St ☎*20019*
GH **Eyre House** Queen St ☎*21455*
GH **Glendare** Fore St ☎*20542*
GH **Mariner's Homestead** Esplanade ☎*20560*
GH **Netherhayes** Fore St ☎*21646*
GH **Thornfield** Scalwell Ln ☎*20039*
SC **Character Cottages (Holidays) Ltd** Sidmouth, Devon ☎*6531*

Restaurant

✕✕ **Copperfields** Fore St ☎*22294*

SIDMOUTH

Sidmouth, the largest of the Lyme Bay towns, is a quiet, rather select Regency-style town with a large residential population. Despite its popularity as a holiday resort Sidmouth has remained generally uncommercialised although the town tends to become very crowded, especially during the first week in August when the well-known Internation Folklore Dance and Song Festival is held in Knowle Arena, attracting teams from all over the world. The eastern part of the beach consists almost entirely of pebbles but further west, below the cliff-top terraces of Connaught Gardens, firm golden sands are to be found where bathing cabins and tents may be hired. Swimming is safe although the eastern beach tends to slope rather steeply. The main promenade has no amusement arcades but provides a pleasant walk between the spot where the River Sid emerges from the eastern cliffs onto the beach and the landscaped area to the west where Jacobs Ladder descends the cliffs to the beach below. Entertainment is provided in the form of band concerts in Connaught Gardens and live theatre at the Manor Pavilion and Arts Centre. There are adequate sports facilities and good opportunities for angling and sailing.

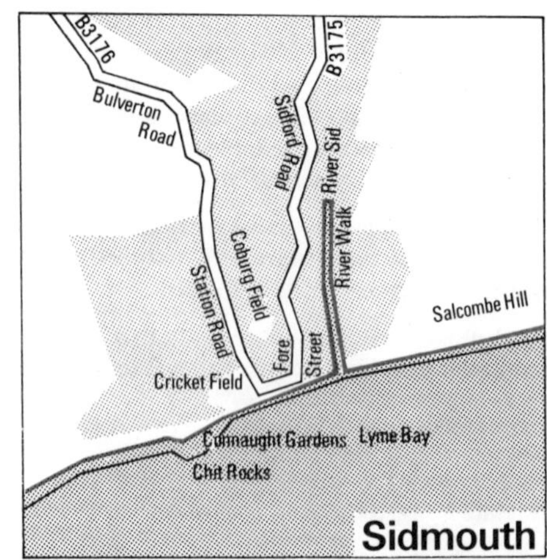

Recreation and Sports

Coburg Field – Bowls, tennis
Esplanade – Cricket, croquet, tennis
Peak Hill – Golf
Sidmouth Bowling Club Coburg Ter ☎ *3082*
Sidmouth Cricket Club Fortfield Ter ☎ *3229*
Sidmouth Golf Club Cotmaton Rd ☎ *3023*
Sidmouth Sailing and Sea Angling Club Esplanade ☎ *2286*

Cinema

Radway Radway Pl ☎ *3085*

Theatre

Manor Pavilion and Arts Centre Manor Rd ☎ *4413*

Places of Interest

Sidmouth Museum Church St ☎ *6139*

Tourist Information

Tourist Information Centre The Esplanade ☎ *6441* (summer)
Tourist Information Centre The District Council Offices, Knowle ☎ *6551* (winter)

Accommodation

The following establishments are recommended by the AA. Further information may be obtained from the Tourist Information Office.

★★★★	**Victoria** Esplanade ☎ *2651*
★★★	**Bedford** Esplanade ☎ *3047*
★★★	**Belmont** Sea Front ☎ *2555*
★★★	**Fortfield** Station Rd ☎ *2403*
★★★	**Riviera** The Esplanade ☎ *5201*
★★★	**Royal York** Esplanade ☎ *3043*
★★★	**Salcombe Hill House** Beatland Rd ☎ *4697*
★★★	**Westcliff** Manor Rd ☎ *3252*
★★	**Abbeydale** Manor Rd ☎ *2060*
★★	**Brownlands** Sid Rd ☎ *3053*
★★	**Byes Links** Sid Rd ☎ *3129*
★★	**Faulkner** Esplanade ☎ *3184*
★★	**Royal Glen** Glen Rd ☎ *3221*
★★	**Woodlands** Station Rd ☎ *3120*
	Wyndham Esplanade ☎ *4167*
GH	**Canterbury** Salcombe Rd ☎ *3373*
GH	**Mount Pleasant Hotel** Salcombe Rd ☎ *4694*
GH	**Southernhay** 3–4 Fortifield Ter ☎ *3189*
GH	**Westbourne Hotel** Manor Rd ☎ *3774*
Inn	**Royal London Hotel** Fore St ☎ *3931*
SC	**Character Cottages (Holidays) Ltd** Sidmouth ☎ *6531*

East Street

Budleigh Salterton
The peaceful town of Budleigh Salterton is famous for its appearance in Millais' painting *The Boyhood of Raleigh*. The beach is of clean white pebbles and is safe for swimming when the conditions are calm. The cliffs above provide fine views of the surrounding coastline. The Fairlynch Arts Centre and Museum in the town contains local history exhibits, a costume museum, a smugglers' cellar and a look-out tower. The River Otter, which flows into the bay, provides good fishing and there are pleasant walks along its banks.

Exmouth *see page 90*

Dawlish Warren
The shelving, sandy beach is backed by a long spit composed of sand dunes. Bathing is safe except near the eastern tip of the spit. There is a small amusement park near the beach and a railway museum at Dawlish Warren Station.

Dawlish *see page 91*

Teignmouth *see page 92*

Shaldon
The village is perched on a steep cliff overlooking the River Teign estuary where there is a pebble beach. A tunnel through the cliff leads to Ness Cove which has a safe, sandy beach. Shaldon offers facilities for golf and putting and a children's zoo.

Maidencombe
A sheltered cove with a beach of reddish sand dotted with slabs of rock. Swimming is safe and there are boats and floats for hire.

Babbacombe
Access to the shingle beach is via a steep, winding path which descends the high, wooded cliffs or by cliff railway. Above the beach on Babbacombe Downs lies an extensive model village in a pleasantly landscaped setting and Babbacombe Pottery is open to the public.

TORQUAY *see page 94*

Paignton *see page 96*

Brixham *see page 97*

Dartmouth
A charming port famous for its maritime history and Royal Naval College. A popular holiday area with ample sporting facilities and many places of interest.
Dartmouth was used as the location for many sequences in the BBC television series *The Onedin Line*.

Torcross
This former fishing village overlooks Slapton Sands, a three-mile stretch of pebble beach backed by meadows and freshwater ponds which attract many species of wildfowl. Part of this area is taken up by a nature reserve.

Hallsands
A steep, but generally safe pebble beach lies before the ruins of an old fishing village which was destroyed by a storm in 1917.

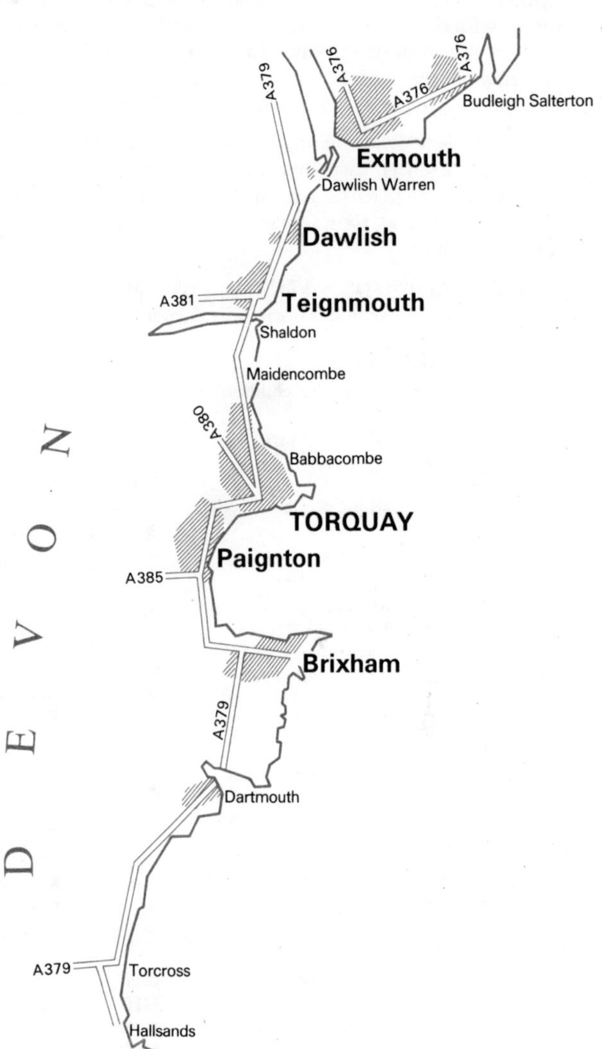

EXMOUTH

The second largest town in East Devon, Exmouth has been a prominent port for the last 700 years and today combines its maritime activities with all the amenities of a popular holiday resort whilst remaining free from excessive commercialisation. Fishing boats and pleasure craft mingle with coastal freighters and the multitude of private dinghies and yachts which are usually to be found around the River Exe estuary, providing the interested visitor with an ever-changing picture of seafaring bustle. Exmouth has extensive sandy beaches where bathing is safe except in areas clearly marked by flags and notices.

Most of the seaside amusement facilities are centred around the Esplanade and include a boating lake, children's pleasure park and a heated open-air swimming pool and the town offers the opportunity to participate in most types of sport. There is an aquarium, a Lifeboat Display Centre and a zoo. Exmouth stages a week long carnival and annual open bowls and tennis championships.

To the north of the town stands A la Ronde, a circular Georgian house with a shell gallery and interesting furnishings, which is open daily throughout the summer.

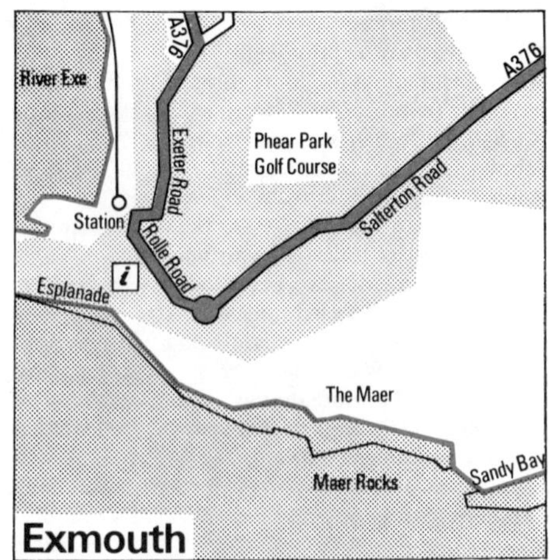

Recreation and Sports

Esplanade – Boating lake, children's pleasure park
Exmouth Amusement Centre 13 Imperial Rd ☎*6933* – Amusement arcade, bingo
Exmouth Swimming Pool Esplanade ☎*4567*
Madeira Bowling Club ☎*73869*
Phear Park – Bowls, children's playground, putting, tennis
Phear Park Golf Course ☎*5800*
Queens Drive – Model railway
Skateboard Centre Imperial Rd ☎*75900*

Cabaret/Dancing

The Pavilion Esplanade ☎*3986 or 3071*

Cinemas

Royal Exeter Rd ☎*72888*
Savoy Rolle St ☎*72866*

Places of Interest

A la Ronde Summer Lane ☎*55142* 2m N on A377
Exmouth Aquarium Esplanade ☎*3016*
Exmouth Lifeboat Display Centre Esplanade
Exmouth Zoo Sandy Bay Leisure Complex ☎*5756*
Steam and Country Museum, Sandy Bay ☎*5333*

Tourist Information

Tourist Information Centre Alexandra Ter ☎*3744*

Accommodation

The following establishments are recommended by the AA. Further information may be obtained from the Tourist Information Office.

★★★	**Devoncourt** Douglas Ave ☎*72277*
★★★	**Imperial** Esplanade ☎*74761*
★★★	**Royal Beacon** ☎*4886*
★★	**Balcombe House** 7 Stevenstone Rd ☎*6349*
★★	**Barn** Foxholes ☎*74411*
★★	**Cavendish** Esplanade ☎*72528*
★★	**Grand** Morton Cres, Explanade ☎*3278*
★★	**Manor** The Beacon ☎*72459*
★	**Carlton Lodge** 15 Carlton Hill ☎*3314*
★	**Isca House** Isca Rd, Off Douglas Ave ☎*3747*
GH	**Anchoria** 176 Exeter Rd ☎*72368*
GH	**Clinton House** 41 Morton Rd ☎*71969*
GH	**Dawson's** 8 Morton Rd ☎*72321*
GH	**Dolphin House** 4 Morton Rd ☎*3832*
GH	**Thornlea** 170 Exeter Rd ☎*72580*
SC	**22 Bradham Lane.** For bookings: Exmouth Holiday Homes, 123 Hulham Rd ☎*4119*
SC	**24 Bradham Lane.** For bookings: Exmouth Holiday Homes, 123 Hulham Rd ☎*4119*
SC	**Character Cottages (Holidays) Ltd** Sidmouth ☎*Sidmouth 6531*
SC	**Easington Court Flat 3/7** Mount Pleasant Ave. For bookings: Exmouth Holiday Homes, 123 Hulham Rd ☎*4119*
SC	**88 Exeter Rd.** For bookings: Exmouth Holiday Homes, 123 Hulham Rd ☎*4119*
SC	**61 Featherbed Lane.** For bookings: Exmouth Holiday Homes, 123 Hulham Rd ☎*4119*
SC	**61a/b Featherbed Lane.** For bookings: Exmouth Holiday Homes, 123 Hulham Rd ☎*4119*
SC	**37 Halsdon Road.** For bookings: Exmouth Holiday Homes, 123 Hulham Rd ☎*4119*
SC	**49 Salisbury Road.** For bookings: Exmouth Holiday Homes, 123 Hulham Rd ☎*4119*

DAWLISH

Developed as a holiday resort during the 19th century, when the coming of the railway rendered the area readily accessible, Dawlish has retained much of its sedate Victorian character and remains one of the least commercialised towns in the area. The beach, separated from the town by the railway line, is mainly sandy and its gentle slope makes it safe for bathing under all but extreme weather conditions.

The town's outstanding feature is the Lawn, a beautifully landscaped garden through which flows Dawlish Water, a wide stream with several waterfalls. Dawlish Water is the home of all kinds of waterfowl including the attractive black swans and the Lawn is the focal point of many of the town's activities such as band concerts, fêtes and carnivals. There is a theatre which stages productions by local groups and Dawlish offers facilities for the pursuit of most outdoor sports. Rowing and motor boats are available for hire, some complete with fishing tackle. There is a museum of local history and the wooded park of Lea Mount, reached by a zig-zag cliff path, affords fine views of the surrounding coastline and countryside.

Annual events include Dawlish Arts Festival, the Dawlish Regatta, bowls and tennis tournaments and a Carnival Week in August.

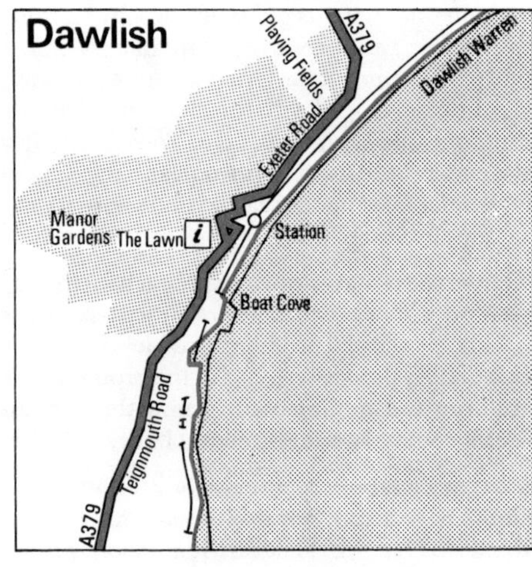

Recreation and Sports

Boat Cove – Boats for hire, pleasure cruises

Dawlish and District Indoor Bowls Association The Pavilion, Playing Fields, Exeter Rd

Dawlish Sailing Club ☎*863201*

Dawlish Swimming Pool Playing Fields, Exeter Rd ☎*864394*

Dawlish Warren Golf Club ☎*862255*

Playing Fields Exeter Rd – Approach-golf, bowls, cricket, football, tennis

Theatre

Shaftesbury ☎*863061*

Places of Interest

Dawlish Museum The Knowle, Barton Ter

Tourist Information

Tourist Information Centre The Lawn ☎*863589* (Etr – Oct)

Accommodation

The following establishments are recommended by the AA. Further information may be obtained from the Tourist Information Office.

★★★ **Langstone Cliff** Dawlish Warren (½m NE off A379) ☎*865155*

★★ **Brooklands** ☎*862226*

★★ **Charlton House** Exeter Rd ☎*863260*

★ **Holcombe Head** Windward Lne (1m S A379) ☎*862130*

GH **Barton Grange Private Hotel** 5 Barton Villas ☎*863365*

GH **Brockington** 139 Exeter Rd ☎*863588*

GH **Broxmore Private Hotel** 20 Plantation ☎*863602*

GH **Fairfield House** Ashcombe Rd ☎*862173*

GH **Lamorna Private Hotel** 2 Barton Ter ☎*862242*

GH **Lynbridge Private Hotel** Barton Villas ☎*862352*

GH **Marldon House Hotel** 6 Barton Villas ☎*862721*

GH **Mimosa** ☎*863283*

SC **Coach House** Holcombe Drive Holcombe. For bookings: Mr & Mrs R W Reed, Edencliffe, Holcombe Drive, Holcombe, Dawlish ☎*863171*

SC **Edencliffe** Holcombe Drive. For bookings: Mr & Mrs R W Reed, address as above

SC **Gaycourt Holiday Flats** 8 Marine Pde. For bookings: Mr & Mrs R A Potter, Lisburne Holiday Flats, Westcliff ☎*862846*

SC Mr K B Richards **Highfield House** Oak Park ☎*862061*

SC R J Richmond **High Trees Holiday Flats** Oak Park Rd ☎*863113*

SC **Lisburne Holiday Flats.** For bookings: Mr & Mrs R A Potter, Lisburne Holiday Flats, Westcliff ☎*863385*

SC **The Lodge** Holcombe Drive, Holcombe. For bookings: Mr & Mrs R W Reed, Edencliffe, Holcombe Drive, Holcombe ☎*863171*

SC R J Richmond **Oak Park Holiday Flats** Oak Park Rd ☎*863113*

SC **Shell Cove House Flats.** For bookings: Mrs A A Jameson, Shell Cove House, Old Teignmouth Rd ☎*862523*

SC **Lee Cliff Park** Dawlish Warren ☎*862269*

WEATHER CHART	Av hours of Sunshine in month	Hottest Av daily Temp °C
April	190	10
May	226	12
June	236	15
July	222	17
August	203	17
September	155	15

TEIGNMOUTH

Teignmouth with its red sandy beach and the added attraction of a beautiful river estuary, has been a port and seaside resort for many years. As with many towns in Devon it became popular with the coming of the Great Western Railway. The harbour, sheltered in the Teign estuary, was first developed with the building of the quay in 1831 for shipping Dartmoor granite to build the Old London Bridge. Today, together with its small fishing fleet it is used mainly for the export of ball clay, mined near Kingsteignton, and by trawlers landing their catch. Sailing is popular both on the sea and in the estuary and Teignmouth Regatta is the major event of the season. Frequent power boat races are also held here.

There is nearly a mile of sandy beach further up the river at Coomb Cellars which is safe except near the estuary mouth where notice boards give warnings of the strong currents. The beach is backed by a broad promenade which, during the summer months, has a glorious display of flowers. At the western end of the promenade is the Children's Corner with trampolines and children's swimming pool. Behind the promenade is the large grass area of Den Green, with tennis courts, bowling greens, children's rides, mini-golf and trampolines.

The sea wall, built to protect the railway, also has a wide footpath providing a pleasant walk along the sea front towards the smugglers' cove at Holcombe and past the Parson and Clerk Rocks to Dawlish. Haldon Moor (800ft) offers splendid views over Teignmouth to the sea.

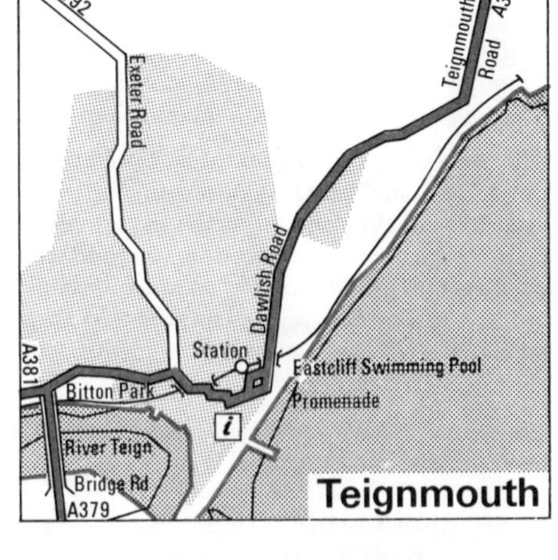

Recreations and Sports

Britton Park – Bowls
Den Green – Bandstand, bowls, children's rides, mini-golf, model boats, tennis, trampolines
Eastcliff Pool and Lido ☎*6271*
Promenade – Children's pool, trampolines
Teign Corinthian Yacht Club Eastcliff, Dawlish Rd ☎*2734*
Teignmouth Golf Course (Haldon) ☎*4194*

Cinema

Rivera The Den ☎*4624*

Theatre

Carlton Theatre The Den ☎*4252*

Places of Interest

Haldon Moor 2m N off B3192
Teignmouth Aquarium Promenade ☎*3383*

Tourist Information Centre

Tourist Information Centre The Den ☎*6271*

Accommodation

The following establishments are recommended by the AA. Further information may be obtained from the Tourist Information Office.

★★	**Glendaragh** Barn Park Rd ☎*2881*
★★	**Ivy House** Seafront ☎*2735*
★★	**London** Bank St ☎*2776*
★	**Belvedere** Barn Park Rd ☎*4561*
★	**Pier** Sea Front ☎*2886*
★	**Portland** Sea Front ☎*2761*
GH	**Bay Cottage Hotel** 7 Marine Pde, Shaldon ☎*2394*
GH	**Bay Hotel** Sea Front ☎*4123*
GH	**Hillsley** Upper Hermonsa Rd ☎*3878*
GH	**New Strathearn Hotel** Bitton Park Rd ☎*2796*
GH	**Ocean View Hotel** Sea Front ☎*2953*
GH	**Overstowey Hotel** Dawlish Rd ☎*4251*
GH	**Westlands Hotel** Reed Vale ☎*3007*
SC	**Bonicliffe and Seascape Holiday Bungalows** Second Drive, Dawlish Rd. For bookings: Mr C W Sharp, Sunningdale, Second Drive, Dawlish Rd ☎*4570*
SC	**Campion** For Bookings: Mrs S Hawkings, Campion, Buckeridge Ave ☎*4574*
SC	**Character Cottages (Holidays) Ltd** Sidmouth, Devon ☎*Sidmouth6531*
SC	**Clifford House** Shaldon (1m S). For bookings: Mr and Mrs Richards, Mews Cottage, Clifford House, Shaldon ☎*Shaldon2334*
SC	Mrs J Graeme **Fonthill** Torquay Rd, Shaldon ☎*Shaldon2344*
SC	Mr and Mrs F R Bass **The Grendons** 58 Combe Vale Rd ☎*3667*
SC	**Holmwood** 58 Ferndale Rd. For bookings: Mr C W Sharp, Sunningdale, Second Dr, Dawlish Rd ☎*4570*
SC	Mr S H Marshall **Lendrick** Sea Front ☎*3009*
SC	Mrs P R Herring **Margaret's Holiday Flats** New Rd ☎*3858*

Restaurants

✕✕	**Churchills** Den Rd ☎*4311*
✕	**Minadab** 60 Teignmouth Rd ☎*2044*

Self Catering Holidays in TORBAY

*** HOUSES, BUNGALOWS, COTTAGES, FLATS, FLATLETS & CARAVANS ***

Harbourside flats near beach, town centre & new Leisure Complex with pool. Accommodating 2-7 persons.

Choice of five selected caravan sites. Whitehill Farm, Paignton. Caravans have main services, shower, TV etc, heated swimming pool, bar & super-market on site.

Balcony view from "Bel Air" Holiday Flats, Paignton, accommodating 2-12 persons.

Various Country Cottages, farm and moorland locations.

* We are confident we can meet your holiday needs from the hundreds of Self-Catering Units we have on offer, all of which have been inspected by our viewing team.
* This service is entirely **FREE** to you the holidaymaker.
* Established in 1965 and members of the West Country Tourist Board & Torquay Chamber of Trade & Commerce.
* Weekly terms from £5 per person off peak. * Hire service available (cots, linen etc,) * Sole Booking Agents for many popular properties * Most properties accept pets. * Let our helpful & experienced staff deal with your enquiry.
* Send now for our extensive **FREE** colour brochure, enclosing large envelope (20p stamp please) to:—

DEPT. 8, THE TORBAY HOLIDAY AGENCY, 58 CADEWELL LANE, TORQUAY, TQ2 7ER. TEL: NO. (STD 0803) 63454.

** Holiday property and caravan owners & self-catering specialists **

TORQUAY

Torquay developed from a fishing village into a fashionable resort during the early 19th century when the Napoleonic Wars discouraged wealthy Englishmen from holidaying on the Continent. Today it is the largest of the Torbay towns occupying the slopes of seven wooded hills and presenting a vista of white-walled villas, luxurious gardens, modern hotels, palm trees and yachts which has a distinctly Mediterranean flavour.

The main beach, Abbey Sands, and the neighbouring bays and coves are mainly sandy and provide safe swimming although Livermead Sands, in the extreme south, is used predominantly by water-skiers. Red flags are displayed when bathing is considered dangerous. Abbey Sands and Corbyn Beach offer floats and motor boats for hire and have changing facilities and showers for public use but tend to be crowded at high-tide. Beacon Cove's pebble beach is a favourite spot for underwater explorers due to its extremely clear water.

Torquay has much to offer the visitor in the way of amusements and entertainments. Concerts, films and shows are all available in the town and there are facilities for most sports. Bowls and tennis championships take place annually and regular regattas and powerboat races are held throughout the summer in addition to the local Torbay carnival. Places of interest include Torre Abbey where art exhibitions are held in an 18th-century mansion and the ruins of the Abbey, founded in 1190, stand beside a 12th-century tithe barn, known as the Spanish Barn as it once housed prisoners washed ashore from the Armada. The Natural History Society Museum contains many items excavated from the neighbouring Kents Cavern, a former Ice Age dwelling where the remains of a sabre-toothed tiger were discovered. The Cavern is open to the public and has fine collections of stalactites and stalagmites which are displayed under floodlights.

Torquay's mild climate is ideal for the cultivation of sub-tropical vegetation and the area abounds in pleasant cliff-top walks and drives which provide fine views of Torbay, particularly after dark when the sea front and harbour are illuminated.

Nearby touring areas include Cockington, a village with many thatched cottages and a 14th-century forge, and Berry Pomeroy with the ruins of its 14th-century castle nestling in a wooded valley.

L — **AA Road Service Centre** Victoria Pde ☎*25903*

Recreation and Sports

J — **Abbey Gardens** – Putting, tennis

J — **Abbey Sands and Corbyn Beach** – Boats and floats for hire, changing and shower facilities

L — **Coral Island Entertainment Centre** Beacon Hill ☎*212525* – Amusements, outdoor pool, sun lounge

J — **Kings Gardens** – Pitch and putt

L — **Royal Torbay Yacht Club** Beacon Ter ☎*27548*

B — **Ten-Pin Bowling** Union St ☎*211821*

Torbay Lawn Tennis Club Belgrave Rd ☎*22786*

J — **Torquay Athletic RFC** Recreation Ground ☎*23842*

F — **Torquay Bowling Club** Belgrave Rd ☎*22100*

J — **Torquay Cricket Club** Recreation Ground ☎*22001*

Torquay Golf Club 30 Petitor Rd, Marychurch ☎*37471*

Torquay United FC Plainmoor ☎*38666* – League Division IV

Cabaret/Dancing

L — **Coral Island Entertainment Centre** Beacon Hill ☎*212525*

L — **La Pigalle Club** Imperial Hotel ☎*24301*

Cinemas

G — **Colony** Union St ☎*22146*

G — **Odeon** Abbey Rd ☎*22324*

Theatres

Babbacombe Theatre Babbacombe ☎*38385*

K — **Princess** Torbay Rd ☎*27527*

Places of Interest

L(1) — **Aqualand** 2 Beacon Quay ☎*24439*

H(2) — **Natural History Society Museum** ☎*23975*

J(3) — **Torre Abbey**

F(4) — **Town Hall and Library**

Kents Cavern Ilsham Rd, Wellswood ☎*24059*

Tourist Information

[i]H — **Tourist Information Centre** Vaughan Pde ☎*27428*

Accommodation

The establishments listed below are a selection of AA-recommended accommodation located in the area covered by the Town Plan. Further information may be found in AA publications or obtained from the Tourist Information Centre.

1SC — Mr and Mrs J M Falcus **Abbey View Holiday Flats** Rathmore Rd, Torquay, Devon TQ2 6NZ ☎*28022*

2GH — **Albaston House Hotel** 27 Marychurch Rd ☎*26758*

3SC — Mr and Mrs J Nelson **Ashfield Rise Holiday Flats** Ruckamore Rd, Torquay, Devon TQ2 6HF ☎*65156*

4SC — Mrs O E Eadie **The Beacon** 15 Braddons Hill Rd East, Torquay, Devon ☎*23048*

5SC — Mr P W Archer-Moy **Chelston Hall** Old Mill Rd, Torquay, Devon TQ2 6NW ☎*65520*

6SC — Mr and Mrs N J P Mills **Clovis Holiday Flats** 14 Thurlow Rd, Torquay, Devon ☎*33203*

7SC — Mr P Jaffa **34 Fleet St** Torquay, Devon ☎*25524* (evenings *Teignmouth 4678*)

8GH — **Fretherne Hotel** St Lukes Rd South ☎*22594*

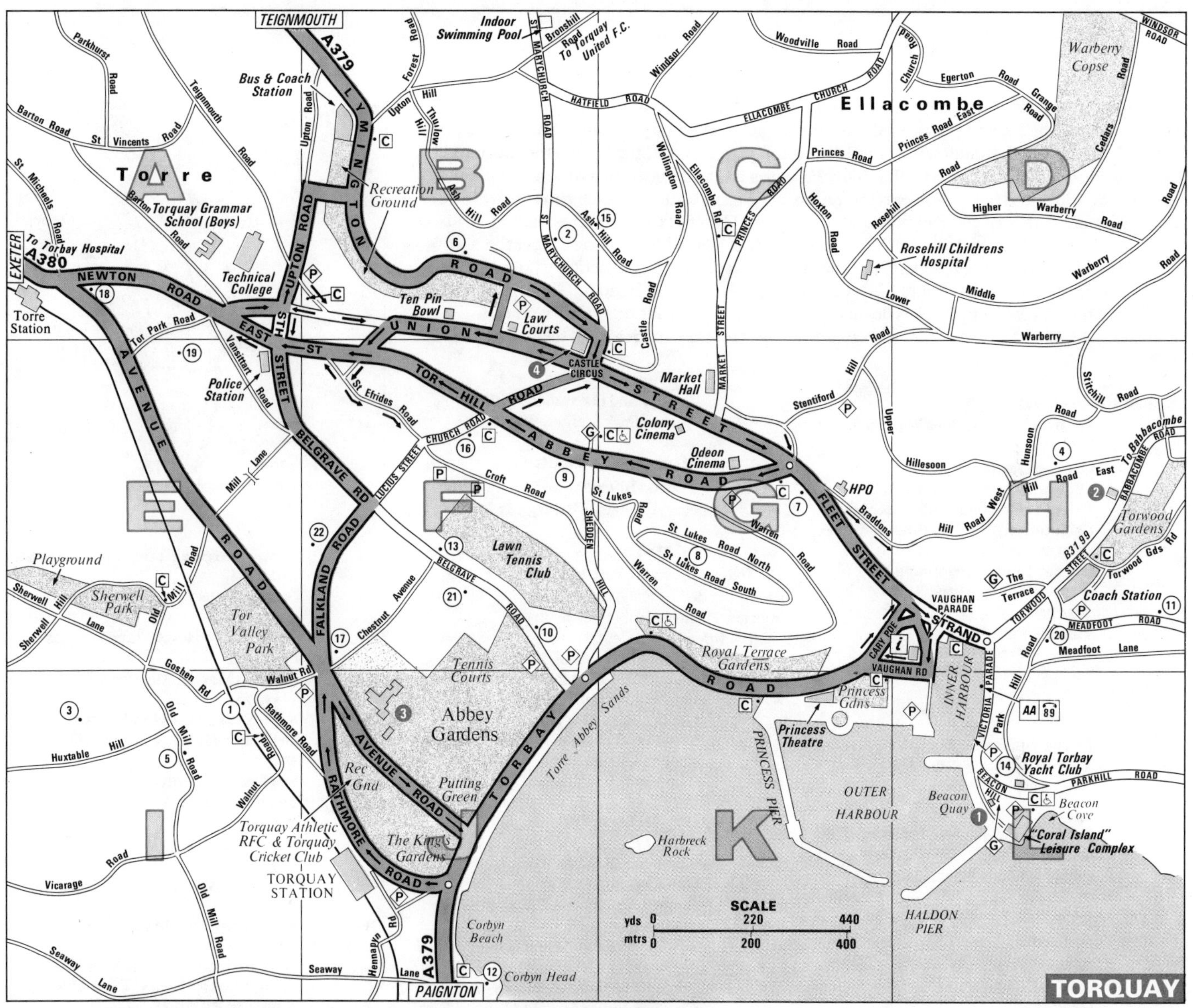

9SC Mr and Mrs R S Watts **Kenton Lodge** Croft Hill (off Abbey Rd), Torquay, Devon TQ2 5NT ☎*27995*

10★★★ **Kiston** Belgrave Rd ☎*23219*

11★★★ **Lincombe Hall** Sea Front ☎*22302*

12★★★ **Livermead House** Sea Front ☎*24361*

13★★★ **Rainbow House** Belgrave Rd ☎*211161*

14★★ **Regina** Victoria Pde ☎*22904*

15SC Mr and Mrs E A Wilson **Sandown Holiday Flats** 27 Ash Hill Rd, Torquay, Devon ☎*26906*

16★★ **Templestowe** ☎*25145*

17★★★ **Toorak** Chestnut Ave ☎*27135*

18GH **Tormohun Hotel** 28 Newton Rd ☎*23681*

PAIGNTON

A resort of predominantly Victorian aspect with long stretches of reddish sands which slope gently towards the sea and provide safe bathing for all, backed by pleasant lawns and playing areas. Beach huts, deck chairs, floats and diving rafts are available for hire on the shore and pleasure trips run from the nearby harbour. Paignton has an aquarium, a zoo and ample sporting facilities and is the terminus for the Torbay Steam Railway which runs on the former Great Western line between Paignton and Kingswear. Other places of interest include Oldway Mansion, built in the mid-19th century after the style of Versailles by Isaac Singer the American sewing machine magnate, Kirkham House, a restored 15th-century house and the Torbay Aircraft Museum at Higher Blagdon. Beyond Roundham Head lie Goodrington Cliff Gardens where a zig-zag path leads down to a sandy beach and a Holiday Centre and amusement area. The gardens are illuminated at night and are an ideal spot for a quiet evening stroll.

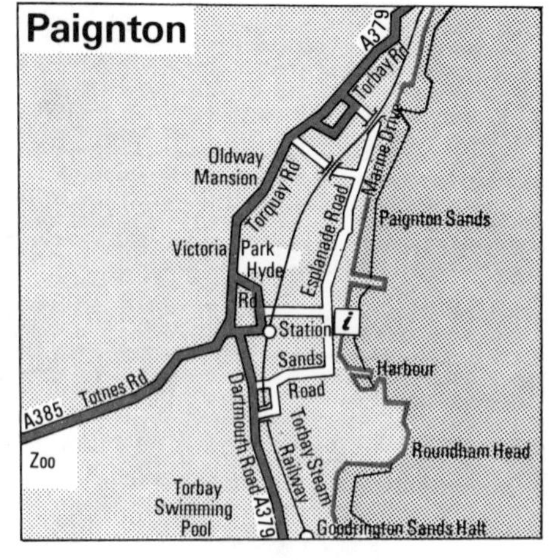

Recreation and Sports

Festival Hall Gardens Esplanade Rd – Mini golf
Oldway Gardens Oldway House, Oldway Rd – Bowls, putting, tennis
Paignton Bowling Club Queens Park
Paignton and Torbay Bowling Club Queens Park
Torbay Indoor Swimming Pool Clennon Valley, Penwill Way ☎*521990*
Victoria Park Torquay Rd – Children's model yacht pond, hockey, playground, tennis

Cinemas

Regent Station Sq ☎*559017*
Torbay Torbay Rd ☎*559544*

Theatre

Festival Hall Theatre Esplanade Rd ☎*558641*
Palace Avenue Theatre Palace Ave ☎*558367*

Places of Interest

Bishops Palace Tower Torquay Rd
Cliff Gardens Roundham Head, Goodrington
Kirkham House Kirkham St
Oldway Mansion Oldway Rd
Paignton Aquarium
Paignton Zoo Totnes Rd ☎*557479*
Torbay Aircraft Museum Barton Pines, Higher Blagdon (3m W off A385) ☎*553540*
Torbay and Dartmouth Railway Queens Park Station ☎*555872*

Tourist Information Centre

Tourist Information Centre Festival Hall, Esplanade Rd ☎*558383*

Accommodation

The following establishments are recommended by the AA. Further information may be obtained from the Tourist Information Centre.

★★★	**Palace** Esplanade Rd ☎*555121*
★★★	**Redcliffe** Marine Pde ☎*556224*
★★	**Hunters Lodge** Roundham Rd, Goodrington ☎*557034*
★★	**St Annes** Alta Vista Rd, Goodrington ☎*557034*
★	**Alta Vista** Alta Vista Rd, Roundham ☎*559580*
★	**Oldway Links** 21 Southfield Rd ☎*559332*
★	**South Sands** Alta Vista Rd, Roundham ☎*557231*
★	**Sunhill** Alta Vista Rd, Goodrington ☎*557532*
☆	**Torbay Holiday Motel** Totnes Rd ☎*558226*
ⓗ	**Amaryllis** Sands Rd ☎*559552*
GH	**Clennon Valley Hotel** 1 Clennon Rise ☎*557736*
GH	**Danethorpe Private Hotel** 23 St Andrews Rd ☎*551251*
GH	**Middle Park Hotel** Seafront, Marine Drive ☎*559025*
GH	**Myllet Private Hotel** Belle Vue Rd ☎*558491*
GH	**Nevada Private Hotel** 61 Dartmouth Rd ☎*558317*
GH	**Orange Tubs** 14 Manor Rd, Preston ☎*551541*
GH	**Oyster Cove Hotel** Three Beaches ☎*556134*
GH	**Roscrea Hotel** 2 Alta Vista Rd ☎*558706*
GH	**Roseville Private Hotel** ☎*550530*
GH	**San Remo Hotel** 35 Totnes Rd ☎*557855*
GH	**Sea Crest** Roundham Cres ☎*559849*
GH	**Sea Verge Hotel** Marine Dr, Preston ☎*557795*
GH	**Shorton House** 17 Roundham Rd ☎*557722*
GH	**Stantor Private Hotel** 7 St Andrews Rd ☎*557156*
GH	**Sunnybank Private Hotel** 2 Cleveland Rd ☎*559153*
Inn	**Gerston Hotel** Victoria St ☎*559016*
SC	Mr and Mrs R Bewley, **Casa Marina** 2 Keysfield Rd ☎*558334*
SC	The Manageress, **Esplanade Court Ltd** 32 Esplanade Ct ☎*556952*
SC	**South Sands Holiday Estate** Cliff Park Rd, Goodrington ☎*22517*
SC	Mr and Mrs K E Watts, **The Top House** 21 Sandringham Gardens, Preston ☎*522481*

BRIXHAM

During the 19th century Brixham was England's premier fishing port with a fleet of nearly 300 trawlers and the industry still survives, although somewhat diminished, thanks to the efforts of a local co-operative. Fishermen, artists and tourists flock to the busy harbour where a statue of William of Orange commemorates the fact that the monarch landed there in 1688. Boats of all kinds are available for hire and a regular ferry service runs to Torquay. Brixham's beaches tend to be pebbly but St Mary's Bay and Man Sands, both accessible only on foot, have a good deal of sand. Shoalstone beach, to the east of the harbour, has a large open-air swimming pool. A replica of Drake's Golden Hind lies beside the quay and the local museum has an interesting display of trawling and maritime exhibits. One resident who achieved fame was the Rev H F Lyte who composed *Abide with me* while he was vicar of All Saints Church. To this day the church bells play this hymn every evening.

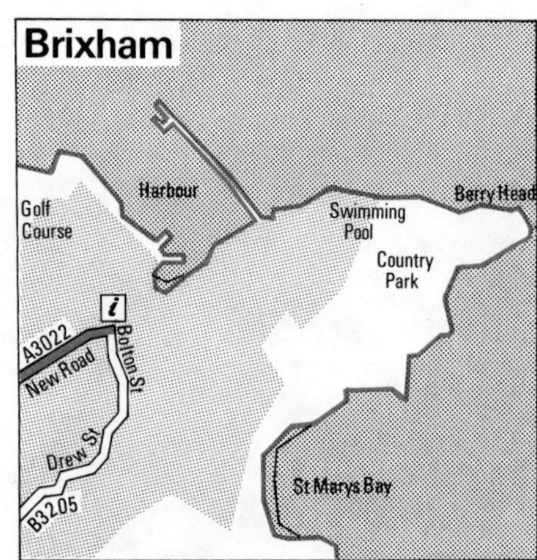

Recreation and Sports

Brixham Indoor Swimming Pool Higher Ranscomb Rd ☎*7151*
Brixham RFC Astley Park ☎*2162*
Brixham Sailing Centre Freshwater Quay ☎*2046*
Brixham Yacht Club Overgang Rd ☎*3332*
Churston Golf Course ☎*Churston842218*

Theatre

Brixham Theatre Market St ☎*2829*

Places of Interest

Aquarium The Quay ☎*2204*
Golden Hind Inner Harbour ☎*6223*
Museum Middle St

Tourist Information

Tourist Information Centre Brixham Theatre, Market St ☎*2861*

Accommodation

The folowing establishments are recommended by the AA. Further information may be obtained from the Tourist Information Office.

★★ **Bolton** ☎*3246*
★★ **Northcliffe** North Furzeham Rd ☎*2751*
★★ **Quayside** King St ☎*3051*
★ **Smugglers' Haunt** ☎*3050*

Mevagissey Bay

Salcombe

The most southerly of Devon's resorts, Salcombe enjoys a favourable climate and bears a close resemblance to some Mediterranean areas. As a bonus, it is surrounded by some beautiful, unmistakably English countryside. The superb natural harbour is a yachtsman's paradise and many attractive creeks branch off the wide main channel. Not surprisingly, Salcombe's origins are in fishing and boat building and even though it has now become a popular resort, it still retains its old character and clings to its seafaring traditions. There are boats for hire, river cruises and sea angling trips. The sandy beaches on the west side of the estuary are sheltered and safe for bathing. There is a yacht regatta in August and a Water Carnival with torchlight procession of boats and a firework display.

Hope Cove

This picturesque fishing village has a small, sandy beach sheltered by two rocky headlands. The extensive cliffs above provide good walking country in either direction.

Thurlestone

An unspoilt village with an 18-hole golf course which overlooks the foreshore. The beaches are sandy and generally provide safe bathing.

Bigbury-on-Sea

A small resort where sandy beaches are exposed at low-tide when Burgh Island may be reached on foot. Swimming near the mouth of the River Avon is very dangerous due to currents.

Newton Ferrers

Forms a small fishing and sailing centre with Noss Mayo from which it is separated by a tidal creek. The coastline is generally rocky.

Wembury

Several sheltered coves lie to the west of the village consisting of silver coloured sand dotted with rock pools and noted for many varieties of shells which may be gathered there. The beach and cliffs to the east are National Trust property.

Plymouth

There are no sandy beaches at Plymouth but this great maritime city compensates by providing facilities for every kind of sport and entertainment. Devastated by wartime bombing, a new city has arisen from the ruins, but there are still parts of the historic city which remain untouched. Its fine seafaring traditions begun by Drake and the Pilgrim Fathers, are upheld today by the presence of one of the premier Royal Naval bases in the country. The waters of Plymouth Sound and the Tamar estuary are dotted with the 'shipside grey' of Her Majesty's vessels. Pleasure craft take visitors around the harbour and dockyard areas, as well as on trips along the Rivers Yealm and Tamar.

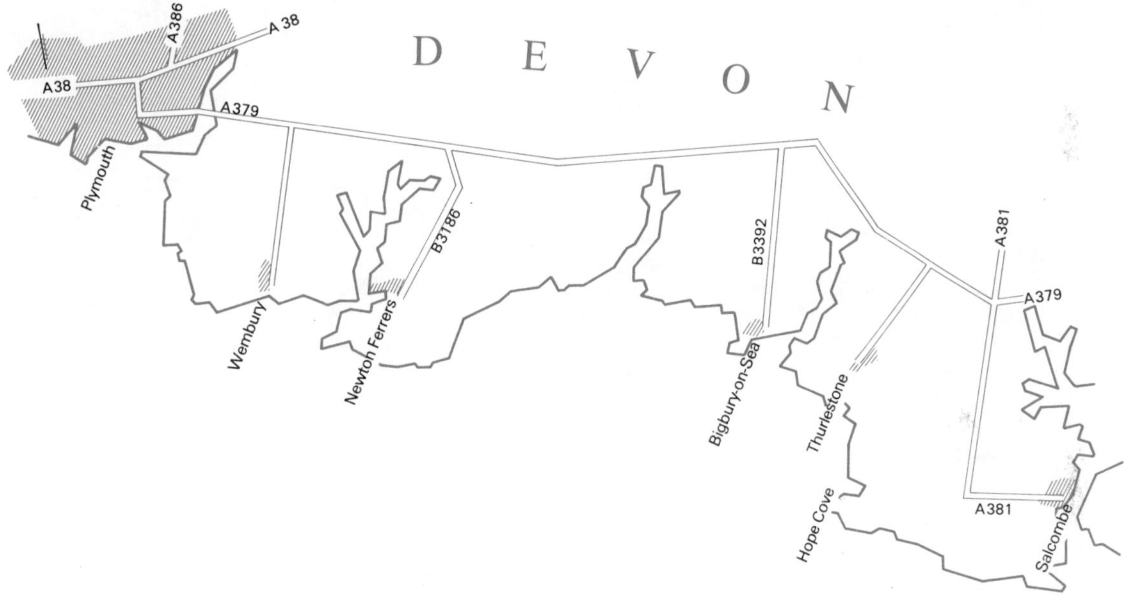

Cawsand
Sheltering behind the headland of Penlee Point, Cawsand was an important port until Plymouth took over this role. Now, its narrow, steep streets lined with colour-washed houses, nestle around a small quay. This is a rocky stretch of coastline with small sandy coves where bathing is generally safe. Cawsand was once the anchorage of Napoleon's ship following his defeat at Waterloo.

Downderry
A beach of silvery sand mixed with shingle. Parking is available in the village and boats are available for hire on the shore.

Looe *see page 101*

Polruan
A village set on a headland above the mouth of the River Fowey. There are many boat-building yards and a small beach at Polruan Quay.

Pentewan
A wide, sandy beach marked by patches of clay. Swimming is safe here.

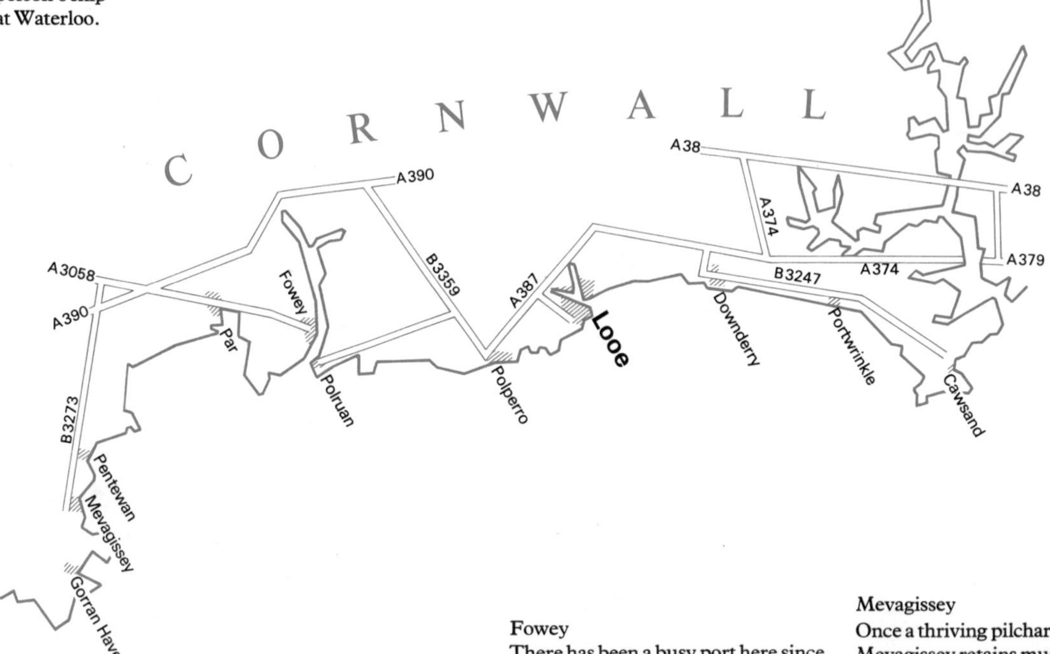

Portwrinkle
At the western end of the wide-sweeping Whitsand Bay, Portwrinkle's beach of greyish sand is sheltered by a stone quay once used by fishing boats. The nearby fort is a monument to the Napoleonic wars and is military property, closed when red flags indicate firing practice. A golf course overlooks Portwrinkle beach.

Polperro
A typical Cornish fishing village attracting many artists. Despite its popularity Polperro has remained relatively uncommercialised and visitors must leave their cars in an inland car park as they are banned from the seafront during the summer. Polperro has a Model Village and a Smugglers Museum.

Fowey
There has been a busy port here since the 15th century when Fowey was a favourite base for pirates. All kinds of commercial craft now use the harbour and the town has become a popular sailing centre. Readymoney Cove provides a sandy beach where swimming is safe.

Par
A large area of sand, whitened by deposits of clay, is revealed at low-tide, backed by dunes and a large clay factory.

Mevagissey
Once a thriving pilchard fishing port, Mevagissey retains much of its former character with steep narrow streets climbing the hills above the harbour. Many of its old fish cellars have been converted into shops and restaurants and the town has now become one of the West Country's foremost shark fishing centres. A Folk Museum is housed in an 18th-century boat builders' workshop.

Gorran Haven
A peaceful village with a safe, sandy beach partly sheltered by a stone pier.

LOOE

This attractive fishing village is situated at the mouth of the deep-wooded valley of the River Looe. It is formed from two separate communities, East and West Looe, which were not amalgamated until the present Victorian bridge was opened in 1855 to replace a medieval bridge which could not cope with the increasing trade. In its heyday the pilchard fishing industry thrived here together with the smuggling activities for which Cornwall is famous. Today these have given way to tourism and rather than negotiate the narrow streets by car it is better to park in the car park in West Looe and continue on foot to explore the twisting thoroughfares filled with old buildings and cottages whose quaint charm and character have remained unaltered for hundreds of years. The harbour is a hive of activity with its brightly-painted fishing luggers, speed boats and yachts and the spectacle of fishing boats unloading their daily catch of crab, lobster, skate and ray is always popular with visitors. Looe is famous for shark fishing and the excitement of the daily 'weigh in' of these great monsters always draws the crowds. The British International Sea Angling Festival is held here annually between September and October.

The sandy beach between Banjo Pier and the cliffs offers safe bathing at all times and Hannafore Beach, on the west bank of the river, is also safe and sandy. For the energetic there is a cliff walk to Polperro (4 miles) passing secluded Port Nadler Beach.

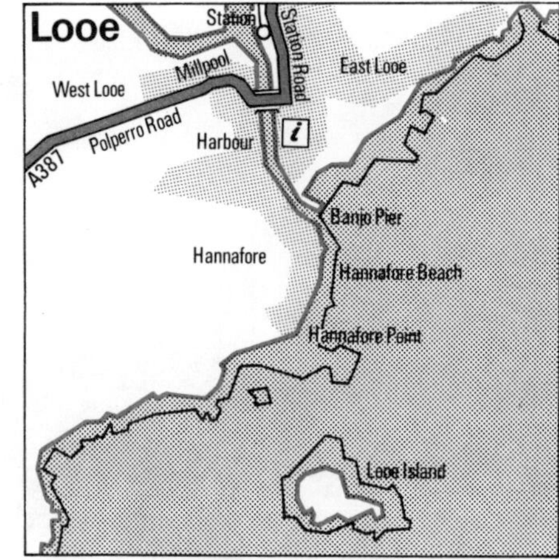

Recreation and Sports

Looe Bin Down Golf Course 3m E off A387 ☎ *Widegates247*
Looe Sailing Club Buller St ☎ *2559*
Millpool Car Park West Looe – Obstacle golf
Seafront Hannafore, West Looe – Bowls, putting
Shark and deep sea fishing Tackle shop, East Looe ☎ *2189*

Places of Interest

Cornish Museum Lower St, East Looe
Looe Aquarium The Quay, East Looe ☎ *2423*
Old Guildhall Museum Higher Market St, East Looe
Paul Corin Musical Collection St Keyne ☎ *Liskeard43108* 4m N off B3254
St Keyne's Well St Keyne
Woolly Monkey Sanctuary Murrayton ☎ *2532* 3m ENE off B3253

Tourist Information

Tourist Information Centre The Guildhall, Fore St, East Looe (summer only) ☎ *2072*

Accommodation

The following establishments are recommended by the AA. Further information may be obtained from the Tourist Information Office.

★★★ **Hannafore Point** Sea Front, Marine Dr ☎ *3273*
★★ **Klymiarven** Barbican Hill ☎ *2333*
★★ **Rock Towers** Hannafore ☎ *2140*
★ **Portbyhan** West Looe Quay ☎ *2071*
GH **Annaclone Hotel** Marine Dr, Hannafore ☎ *2177*
GH **Commonwood Manor Hotel** St Martin's Rd, East Looe ☎ *2929*
GH **Deganwy Hotel** Station Rd ☎ *2984*
GH **Fieldhead Hotel** Portuan Rd, Hannafore ☎ *2689*
GH **Hillingdon** Hannafore ☎ *2906*
GH **Kantara** 7 Trelawney Ter ☎ *2093*
GH **Lemain Hotel** Hannafore ☎ *2073*
GH **Plaidy Beach Hotel** Plaidy ☎ *2044*
GH **Riverside Hotel** ☎ *2100*
GH **Rockwell Hotel** Hannafore ☎ *2123*
GH **Smuggler's House Hotel** Middlemarket ☎ *2397*
SC **Blue Naze** New Barbican. For bookings: Mrs W J M Collins, Brook Cottage, Longcoombe Ln, Polperro ☎ *Polperro274*
SC **Hilldene** West Looe Hill. For bookings: Mrs J Adlam, Trenance Farm, Tideford, Saltash, Cornwall ☎ *Landrake319*
SC Mr D C West, **Millendreath Holiday Village** Millendreath, Looe ☎ *3281*
SC **The Pilchards** Blyth Cottage, Bay Cottages, East Looe. For bookings: Mrs A Lean, Trelean, West Looe Hill ☎ *2530*
SC **Seaview Holiday Village** Polperro Rd. For bookings: Seaview Holiday Village, Central Booking Office, PO Box 8, St Austell Bay ☎ *StAustell61896*
SC **Spindrift** Downs View Rd. For bookings: Mrs W J M Collings, Brook Cottage, Longcoombe Ln, Polperro ☎ *Polperro274*
SC Mrs A Nisbett, **Stoneleigh Villa** Plaidy Beach, Looe ☎ *2538*
SC **Stonerock Holiday Flats** Portuan Rd, Hannafore. For bookings: Mr & Mrs R M C Hore, Green Borders, Marine Dr, Looe ☎ *2928*
SC **Treble 'B' Holiday Centre Ltd** Polperro Rd ☎ *2425*
SC **Up-Aloft** The Quay, West Looe. For bookings: Mrs A Lean, Trelean, West Looe Hill ☎ *2530*

Vista of Looe harbour and town

Portscatho
This unspoilt village clusters around the gently-curving bay with a miniature harbour and launching facilities for small craft. The beach is sandy between the many rocks, and cliff-top walks to the west reveal many more small, safe bathing beaches.

St Mawes
This peaceful village is set on the hillsides around its sheltered harbour where fishing is still a major industry. Henry VIII built the castle in the distinctive 'Clover Leaf' style to help protect the entrance to Falmouth harbour along with its counterpart, Pendennis Castle, on the opposite shore. The two main beaches of sand and shingle provide safe bathing and there are boats for hire, fishing trips and facilities for yachtsmen.

Falmouth *see page 104*

Helford Passage
The Helford River is one of the most attractive stretches of water in the country, its banks extensively wooded and indented with pretty creeks and isolated hamlets. Helford Passage, on the north bank, is a popular sailing centre with a sand and shingle beach where bathing is safe. A passenger ferry operates between here and Helford on the south bank, and boat trips travel along the river to Frenchman's Creek, immortalised by Daphne du Maurier in her novel of the same name.

Coverack
The translucent waters in the rocky bay are the clearest in the area making this an ideal spot for swimming and surfing. The harbour, which provides a haven for small boats, is backed by sea walls. This attractive village, which was once a haunt of smugglers, is now popular with holidaymakers and offers good sea angling.

Kennack Sands
Two shelving beaches of silvery sand provide safe swimming, although the channels near high-water mark might be dangerous for children. This secluded stretch of coastline is backed by Goonhilly Downs, the site of the world's largest communications complex.

Cadgwith
As with so many of the coves and villages around this stretch of coast, Cadgwith was once a smuggler's retreat. The sand and shingle beach with its fishing boats, backed by a truly picturesque scene of thatched cottages set among rocks, is a favourite for picture postcards and calendars. There are several coves in the area and the Devil's Frying Pan, a crater formed by the fall of a cave roof, is accessible by foot.

Lizard
A wild, rocky area where a lighthouse has stood for over 200 years. Swimming is safe in very calm weather only.

FALMOUTH

For as long as Cornishmen have engaged in trade, Falmouth has been a port. The estuaries of seven rivers converge in Carrick Roads creating one of the world's largest natural harbours. Protected at its mouth by the headlands of Pendennis and St Mawes, Falmouth has, over the ages, been host to vessels of all kinds, from Phoenecian traders to oil tankers. A monument stands in The Moor in memory of the packet ships which gave Falmouth her greatest period of prosperity. Still a busy port today, there are also facilities for the countless small craft which use the harbour. The historic old town contains some fine buildings and, for the energetic, there are fine views from the top of Jacob's Ladder – a flight of 111 steps close to the church.

Falmouth is also a popular holiday resort, having four sandy beaches along Falmouth Bay backed by spacious grassy areas and colourful gardens. There are rock pools to explore at low-tide and swimming is safe at all times.

The area around Falmouth contains many pretty little Cornish villages which are well worth a visit, although some are better reached by boat than by road.

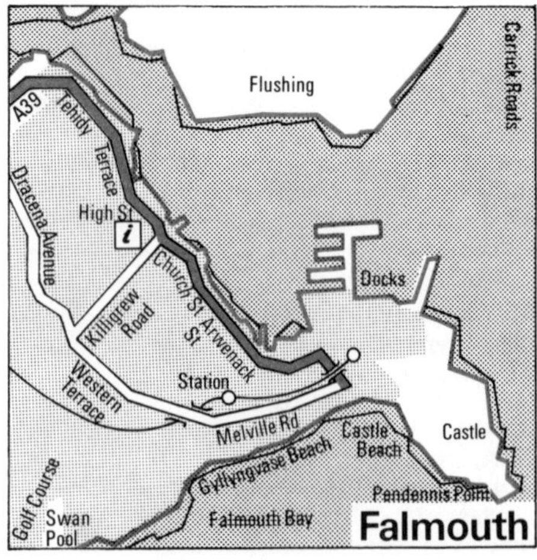

Recreation and Sports

Cornish Diving Centre Bar Rd ☎*311265*
Custom House Quay – Boats for hire
Falmouth Club – Western Ter – Billiards, squash, table tennis, tennis
Falmouth Golf Club Pennance Headland ☎*311262*
Gyllyngvase – Crazy-golf, tennis, trampolines
Prince of Wales Pier – Angling, boat trips
Recreation Ground – Bowls, go-karts
Swanpool – Boating, crazy-golf, miniature railway, pitch and putt

Cinema

Grand Market St ☎*312412*

Dancing

Balcony Club Chapel Ter, Vernon Pl ☎*311202*
Club Internationale St George's Arcade, off Church St ☎*311284*
Desdemona's High St ☎*311819*
Shades Quay St ☎*311323*

Theatre

Arts Theatre Church St ☎*312620*
Princess Pavilion Gyllyngdune Gdns ☎*311277*

Places of Interest

Falmouth Arts Centre Church St ☎*314566*
Gyllyngdune Gardens Biergarten
Impulses Art Gallery Killigrew St ☎*314013*
Maritime Museum Church St
Military Vehicle Museum Lamanva
Pendennis Castle Pendennis Point
Penjerrick Gardens Nr Budock ☎*Mawnan Smith 659* – Open March – May only
Poldark Mining and Wendron Forge Wendron ☎*Helston 3531/3173*
St Mawes Castle
Seal Sanctuary Gweek ☎*Mawgan 361*

Tourist Information

Tourist Information Centre The Moor ☎*312300*

Accommodation

The following establishments are recommended by the AA. Further information may be obtained from the Tourist Information Office.

★★★	**Bay** Cliff Rd ☎*312094*
★★★	**Falmouth** ☎*312671*
★★★	**Green Bank** ☎*312440*
★★★	**Green Lawns** Western Ter ☎*312734*
★★★	**Gyllyngdune** Melville Rd ☎*312978*
★★	**Gwendra** Sea Front ☎*312178*
★★	**Madeira** Sea Front ☎*313531*
★★	**Palm Beach** Gyllyngvase ☎*313812*
★★	**Pendower** Sea View Rd ☎*312108*
★★	**Rosslyn** Kimberley Park Rd ☎*312699*
★	**Carthion** Cliff Rd ☎*313669*
★	**Crill House** Golden Bank ☎*312994*
★	**Lerryn** De Pass Rd ☎*312489*
★	**Melville** Sea View Rd ☎*312134*
★	**Somerdale** Sea View Rd ☎*312566*
★	**Suncourt** Boscowen Rd ☎*312886*
★	**Tresillian House** Stracey Rd ☎*312425*
GH	**Bedruthan** 49 Castle Dr ☎*311028*
GH	**Cotswold House Private Hotel** 49 Melvill Rd ☎*312077*
GH	**Dracaena Hotel** Dracaena Ave ☎*314470*
GH	**Evendale Private Hotel** 51 Melvill Rd ☎*314164*
GH	**Florence** 6 Florence Pl ☎*313494*
GH	**Gyllyngvase House** Gyllyngvase Rd ☎*312956*
GH	**Homelea** 31 Melvill Rd ☎*313489*
GH	**Kelbrook** 8 Florence Pl ☎*312961*
GH	**Langton Leigh** 11 Florence Pl ☎*313684*
GH	**Milton House** 33 Melvill Rd ☎*314390*
GH	**Morvah Hotel** Melvill Rd ☎*311259*

Kynance Cove
A sandy cove with numerous unusual rock formations and some interesting caves which should be explored only at low-tide. Swimming is safe, provided the rocks are avoided. The cove is approached via a toll road.

Mullion Cove
A picturesque little harbour overlooked by high cliffs. A sandy beach is exposed a low-tide.

Porthleven
The large harbour was used by the tin mining industry until 1961 but is now virtually deserted. There is a steeply-shelving beach composed of small flint pebbles but swimming is dangerous due to a strong undertow.

Praa Sands
A long, gently sloping expanse of sand which is sheltered and safe.

Perranuthnoe
The rocky, sandy beach is sheltered on both sides. Ideal bathing for children.

Marazion
A pleasant, sandy beach. Boats take visitors to St Michaels Mount which can also be reached on foot at low-tide. Set in the middle of Mounts Bay, the island contains a Norman monastery which is now a small fortified castle, standing some 300ft above sea level. The island, almost a replica of Mont St Michel in Normandy, is owned by the National Trust.

Penzance *see page 106*

Lamorna Cove
The sheltered, sandy beach is approached via a beautiful wooded valley abounding in wildflowers.

Porthcurno
Not even the rather steep approach can detract from this delightful spot where a safe beach of soft crushed fragments of white shells lies beneath the unique Minack Theatre where open-air performances are given throughout the summer. To the east lies Logan Rock, a precariously balanced granite boulder which is said to be a gathering point for witches.

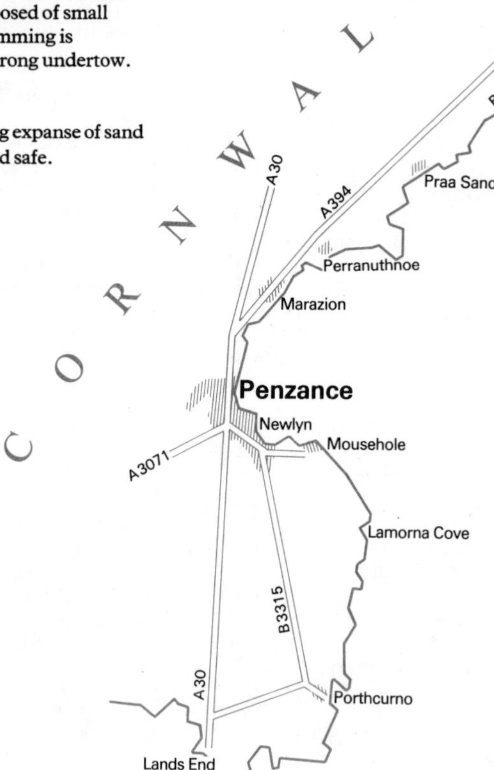

Newlyn
An important international fishing centre with much activity around the harbour. The village, set on the steep hillside overlooking Mounts Bay, attracts large numbers of artists.

Mousehole
Once the chief port of the old Duchy of Cornwall, Mousehole, or 'Mouzel' as it is pronounced locally, has become a popular spot for artists and photographers with its unspoiled ancient quays, cottages and narrow twisting streets.

Lands End
A wild, desolate spot where fascinating rock formations may be viewed. The Longships and Wolf Rock Lighthouses are visable, as are the Isles of Scilly on a clear day.

PENZANCE

Situated at the western end of the wide-sweeping Mount's Bay, Penzance has a south-facing, sheltered position. Going on yearly averages, it is one of the warmest places in the country and is extremely popular with holidaymakers. Its safe, sandy beaches stretch all the way around the bay to Marazion sheltered by grassy sand dunes. As the principal shopping centre of the area, its main road is a hive of activity, dominated by the classically-styled old Market House with its dome and columned façade. In front of the building a statue of Sir Humphry Davy, who invented the miner's safety lamp, looks down on the shoppers below. The picturesque harbour is busy with dinghies, yachts and fishing boats and it is from here that the ferry leaves for the Scilly Isles, some 28 miles offshore. A faster way to the islands is by helicopter from the town's heliport on the eastern outskirts. The coastline around Penzance abounds with small coves where, in days gone by, smugglers would unload their ill-gotten gains under cover of darkness. The area inland is dotted with the gaunt buildings of disused tin mines and the remains of ancient Celtic settlements.

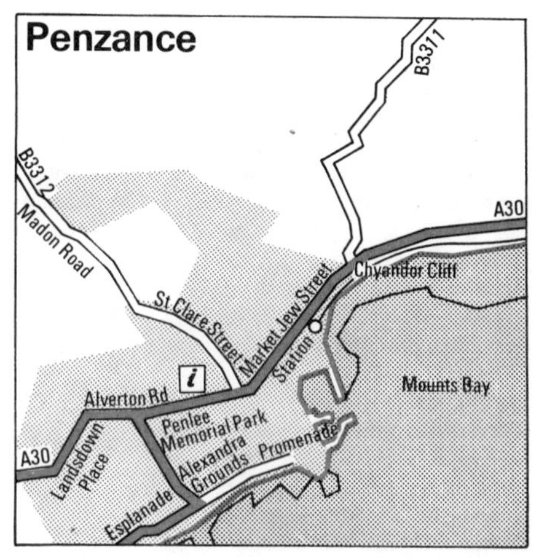

Recreation and Sports

Alexandra Grounds – Bowls, putting, tennis
Bolitho Gardens – Bowls, putting, tennis
Courtwood Squash Court St Michael's St ☎ *4339*
Harbour – Angling, open-air swimming pool, shark-fishing trips.
Mounts Bay Sailing Club Clubhouse, Godolphin Steps, Marazion ☎ *Marazion710620*
Penlee Memorial Park – Children's playground, tennis
Penzance Sailing Club Albert Pier ☎ *4989*

Cinema

The Savoy Causewayhead ☎ *3330*

Dancing

The Barn Eastern Green ☎ *5754*

Theatre

Arts Centre Parade St
St John's Hall

Places of Interest

Age of Steam Rospeath, Crowlas ☎ *Cockwells631*
The Barbican Craft Workshops and Gallery Penzance Harbour
Chysauster Ancient Village
Cornwall Aero Park Culdrose, Helston
Geevor Tin Mining Museum Pendeen, Nr St Just
Geological Museum St John's Hall
Mechanical Music Museum Goldsithney, Nr Marazion ☎ *Marazion710679*
Museum of Nautical Art and Man O' War Display Chapel St
Newlyn Art Gallery ☎ *3715*
Penlee House Museum Penlee Park ☎ *3625*
Trengwainton Gardens Madron

Tourist Information

Tourist Information Centre Alverton St ☎ *2343 or 2207*

Accommodation

The following establishments are recommended by the AA. Further information may be obtained from the Tourist Information Office.

★★★	**Queen's** The Promenade ☎ *2371*
★★	**Minalto** Alexandra Rd ☎ *2923*
★★	**Mount Prospect** Britons Hill ☎ *3117*
★★	**Union** Chapel St ☎ *2319*
★	**Chypons** Newlyn ☎ *2123*
★	**Pentrea** Alexandra Rd ☎ *2711*
★	**Yacht Inn** The Promenade ☎ *2787*
GH	**Alverton Court Hotel** Alverton Rd ☎ *2306*
GH	**Bella-Vista Private Hotel** 7 Alexandra Ter, Lariggan ☎ *2409*
GH	**Camilla Hotel** Regent Ter ☎ *3771*
GH	**Carlton Private Hotel** ☎ *2081*
GH	**Duporth Private Hotel** 1 Mennaye Rd ☎ *2689*
GH	**Essex** 23 Lannoweth Rd ☎ *5129*
GH	**Estoril Private Hotel** 46 Morrab Rd ☎ *2468*
GH	**Glencree Private Hotel** 2 Mennaye Rd ☎ *2026*
GH	**Hansord** Alexandra Rd ☎ *3311*
GH	**Holbein House** Alexandra Rd ☎ *5008*
GH	**Holiday Maker's Rendezvous** Mennaye Rd, Chiverton ☎ *3337*
GH	**Hopedale** 29 Chapel St ☎ *3277*
GH	**Kilindini Private Hotel** Regent Ter ☎ *4744*
GH	**Kirkstone** Penare Rd ☎ *3115*
GH	**Mount Royal Hotel** Chyandour Cliff ☎ *2233*
GH	**Old Manor House** Regent Ter ☎ *3742*
GH	**Penmorvah** Alexandra Rd ☎ *3711*
GH	**Trenant Private Hotel** Alexandra Rd ☎ *2005*
GH	**Revelyan** 16 Chapel St ☎ *2494*
GH	**Willows** Cornwall Ter ☎ *3744*
Inn	**The Longboat Hotel** Market Jew St ☎ *4137*
SC	**Character Cottages (holidays) Ltd**, Sidmouth, Devon ☎ *Sidmouth6531*
SC	**Queens Hotel** The Promenade ☎ *2371*

Sennen
Set amid the rugged scenery of the Lands End Peninsula, Sennen provides a pleasant and somewhat surprising contrast for here, amidst the rocks and rough seas is a sheltered stretch of sandy beach. The southern end of Whitesand Bay is generally safe for swimming, protected by an offshore reef but further north, however, conditions become more dangerous.

Cape Cornwall
Along this desolate stretch of coastline is the only cape in England and Wales. The chimney of an old engine house, a familiar sight in this part of the country, stands on the Cape, a man-made contribution to the naturally stark scenery. Impressive views here rival those of neighbouring Lands End.

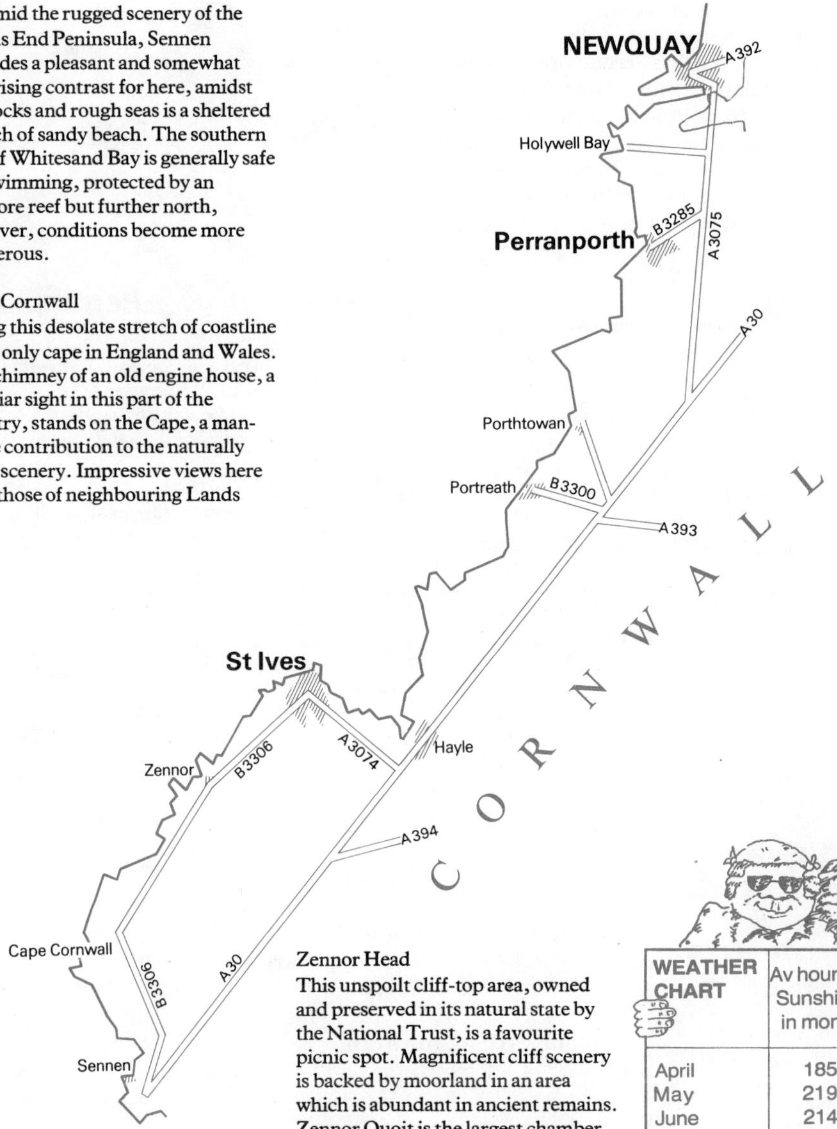

Zennor Head
This unspoilt cliff-top area, owned and preserved in its natural state by the National Trust, is a favourite picnic spot. Magnificent cliff scenery is backed by moorland in an area which is abundant in ancient remains. Zennor Quoit is the largest chamber tomb in the area and the Wayside Museum in Zennor village houses collections illustrating Cornish life.

WEATHER CHART	Av hours of Sunshine in month	Hottest Av daily Temp °C
April	185	9
May	219	12
June	214	14
July	198	16
August	190	16
September	149	15

St Ives *see page 109*

Hayle
This Victorian town which once prospered on the tin-mining industry, clusters around the estuary of the River Hayle, on the mid point of St Ives Bay. Its beautiful stretch of sandy beach, backed by grassy dunes, is extremely popular, but swift currents near the estuary make swimming dangerous at that point.

Portreath
The sandy beach, strewn with pebbles, is a popular surfing area, but swimming can be dangerous near the old pier and the rocks.

Porthtowan
A long sandy beach which can be dangerous at low-tide. Surf boards are available for hire.

Perranporth *see page 108*

Holywell Bay
A National Trust surfing beach backed by high dunes. Swimming is dangerous at low-tide. A neighbouring cave contains rock basins of water reputed to have healing properties.

NEWQUAY *see page 110*

PERRANPORTH

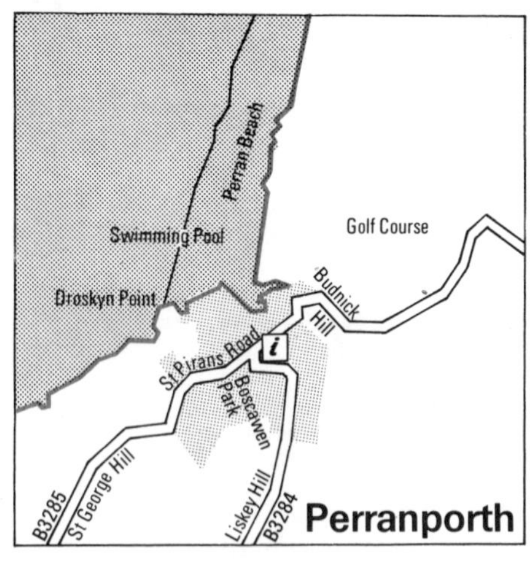

The name of Perranporth conjours up images of a quaint, typically Cornish village which have no substance in reality. Originally a mining settlement, this town has a character of its own. The name is a derivation of St Piran, the patron saint of tinners who founded the town during the 6th century. A wide, three-mile stretch of beautiful sandy beach is Perranporth's main asset, attracting many holidaymakers each year. It is a popular place for surfing, said to compare favourably with the famous surfing beaches of Australia. Another sport for which Perranporth's beach is ideal is sand yachting and championships are held each year on its firm level sands. Bathing is generally safe, except when the red flag is flying. The parish church which is dedicated to the saint is the third to be built here, the other two being overwhelmed by the shifting sands. The first tiny church has been excavated and is now preserved inside an all-enclosed concrete building.

Recreation and Sports

Beach – Angling, children's swimming pool, surfing
Bolenna Field – Children's playground, tennis
Boscawen Park – Boating lake, bowls, model yacht pond, putting
Cornish Gliding and Flying Club Trevellas Airfield ☎ *2124*
Perranporth Golf Club Budnick Hill ☎ *2161*

Cinema

Palace St George's Rd ☎ *3142*

Places of Interest

Cornish Engines Pool
The Holman Mining Museum Camborne ☎ *Camborne 712750*
Perran Round Hill Fort (on Goonhaven Rd)
St Agnes Leisure Park ☎ *St Agnes 2793*
Tolgus Tin Company Portreath Rd, Redruth ☎ *Redruth 215171*
Wheal Coates Engine House (between St Agnes and Chapel Porth)

Tourist Information

Information Bureau Mitchells Corner, Liskey Hill ☎ *2091*

This picturesque village of stone cottages clustered around the harbour was once the site of a prosperous pilchard fishing industry. After its decline in the 1880's when the pilchards mysteriously deserted the inshore fishing grounds, artists, like Whistler and Sickert, attracted by its climate, quality of light and setting, made the town internationally famous, and it has now become a haven for artists and sculptors.

The labyrinth of cobbled streets around the old harbour, known locally as the 'downalong', still retains names such as Fish Street which have survived from a bygone age. On the grassy headland known as 'The Island' stands the fishermans chapel of St Nicholas, which marks the site of the 6th-century shrine of St Ia or Eia, after whom the town is named.

Because of the narrow streets vehicular restrictions operate during the summer. Visitors should take advantage of the large Trenwith car park and either walk down the steep steps to the town or use the frequent 'park and ride' bus service. Alternatively use the new 'park and ride' railway at Lelant Saltings station, 3 miles south of St Ives off the A3074.

St Ives, built on a narrow isthmus, has magnificent sandy beaches. On the north side is the surfing beach of Porthmeor where Malibu surfboards may be hired and trampolines, bowling and putting are available. The other side of the 'island' provides a sheltered swimming area on the fairly steep Porthgwidden Beach. The nearby harbour is shallow and ideal for children and weak swimmers. South of the harbour are the long sands of Porthminster Beach, backed by a putting green. Further round St Ives Bay, below a steep hillside, is the long, sheltered sandy beach of Carbis Bay. All the beaches provide the usual facilities of deck chairs, refreshments etc.

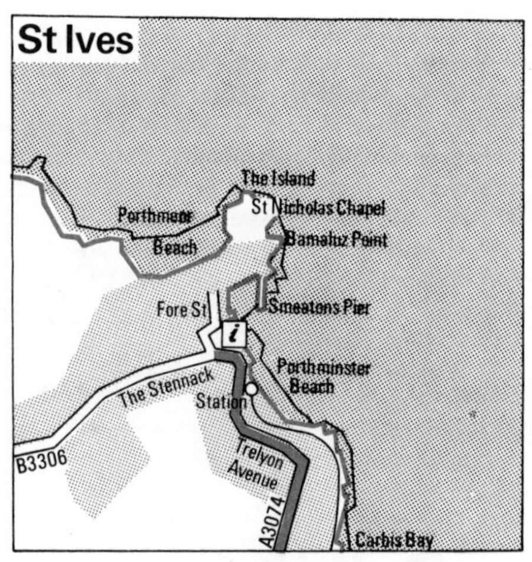

Recreation and Sports

Golf Club West Cornwall Golf Links, Lelant ☎ *Hayle753319*
Porthmeor Beach – Bowls, putting
Porthminster Beach – Putting
St Ives Sailing Club ☎ *6060*

Cinema

Royal Royal Sq ☎ *6843*

Places of Interest

Barbara Hepworth Museum Trewyn St ☎ *6226*
Barnes Museum of Cinematography Fore St
Penwith Society of Arts (Art Gallery), Back Road West ☎ *5579*
St Ives Society of Artists New Gallery, Norway Sq ☎ *5582*
Town Museum Wheel Dream

Tourist Information

Tourist Information Centre The Guildhall, Street-An-Pol ☎ *6297*

Accommodation

The following establishments are recommended by the AA. Further information may be obtained from the Tourist Information Centre.

★★★★	**Tregenna Castle** ☎ *5254*
★★★	**Garrack** Higher Ayr ☎ *6199*
★★★	**Master Roberts** Street-An-Pol ☎ *6042*
★★★	**Porthminster** The Terrace ☎ *5221*
★★	**Chy-An-Albany** Albany Ter ☎ *6759*
★★	**Chy-an-Dour** Treloyan Ave ☎ *6436*
★★	**Chy-an-Drea** The Terrace ☎ *5076*
★★	**Chy-Morvah** The Belyars ☎ *6314*
★★	**Pedn-Olva** ☎ *6222*
★★	**Western** 1 Royal Sq ☎ *5277*
GH	**Aquitaine** 4 Ocean View Ter ☎ *5049*
GH	**Cortina** 26 The Warren ☎ *6183*
GH	**Dolphin** 3 Draycott Ter ☎ *5669*
GH	**Island View** 2 Park Av ☎ *5363*
GH	**Kandahar** 11 The Warren ☎ *6183*
GH	**Lonships Hotel** 2 Talland Rd ☎ *6263*
GH	**Lyonesse Hotel** 5 Talland Rd ☎ *6315*
GH	**Pondarosa** 10 Porthminster Ter ☎ *5875*
GH	**Rosemorran Private Hotel** The Belyars ☎ *6359*
GH	**St Margarets** 3 Parc Ave ☎ *5785*
GH	**St Merryn Hotel** Trelyon ☎ *5767*
GH	**Shun Lee Private Hotel** Trelyon Ave ☎ *6284*
GH	**Sunrise** 22 The Warren ☎ *5407*
GH	**Trelissick Hotel** Bishops Rd ☎ *5035*
GH	**Verbena** Ocean View, Orange Ln ☎ *6396*
GH	**Woodside Hotel** The Belyars ☎ *6282*
SC	Mr R D Baragwanath, **Ayr Holiday Park** ☎ *5855*
SC	Mr and Mrs F Lipman, **Beaumont Holiday Flats** 4–5 Albany Ter ☎ *6420*
SC	Mr A Luke, **Cheriton House** Market Pl ☎ *5083*
SC	**Hayeswood and Rocky Close** Higher Ayr. For bookings: Mr Baragwanath, Ayr Holiday Park, Ayr, St Ives ☎ *5855*
SC	**Palm Court** Chyangweal. For bookings: F W Smith, Lamorna, St Ives Rd, Carbis Bay, St Ives ☎ *7229*
SC	Mr and Mrs P Stokes, **Rockcliff Holiday Flats** Island Rd ☎ *7165*
SC	**Talland House Holiday Flats** For bookings: Mr and Mrs S O Scott, Talland House, St Ives ☎ *6368*

Restaurants

✕	**Outrigger** Street-An-Pol ☎ *5936*

NEWQUAY

Newquay harbour was enlarged to its present size during the 16th century when the town began to prosper as a centre for pilchard fishing. The 'Huers House', on a headland overlooking the harbour dates from this period when 'Huers' scanned the seas and alerted the fishermen when a shoal was sighted. When pilchards were no longer plentiful, the town was able to survive as the main port for the export of china clay and minerals. Ships were built in the area and a good deal of smuggling took place. It was not until the late 19th century that Newquay began to realise its potential as a holiday centre but it is now firmly established as one of the five most popular resorts in the country.

Fine sandy beaches lie on either side of Towan Head, all of them safe, provided that adequate care is taken. Lifeguards patrol the sands throughout the summer and red and yellow flags are erected to indicate safe bathing areas. Plain red flags are flown when bathing is considered dangerous. Surf boards are available for hire and Great Western Beach and Fistral Beach are the favourite locations for indulging in this sport. Towan Beach is sheltered and generally more suitable for children. A curious island, linked to the mainland by a bridge, lies in one corner of the beach with a salt-water paddling pool at its foot. The pounding Atlantic waves have created numerous rock pools and caves along this part of the coast and Cathedral Cavern and the Banqueting Hall at Porth may be visited when the tide is favourable. The main amusement area is centred around Trenance Park and Gardens where a boating lake, miniature railway, outdoor swimming pool, trampolines and a zoo are to be found. Other attractions include a golf driving range, a toboggan run and facilities for bowls, pitch and putt and tennis. There is a golf course on the cliffs above Fistral Bay, the Newquay Sports Centre caters for most activities and deep-sea fishing boats may be chartered from the harbour. Regattas and races take place regularly, including 'gig' races, featuring 30ft former pilot boats. There is a museum in Trenance Gardens and an aquarium near the harbour. There are ample opportunities for pleasant coastal walks and the rocky headlands such as Porth with its island which was once a prehistoric camp, all offer fine views of the surrounding area.

Newquay is an ideal centre for touring Cornwall. The villages of Crantock, St Columb Major and St Mawgan, all possessing interesting churches, are only a short distance away. Further afield lie Bedruthan Steps with its imposing rock formations, the ancient town of Truro, Bodmin in its bleak moorland setting and the many coastal resorts which are described elsewhere in this book.

Recreation and Sports

F **Barrow Fields** – Putting
E **Killacourt** – Putting
D **Newquay Golf Club** ☎*4354*
F **Newquay Indoor Bowling Club** Tretherras ☎*4368*
F **Newquay Sports Centre** Tretherras ☎*5533* – Most indoor and outdoor sports
I **Newquay Swimming Pools** Trenance Park ☎*5982* – Indoor and open-air heated pools
Pentire Head – Pitch and putt
I **Trenance Gardens** – Boating lake, bowls, golf-driving range, miniature railway, pitch and putt, putting, tennis, toboggan run

Cabaret/Dancing

E **Cabaret Club** 42 Cliff Rd ☎*4631*

Cinemas

F **Astor** ☎*2023*
E **Camelot** ☎*4222*

Theatres

E **Cosy Nook** ☎*3365*
E **Newquay Theatre** St Michaels Rd ☎*3379*

Places of Interest

D **Aquarium** Newquay Harbour
A(1) **Huer's House**
I **Museum** Trenance Gdns
I **Newquay Zoo** Trenance Gdns ☎*3342*

Tourist Information

[i]E **Tourist Information Centre** Cliff Rd ☎*2119*

Accommodation

The establishments listed below are a selection of AA-recommended accommodation located in the area covered by the Town Plan. Further information may be found in AA publications or obtained from the Tourist Information Centre.

1GH **Arundell Hotel** Mount Wise ☎*2481*
2★★★ **Atlantic** Dane Rd ☎*2244*
3★ **Barrowfield** Hillgrove Rd ☎*2560*
4★★ **Beachcroft** Cliff Rd ☎*3022*
5★★ **Bewdley** Pentire Rd ☎*2883*
6★★★ **Bristol** Narrowcliff ☎*5181*
7GH **Castaways Hotel** 39 St Thomas Rd ☎*5002*
11★★★ **Edgcumbe** Narrowcliff ☎*2061*
12GH **Gentle Knight** 6 Treloggan Rd ☎*2419*
13★★★ **Glendorgal** Lusty Glaze Rd ☎*4937*
14GH **Gluvian** 12 Edgcumbe Gdns ☎*3133*
15Inn **Godolphin Hotel** Henver Rd ☎*2572*
16★★ **Great Western** Cliff Rd ☎*2010*
17★★★★ **Headland** ☎*2211*
18★★★ **Hotel Riviera** Lusty Glaze Rd ☎*4251*
19★★★ **Kilbirnie** Narrowcliff ☎*5155*
20★★ **Marina** Narrowcliff Prom ☎*3012*
21GH **Mellanvrane Hotel** Trevemper Rd ☎*2593*
22GH **Mount Wise Hotel** Mount Wise ☎*3080*
23GH **Ocean Hill Lodge Private Hotel** Trelawney Rd ☎*4595*
25GH **Ranelagh Court Hotel** 101A Henver Rd ☎*4922*
26★ **Sandy Lodge** Hillgrove Rd ☎*2851*
27★★★ **Trebarwith** Island Estate ☎*2288*
27aSC **Trevelga Flats** Lusty Glaze Rd For bookings: Mr & Mrs Pearce, 1 Tredour Rd, Rawley Ln, Newquay, Cornwall ☎*3792*
28★★ **Trevelgne** Porth ☎*2864*

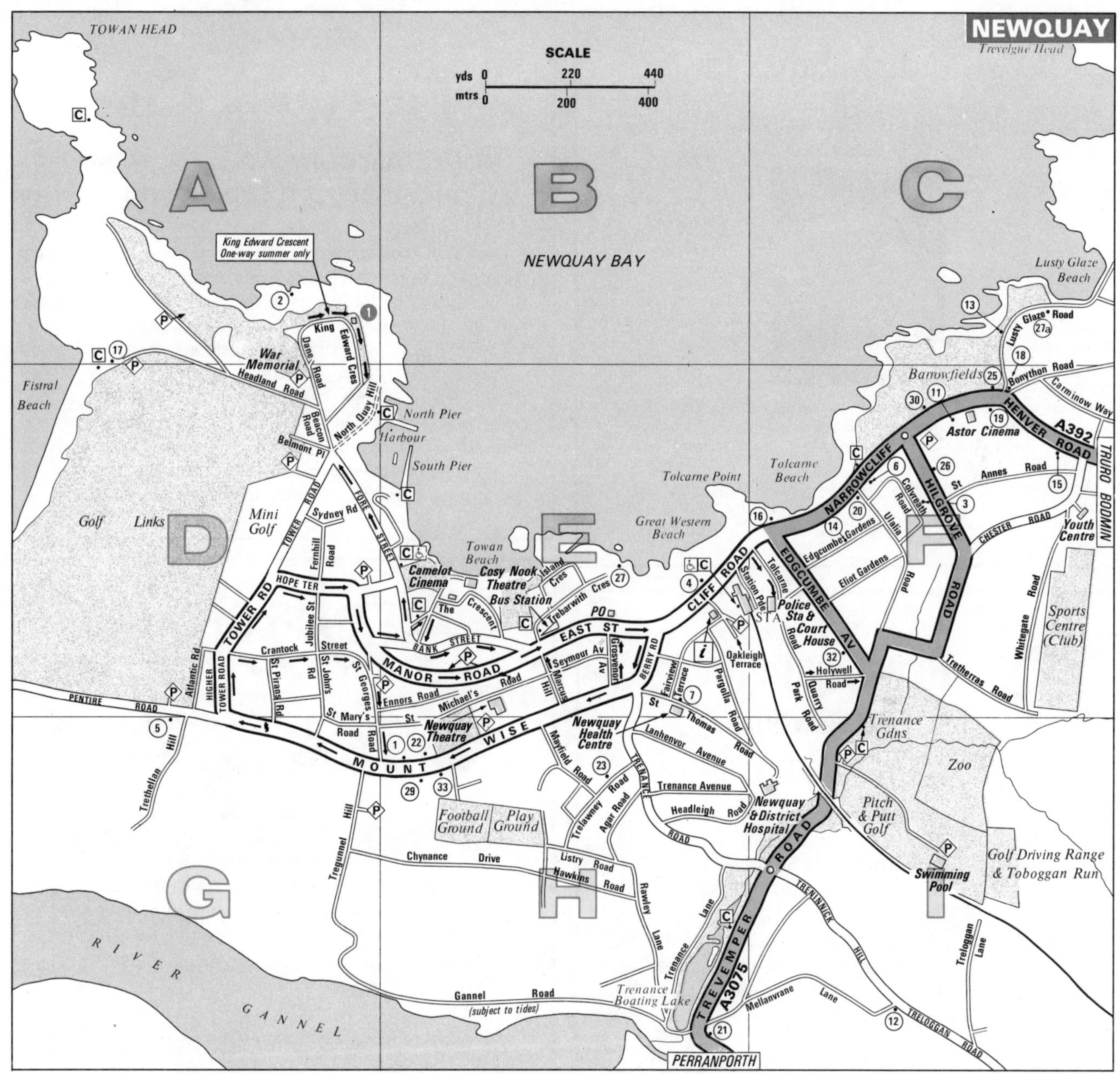

29GH **Trevane Hotel** Mount Wise ☎*3039*
30GH **Viewpoint Hotel** 89 Henver Rd ☎*2170*
32GH **Wheal Treasure** 72 Edgcumbe Av ☎*4136*
33★★★ **Windsor** Mount Wise ☎*5188*

Watergate Bay
A flat, unspoilt, sandy surfing beach. Surf-boards are available for hire and an area is set aside for surfers.

Mawgan Porth
This rocky cove has a beach of fine white sand but swimming can be dangerous, especially at low-tide. Amusements are available nearby.

Bedruthan Steps
Huge outcrops of jagged rock stand on the sandy foreshore, presenting a magnificent view from the cliffs above, reminiscent of Portugal's Algarve.

Treyarnon Beach
A sandy surfing beach which can be dangerous for swimmers at low-tide. There is a tidal swimming pool among the rocks.

Constantine Bay
There is a good, sandy beach here, backed by dunes, but swimming is generally considered to be dangerous.

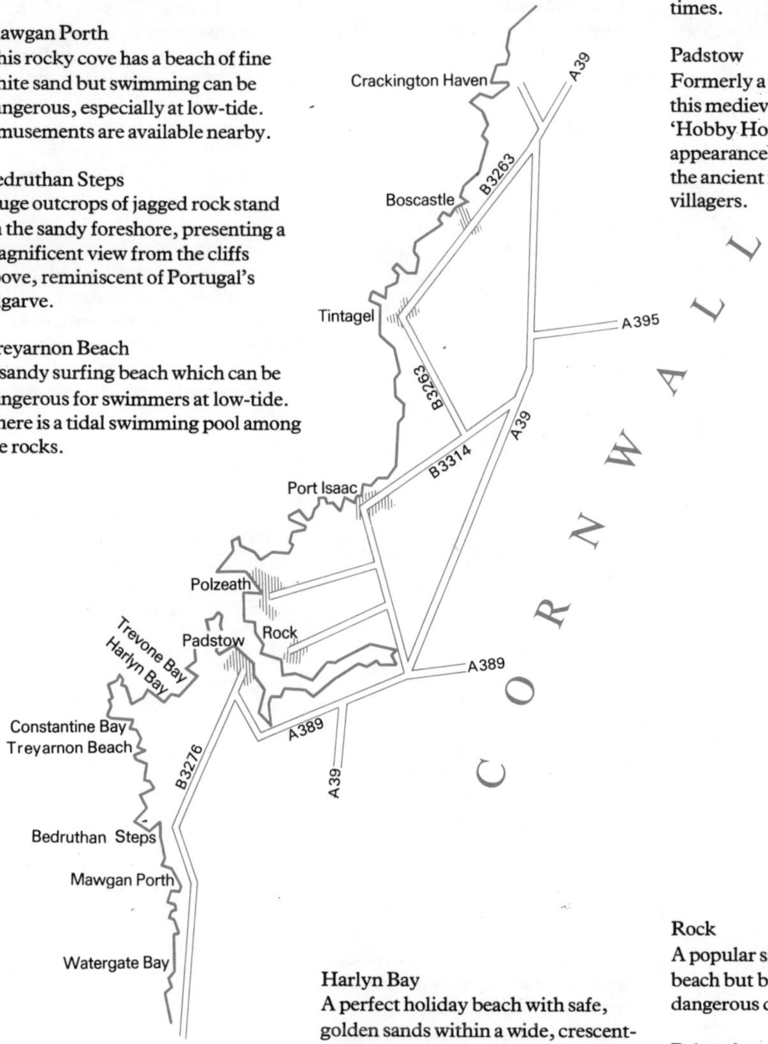

Harlyn Bay
A perfect holiday beach with safe, golden sands within a wide, crescent-shaped bay. There is a small museum exhibiting finds from an Iron Age cemetery which was excavated around the beginning of the century.

Trevone Bay
The beach here is ideal for surfing but care should be taken as there are exceptionally strong currents at most times.

Padstow
Formerly a prominent trading port this medieval village is famous for its 'Hobby Horse' which makes its appearance each May Day to join in the ancient festivities held by the villagers.

Rock
A popular sailing centre with a sandy beach but bathing is generally dangerous due to strong currents.

Polzeath
An ideal spot for a family holiday with a safe, sandy beach dotted with rock pools.

Port Isaac
The village is a fishing centre renowned for its fresh crabs and lobsters. Some sand is exposed at low-tide.

Tintagel
The imposing ruins of a 12th-century castle stand above the shore on a rocky promontory. It is said to have been the legendary site of King Arthur's Court. There is a small shingle beach below the bridge which links the castle with the mainland.

Boscastle
An unspoilt village with a small harbour. There is a small swimming pool among the rocks on the foreshore and a Museum of Witchcraft in the village.

Crackington Haven
A remote, sandy beach below sheer cliffs. Surf-boards are available for hire.

Widemouth
A popular surfing beach with a wide expanse of sand. Bathing is restricted to the northern part of the beach and red flags are displayed when conditions are considered dangerous.

Bude *see page 115*

Hartland Quay
A ruined quay and an hotel stand here amid rugged coastal scenery. The hotel has a swimming pool which is open to the public. There are fine views of the Cornish coast to the south. One mile inland lies Spekes Mill where there is a spectacular waterfall.

Clovelly
A quaint village set on the face of a sheer cliff with a steep cobbled and stepped path winding down among the ancient houses to a small harbour. Vehicles must be left in the car park at the top of the cliff and a Land Rover service is available for those who do not care for a stiff climb on their return journey. Boat trips run from the quay and the famous Clovelly donkeys give rides around the paths near the car park. The most picturesque approach to Clovelly is via the three- mile Hobby Drive which runs fom the main road near Bucks Cross to Clovelly car park through some pleasant woodland and provides panoramic views of the coastal surroundings.

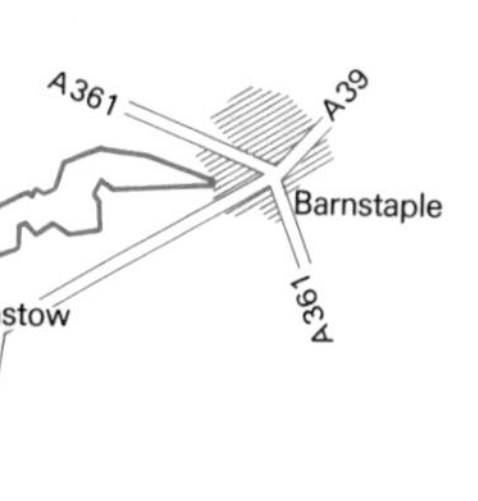

Westward Ho!
A fine expanse of safe, gently sloping sand which is ideal for young children, backed by a high ridge of large grey pebbles. There are rock pools on the western shore and the beach is backed by Northam Burrows, an extensive area of grassland containing the Royal North Devon Golf Course. Westward Ho! has a small funfair and several amusement arcades. The town was founded as a holiday resort in the mid 18th century and named after Charles Kingsley's seafaring novel which was set in the area. Kipling Tors rise behind the town, providing popular walking country. Rudyard Kipling attended the old United Services College here, obtaining much of the material for his novel *Stalky and Co.*

Appledore
An ancient seaport at the mouth of the River Torridge containing fascinating shipyards where replicas of famous vessels such as the *Golden Hind* are built. Swimming is dangerous due to strong currents in the estuary. Boat trips operate to Lundy Island and fishing trips are available. A few miles to the south lies the historic town of Bideford with pleasant riverside walks, a museum and an art gallery.

Instow
A small resort on the Torridge estuary with a fine sandy beach backed by dunes. Although the sands are popular with children swimming is inadvisable due to strong currents. Instow is accessible by a ferry from Appledore on the opposite side of the river.

Barnstaple
The largest town in North Devon, Barnstaple can claim to be one of the oldest Boroughs in existence with a recorded history stretching back to the 9th century. It is a busy market town with fine shopping and entertainment facilities and many interesting buildings including the Three Tuns Tavern, a restored medieval house dating from 1450. Barnstaple is also ideally situated for exploring the surrounding coastal resorts.

BUDE

This is the principal resort of north-east Cornwall, a small town which takes pride in its unspoilt natural beauty and its reputation for peace and quiet. Its main attraction is the beautiful, lifeguard patrolled, sandy beaches set in a stretch of wild coastline which is a haven for birds and wildlife and where seals can sometimes be seen. There are tiny caves to explore and rock pools and an unusual feature is the tide-washed, sea-water swimming pool. The harbour's breakwater at Summerleaze Beach is the scene of the annual Sea Blessing Ceremony, just one of many traditional events in the area. Bude, like so many other towns has its Carnival and the town band, as well as giving regular concerts in the Castle grounds, leads Furry Dances through the town during the summer.

Recreation and Sports

Beach – Angling, surfing, swimming pools
Bude and North Cornwall Golf Club Burns View ☎*2006*
Recreation Ground – Bowls, putting, squash, tennis

Cinema

Bude Picture House Belle Vue ☎*2016*

Dancing

Flexbury Lodge ☎*2344*

Places of Interest

Bude Museum The Wharf ☎*3576*
Ebbingford Manor Bude ☎*2808*

Tourist Information

North Cornwall District Council The Castle ☎*3111*

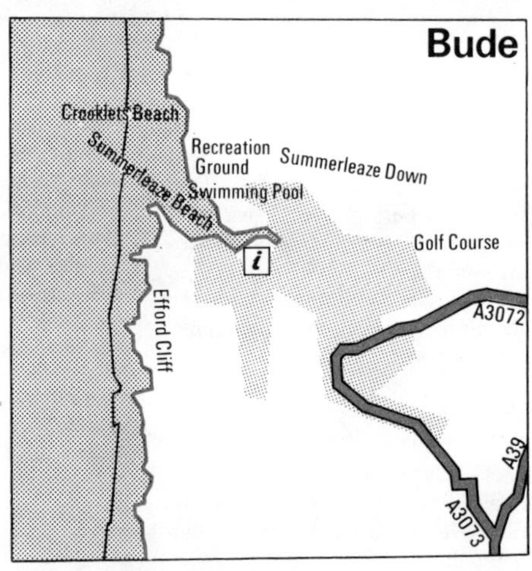

Accommodation

The following establishments are recommended by the AA. Further information may be obtained from the Tourist Information Office.

★★★ **Falcon** ☎*2005*
★★ **Grosvenor** Summerleaze Cres ☎*2062*
★ **Summerleaze Beach** Summerleaze Cres ☎*2502*

Saunton Sands
A three-mile stretch of surfing beach which is generally safe for swimming provided the rocks at the northern end and the mouth of the River Taw are avoided. The sands are backed by Braunton Burrows which contain Saunton Golf Course.

Croyde Bay
Good, level sands within a wide bay backed by towering sandhills. Swimming can be dangerous at low-tide. The village of Croyde contains many thatched cottages and some quaint cafes and gift shops.

Combe Martin
A stoney beach where level sand and rock pools are uncovered at low-tide. Bathing is safe and there is a heated swimming pool and a bowling alley. The village lies on the edge of the Exmoor National Park and is noted for its fine strawberries.

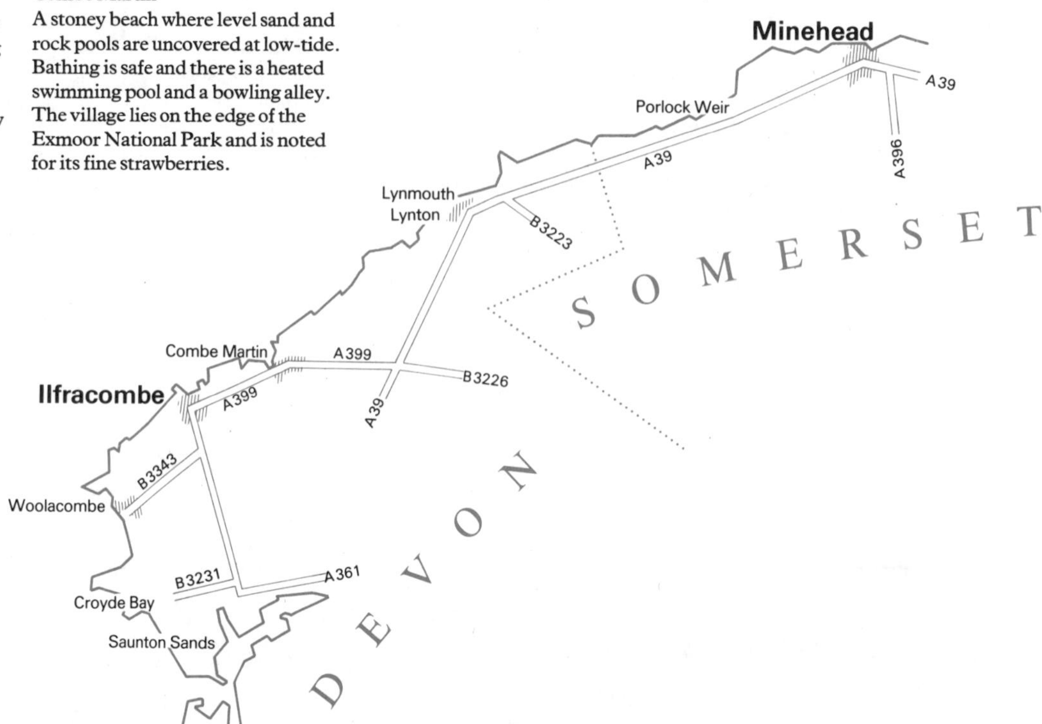

Woolacombe
The fine beach covers two miles of coastline. Flags indicate the safest surfing and swimming areas and the dunes behind the beach contain spacious car parks. Surf-boards are available for hire and Woolacombe has good entertainment and sporting facilities.

Ilfracombe *see page 117*

Lynton and Lynmouth
Lynton, poised on a 600 foot cliff, is connected by a cliff railway to Lynmouth which lies far below on the banks of the river. The towns are renowned for their setting amid sweeping moorland and rugged wooded cliffs which earned them the title of the 'Switzerland of England' in the Victorian era. Much of Lynmouth has been rebuilt following the devastation caused by the severe flooding which the town suffered in 1952. The beach is mainly stoney but has tidal pools which provide the safest swimming areas. Boat trips and amusements are available. The Lyn and Exmoor Museum, housed in an ancient cottage, is devoted to the history of the region and the famous Valley of Rocks, containing several unusual rock formations is located a mile to the north-west of Lynton.

Porlock Weir
A quaint old dock set on a small channel strewn with boulders. Two cottages have been converted into teashops and boat trips run from the dock.

Minehead *see page 118*

ILFRACOMBE

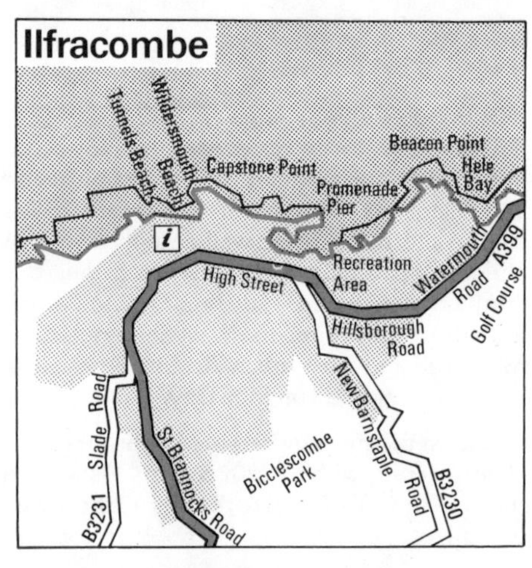

A friendly town which developed into a busy port between the 14th and 16th centuries, with steep streets all converging on the seafront and harbour. It has a majestic coastline with the harbour, situated in a picturesque setting, offering a safe anchorage to pleasure craft. The rocky coastline has numerous sand and shingle coves and beaches with rock pools which are reached by walks or through tunnels. Two have children's paddling pools and canoes can be hired at Hele Bay which is also safe for both the experienced swimmer and the learner. Tunnels Beach has bathing pools set in natural rock surrounds. It is privately owned and visitors must pay for the use of facilities.

The town has all the amenities to make the family holiday enjoyable and there are boat trips and cruises from the harbour. It is an ideal starting point for exploring both Exmoor and the adjoining coastline. There are some excellent walks in and around the town. A Fishing Festival, and golf and bowls tournaments are held annually. There are also facilities for horse riding in the area.

Recreation and Sports

Bicclescombe Park – Boating pool, tennis, wildlife corner
Hele Bay – Canoes, paddling pool
Highfield Road – Bowls
Hillsborough Road – Golf Drive, indoor pool, tennis
Ilfracombe Golf Club West Hagginton ☎62176
Ilfracombe Yacht Club The Quay ☎63969
Marine Drive – 'Karting', pitch and putt
Tunnels Beach – Bathing pool
Wildersmouth Beach – Paddling pool
Wilder Road – Children's 'karts', crazy-golf, putting

Cinemas

Clifton 1 and 2, High St ☎62626
Embassy High St ☎63484

Theatre

Pavilion Theatre Victoria Pavilion, Wilder Rd ☎62228
Top of the Town Market St ☎62123

Places of Interest

Chambercombe Manor Chambercombe ☎62624
Corn Mill Bicclescombe Park
Museum Wilder Rd ☎63541
Wild-Life Corner Bicclescombe Park

Tourist Information

Tourist Information Centre The Promenade ☎63001

Accommodation

The following establishments are recommended by the AA. Further information may be obtained from the Tourist Information Office.

★★	**Carlton** Runna Cleave Rd ☎62446
★★	**Cliffe Hydro** Hillsborough Rd ☎63606
★★	**Collingwood** Wilder Rd ☎63621
★★	**Dilkhusa Grand** Wilder Rd ☎63505
★★	**Harleigh House** Wilder Rd ☎63850
★★	**Imperial** ☎62536
★★	**Mount** Highfield Rd ☎62308
★★	**St Helier** Hillsborough Rd ☎63862
ap	**Seven Hills** Torrs Park ☎62207
GH	**Avenue Private Hotel** Greenclose Rd ☎63767
GH	**Bickleighscombe House** 41 St Brannocks Rd ☎63899
GH	**Carbis** 50 St Brannocks Rd ☎62943
GH	**Cheddar** Montpelier Ter ☎63322
GH	**Clovelly Private Hotel** 1 Oxford Park ☎63720
GH	**Clutha Private Hotel** Hillsborough Ter ☎62798
GH	**Craigmillar** 22 Crofts Lea Park (New Barnstaple Rd) ☎62822
GH	**Cresta Private Hotel** Torrs Park ☎63742
GH	**Darnley Private Hotel** Belmont Rd ☎63955
GH	**Dedes Hotel** 1–2 The Promenade ☎62545
GH	**Elmfield** Torrs Park ☎63377
GH	**Headlands Hotel** Capstone Crescent ☎62887
GH	**Laston House Private Hotel** Hillsborough Rd ☎62627
GH	**Lympstone Private Hotel** Cross Park ☎63038
GH	**Marlyn** 7 and 8 Regent Place ☎63785
GH	**Merrydene Private Hotel** 10 Hillsborough Ter ☎62141
GH	**New Cavendish Hotel** 9–10 Larkstone Ter ☎63994
GH	**Queen's Court Hotel** Sea Front ☎63764
GH	**Riversdale Hotel** Torrs Park ☎62535
GH	**Rockcliffe Hotel** Capstone Parade ☎62267
GH	**Southcliffe** Torrs Park ☎62958
GH	**South Torr Hotel** Torrs Park ☎63750
GH	**Strathmore Private Hotel** 57 St Brannocks Rd ☎64301
GH	**Sunny Hill** Lincombe, Lee ☎62953
GH	**Tamaris** 17 Larkstone Ter ☎62223
GH	**Torrsvale Private Hotel** Torrs Park ☎63102
GH	**Wentworth House Private Hotel** Belmont Rd ☎63048
GH	**Westbourne Private Hotel** Wilder Rd ☎62120
GH	**Westwell Hall Private Hotel** Torrs Park ☎62792
GH	**Wilson** 16 Larkstone Ter ☎63921
Inn	**Royal Britannia** The Quay ☎62939

MINEHEAD

This popular seaside resort with its sandy beach and small harbour was a busy port until the latter part of the 18th century. The extensive sands are ideal for all the family, although the sea should not be entered when red flags are flying. Those wishing to enjoy a swim at low-tide will find an alternative in the well-equipped open-air pool with its filtered sea water, and there is a children's paddling pool on the beach. There are facilities for all kinds of sport, boat trips, pony and donkey rides and horse riding. Minehead has a model village surrounded by a miniature railway and the West Somerset Railway operates a steam and railcar service between Minehead and Stogumber. An Arts Festival is held each year and the famous Hobby Horse Festival takes place on May Day.

The most picturesque part of Minehead is around the harbour, now used as an anchorage for pleasure craft, with its 17th-century Fisherman's Chapel and cottages, and the old village on the slopes of North Hill to the west of the town. This includes the 14th- to 15th-century church reached by a flight of cobbled steps with white-washed cottages on each side.

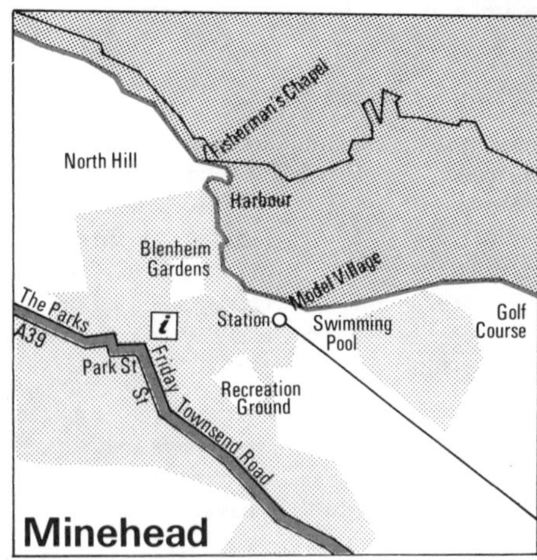

Recreation and Sports

Beach – Paddling pool
Blenheim Gardens – Band concerts, open air dancing (summer), putting
Irham Road – Bowls
Minehead and West Somerset Golf Club The Warren ☎2057
Minehead Sailing Club The Harbour, Quay West
Recreation Ground – Cricket, putting, tennis
Seafront – Mini-golf, miniature railway, open-air seawater swimming pool

Cinema

Regal The Ave ☎2439

Theatre

Gaiety Theatre The Esplanade ☎2776

Places of Interest

Almhouses
Fisherman's Chapel
Model Village Seafront
St Michael's Church
West Somerset Railway Station ☎4996

Tourist Information

Exmoor National Park Information Centre The Market House, The Parade ☎2984
Information Centre The Market House, The Parade ☎2624.

Accommodation

The following establishments are recommended by the AA. Further information may be obtained from the Tourist Information Office.

★★★	**Beach** The Avenue ☎2193
★★	**Benares** Northfield Rd ☎2340
★★	**Wellington** Wellington Sq ☎4371
★★	**Winsor** The Avenue ☎2171
★★	**York** ☎2037
★	**Edinor** Martlet Rd ☎2100
★	**Kingsway** Ponsford Rd ☎2313
★	**Merton** Western Lane, The Parks ☎2375
GH	**Carbery** Western Ln, The Parks ☎4617
GH	**Dorchester Hotel** 38 The Avenue ☎2052
GH	**Glen Rock Hotel** The Avenue ☎2245
GH	**Lambrook House** 34 Tregonwell Rd ☎4858
GH	**Mayfair Hotel** The Avenue ☎2719
GH	**Mentone Hotel** The Parks ☎2549
GH	**Wyndcott Hotel** Martlet Rd ☎4522
Inn	**Red Lion Hotel** The Esplanade ☎2653
SC	**Flats 2 and 3 Dunboyne** For Bookings: Miss O Sellick, Dunboyne Bratton Ln ☎3062.

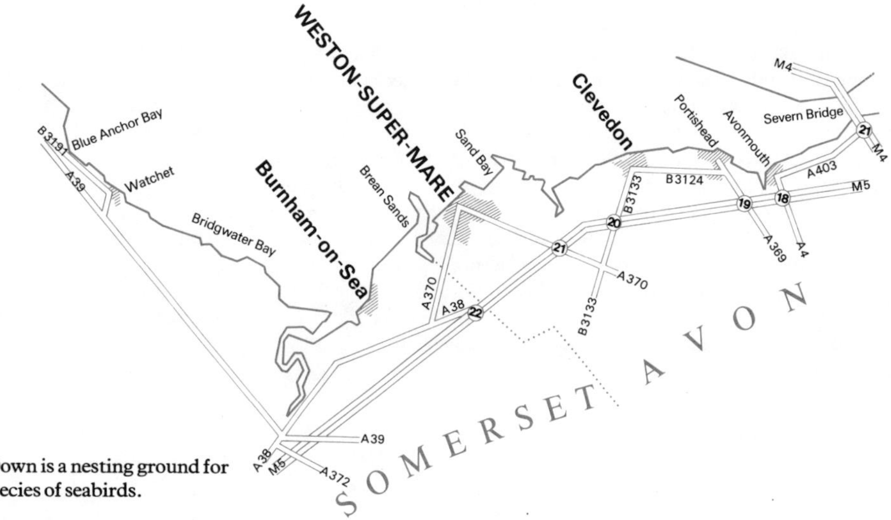

Blue Anchor Bay
A long, open beach of firm sand where swimming is safe at all times under normal weather conditions. A short distance inland lies Dunster, a village nestling among wooded hills which retains its medieval appearance. It has a castle dating from Norman times which is now owned by the National Trust and a picturesque Yarn Market built in the early 17th century to promote the sale of locally produced cloth.

Watchet
An old seaport, situated at the foot of the Quantock and Brendon Hills, with a busy harbour surrounded by old cottages. It was here that Coleridge acquired the inspiration for his famous poem *The Ancient Mariner* after listening to the tales of seafaring men. The beach contains many rock pools and is safe for bathing. The 'Watchet Society' caters for the entertainment of both residents and visitors and Watchet is ideally situated for touring Blackmore's 'Lorna Doone Country' which lies a few miles inland.

Bridgwater Bay
A vast area of mudflats and saltings containing a nature reserve under the control of the National Nature Conservancy. Many species of birds may be seen in the reserve, particularly shelduck which congregate there during the early autumn. The fishing villages of Stolford and Steart (both noted for their abundance of shrimps) overlook the bay.

Burnham-on-Sea *see page 122*

Brean Sands
A beach of firm sand backed by high grassy dunes. Vehicles are allowed on the sands and can be a hazard to the unwary. To the north, the headland of Brean Down is a nesting ground for many species of seabirds.

WESTON SUPER MARE *see page 120*

Sand Bay
The southern foreshore is mainly sandy and swimming is safe. The tide recedes for almost a mile.

Clevedon *see page 122*

Portishead
This ancient port, built upon two hills, was once an anchorage used by ships awaiting favourable winds to carry them on to Bristol or out into the Atlantic. Portishead is now a thriving holiday resort with amusement facilities, a boating lake and a heated outdoor swimming pool. The beach tends to be marshy but a pleasant park overlooks the sea. A lighthouse stands to the north on Battery Point, a headland affording fine coastal views.

Avonmouth
A busy modern port serving Bristol. Guided tours of the dockyard, which accommodates vessels from all over the world, may be arranged.

WESTON-SUPER-MARE

This former fishing village has been developed over the last century into one of Britain's principal resorts. The safe, sandy beach has a gentle slope and is wide enough to accommodate two large parking areas. Donkey and pony rides and a Punch and Judy Show are regular features on the sands. A salt-water swimming pool and model boating pools are to be found on the beach. The Grand Pier has a large covered amusement park, and an aquarium, model railway, mini-zoo and model village are situated close to the seafront. Boat trips depart from the Old Pier and the visitor may enjoy the regular spectacles of regattas, flower shows, carnivals, folk dancing and pedal-car racing along Marine Parade. The Woodspring Museum contains a number of unusual features including the reconstruction of an old-fashioned chemist's shop, a dairy and a Victorian seaside holiday display. Outdoor art exhibitions are held in the Winter Gardens. There are a number of pleasant seafront gardens and several well-landscaped parks within the town. Weston Woods occupy much of the headland at the northern corner of the bay. A toll road runs through these woods along the edge of the cliff and a huge Iron Age encampment, complete with ramparts, ditches and storage pits, stands among the trees at the seaward end.

Weston-super-Mare is a good base for touring the Avon/Somerset area with the Mendip Hills, Cheddar Gorge and Wookey Hole less than an hour's drive away. Longer trips could include the splendours of Bath and Wells, the Arthurian mystique of Glastonbury or the more modern attractions of Bristol.

Recreation and Sports

	Ashcombe Park – Bowls, pitch and putt, putting, tennis
F	**Beach Lawns** – Putting
F	**Clarence Park** – Bowls, County Cricket
A	**Cove Pavilion** – Model railway
D	**Dolphin Bowling Centre** Dolphin Sq ☎*26480*
C	**Grand Pier** – Amusements
B	**Grove Park** – Multi-sports area, tennis
A(1)	**Knightstone Baths** ☎*29011* – Indoor Pool
A	**Knightstone Causeway** – Aquarium, mini-zoo
C/E	**Marine Parade** – Model yacht pools, outdoor swimming pool
A	**Park Place** – Putting
A	**Royal Parade** – Model village
D	**Victoria Square** – Crazy-golf
	Weston Bay Yacht Club Knightstone
	Weston-super-Mare Golf Club ☎*21360* S off A370
A(2)	**Winter Gardens** – Putting, tennis
	Worlebury Golf Club – ☎*23214*

Cabaret/Dancing

B	**Sloopys** North St ☎*32570*
A(2)	**Winter Gardens** ☎*413040*

Cinema

D	**Odeon Film Centre** ☎*21784*

Theatres

A(1)	**Knightstone Theatre** ☎*29075*
B	**Playhouse** ☎*23521*

Places of Interest

B(3)	**Library**
D(4)	**Town Hall**
B(5)	**Woodspring Museum** Burlington St ☎*21028*

Tourist Information

ℹD	**Tourist Information Centre** Beach Lawns ☎*26838*

Accommodation

The establishments listed below are a selection of AA-recommended accommodation located in the area covered by the Town Plan. Further information may be found in AA publications or obtained from the Tourist Information Centre.

1★★	**Albert** Beach Rd ☎*21363*
SC	Mrs and Mrs B J T Smart, **Dalmeny Holiday Accommodation** 4 Claremont Cres, Sea Front, Weston-super-Mare, Avon ☎*31595*
3GH	**Glenelg** 24 Ellenborough Pk South ☎*20521*
4★★★	**Grand Atlantic** Beach Rd ☎*26543*
5GH	**Kew Dee** 6 Neva Rd ☎29041
6SC	Mr and Mrs Dinham, **Merrymead Holiday Flats** 1 Ellenborough Pk Rd, Weston-super-Mare, Avon BS23 1XT ☎*29030*
7★	**Monte Bello** 48 Knightstone ☎*22303*
8★★★	**Royal** ☎*23601*
9SC	**Mr and Mrs T Gee, Russell Holiday Flats** 15/17 Clevedon Rd, Weston-super-Mare, Avon ☎*20195*
10GH	**Russell Hotel** 15/17 Clevedon Rd ☎*20195*
11GH	**St Annes Hotel** 35 Severn Rd ☎*20487*
12GH	**Scottsdale Hotel** 3 Ellenborough Pk North ☎*26489*
13GH	**Tower House Hotel** Ellenborough Pk North ☎*21393*
14GH	**Westgate Private Hotel** 5 Ellenborough Cres ☎*21952*

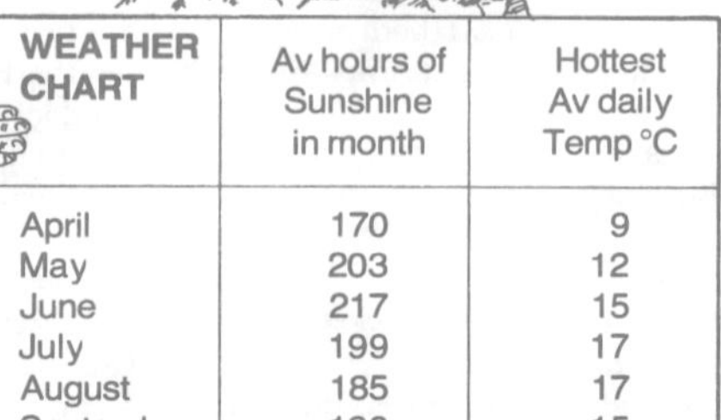

WEATHER CHART	Av hours of Sunshine in month	Hottest Av daily Temp °C
April	170	9
May	203	12
June	217	15
July	199	17
August	185	17
September	138	15

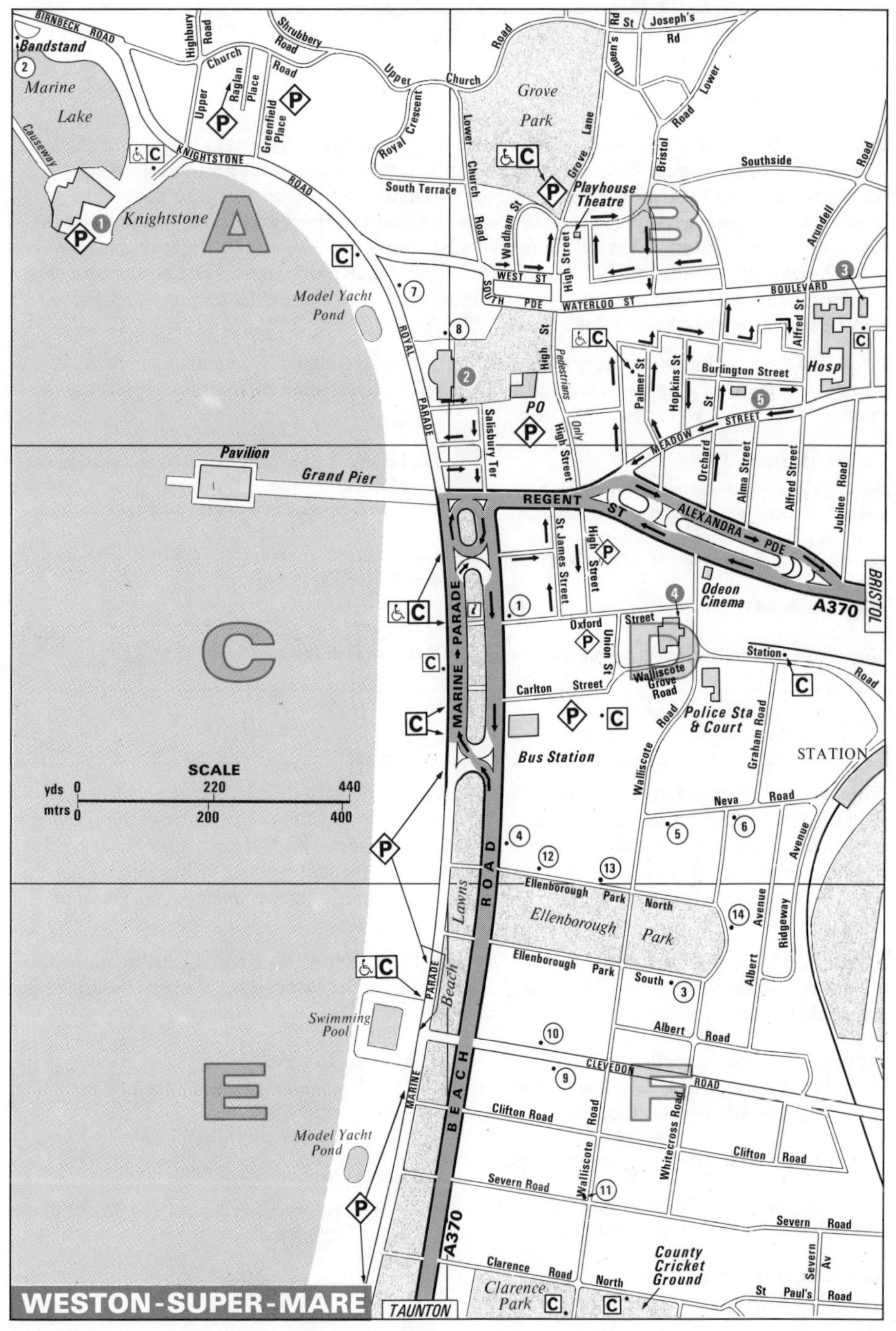
WESTON-SUPER-MARE
SCALE
yds 0 220 440
mtrs 0 200 400
Bandstand
Marine Lake
Causeway
Knightstone
Model Yacht Pond
Pavilion
Grand Pier
Swimming Pool
Grove Park
Playhouse Theatre
PO
Odeon Cinema
Police Sta & Court
Bus Station
STATION
Hosp
Ellenborough Park
County Cricket Ground
Clarence Park
Lawns
Beach
BRISTOL
TAUNTON
A370

BURNHAM-ON-SEA

This seaside resort, north of the mouth of the River Parrett and Brue, is popular because of the wide sandy beach which stretches northwards for approximately 7 miles as far as Brean Down. The gently sloping beach, sheltered by sand dunes, is safe for swimming and the beautiful Manor Gardens and Marine Cove are ideal settings in which to relax. The young are well catered for with swings, trampolines, roundabouts, paddling pool and donkey rides all on the sea front. There is an excellent golf course which features some championship events. The King Alfed Sports Centre at Highbridge has facilities for all indoor sports and equipment can be hired. Burnham is a superb area for sea angling and for coarse and fly fishing. Craftsmen may be seen at work in Haven Pottery at Highbridge.

Brean Down, a rocky promontory at the northern end of the beach, is an excellent viewpoint and is also the site of a Roman Temple and ancient fort. The Brean Bird garden is well worth a visit.

Recreation and Sports

Berrow Road – Indoor heated swimming pool
Brean Leisure Centre – Greyhound racing, model boating, pitch and putt
Burnham and Berrow Golf Club Berrow Road ☎*783137*
Burnham Road Highbridge – King Alfred Sports Centre
Crosses Pen – Children's playground, putting, tennis
Esplanade – Crazy-golf, model boats, trampolines
Highbridge – Tennis
Pavilion Leisure Centre – Amusement arcade

Cinema

Ritz Victoria St ☎*782871*

Theatre

Princess Hall Princess Street ☎*787852*

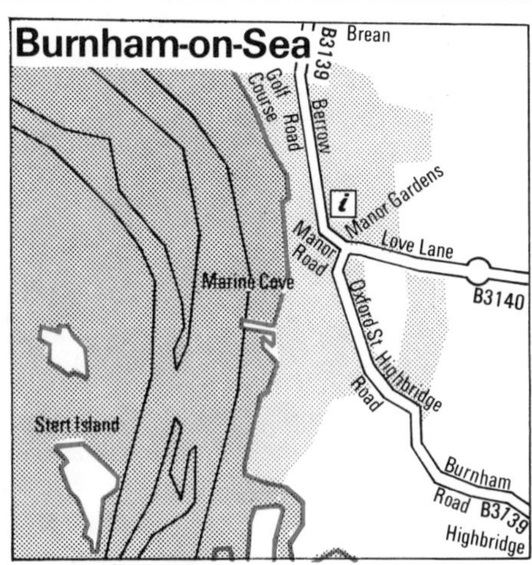

Tourist Information

Tourist Information Centre Berrow Road ☎*787852* or ☎*782377 Ext 44*.

This quiet picturesque town with its beautiful gardens and varied rocky coastline with small coves, has all the amenities of the family holiday resort. The pebble beach close to the pier with its small rocks is very popular and there is also a slipway from which yachts, motorboats and dinghies can be launched. Ladye Bay at the north end of the seafront can be reached by a leisurely walk along the cliff top and offers a sheltered secluded beach reached by a flight of steps.

Medieval Clevedon Court, owned by the National Trust, is furnished with beautiful antique furniture and has a collection of Nailsea glass. It stands at the foot of The Warrens (300ft) from which there is an excellent view.

Recreation and Sports

Clevedon Golf Club Walton ☎*873140*
Clevedon Sailing Club The Alcoves, The Beach ☎*875916*
Elton Road – Amusements, Marine Lake
Salthouse Fields – Bowls, crazy-golf, miniature railway, putting, tennis

Cinema and Bingo Hall

Curzon Old Church Rd ☎*872158*

Places of Interest

Clevedon Court Tickenham Rd ☎*873180*
St Andrew's Church West End

Tourist Information

Information Bureau The Beach Office ☎*873208*

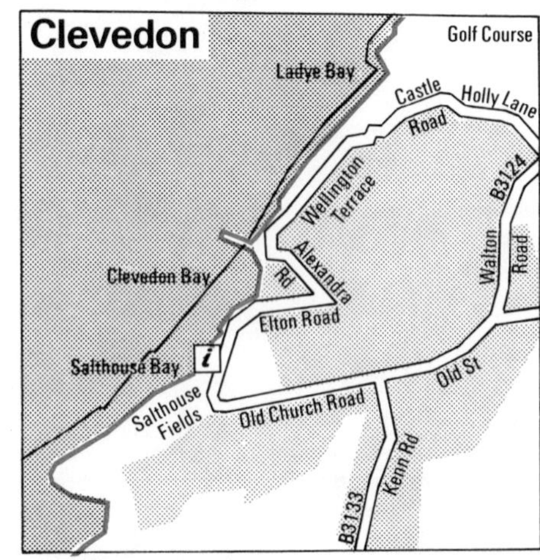

Accommodation

The following establishments are recommended by the AA. Further information may be obtained from the Tourist Information Office.

★★★ **Walton Park** Wellington Ter ☎*874253*
★ **Highcliffe** Wellington Ter ☎*873250*

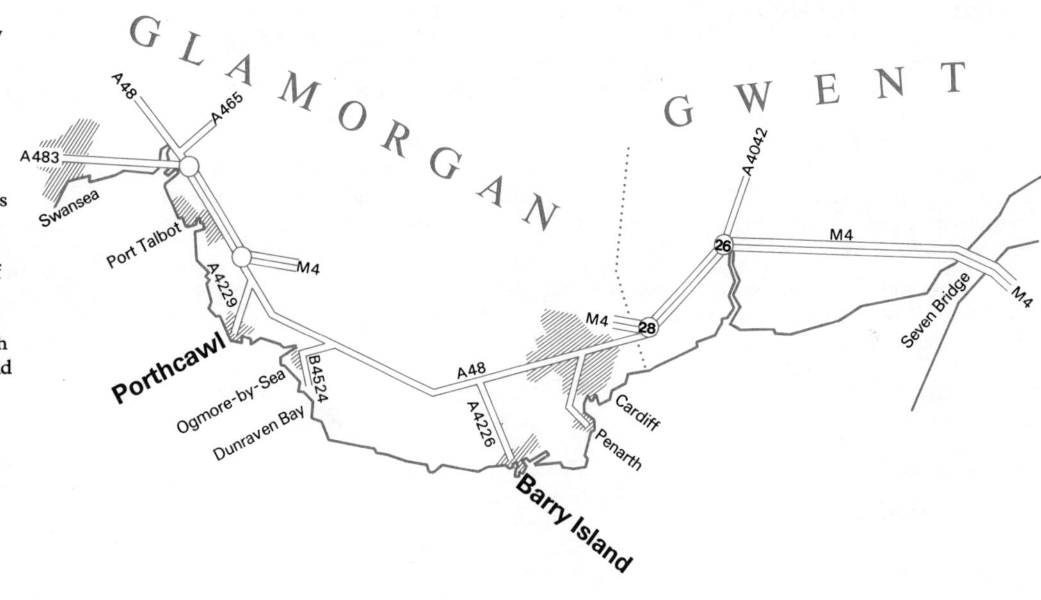

Cardiff

The capital of Wales has a lengthy history. The Romans established a settlement here and were followed by the Normans who founded the castle in 1090 and elevated Cardiff to borough status some ten years later. The city's industrial expansion followed the growth of the coal and iron production in South Wales and the dockyard was established towards the end of the 18th century to cope with the increased trade. Cardiff has much to offer the visitor in the way of entertainment and sports and the city's many places of interest include the National Museum of Wales which covers all aspects of Welsh culture and history.

Penarth

A former fishing village involved in coastal shipping Penarth is now an active seaside resort. The beach, composed of shingle and flat rocks, gives way to sand at low-tide but swimming can be dangerous due to strong currents. The landscaped gardens which lie behind the promenade have earned Penarth the title of the 'Garden by the Sea' and the surrounding cliffs provide some fine walks. Boat trips are available and there are ample amusement and entertainment facilities.

Barry Island *see page 124*

Dunraven Bay

A fine sandy beach, backed by a shingle bank, below towering cliffs. Bathing is safest inshore at high-tide and the rocks at the southern end should be avoided.

Ogmore-by-Sea

There is a sandy beach here beneath impressive cliffs with caves which may be explored at low-tide. Flags mark the safest bathing area. Swimming near the river mouth is not permitted. One mile offshore lies Tusker Rock, a reef which claimed many victims in the days of sail and is still a potential hazard to shipping. Ogmore Castle, dating from the 12th century, stands on the river bank about half a mile inland.

Porthcawl *see page 125*

Port Talbot

One of the largest towns in Wales with a dockyard servicing the local steel and chemical works. Port Talbot has a fine shopping centre and good entertainment and sports facilities including a modern Lido Complex. Aberavon Sands lie to the north and Margam Sands to the south, making the town an ideal centre for a family holiday. Margam Sands are rarely crowded and give access to neighbouring Kenfig Sands backed by dunes.

Swansea

Swansea, the second largest city in Wales, is very heavily industrialised around the busy dockyard. Much of the city was destroyed during World War II bombing but Swansea has its fair share of museums and entertainment facilities. There is a sandy beach below Black Pill and many acres of public parks and gardens and the city is ideally situated for exploring the delightful Gower Peninsula. A local delicacy is Laver Bread, made from seaweed, which all visitors are urged to sample.

BARRY ISLAND

This former fishing village was developed into a popular seaside resort during the latter part of the 19th century. It now has a large residential population and a busy harbour. Barry Island, joined to the town by the Harbour Road causeway, has an extensive sandy beach at Whitmore Bay backed by a large pleasure and amusement park. There are many fascinating rock pools at each end of the bay and pony rides and trampolines are available. Beyond the holiday camp lies the sandy, rocky Jacksons Beach. The Knap, to the west of Barry, with its long pebble beach, has facilities for water sports and an open-air swimming pool. Porthkerry Country Park, with its attractive viaduct, is close by and has a pitch and putt course. It is also used for the horse and agricultural shows which take place annually. There is a good shopping and sports centre, and a zoo and wildlife park at Weycock Cross to the north of the town. For those who prefer to delve into the past there are the ruins of Barry Castle gatehouse and the early – 13th-century Merthyr Dyfan church.

Water-skiing and powerboat racing competitions take place in Old Harbour, Watch-house Bay and Knap Beach most weekends. Standing off-shore at the picturesque village of Sully, to the east of Barry, is the Island of Sully which can be reached only at low-tide.

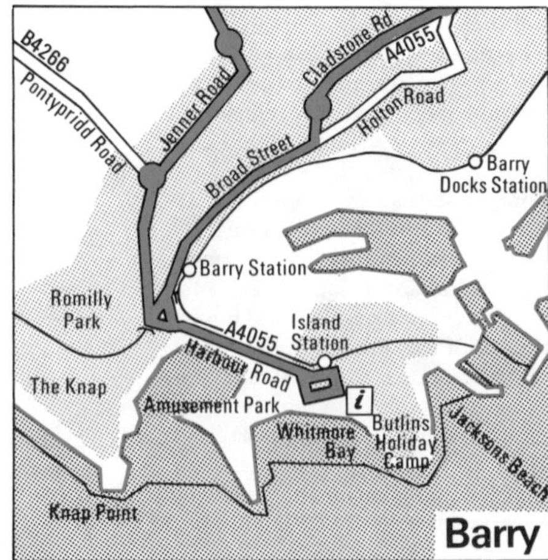

Recreation and Sports

Alexandra Gardens – Tennis
Barry Sports Centre – Facilities for most sports
Barry Yacht Club The Harbour, Pier Head, Barry Docks, ☎735511
The Brynhill Golf Club The Colcot ☎735061
Central Park – Bowls
Gladstone Park – Tennis
Jenner Park Stadium – Athletics
Knap Point – Boating lake, open-air swimming and paddling pool
Porthkerry Country Park – Pitch and putt
Romilly Park – Bowls, tennis
Victoria Park Cadoxton – Bowls, tennis

Cinema

Theatre Royal Broad St ☎735019

Places of Interest

Barry Castle (ruins)
Merthyr Dyfan Church
Sully Island (low-tide only)
Weycock Cross – Wildlife Park

Tourist Information

Town Hall Kings Sq ☎730311 *Ex16*

Accommodation

The following establishments are recommended by the AA. Further information may be obtained from the Tourist Information Office.

★★★ **International** Port Rd, Rhoose (2½m W A4226) ☎*Rhoose710787*
★★★ **Water's Edge** The Knap ☎733392
★★ **Mount Sorrel** ☎*740069*

Restaurant

✕✕ **Casa Paco** 1–2 Broad St Pde ☎*2009*

PORTHCAWL

Once the playground of the local industrial communities, Porthcawl now draws visitors from much further afield and has developed into one of the most popular resorts in South Wales. Its sandy bays are sheltered by rocky headlands and small outcrops of rocks on the beaches add interest to the scenery and contain tiny pools at low-tide. Bathing is safe from many of the beaches, but care should be taken near the headlands. There is a lifeguard station at Black Rocks between Sandy Bay and Trecco Bay. Coney Beach has a large fun-fair and was named after its counterpart in New York, Coney Island. Harbours are always an attraction and the one in Porthcawl is no exception, always busy with small craft and the pleasure steamers which operate cruises along the Bristol Channel.

To the east of Porthcawl a 5½-mile stretch of coastline has been designated an "area of outstanding natural beauty" by the Countryside Commission. Along the coast to the west, part of an old castle can be seen among the sand dunes. This marks the place where the town of Kenfig lies buried beneath the sand, the result of a violent sandstorm in the 15th century and subsequent years of shifting sands. Some say that at times the bells of Kenfig church can be heard tolling beneath the water.

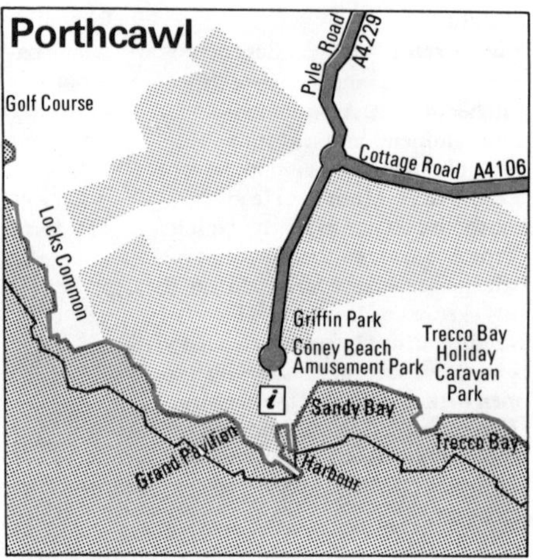

Recreation and Sports

Coney Beach – Amusements, fun-fair
Esplanade – Swimming pool and paddling pool
Griffin Park – Bowls, putting, tennis
Porthcawl Powerboat and Ski Club 4 Bay View Rd, Newton ☎*8593*
Royal Porthcawl Golf Club ☎*2251*

Cinema

Caesar's Palace and Cinema 2 Trecco Bay Holiday Caravan Park ☎*2103*

Dancing

The Grand Pavilion Esplanade ☎*3860*

Theatre

The Grand Pavilion Esplanade ☎*6996*

Places of Interest

Newcastle Bridgend – Ruins of a 12th-century castle
Stones Museum Margam – A collection of carved prehistoric stones and crosses

Tourist Information

Ogwr District Council Publicity Officer, ☎*Bridgend62141 ex3282*
Wales Tourist Office Old Police Station, St Johns St ☎*6639*

Accommodation

The following establishments are recommended by the AA. Further information may be obtained from the Tourist Information Office.

★★	**Fairways** Sea Front ☎*2085*
★	**Rose and Crown** Nottage (2m N B4283) ☎*4849*
GH	**Collingwood Hotel** 40 Mary Street ☎*2899*
GH	**Graig-y-Don Private Hotel** 30 The Esplanade ☎*3259*
GH	**Gwalia Private Hotel** 40 Esplanade Ave ☎*2751*
GH	**Seaways Hotel,** 28 Mary St ☎*3510*

Mumbles
A lively resort with beaches composed of dark brown sand strewn with patches of rock. Amusements, entertainments and sea cruises are available and the area is popular with water-skiers. Mumbles Head lighthouse is famous for the exploits of the Ace sisters – the daughters of a lighthousekeeper who waded into the surf to rescue a drowning sailor. Neighbouring Oystermouth has a ruined 12th-century castle which is open to the public and the parish churchyard contains the grave of Thomas Bowdler, the well-known expurgator of Shakespeare and Gibbon.

Langland Bay
This fine sandy beach is safe for swimming or surfing except on the ebbing tide.

Caswell Bay
A popular, sheltered surfing beach backed by a wooded valley. Red flags are flown when conditions make swimming unsafe. The bay is accessible from Langland Bay via the dividing cliffs.

Oxwich
A small seaside resort overlooking a long sandy beach backed by a nature reserve. Swimming is generally safe.

Port-Eynon
Safe dune-fringed sands lie below high cliffs. Around the western headland lies Culver Hole, a sheer wall sealing a cleft in the cliff with openings in the shape of doors and windows. The purpose of this structure has never been satisfactorily explained but as the area is said to have been a smuggling centre it is thought to have been linked with some nefarious activities.

Rhossili
A long bay with fine, safe sands ideal for surfing. Worms Head, two elongated islands, lie in the southern corner and are accessible at low-tide.

Burry Port
This former seaport has a sand and shingle beach but strong currents can make swimming hazardous.

Pembrey
Extensive sands, backed by dunes and a pine forest, provide safe swimming. The beach is sometimes closed while the RAF are engaged in target practice.

Llanstephan
Bathing from the sandy shore of the River Loughor estuary is safe when the tide is coming in but dangerous at other times because of fast currents. A ruined 11th-century castle stands on a hill above the shore.

Pendine
One of the best beaches in Britain with flat, firm sands which extend for almost seven miles in the shelter of the Carmarthen Bay Hills.

Amroth
A sandy beach backed by a ridge of shingle. The stumps of a submerged prehistoric forest are revealed at low-tide.

Saundersfoot
The harbour of this small resort is usually crowded with small craft. There are sandy beaches nearby with some shingle and patches of rock. Amusements are available and there are boats for hire.

Tenby *see page 127*

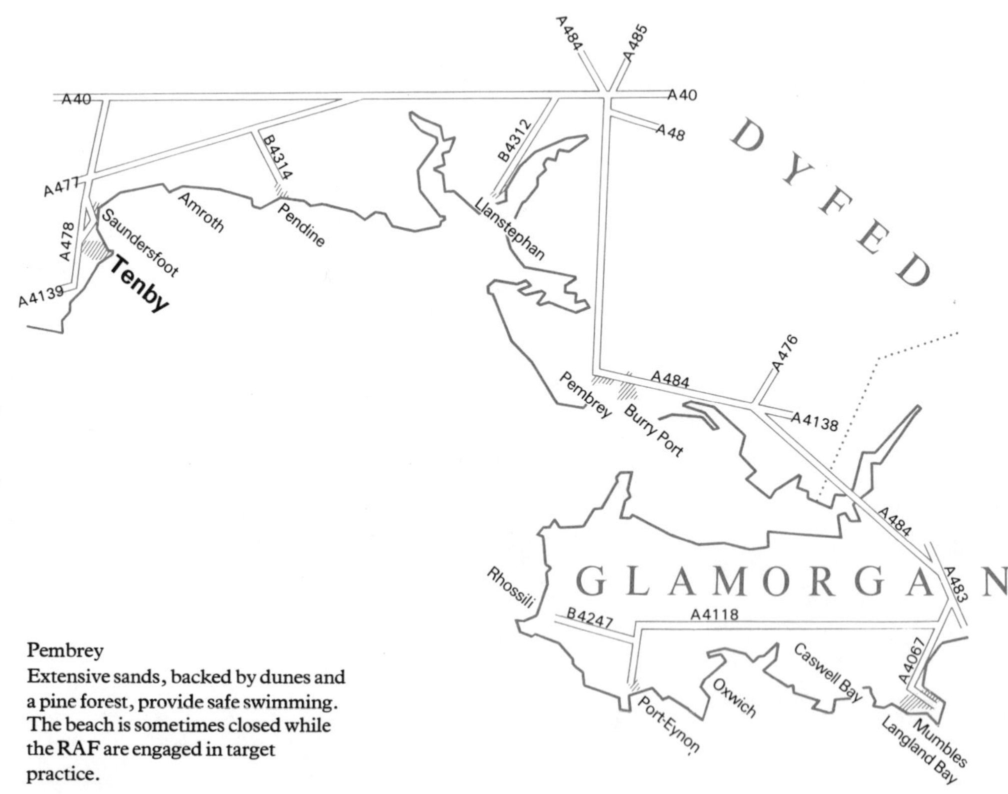

A picturesque seaside resort with a distinctive charm established early in the last century. Tenby is an important yachting centre and provides facilities for most forms of outdoor sport including fishing, golf, water ski-ing and underwater swimming. There are four sandy beaches all with safe bathing. Castle Hill and the restored keep of Tenby Castle, containing a museum, overlook the attractive and secluded old harbour with its stone pier and lifeboat station. Nearby St Catherine's Rock houses a small zoo in its Napoleonic Fort.

Situated on a narrow rocky promontory on the west side of Carmarthen Bay which Victorians likened to the bay of Naples, Tenby is rich in history. The essence of the town is contained inside the extensive remains of the finely-preserved 13th-century town walls which probably contained twenty towers and five gateways. The narrow streets with their interesting shops and houses grouped about St Mary's, the largest parish church in Wales dating from the 13th century, all convey an old world atmosphere.

A regular service runs from Tenby harbour to nearby Caldy Island with its Cistercian monastery where the monks produce the well-known Caldy perfume.

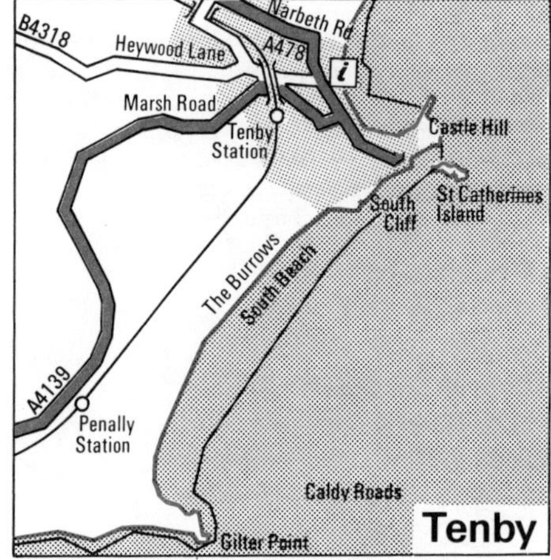

Recreation and Sports

De Valence Pavilion – Air-conditioned recreation centre with bars and restaurant holding dances and concerts
North Beach – Amusement arcades
South Cliff Gardens – Bowls
South Beach – Donkey rides
Tenby Golf Club The Burrows ☎*2787*
Tenby Swimming Pool Marsh Road ☎*3852*

Cinema

The Royal Playhouse Cinema White Lion St ☎*2093*

Places of Interest

Manor House Wildlife and Leisure Park St Florence ☎*Carew201* On the Pembroke road (B4318) – Aquarium, bird and animal gardens, children's playground, exhibitions, mini-marina, model railway exhibition
Tenby Museum Castle Hill, ☎*2809*

Tourist Information

Tourist Information Bureau The Croft ☎*2404*

Accommodation

The following establishments are recommended by the AA. Further information may be obtained from the Tourist Information Office.

★★★	**Imperial** The Paragon ☎*3737*
★★	**Atlantic** Esplanade ☎*2881*
★★	**Royal Lion** ☎*2127*
★★	**Tenby House** Tudor Sq ☎*2000*
★	**Fourcroft** The Croft ☎*2516*
ⓐ	**Croft** ☎*2576*
GH	**Belvedere Private Hotel** Serpentine Rd ☎*2549*
GH	**Harbour Heights Hotel** 11 The Croft ☎*2264*
GH	**Heywood Lodge** Heywood Ln ☎*2684*
GH	**Norton** ☎*2460*

Manorbier
A sandy beach scattered with shingle lies behind the curiously named 'Priest's Nose' headland, and provides good bathing. The historic village of stone houses contains an impressive, well-preserved Norman Castle which is open to the public.

Angle
A quiet fishing village situated between two bays. Angle Bay to the east is a mixture of sand and shingle while West Angle Bay has fine sands dotted with rock pools.

Bosherton
To the south of the village a lane and a steep path lead to a sheltered, sandy beach at Broad Haven. Nearby, at St Govan's Head, a tiny 13th-century chapel nestles below huge limestone cliffs.

Pembroke
This small, riverside town gave its name to the old county and gave one of its sons to the throne of England. Henry Tudor, later Henry VII, was born in Pembroke Castle in 1457. Still the outstanding feature of the town, this impressive Norman castle overlooks the Pembroke River. Boats are available for hire.

Pembroke Dock
An historic naval town where many warships and royal yachts were built between 1816 and 1922. Today, the docks have fallen into virtual disuse and the town is now a sailing centre.

Neyland
The terminus for the Irish ferry service until the completion of Fishguard harbour in 1906. Neyland is now a quiet yachting centre with a sand and shingle beach.

Milford Haven
Founded in the late 18th century, Milford Haven is now the principal oil port of Europe. There is a fine open-air sea water swimming pool.

Dale
A popular sailing centre with a sheltered shingle beach giving way to sand at low-tide.

Broad Haven
One of the most popular resorts in the area with fine sands and rock pools sheltered by cliffs.

Newgale
An unspoilt holiday resort with a long sandy beach backed by a bank of shingle.

Solva
The most popular yachting centre on St Brides Bay, where steep grassy slopes shelter a creek.

St Davids
The tiny city of St Davids holds a special romanticism for all Welshmen, for it was here that their Patron Saint was born. The beautiful cathedral, built on the site of earlier ecclesiastical foundations, contains St David's shrine and nearby are the ruins of the one-time Bishop's Palace. There is a small sandy beach nearby at Caerfai Bay.

Strumble Head
Ancient volcanic action beneath the sea formed the strange black rocks of the coastline around Strumble Head where a lighthouse now stands. A secluded shingle cove lies to the south-east and can be reached by a cliff path.

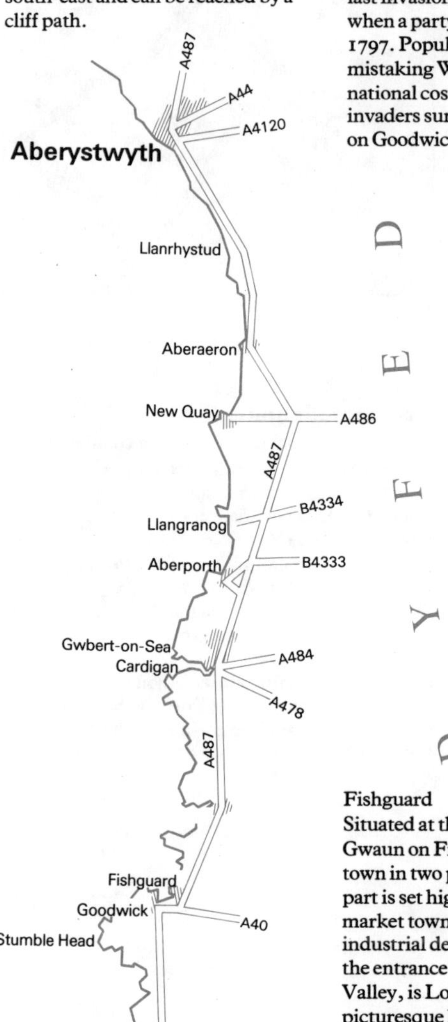

Goodwick
The twin town of Fishguard, Goodwick is the port for the Irish Ferries to Rosslare and Cork. There is a shingle beach. Just around the headland at Carreg Wastad Point the last invasion of Britain took place when a party of Frenchmen landed in 1797. Popular legend claims that, mistaking Welsh women in their national costume for soldiers, the invaders surrendered without a fight on Goodwick beach.

Fishguard
Situated at the mouth of the River Gwaun on Fishguard Bay, this is a town in two parts. The more modern part is set high above the bay, a market town with some light industrial development. Below, near the entrance to the lovely Gwaun Valley, is Lower Town with its picturesque harbour made famous by the filming here of Dylan Thomas's *Under Milk Wood. Moby Dick* was also filmed in the area. Reminders of the last invasion of Britain (see Goodwick) are apparent around the town and the Royal Oak pub was the scene of the signing of the surrender documents. The sandy beach is backed by rocks and swimming is safe except when the tide is ebbing.

Cardigan
An historic market town at the mouth of the River Teifi, Cardigan was once a prominent port but is now mainly a boating and fishing centre.

Gwbert-on-Sea
The shingle beach gives way to sand at low-tide and can be dangerous for swimmers when the tide is ebbing.

Aberporth
The sheltered, sandy beaches are generally safe. Boat trips are available.

Llangranog
An attractive village in a steep valley leading to a sandy, rocky beach. Bathing is safe, provided the rocks are avoided.

New Quay
This quiet fishing town has gently sloping sandy beaches. New Quay is a popular sailing centre and boats are available for hire.

Aberaeron
A charming harbour town with shingle beaches, where some sand is exposed at low-tide, backed by attractive countryside.

Llanrhystud
Two mainly shingle beaches with low-tide sand. The northern shore is accessible only on foot.

Aberystwyth *see page 130*

ABERYSTWYTH

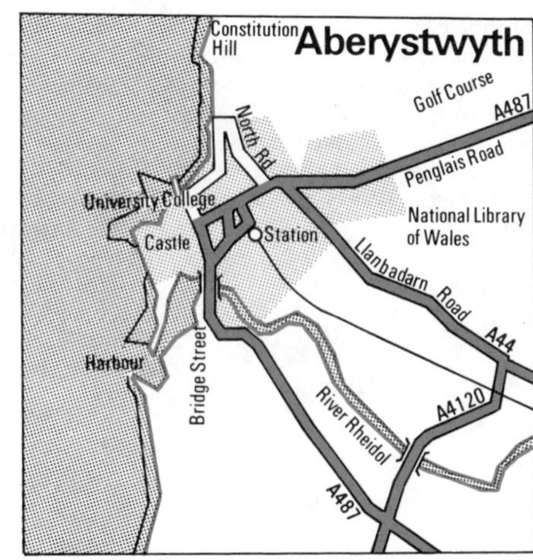

A popular holiday resort and University town, Aberystwyth has a history which can be traced back to 4,000BC. It is situated in an ideal position in the centre of the Welsh coastline with the whole country within motoring distance and offering amenities for almost all sports including angling, bowls, golf, putting, riding and tennis. There are some interesting buildings including the ruins of the 13th-century castle, the mid-19th-century Old University College on the seafront, the early-20th-century building housing the National Library of Wales and the modern Arts Centre. The University of Wales is located on the Penglais Hill Campus and it was here that Prince Charles studied in 1969. The castle stands on the promontory which divides the main beach from the Harbour beach. The Ceredigion Museum depicts all aspects of regional life and local crafts.

The beaches, mainly pebble, have patches of rock and shingle and the area adjoining the centre of the promenade is recommended for bathing. Lifeguards patrol the beach and warning flags are flown when it is dangerous to bathe. Alternatively there is the indoor pool at Plas Crug. The northern part of the town is shelterd by Constitution Hill and the summit, from which there is a fine view, can be reached by a cable railway. At the southern end of the town is the harbour, into which flow the Rivers Rheidol and Ystwyth, with its anchorage for pleasure craft and facilities for launching. For railway enthusiasts, a narrow-gauge railway runs from Aberystwyth to Devil's Bridge at the end of the Rheidol Valley, one of the beauty spots of Wales. There is hymn singing by the castle choir, at the castle, on Sunday evenings in summer.

Recreation and Sports

Aberystwyth Golf Club Brynmor ☎*615104*
Aberystwyth Sea Angling and Yacht Club The Harbour
Castle Grounds – Crazy-golf
Harbour – Fishing trips
Plus Crug – Bowls, indoor swimming pool and learner pool
Queens Road – Bowls, putting, tennis

Cinema

Commodore Bath St ☎*612421*

Theatre

Theatr Y Werin Penglais Campus ☎*4277*

Places of Interest

Arts Centre University Campus, Penglais
The Castle Marine Ter
Ceredigion Museum
National Library of Wales
Old University College Sea front
Vale of Rheidol Light Railway

Tourist Information

Tourism and Amenities 6 Park Ave ☎*617911 ex 254*
Wales Tourist Board Information Centre The Promenade (summer only) ☎*612125*

Accommodation

The following establishments are recommended by the AA. Further information may be obtained from the Tourist Information Office.

★★★	**Conrah** Chancery ☎*7941*
★★	**Belle Vue Royal** Marine Ter ☎*617558*
★★	**Seabank** Victoria Ter ☎*617617*
ⓐⓟ	**Groves** North Pde ☎*617435*
ⓐⓟ	**Marine** Marine Pde ☎*612444*
GH	**Four Seasons Hotel** 50–54 Portland St ☎*2236*
GH	**Glanaber Hotel** Union St ☎*7364*
GH	**Shangri-La** 36 Portland St ☎*7475*
GH	**Swn-y-Don** 40–42 North Pde ☎*2647*
GH	**Windsor Private Hotel** 41 Queens Rd ☎*7548*

Borth
A long sandy beach backed by shingle with rock pools at the southern end. The remains of a petrified forest are visible at low-tide, and Ynyslas Nature Reserve lies at the northern end of the beach.

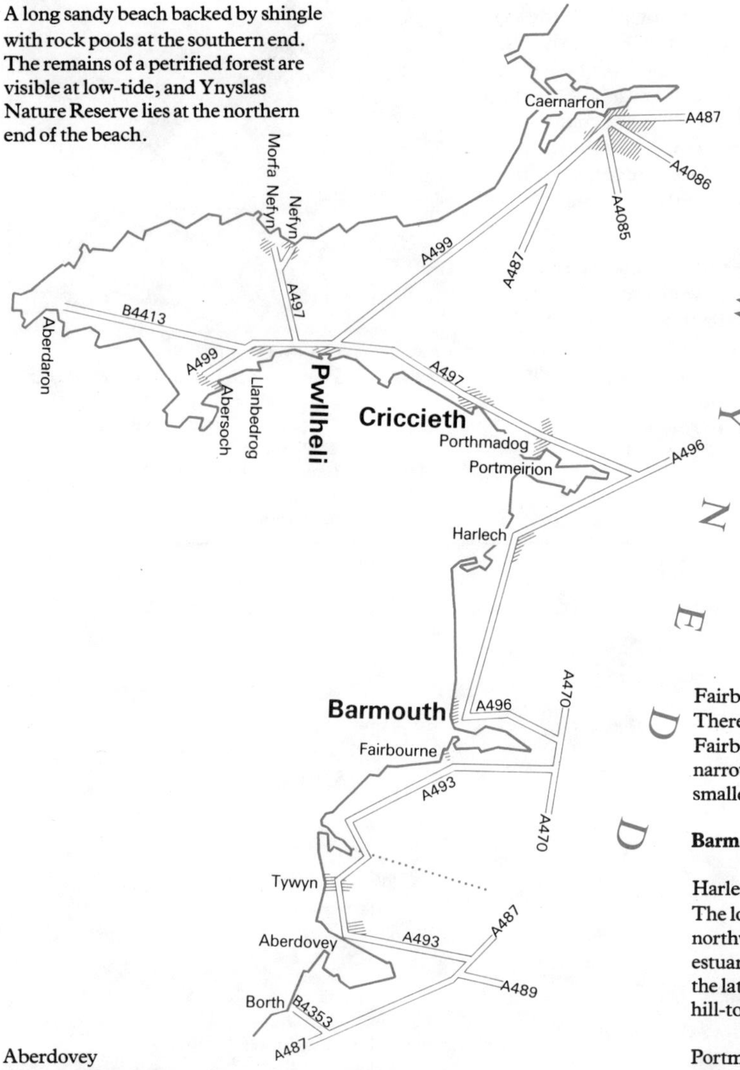

Aberdovey
This picturesque village has remained largely unspoilt despite its popularity with holidaymakers. There is a wide sandy beach which is safe for swimming provided the river estuary is avoided.

Tywyn
A popular resort with a long sweep of safe sandy beach. Tywyn is the terminus for the Talyllyn narrow-gauge railway and there is a railway museum in the station.

Fairbourne
There is a safe sandy beach here, but Fairbourne is better known for its narrow-gauge railway, which has the smallest track width in Wales.

Barmouth *see page 132*

Harlech
The long, sandy beach extends northwards to the River Glaslyn estuary. Harlech Castle, dating from the late 13th century, stands on a hill-top overlooking the shore.

Portmeirion
This Italian-style village built on a wooded peninsula was designed by Mr Clough Williams-Ellis. Visitors may tour this impressive estate, which featured in the television series *The Prisoner*, on payment of a toll.

Porthmadog
A market town and popular holiday resort. There are sandy coves to the east around Borth-y-Gêst. The oldest of the Welsh narrow-gauge railways operates from Porthmadog running inland through the Vale of Ffestiniog.

Criccieth *see page 133*

Pwllheli *see page 134*

Llanbedrog
This attractive village lies above a safe, sandy beach.

Abersoch
This popular, unspoilt resort has a safe, sandy beach and an exceptionally mild climate.

Aberdaron
A quiet, remote fishing village with a long, sheltered, sandy beach where the bathing is generally safe. Boat trips are available to Bardsey Island when conditions are suitable.

Morfa Nefyn
The long stretch of sandy beach offers safe bathing in the shelter of rugged headlands.

Nefyn
Two miles of safe sandy beach lie below 100 foot cliffs. There are rock pools on the eastern sands and boat trips are available.

Caernarfon
An ancient town dominated by its massive 13th-century castle where Prince Charles' investiture as Prince of Wales took place in 1969. A museum of Roman remains and a ruined Roman fort are open to the public.

BARMOUTH

The small picturesque resort of Barmouth stands on a strip of land beside the shores of Cardigan Bay overshadowed by the cliffs of the 870ft Garn Gorllwyn. The town lies huddled between the Rhinog Mountains and the sea with the quaint Old Town, at the back of the High Street, clinging to the slopes above the harbour with its pleasure craft and life-boat house. A fascinating jumble of steps and terraces, where the houses seem to be jostling one another for a precarious hold on the steep slopes, the town has a quiet charm but still offers the traditional attractions associated with the seaside. A spacious main promenade extends over the whole length of the seafront, said to be one of the finest on the Welsh coast. There are some two miles of sandy beach, but bathers must exercise caution because of a strong tidal race in the Mawddach estuary.

A feature of Barmouth is the half-mile-long wooden railway bridge which spans the estuary. A footpath alongside the bridge forms a promenade from which magnificient views of Friar's Island and The Mawddach may be obtained. Fine views are also available along Panorama Walk, a series of terraced paths overlooking the estuary. Beyond the Old Town lies Dinas Oleu, 4½ acres of cliffs where the National Trust acquired its first property in 1895. Across the estuary, some five minutes by ferry from the quayside to Penrhyn Point, is the Fairbourne narrow-gauge miniature railway, steam operated and 1½ miles long. Barmouth has facilities for boating and fishing and the golf clubs of Dolgellau and Harlech are only 10 miles away.

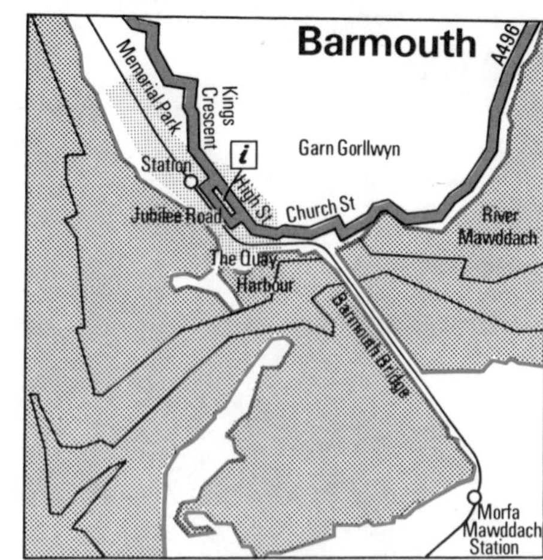

★★ **Cors-y-Gedol** ☎*280402*
★★ **Plas Mynach** Llanaber Rd ☎*280252*
(AP) **Min-Y-Mor** Promenade ☎*280555*
(AP) **Ty'r Craig Castle** Llanaber Rd ☎*280470*
GH **Lawrenny Lodge** ☎*280466*
GH **Morwendon** Llanaber (1m N A496) ☎*280566*

Recreation and Sports

Beach – Bathing huts, chalets, and deck chairs for hire
Memorial Park – Bowls, children's amusements, putting, tennis
Merioneth Yacht Club The Quay ☎*280000*

Theatre

The Dragon Theatre Jubilee Rd (performances of music and drama by professional companies and local amateurs)

Places of Interest

Ty Crwn The Quay – Old Lock-up
Ty Gwyn The Quay – Building reputed to have been built for Henry VII when, as Henry Tudor, Earl of Richmond, he landed to begin his campaign against Richard III

Tourist Information

Tourist Information Centre The Promenade ☎*280787*

Accommodation

The following establishments are recommended by the AA. Further information may be obtained from the Tourist Information Office.

CRICCIETH

Criccieth lies on the shores of Tremadoc Bay, cradled in the coastline of the Lleyn Peninsula. An attractive, compact resort built on a slope descending to the sea, Criccieth was first made popular by the Victorians in the 19th century. The town is a mixture of Victorian buildings interspersed with older cottages and has fine views of the Snowdon range of mountains to the north, especially from the castle ruins. The ruins of Criccieth Castle, on its rocky headland, dominate the surrounding area. Set on what is reputed to have been the site of fortifications since pre-Roman times, the castle itself dates from the 13th century when it was captured and strengthened by Edward I. In 1933 it was placed under the guardianship of the government and is now cared for by the Department of the Environment.

The sea front consists of two short promenades divided by the castle ruins. Two sand and pebble beaches, The Esplanade and Marine Terrace, each offering safe bathing, lie to the east and west of the headland. Criccieth is a centre for both freshwater and sea angling and also has facilities for golf, sailing and tennis. Licences are required for river fishing and details of how to apply for these may be obtained from the Tourist Association.

B4411
Golf Course
A497
Caernarfon Road
Memorial Hall
Porthmadog Road
Pwllheli Road
High St
Criccieth Station
Castle
Black Rock Station
Tremadog Bay
Criccieth

Recreation and Sports

Footpath behind Railway Station leading to – Bowls, children's playground, mini-golf
Golf Club ☎ *2154*
Memorial Hall – Concerts and dancing

Places of Interest

The Lloyd George Museum
Llanystumdwy, nr Criccieth (1½m from Criccieth)

Tourist Information

The Secretary, Criccieth Tourist Association ☎ *2888*
(An information caravan is also located on The Green at the entrance to the car park during June, July and August).

Accommodation

The following establishments are recommended by the AA. Further information may be obtained from the Tourist Information Office.

★★★	**Bron Eifion Country House** ☎ *2293*
★★	**George IV** ☎ *2168*
★★	**Lion** Y Maes ☎ *2460*
★★	**Marine** Marine Cres ☎ *2409*
★★	**Parclau Mawr** High St ☎ *2368*
★★	**Plas Gwyn** Pentrefelin (1m NE A497) ☎ *2559*
★	**Bondlondeb** Porthmadog Rd ☎ *2249*
★	**Caerwylan** ☎ *2547*
★	**Henfaes** Porthmadog Rd ☎ *2396*
(ap)	**Bron Aber** Pwllheli Rd ☎ *2539*
(ap)	**Glyn-y-Coed** Porthmadog Rd ☎ *2870*
(ap)	**Min-y-Gaer** Porthmadog Rd ☎ *2151*
GH	**Mor Heli Private Hote** ☎ *2794*
GH	**Neptune Private Hotel** ☎ *2878*
SC	Mrs Broadley, **Vista Marina** 30 Marine Ter, Criccieth ☎ *2139*
SC	Mr A Murray, **Clifton House** 27 Marine Ter, Criccieth ☎ *2220*

PWLLHELI

Pwllheli, a small harbour resort and market town, has a history as a Welsh borough dating back to the 14th century when it received its charter from the Black Prince. Hundreds of years ago its fine natural harbour was the only port in the area and in the days of the tall ships it had considerable importance. Ships were built there and the harbour was filled with ocean-going and coastal vessels. Today the harbour affords a safe anchorage for pleasure boats. Recently its importance as the main town of the Lleyn Penisnsula has somewhat overshadowed its role as a resort.

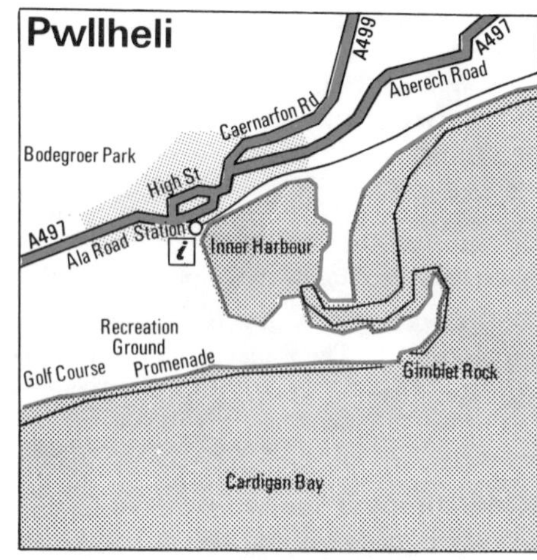

Sheltered by a semi-circle of mountains, Pwllheli enjoys a mild climate and offers safe bathing. The three crescent-shaped beaches are extensive and consist of sand and shingle. A broad promenade about a mile in length runs along the sea front between South Beach and West End. The old town, about half a mile from the sea, is the shopping and business centre. Pwllheli has facilities for freshwater and sea angling, golf and pony trekking. It is a centre for sailing, water-skiing and powerboats and fishing trips are available around Cardigan Bay.

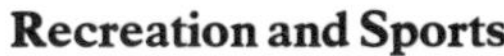

Recreation and Sports

Marina Boat Club Marinaland, Outer Harbour ☎*2271*
Pwllheli Golf Club ☎*2520*
Pwllheli Sailing Club Gimblet Rock ☎*2219*
Pwllheli Sports Club Bodegroes Park, Efail Newydd ☎*3676*
Recreation Ground – Bowls, tennis

Cinema

Palladium ☎*2892*

Places of Interest

Penlan Fawr Inn Penlan Street – Inn dating from 13th century

Tourist Information

Information Kiosk Station Sq ☎*2044*

Accommodation

The following establishment is recommended by the AA. Further information may be obtained from the Tourist Information Office.

GH **Seahaven Hotel** West End Pde ☎*2572*

Aberffraw
A quiet resort with a good beach flanked by sand dunes.

Rhosneigr
This former fishing village is now a popular holiday centre with a long, safe sandy beach dotted with outcrops of rock. Boat trips are available.

Holyhead
The largest town on the Isle of Anglesey and the main ferry terminal for Irish steamers and ferries. There is a shingle beach and boats are available for hire.

Cemaes Bay
A fishing village with a sheltered, sandy beach which is completely covered at high-tide.

Amlwch
This former copper-mining town has an old harbour set in a narrow rocky cleft and a sandy beach where rock pools are revealed at low-tide.

Benllech
A popular but unspoilt resort with a long, shelving sandy beach.

Red Wharf Bay
There are extensive sands here, backed by wooded hills. Bathing is safe, but the ebbing tide creates strong currents.

Beaumaris
An ancient town which has become the boating centre of the Menai Straits. The shingle beach gives way to sand at low-tide and there are strong currents.

Bangor
A busy university town with many places of interest. There is a mainly shingle beach and amusements and entertainments are available.

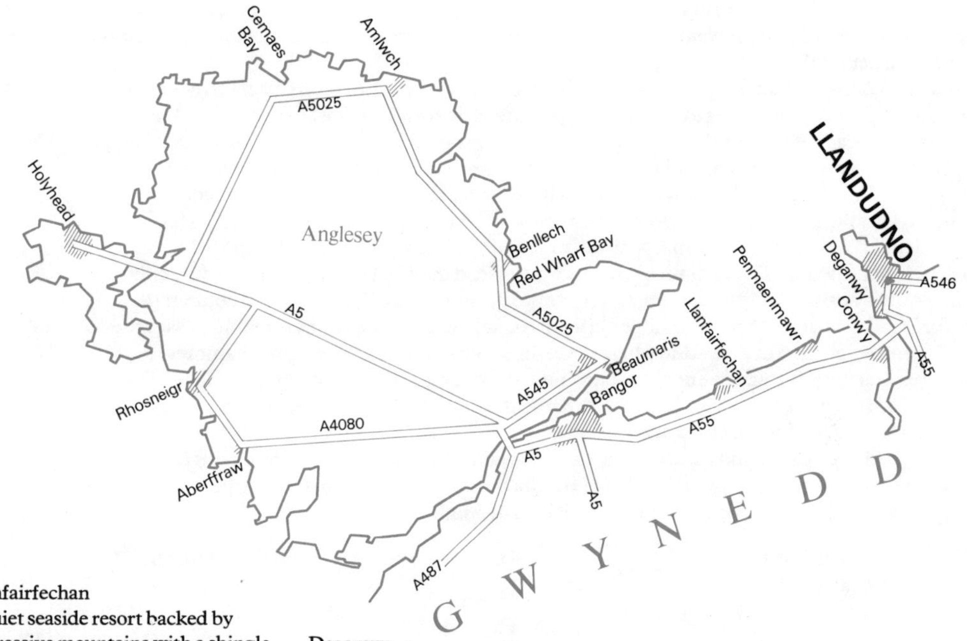

Llanfairfechan
A quiet seaside resort backed by impressive mountains with a shingle beach where extensive sands are exposed at low-tide.

Penmaenmawr
This busy port has a fine sandy beach backed by shingle. Amusements are available.

Conwy
Conwy stands guard over the estuary of the River Conwy, presenting the visitor with an almost perfect example of a medieval fortified borough, set against a backdrop of wooded hills. The well-preserved castle was established by Edward I in the late 13th century and the old town walls, incorporating twenty-one towers, can also be visited. Sandy Morfa Beach to the north-west, provides safe swimming. River trips are available and local events include the Seed Fair in March and the Honey Fair in September.

Deganwy
This old town is now a popular sailing centre. There is a sandy beach and bathing is safe provided the mouth of the River Conwy is avoided.

LLANDUDNO *see page 136*

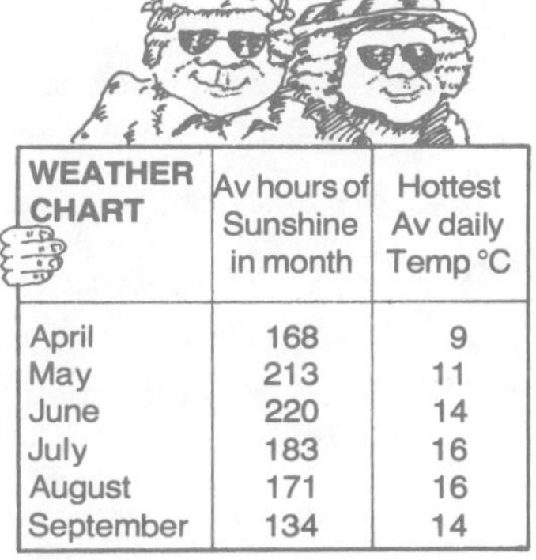

WEATHER CHART	Av hours of Sunshine in month	Hottest Av daily Temp °C
April	168	9
May	213	11
June	220	14
July	183	16
August	171	16
September	134	14

LLANDUDNO

Prior to the middle of the 19th century Llandudno was little more than a cluster of cottages between two headlands. It was then decided to develop the area as a holiday resort with results which border on the spectacular.

Broad promenades and boulevards follow the sweep of the bay, between Great Ormes Head and Little Ormes Head, overlooked by rows of Edwardian and Victorian buildings. The town's two beaches lie on either side of Great Ormes Head. Maine Shore, within Ormes Bay, is a pleasure beach in every sense of the word – two miles of safe sand. Boat trips run from the jetty and a Punch and Judy Show, presented by members of the same family for over a hundred years, gives regular performances on the sea front. West Shore, generally less crowded, is backed by sand dunes with only a café and children's play area imposed upon nature's handiwork. The summit of Great Ormes Head may be reached either by funicular railway or by cable railway, the longest passenger lift in Britain. The headland contains a nature trail. Marine Drive, accessible via a toll road, provides splendid views and passes the 17th-century church of St Tudno where open-air services are held during the summer. A summer Carnival is staged annually including arena events and folk dancing displays. The Rappallo House Museum stands among ornamental gardens and contains a traditional Welsh kitchen and collections of china and glassware.

Touring areas in the vicinity include the historic walled town of Conwy with its huge 13th-century castle, the varied delights of the Snowdonia National Park or the possibility of a trip across the Menai Bridge to explore the island of Anglesey.

Recreation and Sports

I	**Craig-y-don** – Bowls, tennis
A	**Great Ormes Head** – Children's playground, pitch and putt
F	**Gwynedd Road** – Kiddies Funland
B(1)	**Happy Valley Gardens** – Children's playground, mini-golf
A	**Haulfre Gardens** – Mini-golf
G	**Llandudno Golf Club (Maesdu)**, ☎76016
E	**Llandudno Sailing Club** ☎76083
E	**Llandudno Swimming Pool** Mostyn Broadway, ☎78838 – Indoor pool
B	**Marine Drive** – Children's playground
G	**North Wales Golf Club** West Shore, ☎75325
D	**Oval** – Bowls, cricket, tennis
B	**Pier** – Amusements, fishing, pleasure cruises
F	**Seafront (East)** – Children's playground, mini-golf, paddling pool
B	**Seafront (North)** – Bandstand, donkey rides, Punch and Judy
	West Shore – Children's playground, model yacht pond, pony rides, putting.

Cabaret/Dancing

B	**Dolphin Bar** Llandudno Pier
D	**Winter Gardens** Gloddaeth St, ☎77626

Cinemas

D	**Astra** Gloddaeth St, ☎76666
E	**Palladium** Gloddaeth St, ☎76244
E	**Savoy** Mostyn St, ☎76398

Theatres

F	**Arcadia** ☎76570
F	**Grand** Mostyn Broadway, ☎77327
B	**Happy Valley Open Air Theatre** ☎75649
B	**Pier Pavilion** ☎75259

Places of Interest

E(2)	**Doll Museum and Model Railway** Masonic St
I(3)	**Rapallo House Museum** Fferm Bach Rd, ☎76517
	St Tudno's Church, Great Ormes Head

Touring Information

[i]E	**Main Tourist Information Centre** 1–2 Chapel St, ☎76413
[i]B	**Seafront Tourist Information Centre** ☎76572 (Summer only)

Accommodation

The establishments listed below are a selection of AA-recommended accommodation located in the area covered by the Town Plan. Further information may be found in AA Publications.

1SC	Mrs McVey, **Augusta Holiday Flats** 7 Augusta St, Llandudno, Gwynedd ☎78330
2GH	**Bella Vista Private Hotel** 72 Church Walks ☎76855
3GH	**Braemar Hotel** St David's Rd ☎76257
4GH	**Brigstock Private Hotel** 1 St Davids Place ☎76416
5Ⓟ	**Bron Orme** Church Walks ☎76735
6GH	**Buile Hill Private Hotel** St Mary's Rd ☎76972
7★★	**Clarence** Gloddaeth St ☎76485
8GH	**Cleave Court Private Hotel** 1 St Seiriols Rd ☎77849
9GH	**Cliffbury Private Hotel** 34 St Davids Rd ☎77224
10★	**Clontarf** West Shore ☎77621
11GH	**Cornerways Private Hotel** 2 St Davids Place ☎77334
12GH	**Craig Ard Private Hotel** Arvon Av ☎77318
13★	**Cranleigh** Gt Ormes Rd ☎77688
14GH	**Cumberland Hotel** North Pde ☎76379
15★★★	**Empire** Church Walks ☎77260
16Ⓟ	**Esplanade** Prom ☎76687
17★	**Gwesty Leamore** 40 Lloyd St ☎75552
18★	**Headlands** Hill Ter ☎77485
19GH	**Heatherdale** 30 St Davids Rd ☎77362
20★★★	**Hydro** Prom ☎77241
21★★★	**Imperial** The Prom ☎77466
22GH	**Lynwood Private Hotel** Clonmel St ☎76613
23★★★	**Marine** Prom ☎77521
24★	**Min-y-Don** North Pde ☎76511
25GH	**Montclare** North Pde ☎77061
26★★	**Ormescliffe** Prom ☎77191
27★	**Osborne** North Pde ☎77087
28SC	**The Penthouse** 17A Bodafon St, for bookings Mrs McVey, Augusta Holiday Flats, 7 Augusta St, Llandudno, Gwynedd ☎78330
29GH	**Plas Madoc Private Hotel** 60 Church Walks ☎76514
30★	**Ravenshurst** West Pde ☎75525
31★	**Richmond** St Georges Pl ☎76347
32GH	**Rosaire Private Hotel** 2 St Seiriols Rd ☎77677

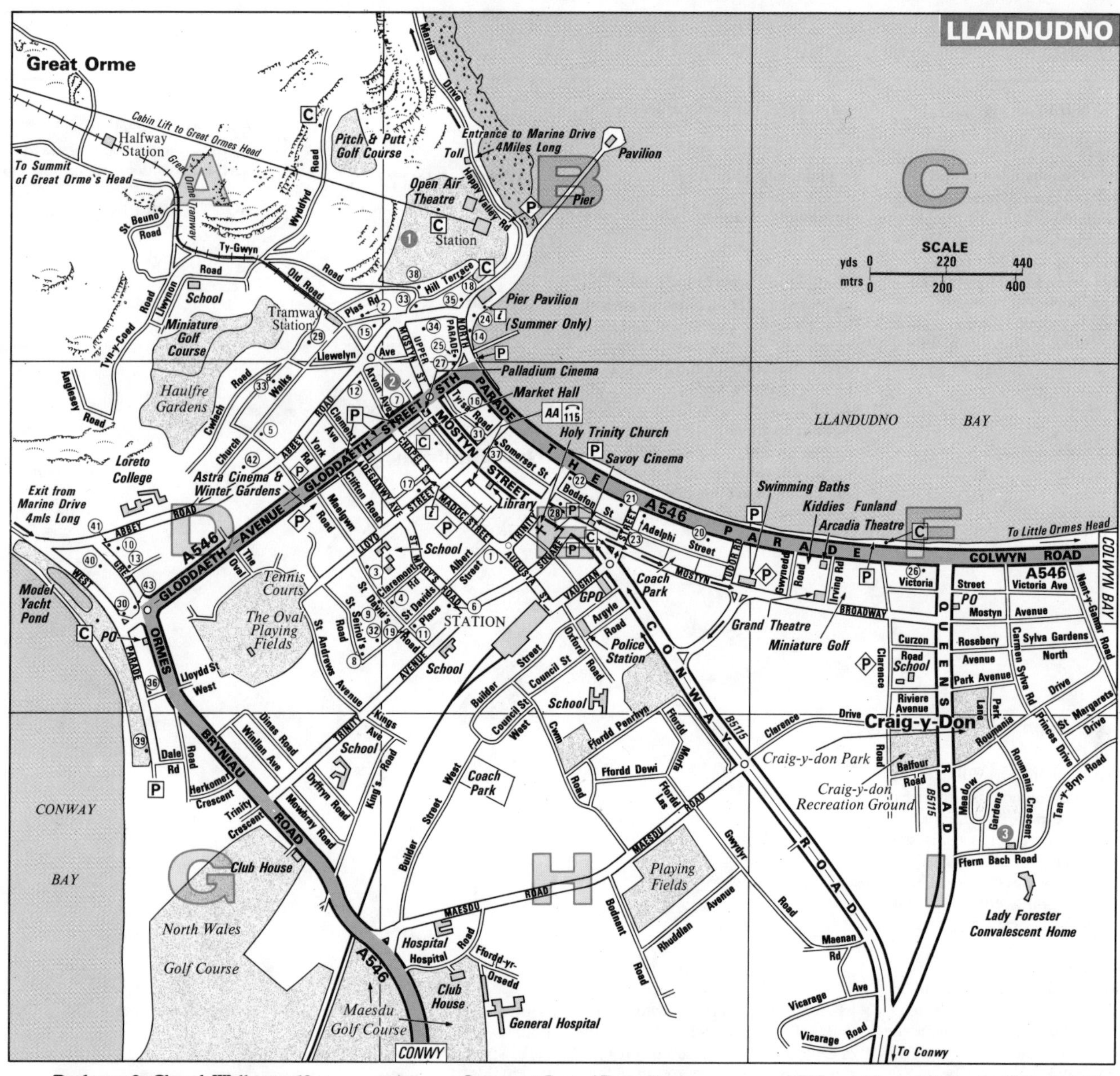

33★ **Rothesay** 83 Church Walks ☎*76844*
33a★★ **Royal** Church Walks ☎*76476*
34★★★ **St Georges** Prom ☎*77544*
35★ **St Tudno** North Pde ☎*76309*
36GH **Sandilands Private Hotel** Dale Rd ☎*75555*
37★ **Somerset** Central Prom ☎*76540*
38★ **Southcliffe** Hill Ter ☎*76277*
39Ⓡ **Sunnymede** West Pde ☎*77130*
40GH **Tan Lan** Great Ormes Rd, West Shore ☎*75981*
41GH **Tan-y-Marian** 87 Abbey Rd, West Shore ☎*77727*
42GH **Westdale Private Hotel** 37 Abbey Rd ☎*77996*
43GH **West Shore Hotel** Great Ormes Rd ☎*76833*

COLWYN BAY *see page 140*

Pensarn

This quiet resort, now a suburb of Abergele, has a steep beach of shingle with sands exposed at low-tide. It was here that the famous Captain Webb trained for his successful cross-Channel swim, the first ever to be achieved, in 1875. The short promenade provides amusements and there are donkey rides along the beach.

Rhyl *see page 139*

Prestatyn *see page 142*

Flint

Once a prominent port, Flint lost its trade when the extensive silting up of the River Dee made its continued use impossible. Now an industrial town, its main feature is its ruined castle overlooking the Dee estuary. There is a modern shopping centre and good indoor and outdoor sporting facilities.

West Kirby

Overlooking the wide estuary of the River Dee, West Kirby enjoys fine views over this stretch of water to the hills of North Wales. There are extensive sands which can be dangerous when the tide is coming in due to deep channels. A man-made embankment encloses the thirty-two acres of the Marine Lake which provides boating and sailing facilities and there is a children's paddling pool.

Hoylake *see page 143*

New Brighton *see page 146*

Liverpool

This great city with its long and impressive seafaring traditions is now Britain's second largest port and the premier transatlantic port in Europe. Seven miles of docks and quays line the shore and, backed by such buildings as the Royal Liver and Cunard, create a most distinctive skyline. Steamer trips along the Mersey are available. This one-time fishing village saw a period of rapid development during the 18th century when the quays were lined with the great sailing vessels which traded out of Liverpool. The romanticism of those days of sail lingers on amid the modern development and industrial diversification. The city is also a major centre for shopping, commerce and culture. Its museums and art galleries are second to none and there is music of every kind from the Philharmonic to the humblest folk club. Sport, too, plays an important part in this, the home of the Grand National at Aintree. There are over three thousand acres of parks and gardens in Liverpool and the many places of interest include the 16th-century, half-timbered Speke Hall.

Crosby

A long sandy beach extends northwards, backed by sand dunes. There is an indoor swimming pool.

SOUTHPORT *see page 144*

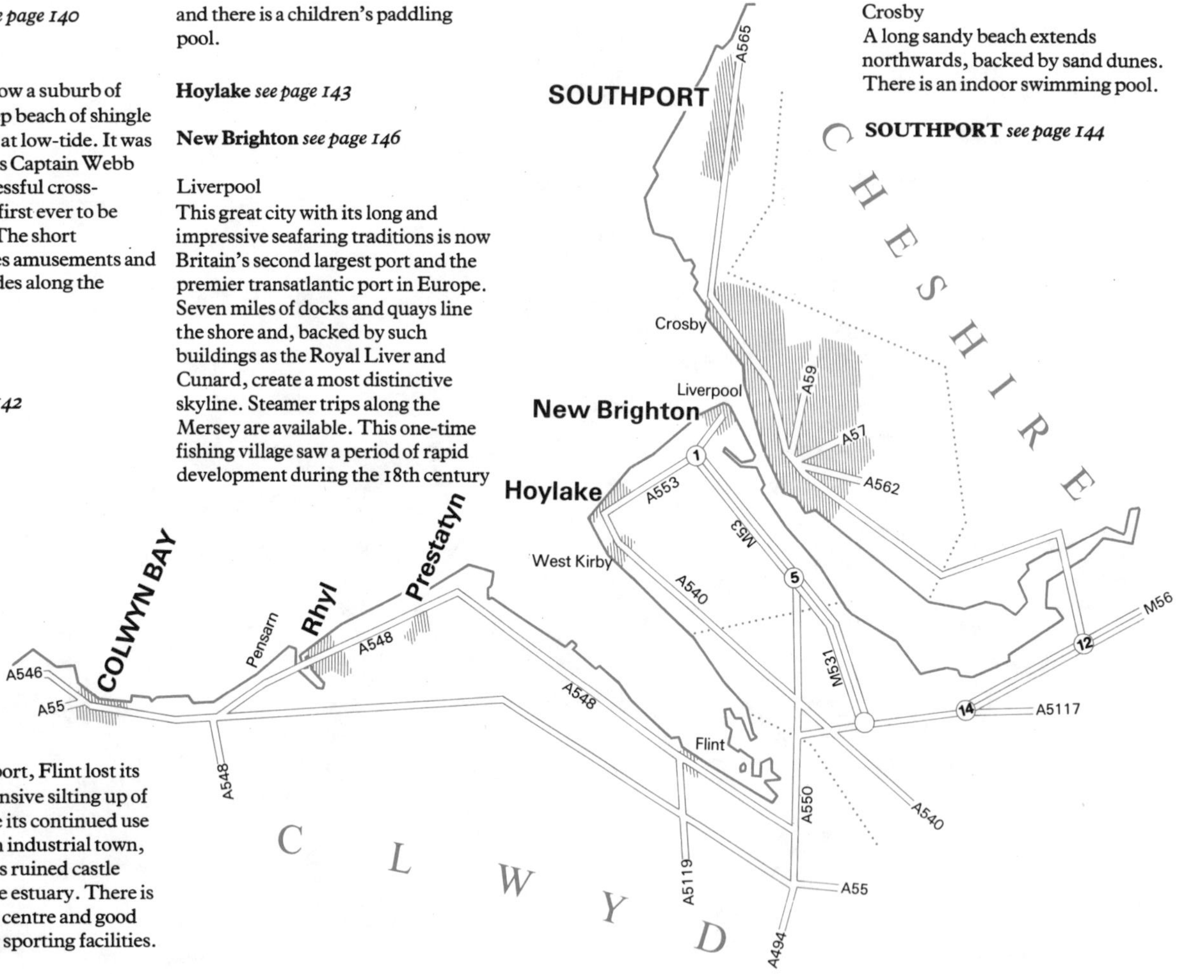

RHYL

Developed from a few fishermen's cottages into a very popular seaside resort, Rhyl has several miles of golden sand, which is generally safe for bathing with the exception of the area near the harbour, at the mouth of the River Clwyd, where there are fast currents. In fact before venturing into the sea it is advisable to read the notices and familiarise oneself with the instructions to swim within the areas patrolled by lifeguards. Children are well catered for with various types of boats for hire, donkey rides, go-karts, Skateworld for roller-skating and skateboarding, cycle track, paddling pools and trampolines. Rhyl also has facilities for all types of sporting activities.

There are pleasant gardens, notably the Royal Floral Hall with its wealth of sub-tropical plants, and the Botanical Gardens with its lawns and flowerbeds.

Just south of the town on the bank of the River Clwyd is 13th-century Rhuddlan Castle built by Edward I.

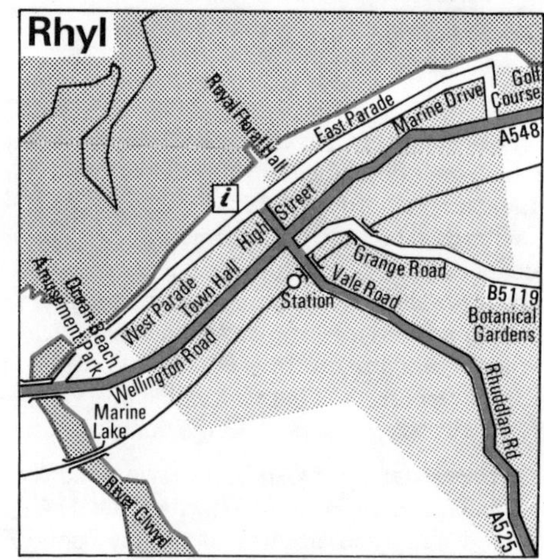

Recreation and Sports

Botanical Gardens – Bowls, putting, tennis
East Promenade – Bowls, pitch and putt
Marine Lake Leisure Park – Amusements, boating lake, go-karts, miniature steam railway
Ocean Beach – Amusement Park
Rhyl Golf Club Coast Rd – 9 holes
Rhyl Yacht Club Foryd Harbour ☎*4365*
Sport and Recreation Centre – Indoor heated pool, learner pool and sports facilities
West Promenade – Children's boating lake, children's cycle track, paddling pool, putting, Skateworld

Cinemas

Astra 1, 2 and 3 High St
Plaza High St ☎*53442*

Theatres

Coliseum Theatre West Prom ☎*51126*
Gaiety Theatre East Prom ☎*51251*
Little Theatre Vale Rd ☎*2229*

Places of Interest

Botanical Gardens
Floral Hall

Tourist Information

Tourist Information Centre Town Hall, Wellington Rd ☎*31515*

Accommodation

The following establishments are recommended by the AA. Further information may be obtained from the Tourist Information Office.

★★ **Westminster** East Pde ☎*2241*
GH **Anchorage** 25 Seabank Rd ☎*50698*
GH **Ashurst Private Hotel** 7 Seabank Rd ☎*50417*
GH **Ingledene Hotel** 6 Bath St ☎*4872*
GH **Pier Hotel** 23 East Pde ☎*50280*
GH **Toomargoed Private Hotel** 31–33 John St ☎*4103*

COLWYN BAY

The borough of Colwyn Bay has been gradually established, over the last century, on land which once contained no more than a manor house, three farms and a few cottages. Landscaped gardens, which have twice won the town 'Wales in Bloom' awards, lie behind the sheltered sands and long promenade presenting the visitor with a colourful and largely unspoiled resort which is also one of the largest towns in North Wales. Donkey and pony rides are available on the clean, safe sands and there are plentiful amusements on the pier. A large funfair adjoins the promenade and boating, a children's playground and Dinosaur world where a miniature railway operates, bowls and tennis are available in Eirias Park together with a large restaurant. There is a varied programme of entertainment and Rhos-on-Sea has a fine open-air swimming pool. Opportunities exist for fishing, golf, sailing and pony-trekking.

On the western outskirts of the town is the Welsh Mountain Zoo, containing a large variety of animals, and the Botanical Gardens. Daily falconry displays and a penguin pool which allows underwater observation are two of the Zoo's unusual features. St Trillo's Chapel, the smallest in Wales measuring only 12ft by 6ft, stands above the beach at Rhos-on-Sea, built on the site of an ancient well. Regular services are still held there.

Local beauty spots include Pwll-y-Crochan Woods, the Fairy Glen at Dwygyfylchi at the foot of the Sychnant Pass and the National Trust property of Bodnant Gardens. To the east lies Gwrych Castle, a fortress of many towers and battlements established in the early 19th century. The grounds are open to the public and medieval jousting and archery displays are staged here. Pony rides, a miniature railway and a restaurant are also available. Other touring areas include Conwy, Snowdonia and the castles of Beaumaris and Rhuddlan.

Recreation and Sports

A **Colwyn Bay Cricket Club** Rhos-on-Sea ☎*44103*
K/O **Eirias Park**–Boating, bowls, children's playground, Dinosaur World, model yachting, sports arena, tennis
J **Happy Hour Pleasure Park** Victoria Ave–Amusements, funfair
L **Min-y-don Park**–Bowls, putting, tennis
P **Old Colwyn Golf Club**☎*55581*
A **Rhos-on-Sea Golf Club** Penrhyn Bay ☎*Llandudno49641* W off Marine Drive
A **Rhos-on-Sea Recreation Ground**–Bowls, tennis
A **Rhos-on-Sea Swimming Pool** Rhos Promenade ☎*44113*–Outdoor pool, sauna, solarium, squash
J **Victoria Pier**–Amusements

Cabaret/Dancing

J **Dixieland Showbar** Victoria Pier
O **4 Oaks Restaurant** Eirias Park ☎*30478*

Cinemas

E **Astra Entertainment Centre** Conwy Rd ☎*30803*
J **Princes** Princes Dr ☎*2557*
J **Wedgwood Cinema** Princes Drive ☎*2765*

Theatres

A **Harlequin Puppet Theatre** Rhos-on-Sea ☎*48166*
J **Prince of Wales Theatre** Abergele Rd ☎*2668*

Places of Interest

K(1) **Civic Centre**
J(2) **Library**
A(3) **St Trillo's Chapel**
I(4) **Welsh Mountain Zoo**

Tourist Information

[i]J **Information Bureau** ☎*30478*
A **Information Bureau** Rhos-on-Sea ☎*48778*

Accommodation

The establishments listed below are a selection of AA-recommended accommodation located in the area covered by the Town Plan. Further information may be found in AA publications or obtained from the Information Bureau.

1GH **Brompton Lodge Hotel** Rhos-on-Sea ☎*44784*
2GH **Cabin Hill Private Hotel** College Ave, Rhos-on-Sea ☎*44568*
3GH **Clevedon Private Hotel** Hawarden Rd ☎*2368*
4(ap) **Commodore** Conwy Rd ☎*2720*
5(ap) **Edelweiss** Lawson Rd ☎*2314*
6GH **Green Lawns** 14 Bay View Rd ☎*2207*
7★★ **Hopeside** Princes Dr ☎*30328*
9(ap) **Marine** West Prom ☎*30295*
11SC **Nant-y-Glyn Hall, Garden Cottages**. For bookings: Nant-y-Glyn Hall Ltd, Colwyn Bay, Clwyd ☎*Llanddulas212*
12SC **Nant-y-Glyn Hall, Tree Tops**. For Bookings: Nant-y-Glyn Hall Ltd, Colwyn Bay, Clwyd ☎*Llanddulas212*
13★★★ **Norfolk House** Princes Dr ☎*31757*
14★★★ **Rhos Abbey** 111 Rhos Prom ☎*46601*
15★ **St Enoch's** Prom ☎*2031*
16(ap) **St Margarets** Princes Dr ☎*2718*
17GH **Southlea** 4 Upper Prom ☎*2004*
18GH **West Mains Private Hotel** Trillo Ave, Rhos-on-Sea ☎*44664*
19GH **Whitehall Hotel** Cayley Prom, Rhos-on-Sea ☎*47296*

WEATHER CHART	Av hours of Sunshine in month	Hottest Av daily Temp °C
April	168	9
May	212	11
June	217	14
July	184	16
August	171	16
September	134	14

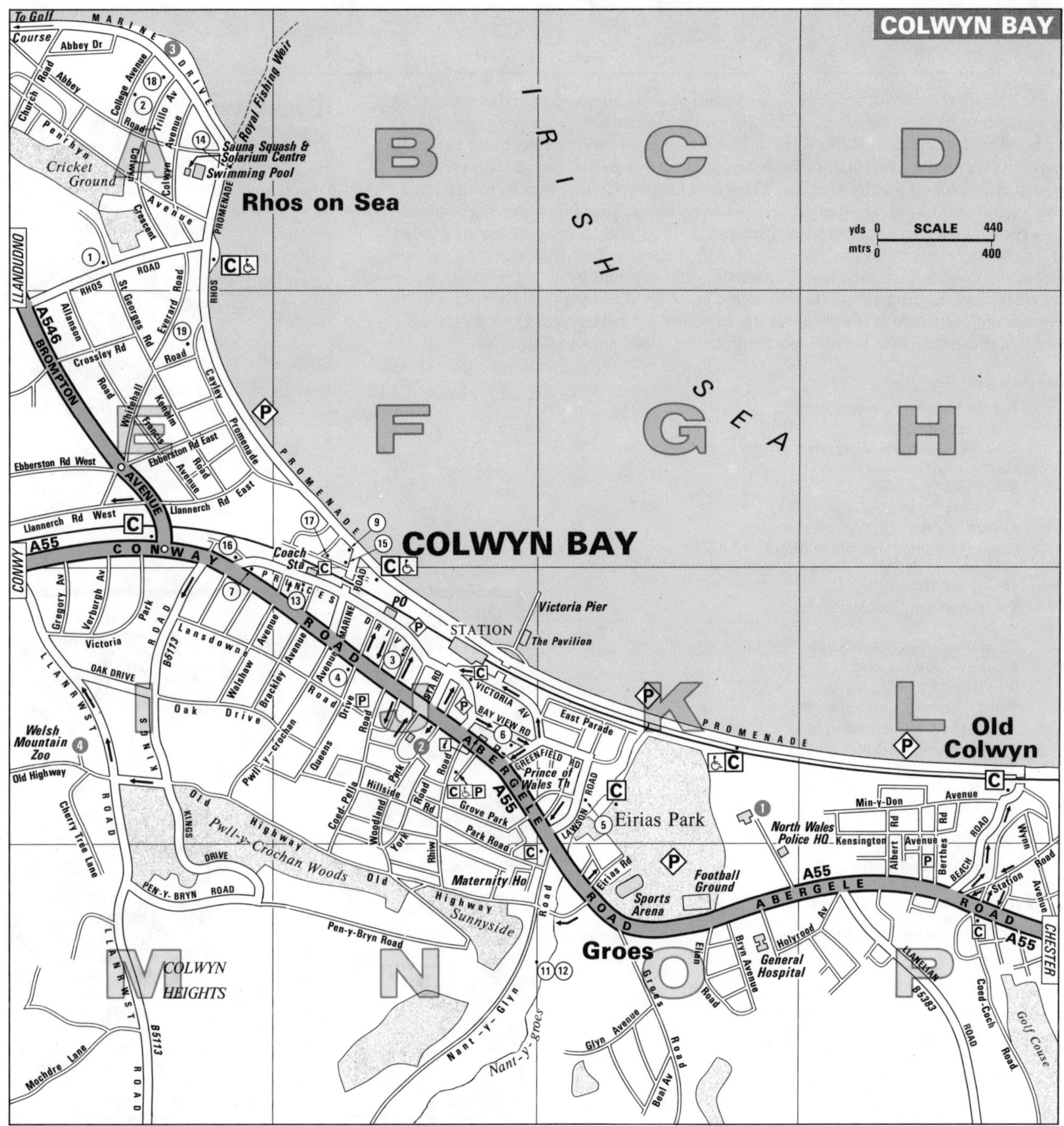
COLWYN BAY
Rhos on Sea
COLWYN BAY
Old Colwyn
Groes
IRISH SEA
Cricket Ground
Sauna Squash & Solarium Centre
Swimming Pool
Royal Fishing Weir
Victoria Pier
The Pavilion
STATION
Coach Sta
PO
Welsh Mountain Zoo
Prince of Wales Th
Eirias Park
North Wales Police HQ
Football Ground
Sports Arena
General Hospital
Maternity Ho
Pwll-y-Crochan Woods
Sunnyside
COLWYN HEIGHTS
Golf Course
To Golf Course
LLANDUDNO
CONWY
CHESTER
yds 0 SCALE 440
mtrs 0 400
A55
A546
B5113
B5383

PRESTATYN

A popular holiday resort with a background of steep wooded hills at the northern end of Offa's Dyke, an earth-work which was built in the 8th century to mark the boundary between England and Wales. To the east, the three-mile-long sandy beach stretches as far as the Point of Air with its lighthouse, and offers safe bathing at most times. Red flags are flown when safety patrols consider it unwise to bathe. The Royal Lido, at Central Beach, has a large open-air heated swimming pool and the sports centre has facilities for most indoor sports. Outdoor sports are well catered for with amenities for mini-golf, crazy-golf, putting, bowls, tennis, cricket, football and rugby. The sailing club at Barkby Beach has a jetty for launching pleasure craft. Boating and canoe lakes, a miniature railway, children's playground, go-karts, donkey rides, amusement parks and a fairground are to be found at Ffrith Beach. Band concerts are regularly held in the town during the summer. Gwaenysgor Church, one mile south-east of the town, has some noteable features and is well worth a visit.

Recreation and Sports

Barkby Beach – Pitch and putt, pleasure craft launching
Central Beach – Paddling pool
Coronation Gardens Station Rd – Bowls, putting
Ffrith Beach Entertainment Centre – Crazy-golf, golf, go-karts, miniature train, motor boats, picnic area, pitch and putt, play area
Gronant Road – Tennis
Prestatyn Golf Club Marine Rd East ☎*4320*
Prestatyn Sailing Club Barkby Beach
Roundwood Avenue Meliden – Bowls
The Royal Lido Central Beach – Boating, entertainment, outdoor heated swimming pool
St Melyd Golf Club Meliden (9 hole) ☎*4405*
Sports and Recreation Centre Princes Ave – Most indoor sports, tennis

Cinema

Scala High St ☎*4365*

Tourist Information

Information Centre Nant Hall Rd ☎*2484*

Accommodation

The following establishments are recommended by the AA. Further information may be obtained from the Tourist Information Office.

GH **Bryn Gwalia** 17 Granant Rd ☎*2442*
SC Pontin's Ltd, **Prestatyn Holiday Village** Central Beach ☎*2267*

Situated on the north coast of the Wirral Peninsula, this residential seaside town was originally a busy port for traffic to Ireland and it was from here that William III set sail in 1690. The air is bracing, the long sandy beach is washed by the Irish Sea and there is an attractive two-mile-long promenade. There are parks and gardens which have facilities for bowls, putting, tennis and swimming. Picturesque Market Street is the main shopping area.

To the west of the town, in the north-west corner of the peninsula, is the famous Royal Liverpool Golf Course. Neighbouring Red Rocks is an ideal picnic spot.

For the ornithologist, the islands in the Dee estuary at West Kirby are well worth a visit and can be reached on foot when the tide is ebbing. The only inhabitants are seabirds and, on Hilbre, seals. Permits to land can be obtained from Leisure Services, 8 Riversdale Road, West Kirby *tel* 625 9441.

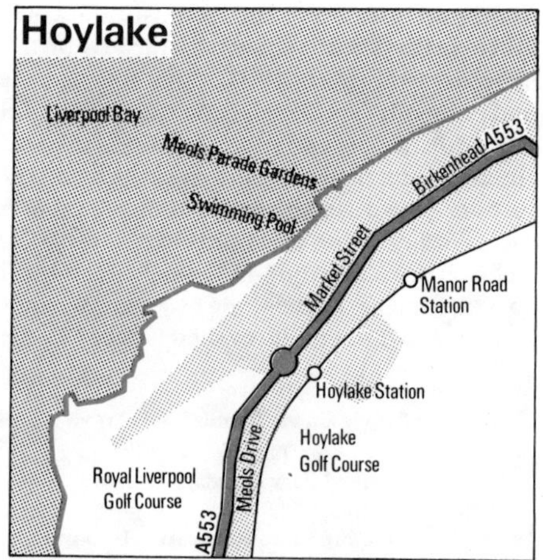

Recreation and Sports

Hoylake Sailing Club Parade ☎*632 2616*
Meols Parade Gardens – Bowls, putting, tennis
Municipal Golf Course Carr Ln ☎*632 2956*
North Parade – Open-air swimming pool
Queens Park – Bowls, putting, tennis
Royal Liverpool Golf Club Meols Dr ☎*632 3101*

Cinema

Classic Alderley Rd ☎*632 1345*

Tourist Information

Public Relations Officer Town Hall, Brighton St, Wallasey ☎*632 8488*

Accommodation

The following establishments are recommended by the AA. Further information may be obtained from the Tourist Information Office.

★★ **Stanley** Kings Gap ☎*632 3311*
GH **Sandtoft Hotel** 70 Alderley Rd ☎*632 2204*

Restaurant

✕ **Bistro 2** 36 Market St ☎*632 5101*

SOUTHPORT

Southport offers the visitor some six miles of fine sand, backed by dunes. The beach is so large and firm that vehicles may park directly on the sands near the base of the dunes. Swimmers should use the prescribed bathing area patrolled by lifeguards during the summer. Donkey and pony rides are available on the sands and children's sports and competitions are organised there during July and August. Most of the traditional seaside amusements are concentrated in the area immediately inland from the pier. The 86-acre Marine Lake has all kinds of boats for hire and is also used for water-skiing demonstrations and races, including a 24-hour dinghy race. An airstrip on the shore near the esplanade is used for pleasure flights and an electric railway runs along the ¾-mile-long pier. The Floral Hall and Southport Theatre provide a varied, constantly-changing programme ranging from wrestling to shows by international stars and are renowned for their conference facilities.

Recreation and Sports

K	**Argyle Lawn Tennis Club** Argyle Rd ☎*30132*–Championship Tennis
	Bedford Park Birkdale–Bowls, putting
H	**Canning Road Recreation Ground** Blowick–Bowls
H	**Foreshore Aerodrome**–Pleasure flights
C	**Happiland** Marine Pde–Children's funfair
E	**Hesketh Golf Club** ☎*36897*
M	**Hillside Golf Club** ☎*67169* S off Waterloo Rd
C	**Kings Gardens**–Bowls, putting
I	**Masters Putting Course** Lower Prom
C	**Marine Drive**–Go-karts
C/D	**Marine Lake**–Boating, racing, water-skiing
C/I	**Pier**–Amusements, Leisure Centre, miniature railway
C	**Pleasureland**–Amusement Park
C	**Princes Park**–Model yachting, paddling pool, pitch and putt, Sea Bathing Lake, trampolines
M	**Royal Birkdale Golf Club** Waterloo Rd ☎*69928*
C	**Sands** (nr pier)–Children's playground
M	**Southport and Ainsdale Golf Club** ☎*78092* S off Waterloo Rd
N	**Southport and Birkdale Cricket Club** Trafalgar Rd, Birkdale ☎*69951*
E	**Southport Municipal Golf Course** ☎*35286*
R	**Southport Old Links** Moss Ln ☎*28207*–9 holes
D	**Southport Sailing Club** Marine Dr ☎*30619*
I	**Southport Swimming Baths** Esplanade ☎*37160*
H	**Victoria Park**–Bowls, tennis (Site of the 3-day Southport Flower Show each August)

Cabaret/Dancing

I	**Dixieland Showbar** Pier Entrance ☎*40577*
J(1)	**Floral Hall** Promenade ☎*40404*

Cinemas

I	**ABC** Lord St ☎*32797*
I	**Classic 1 and 2**, Lord St ☎*30627*
J	**Odeon** Lord St ☎*35582*

Theatres

I(2)	**Arts Centre** Lord St ☎*40004*
J(1)	**Floral Hall** Promenade ☎*40404*
J	**Little Theatre** Hoghton St ☎*30521*
J(1)	**Southport Theatre** Promenade ☎*40404*

Places of Interest

C	**Aquarium** Marine Dr ☎*32553*
I(2)	**Arts Centre and Atkinson Art Gallery** Town Hall ☎*33133*
R(6)	**Botanic Gardens Museum** ☎*27547*
I(3)	**Model Village and Garden Centre** ☎*42133*
C(4)	**Southport Zoo** ☎*38102*
J(5)	**Steamport Transport Museum** ☎*30693*

Tourist Information

[i] I	**Tourist Information Centre** Cambridge Arcade ☎*33133*

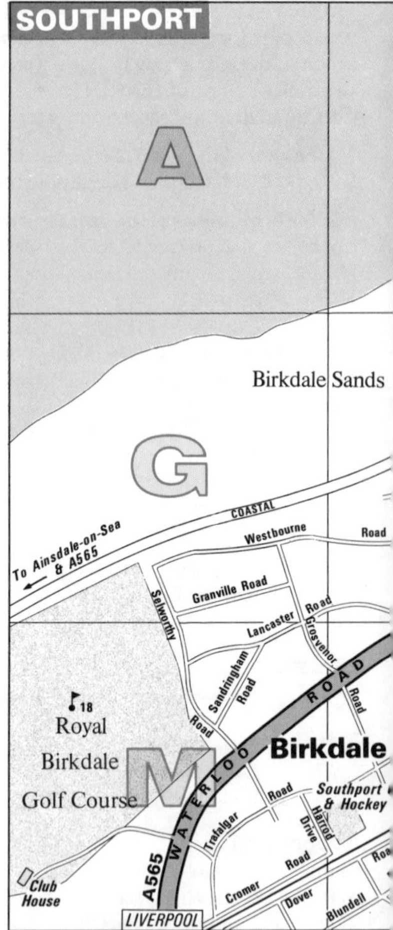

Accommodation

The establishments listed below are a selection of AA-recommended accommodation and restaurants located in the area covered by the Town Plan. Further information may be found in AA publications or obtained from the Tourist Information Centre.

1aGH	**Abbey Hotel** 6 Lathom Rd ☎*38430*
1SC	**7 Albany Road.** For bookings: Mrs E Baines, 10 Derby Rd, Southport, Merseyside ☎*31546*
2★★	**Bold** Lord St ☎*32578*

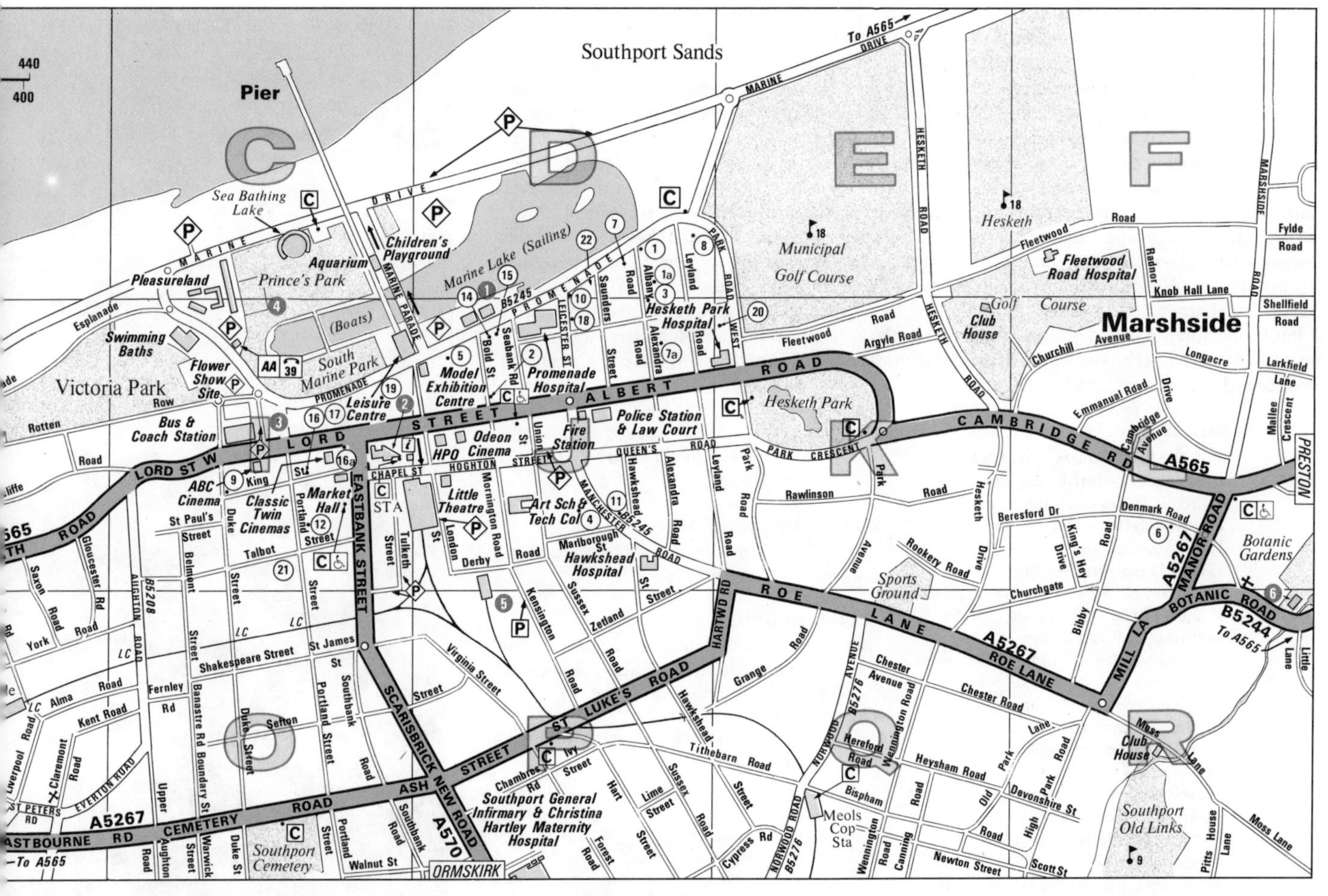

3SC Mrs J Gregory, **Cairn House** 18 Knowsley Rd, Southport, Merseyside PR9 0HQ ☎*42878*

4SC Mr Ward, **Conway Holiday Flats** 2 Arnside Rd, Southport, Merseyside PR9 0QX ☎*37170*

5✕ **Le Coq Hardi** 1 Royal Ter, West St ☎*38855*

6SC Mrs M M Brown, **41 Denmark Road** Churchtown, Southport, Merseyside PR9 7LL ☎*25270*

7GH **Fernley Private Hotel** 69 The Promenade ☎*35610*

7aGH **Fulwood Private Hotel** 82 Leyland Rd ☎*34597*

8GH **Garden Hotel** 19 Lathom Rd ☎*30244*

9GH **Glenwood Private Hotel** 98–102 King St ☎*35068*

10GH **Knowsley Private Hotel** Promenade, 2 Knowsley Rd ☎*30190*

11SC Mrs Gill, **101 Manchester Road** Southport, Merseyside ☎*42150*

12★ **Metropole** Portland St ☎*36836*

14GH **Ocean Bank** 16 Bank Sq ☎*40988*

15SC Mrs A Barnard, **Pomme D'or** 58 Promenade, Southport, Merseyside PR9 0DY ☎*38003*

16★★★★ **Prince of Wales** Lord St ☎*36688*

16a★★ **Red Rum** 86–88 Lord St ☎*35111*

17★★★ **Royal Clifton** Promenade ☎*33771*

18GH **Savoia Hotel** 37 Leicester St ☎*30559*

19★★ **Scarisbrook** Lord St ☎*38321*

20GH **West Point Hotel** 6 Park Rd ☎*30474*

21GH **Westwood House** 30 Talbot St ☎*30655*

22GH **Windsor Lodge Hotel** 37 Saunders St ☎*30070*

NEW BRIGHTON

New Brighton, situated at the north-eastern corner of the Wirral peninsula, has been a popular holiday area since the 19th century, with a partially traffic-free promenade, and a wide variety of amusement, entertainment and sporting facilities. There are donkey rides on the sands, numerous amusement arcades and the New Palace Amusement Park, the largest indoor amusement centre in the north-west, contains the expected dodgems and large scale rides in addition to bingo and refreshment areas. A special children's entertainment is staged at Vale Park during the summer. There are three golf courses in the vicinity and ample facilities for bowls, putting and tennis. A Festival of Sport is held each June, attracting several thousand competitors and regattas and power boat races take place at regular intervals. New Brighton has a huge open-air swimming pool, complete with catering and shopping facilities and an artificial beach. The heats and final of the 'Miss New Brighton' beauty contest are held here each year. A number of ferry cruises are available from Seacombe Ferry. The *Royal Iris*, a vessel with bars, restaurants and a disco, provides daily tours on the River Mersey and trips to Llandudno and the Isle of Man also operate regularly from Liverpool. New Brighton is well situated for touring the surrounding area and cities such as Liverpool and historic Chester can be reached in a comparatively short time.

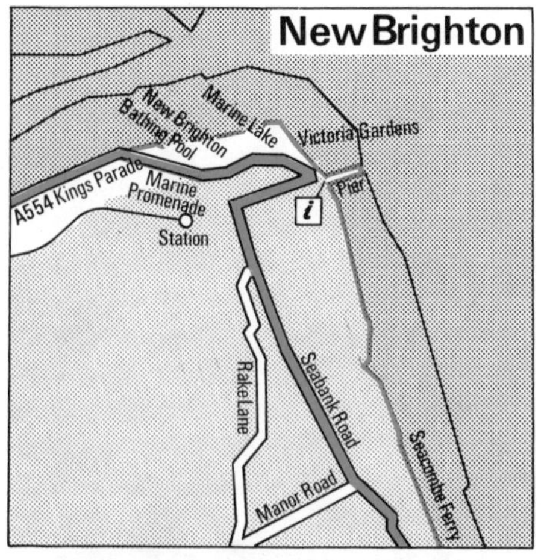

Recreation and Sports

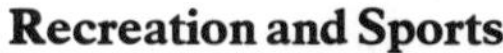

Bidston Golf Course ☎ *638 3412*
Central Park – Bowls, cricket, football, model yachting, tennis
Fort Perch Rock Marine Pde – Amusements
Granada Bowling Marine Pde ☎ *639 1238* – Ten-pin bowling
Kings Parade – Crazy-golf, model yachting, putting, tennis
Leasowe Golf Course Leasowe ☎ *677 5852*
Marine Park – Bowls, tennis
Marine Promenade – Trampolines
New Brighton Bathing Pool ☎ *639 3482* – Outdoor swimming pool
New Palace Amusement Park Marine Prom – Indoor funfair
Victoria Gardens – Crazy-golf, funfair, trampolines
Wallasey Golf Course Bayswater Rd ☎ *639 3630*
Wallasey Yacht Club Hope St ☎ *639 1427*
West Cheshire Sailing Club Harrison Dr ☎ *639 6473*

Dancing

Golden Guinea Club Marine Prom ☎ *639 6599*
Grosvenor Ballroom Liscard Village ☎ *638 4431*

Theatres

Floral Pavilion Theatre Victoria Gdns ☎ *639 4360*

Tourist Information

Information Bureau New Brighton Pier ☎ *639 3929*

Accommodation

The following establishments are recommended by the AA. Further information may be obtained from the Tourist Information Centre.

★★ **St Hillary** Grove Rd ☎ *639 3947*
GH **Divonne Private Hotel** 71 Wellington Rd ☎ *639 4727*

WEATHER CHART	Av hours of Sunshine in month	Hottest Av daily Temp °C
April	168	8
May	212	11
June	216	14
July	184	16
August	173	16
September	131	14

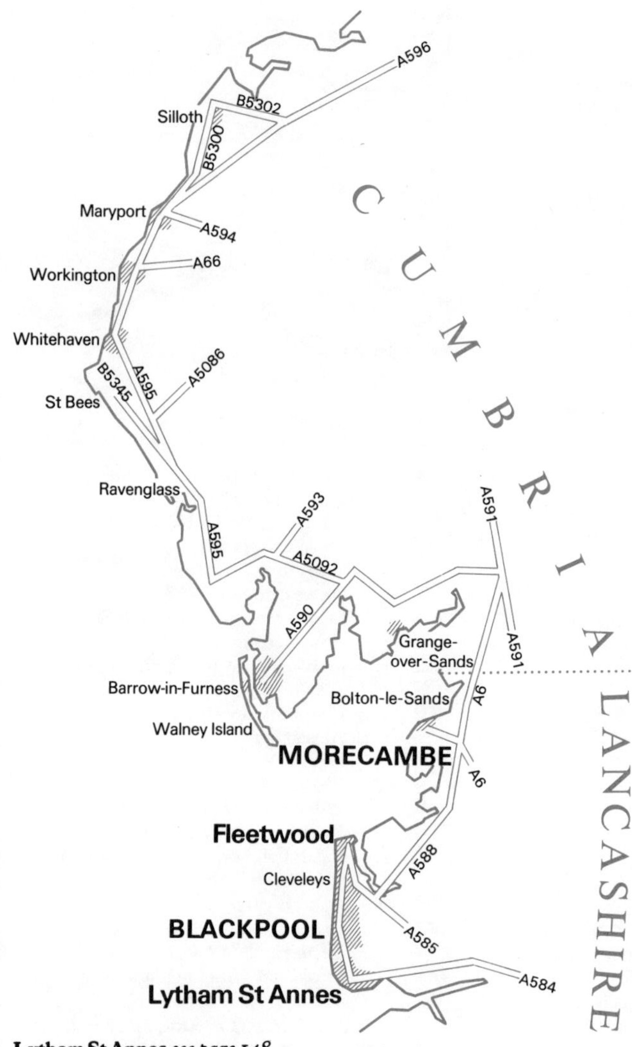

Lytham St Annes *see page 148*

BLACKPOOL *see page 150*

Cleveleys
There is a sand and shingle beach which is generally safe for swimming. Amusements are available.

Fleetwood *see page 152*

MORECAMBE *see page 154*

Bolton-le-Sands
A modern village resort with a wide expanse of sandy beach.

Grange-over-Sands
A quiet little resort with a sand and shingle foreshore backed by gardens. Bathing is unsafe due to strong currents but an open-air sea water swimming pool is available during the summer months.

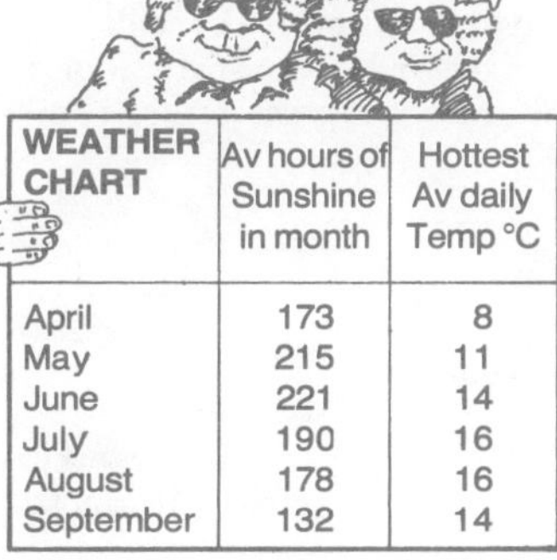

WEATHER CHART	Av hours of Sunshine in month	Hottest Av daily Temp °C
April	173	8
May	215	11
June	221	14
July	190	16
August	178	16
September	132	14

Walney Island
The island is linked to the mainland by a bridge and its southern extremity is a nature reserve. The western shore has a fine stretch of safe, sandy beach backed by dunes.

Barrow-in-Furness
An ancient settlement which developed into a highly industrialised port during the late 18th century, mainly concerned with the production of iron and shipbuilding. Forests of cranes, rising from the busy dockyard which lies in the shelter of Walney Island, are often the visitors' first sight of Barrow. Despite its industrial activities the town has much to offer the holidaymaker in the way of entertainment and sports. The remains of Furness Abbey, dating from 1127, stand in a wooded valley on the northern outskirts of the town.

Ravenglass
An unspoilt fishing village which is the starting point for the Ravenglass and Eskdale narrow gauge railway. The sand and shingle beach is unsafe for swimming due to strong currents.

St Bees
The village lies in a sheltered valley behind a safe, sandy beach. There are fine views from the surrounding cliffs.

Whitehaven
An industrial town which has been a leading port since the 15th century. There are facilities for sports and entertainment.

Workington
This mining town is a popular boating centre and has numerous parks and playing fields. There is a sand and shingle beach and amusements etc are available.

Maryport
A former Roman settlement, Maryport has fine safe beaches and is now a small resort and a good touring centre.

Silloth
This popular holiday resort has a sandy beach which is safe for bathing except when the tide is ebbing.

LYTHAM ST ANNES

A large residential resort, Lytham St Annes is laid out on garden city lines and its cool, tree-lined streets and quiet paths make it an ever-popular setting for family holidays. At one time Lytham was a port used by sailing ships but the dock has long since disappeared. Now, although the tall ships have gone, yachts and other pleasure craft may be seen moored at Lytham Dock Creek. A feature of the town is the windmill standing on Lytham Green next to the old life-boat house. Built in the early 19th century and damaged by fire in 1918, the windmill has recently been restored.

Lytham St Annes is noted for its flowered gardens and famous for its four championship golf courses, particularly The Royal Lytham St Annes. The beach, fringed with grass-covered dunes, comprises firm sand which is completely covered by shallow water at high tide. An extensive range of recreational facilities are available and natural amenities include medicinal baths. Lytham is an ideal touring centre having easy access to the Forest of Bowland, the Lake District and North Wales.

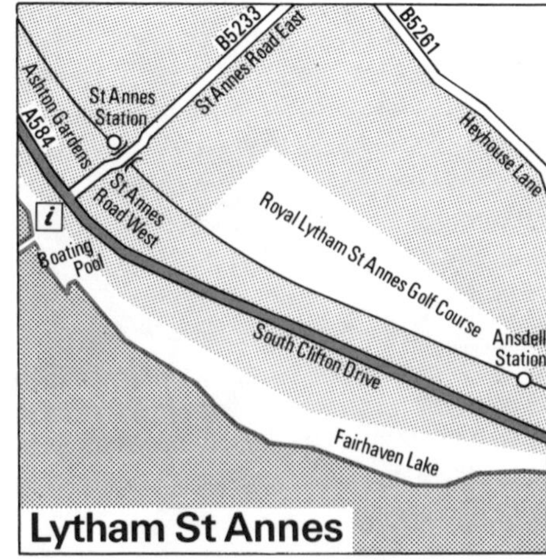

Recreation and Sports

Ashton Gardens – Aviary, bowls, putting, tennis

Fairhaven Golf Club Blackpool Rd, Ansdell ☎ *722637*

Fairhaven Lake – Bowls, boating, crazy-golf, mini-golf, putting, tennis, water-skiing

Fylde International Sand Yacht Club ☎ *St Annes725981*

Hope Street Recreation Ground – Tennis

Lowther Gardens – Aviary, bowls, putting, tennis

Lytham Cricket and Sports Club Pavilion, Church Rd ☎ *734137*

Lytham Green Drive Golf Club Ltd Ballam Rd ☎ *734782*

Lytham Swimming Baths ☎ *736258*

Lytham Yacht Club ☎ *735223*

North Promenade – Beach chalets for hire

Pier – Amusement arcade, deck games

Royal Lytham St Annes Golf Club Club House, Links Gate ☎ *St Annes724206*

St Annes Old Links Golf Club ☎ *St Annes721826*

St Annes Open Air Heated Swimming Baths ☎ *St Annes721325*

St Annes-on-Sea Lawn Tennis Club Avondale Rd ☎ *St Annes722637*

South Promenade – Boating, mini-golf, putting

Cinema

Studios 1, 2 and 3 St Georges Rd ☎ *St Annes726235*

Theatre

Lowther Pavilion Lytham ☎ *St Annes721222*

Places of Interest

Motive Power Museum and Lytham Creek Railway Dock Rd, Lytham

Tourist Information

Lytham Information Bureau Lytham Baths, Dicconson Ter ☎ *736258*

Publicity and Information Services Dept Town Hall ☎ *St Annes721222*

St Annes Information Bureau Junction Clifton Dr North and St Annes Rd West ☎ *St Annes725610*

Accommodation

The following establishments are recommended by the AA. Further information may be obtained from the Tourist Information Office.

★★★★	**Clifton Arms** West Beach ☎ *739898*
★★	**Chadwick** South Prom ☎ *St Annes720061*
★★	**Fernlea** 15 South Prom ☎ *St Annes726726*
★★	**Grand** South Prom ☎ *St Annes722155*
★★	**Hotel Glendower** North Prom ☎ *St Annes723241*
★★	**Knights** 365–367 Clifton Dr North ☎ *St Annes720421*
★★	**Princes** North Prom ☎ *St Annes725161*
★★	**Savoy** Clifton Dr North ☎ *St Annes728441*
★	**Carlton** 61 South Prom ☎ *St Annes721036*
★	**Oceandene** South Prom ☎ *St Annes726249*
GH	**Gables Hotel** 35 Orchard Rd ☎ *St Annes729851*
GH	**Harcourt Hotel** 21 Richmond Rd ☎ *St Annes722299*
GH	**Heath House Private Hotel** 4 Bromley Rd ☎ *St Annes723109*
GH	**Westbourne Hotel** 10–12 Lake Rd, Fairhaven ☎ *734736*
SC	R & E Fallows, **Argyll Holiday Flats** 336 Clifton Dr North ☎ *St Annes721810*
SC	**Beach Holiday Flats** 362/364 Clifton Dr North ☎ *St Annes727915*
SC	**Fern Bank Holiday Flats** 28 St Thomas' Rd. For bookings: Mrs Kember, 50 Laverton Rd ☎ *St Annes725350*
SC	Mrs W Ettenfield, **Greenways** 7 Victoria Rd, St Annes ☎ *St Annes726204*
SC	Mrs E Crowther, **Harcourt Holiday Flats** 22 Victoria Rd ☎ *St Annes720659*
SC	Mr and Mrs Buttery, **Monterey** 26 North Prom ☎ *St Annes725080*

CHANNINGS HOTEL

BLACKPOOL

A first class, private hotel commanding one of the finest positions on the promenade, overlooking the Irish Sea, enabling our visitors to bathe from the hotel.
The hotel has 20, well furnished bedrooms with electric fires & shaver sockets. Ample bath & shower facilities are available. All public rooms are centrally heated, newly decorated and tastefully furnished and include cocktail bar, dining room, colour TV lounge and sun lounge.
Free car parking.
The Hotel is open throughout the year under the personal supervision of the proprietors Mr & Mrs Holden.

**557 New South Promenade, Blackpool FY4 1NF.
Tel. 41380.**

SUNRAY PRIVATE HOTEL

One of the only 36 Guest Houses in England so far awarded a special commendation by the British Tourist Authority for the outstanding quality of service offered to visitors. Quiet residential area, off Queens Promenade by North Shore Golf Club. All bedrooms first floor. Full central heating. Electric blankets. Good food and service. Free car park.

**42 Knowle Avenue, North Shore,
Blackpool, FY2 9TQ Tel: 51937.**

Beaucliffe Hotel

**22 Holmfield Road, North Shore, Blackpool
Tel: 51663**

Adjacent to Gynn Square and Queens Promenade. Large lounge with colour TV. Separate dining room. Private car park. Part central heating. Keys to all bedrooms. Divan beds. Hot and cold water. Shaver sockets. Bed lights. Electric heaters in all bedrooms. Open all year. Conference delegates welcome. Special fare and tariff during Christmas period.
There are electric blankets.

Under the personal supervision of the proprietors:
Mr and Mrs C Jamieson.

Arandora Star
Private Hotel

559 New South Promenade.
Blackpool, Lancs. FY4 1NF.
Tel 0253 41528.

Licensed to Residents.
Free parking. Garage.
Res Prop Mr and Mrs A E Trow.

Offers you the finest position overlooking the beach and promenade. Bathing from hotel. Lounges with television.

Hot and cold services in all rooms. All bedrooms fitted with divans and spring-interior beds. Bedhead lighting. Room keys. Shaving points and electric fires. Twin beds available if desired. Central heating in most rooms.

Christmas festivities. Fire certificate obtained. Modern bathrooms and separate shower room available. Cocktail bar. Established 32 years ago. Finest English cuisine and personal service.

BLACKPOOL

Blackpool is the largest and perhaps the best known resort in Britain welcoming many millions of visitors each year and typifying the popular conception of the English seaside with its gaily illuminated Golden Mile and acres of amusement parks and arcades.

Seven miles of promenade span broad, safe sands where beach huts may be hired and donkey rides and Punch and Judy Shows are available. The Pleasure Beach Amusement Park, near South Pier, is one of the largest of its kind in Europe. It has grown, under the management of one family, from a cluster of roundabouts in the late 19th century into a huge complex containing a cable railway, monorail, numerous ingenious and unusual rides and exhibits, a separate children's park with scaled-down rides and leisure facilities in the shape of the Ice Drome, where a 'Spectacular' is staged and the new "Wonderful World" with bars and restaurants where cabaret-type entertainment is provided.

Five miles of the town's sea front is illuminated from early September until late October at a cost of more than £1 million per year, providing the evening stroller with an enchanting vista of coloured lights, imaginative decorations, animated tableaux and even passenger carrying tram-cars disguised as moon rockets, paddle steamers and the like.

In Blackpool it would be possible to see a different Summer Show every night of the week with famous artists appearing at all of the town's theatres. Add to this the renowned International Tower Circus, family entertainment at the Tower Ballroom, cinemas and numerous bars and clubs providing cabaret and dancing, not to mention regular band concerts, dog shows, veteran car rallies, the Miss United Kingdom beauty contest, greyhound racing and League football and you have an idea of what Blackpool has to offer.

Recreation and Sports

C	**Blackpool Cricket Club** Stanley Pk ☎*33347* – County and Northern League matches
G	**Blackpool FC** Bloomfield Rd ☎*46118* League Division III
D	**Blackpool Greyhound Stadium** Rigby Rd ☎*22057*
G	**Blackpool Open-Air Swimming Pool** ☎*41530*
C	**Blackpool Park Golf Club** Stanley Pk ☎*33960*
E	**Central Drive Recreation Ground** – Bowls, putting, tennis
A	**Coral Island Entertainment Centre** – Amusements, bingo
G	**Lido Swimming Pool** ☎*41593*
A	**Olympia** Coronation St – Amusement Park
	Pleasure Beach – Amusement Park S on A584
F	**Stanley Park** – Boating, bowls, crazy-golf, pitch and putt, putting, tennis, table tennis

Cabaret/Dancing

A	**Coral Island Entertainment Centre** ☎*29133*
D	**Dixieland Showbar** Central Pier
A	**Hofbrauhaus** Star Entertainment Centre, North Prom ☎*25961*
	Horseshoe Theatre Nite-Spot Casino, Pleasure Beach
A	**Merrie England Showbar** North Pier
A	**Scamps Discotheque** Star Entertainment Centre, North Prom ☎*25952*
D	**Tiffanys** Central Dr ☎*21572*
A(1)	**Tower Ballroom** Lounge and Ocean Room
A	**Winter Gardens** Planet Room
	Wonderful World Pleasure Beach

Cinemas

A	**ABC** Church St ☎*24233*
A	**Odeon** Dickson Rd ☎*23565*
G	**Palladium** Waterloo Rd ☎*42023*
A	**Princess** North Prom ☎*20467*
G	**Rendezvous** Bond St
D	**Royal Pavilion** Rigby Rd ☎*25313*
A	**Studio 1, 2, 3, 4** Princess Pde ☎*25957*
A	**Tivoli** Clifton St ☎*20508*

Theatres

D	**Central Pier**
	Ice Drome Pleasure Beach
A	**North Pier** ☎*20980*
A	**Opera House** ☎*25252*
G	**South Pier** ☎*43096*
A(1)	**Tower Circus** ☎*25252*

Places of Interest

A(1)	**Blackpool Tower**
A(2)	**Grundy Art Gallery and Central Library** ☎*23977*
D(3)	**Louis Tussaud's Waxworks** Central Prom ☎*25953*
F	**Model Village** Stanley Pk ☎*63827*
G(4)	**Platform 3 Model Railway** South Station ☎*401150*
	Seafront Tramway – Squires Gate (Blackpool – Fleetwood)
	Venetian Glass Co Sycamore Trading Estate
F	**Zoo Park** East Pk Dr ☎*65027*

Tourist Information

[i] A	**Information Bureau** Promenade ☎*21623*

Accommodation

The establishments listed below are a selection of AA-recommended accommodation located in the area covered by the Town Plan. Further information may be found in AA publications or obtained from the Information Bureau.

1SC	Mr and Mrs McQuillan, **Charnley Holiday Flats** 5 Charnley Rd, Blackpool, Lancs FY1 4PE ☎*23643*
2★★★	**Clifton** Talbot Sq ☎*21481*
3SC	Mr and Mrs Battersby, **Havelock Flats** 117 Coronation St, Blackpool, Lancs ☎*64204*
4GH	**Motel Mimosa** 24A Lonsdale Rd ☎*41906*

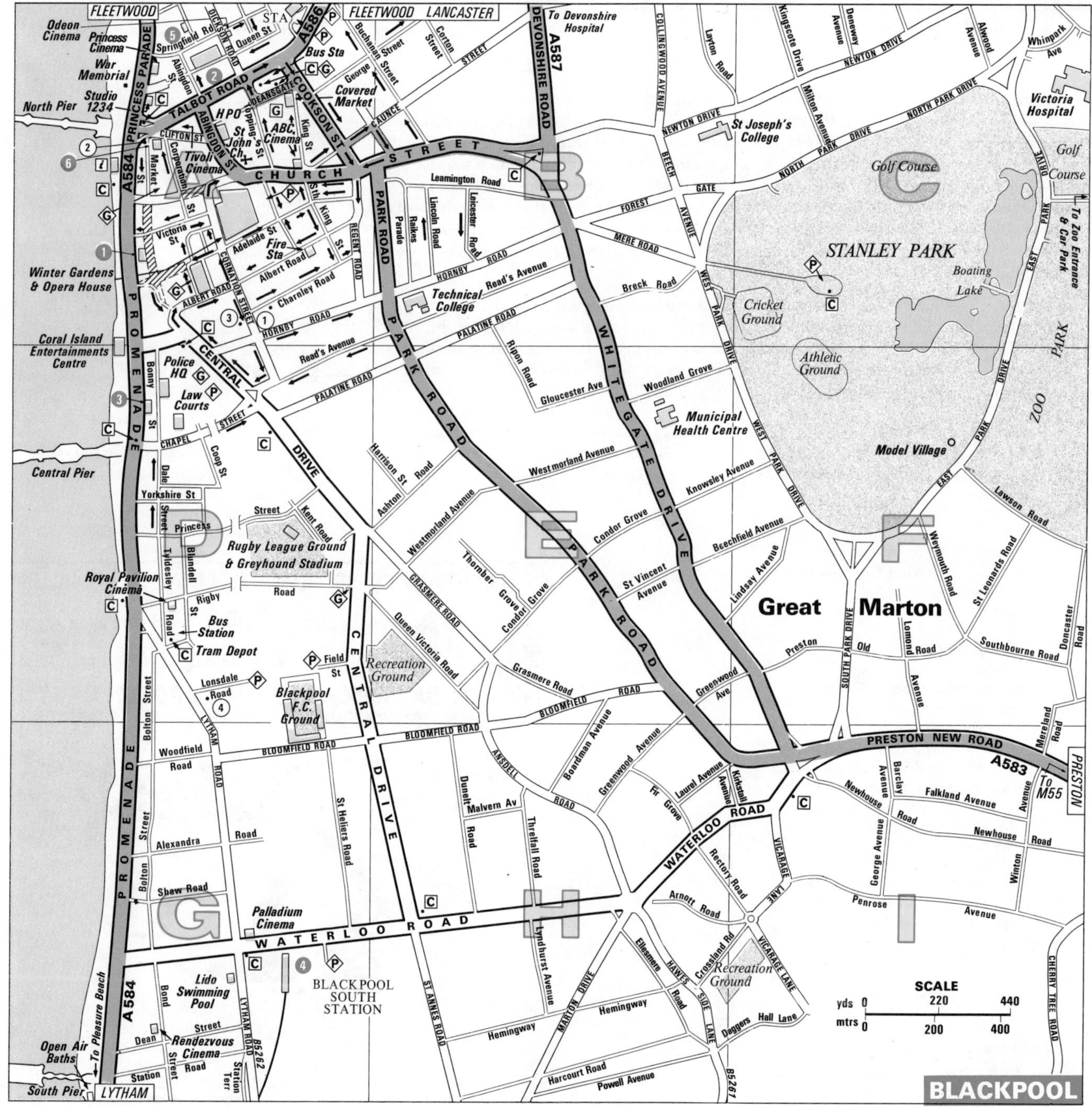

BLACKPOOL
FLEETWOOD
FLEETWOOD LANCASTER
To Devonshire Hospital
A587
DEVONSHIRE ROAD
A586
STA
Bus Sta
Odeon Cinema
Princess Cinema
War Memorial
Studio 1234
North Pier
Springfield Rd
Queen St
DICKSON ROAD
Abingdon St
TALBOT ROAD
DEANSGATE
COOKSON ST
Buchanan Street
George Street
Covered Market
Corton Street
STREET
CAUNCE
HPO
ABC Cinema
St John's Ch.
King St
CLIFTON ST
Corporation
Market St
Tivoli Cinema
ABINGDON ST
CHURCH
STREET
PRINCESS PARADE
A584
Leamington Road
Parade
Raikes
Lincoln Road
Leicester Road
PARK ROAD
REGENT ROAD
Victoria St
Adelaide St
Fire Sta
Albert Road
Charnley Road
ALBERT ROAD
CORONATION STREET
Winter Gardens & Opera House
HORNBY ROAD
Read's Avenue
Technical College
PALATINE ROAD
Coral Island Entertainments Centre
Police HQ
Law Courts
Bonny St
CENTRAL
CHAPEL
STREET
Coop St
Central Pier
DRIVE
Dale Street
Yorkshire St
Street
Princess
Kent Road
Rugby League Ground & Greyhound Stadium
Tyldesley
Blundell
Royal Pavilion Cinema
Rigby
Road
Bus Station
Tram Depot
Field St
Lonsdale Road
Blackpool F.C. Ground
Recreation Ground
Queen Victoria Road
GRASMERE ROAD
Grasmere Road
CENTRAL DRIVE
PROMENADE
Bolton Street
Woodfield Road
LYTHAM ROAD
BLOOMFIELD ROAD
St Heliers Road
Alexandra
Road
Shaw Road
Palladium Cinema
WATERLOO ROAD
BLACKPOOL SOUTH STATION
Lido Swimming Pool
Bond Street
Dean Street
Rendezvous Cinema
Station Road
Station Terr
B5262
Open Air Baths
To Pleasure Beach
South Pier
LYTHAM
Ripon Road
Gloucester Ave
Woodland Grove
Municipal Health Centre
Harrison St
Road
Ashton
Westmorland Avenue
Thornber Grove
Condor Grove
St Vincent Avenue
Knowsley Avenue
Beechfield Avenue
Lindsay Avenue
PARK ROAD
WHITEGATE DRIVE
Greenwood Ave
Boardman Avenue
Greenwood Avenue
ANSDELL ROAD
Dunelt Road
Malvern Av
Threlfall Road
Fir Grove
Laurel Avenue
Kirkstall Avenue
WATERLOO ROAD
Rectory Road
Arnott Road
VICARAGE LANE
Lyndhurst Avenue
MARTON DRIVE
Ellesmere Road
HAWES SIDE LANE
Crossland Rd
Hemingway
Harcourt Road
Powell Avenue
Daggers Hall Lane
B5261
ST ANNES ROAD
COLLINGWOOD AVENUE
Layton Road
Kingscote Drive
Deneway Avenue
Alwood Avenue
NEWTON DRIVE
Milton Avenue
St Joseph's College
BEECH AVENUE
NORTH PARK DRIVE
FOREST GATE
MERE ROAD
Breck Road
WEST PARK DRIVE
Whinpark Ave
Victoria Hospital
Golf Course
STANLEY PARK
Boating Lake
Cricket Ground
Athletic Ground
Model Village
EAST PARK DRIVE
ZOO
PARK
To Zoo Entrance & Car Park
Lawson Road
Weymouth Road
St Leonards Road
Great Marton
SOUTH PARK DRIVE
Preston Old Road
Lomond Avenue
Southbourne Road
Doncaster Road
Mereland Road
PRESTON NEW ROAD
A583
PRESTON
To M55
Barclay Avenue
Falkland Avenue
Newhouse Road
George Avenue
Winton Avenue
Penrose Avenue
CHERRY TREE ROAD
SCALE
yds 0 220 440
mtrs 0 200 400
A B C D E F G H I

FLEETWOOD

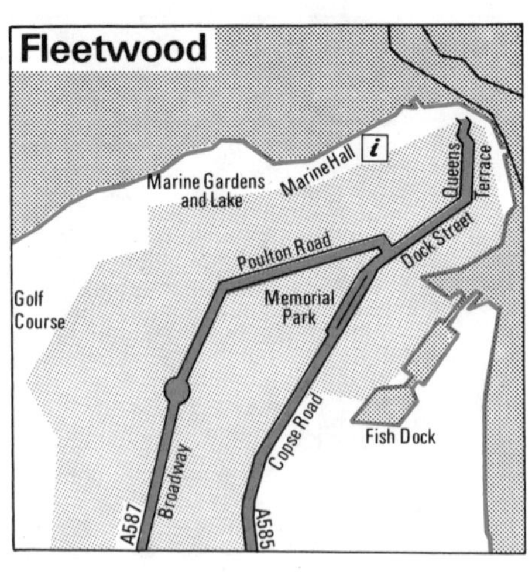

Situated on the Fylde peninsula, Fleetwood lies at the mouth of the Wyre Estuary in Morecambe Bay. A popular resort, the town is one of Britain's largest fishing ports where anything from small inshore fishing boats to larger trawlers may be seen. Ferry vessels operate from the port to Douglas, Isle of Man; the crossing taking about 3 hours according to tidal conditions. Presiding over all this traffic are two lighthouses, the lower lighthouse near the Lifeboat Station and the larger Pharos Lighthouse, rising high above the trams and traffic of a busy street. Wonderful panoramic views of the Lake District peaks can be seen to the north across Morecambe Bay in clear weather. To the east views extend over the Lune Valley to the distant Pennines.

Fleetwood has 4 miles of coastline with splendid sand and shingle beaches. Sea bathing is allowed from the patrolled Marine Hall Beach when green flags are displayed, but prohibited when a red flag is flying. The sea front is unique in that it has gardens and amenities between the two promenades away from the traffic. Facilities exist for most forms of sport including angling, boating, yachting and golf.

Recreation and Sports

Blackpool and Fleetwood Yacht Club Tatham House, Skippool ☎ *Poulton-le-Fylde884205*
Cala Gran Country Club – Ten Pin Bowling
Euston Park – Recreation ground
Fleetwood Bowling Club Ltd Lune St ☎ *3903*
Fleetwood Golf Club Ltd Princess Way ☎ *3114*
Fleetwood Cricket Club Broadwaters ☎ *2132*
Fleetwood Swimming Centre Esplanade ☎ *71505*
Marine Gardens – Band concerts (Sunday afternoons), boating, bowls, crazy-golf, model yachting, model railway, paddling pool, pitch and putt, table-tennis, trampolines
Marine Hall – Cafe, ballroom, sun parlour
Marine Lake – Boating
Memorial Park – Bowls, tennis
Mount Grounds – Recreation ground
Pier – Bingo

Cinema

Regent Lord St ☎ *3667*

Places of Interest

Dock Street Museum Fleetwood – Local history

Tourist Information

Tourist Information Centre Marine Hall ☎ *71141*

Accommodation

The following establishments are recommended by the AA. Further information may be obtained from the Tourist Information Office.

★★ **North Euston** The Esplanade ☎ *3375*
Ⓖ **Boston** Esplanade ☎ *4644*

MORECAMBE

The ancient villages of Morecambe and Heysham have gradually been merged into one large, enterprising holiday resort although both retain a degree of their former maritime trade; Heysham as a port serving Belfast and the Isle of Man, and Morecambe as the centre of the local shrimp fishing industry.

The northern part of the beach near Morecambe jetty tends to be muddy with some shingle, but becomes much sandier in the south towards Heysham and bathing is generally safe. There are several paddling pools along the beach. A beach "train" runs from West End Beach to Heysham and boat trips around the bay are available from the seafront. Central Pier has the usual amusement arcade and two large amusement parks stand side by side on the sea front near Morecambe jetty which contains the Marineland complex with dolphins, an aquarium and a reptile house. There is a large entertainment centre at Heysham Head composed of a funfair, a free-flight tropical bird collection, a zoo and animal walk, a go-kart track where international events are held and several bars. Morecambe's three parks all contain facilities for tennis, bowls, putting etc and Happy Mount Park has a miniature railway and an 'Enchanted Garden' display which is illuminated at night, along with a four-mile stretch of the main sea front, from August to October. Sports enthusiasts are well catered for and Morecambe offers the visitor ample facilities for evening entertainment with shows, films and dancing. The Harbour Band Arena offers family entertainment throughout the season, including heats of the famous Miss Great Britain beauty contest and the carnival parade is an annual seafront event. An unusual route for walkers is the low-tide crossing of the bay to Grange-over-Sands under the supervision of an official guide.

Neighbouring places of interest include historic Lancaster with its 11th-century castle and Hornsea Pottery Factory, the neo-Gothic mansion of Leighton Hall with its bird collection, the Steamtown Railway Museum at Carnforth and the picturesque Lake District which lies little more than 30 miles away.

Recreation and Sports

C **Central Pier** – Amusements
Douglas Park – Bowls, tennis
Half Moon Bay Heysham – Mini-golf
Happy Mount Park – Boating, bowls, crazy-golf, mini-golf, miniature railway, putting, tennis, trampolines E off A589

F **Harbour Band Arena** – Band concerts, beauty contests, open air swimming pool
Heysham Golf Club Trumacar Pk ☎*Heysham51011*
Heysham Head Holiday Park ☎*Heysham52391* – Amusement Park, disco, entertainment, kart-racing, trampolines

B **Marine Road Central** – Boating and paddling pool
Morecambe FC Christie Pk ☎*411797* – Northern Premier League E off B5321
Morecambe Golf Club ☎*412841* E off A589

D **Morecambe and Heysham Yacht Club** Back Carlton Ter ☎*418206*

I **Regent Park** – Bowls, putting, tennis SE on Regent Rd
Sandylands Promenade – Boating and paddling pool S on A589

I **West End Esplanade** – Paddling pool, trampolines

I **West End Gardens** – Mini-golf, putting

F **West End Pleasure Park** – Amusement Park
Whinnystye Lane – Mini-golf, putting S on A589

F **Winter Gardens Pleasure Park** – Amusement Park

Cabaret/Dancing

C **Central Pier**

I **Inn on the Bay** Marine Rd West ☎*414224*

D **Miami Entertainment Centre**

Cinema

F **Empire 1, 2 and 3** Promenade ☎*412518*

F **Arcadian** Promenade ☎*412518*

Theatres

C **Dukes Comedy Playhouse** Central Pier ☎*410039*

I **Palace Theatre** Promenade, Sandylands ☎*410601*

Places of Interest

B **Marineland Oceanarium and Aquarium** ☎*414727*
Zoo Heysham Head Holiday Park

Tourist Information

C(1) **Information Bureau** Central Promenade ☎*414110*

Accommodation

The establishments listed below are a selection of AA-recommended accommodation located in the area covered by the Town Plan. Further information may be found in AA publications or obtained from the Information Bureau.

1SC **The Anchorage** 19 Clarence St. For bookings: Mrs M Woodcock 99 Regent Rd, Morecambe, Lancs LA3 1AF ☎*413466*

2SC **Delamare Flats** 10 Skipton St. For bookings: Mrs A Willoughby 7 Scafell Ave, Morecambe, Lancs ☎*416858*

3SC Mr and Mrs R E Singleton **Eden Vale Holiday Flats** 338 Marine Rd, Morecambe, Lancs ☎*415544*

4SC **J and E Pearson Holiday Flats** 301 Marine Rd Central. For bookings: Mrs E Palmer and Mrs J Charnley 298 Marine Rd Central, Morecambe, Lancs LA4 5BY ☎*412521*

5★★★ **Midland** Marine Rd ☎*417180*

6GH **Hotel Prospect** 363 Marine Rd, East Prom ☎*412133*

7GH **Rydal Mount Private Hotel** 361 Marine Rd East ☎*411858*

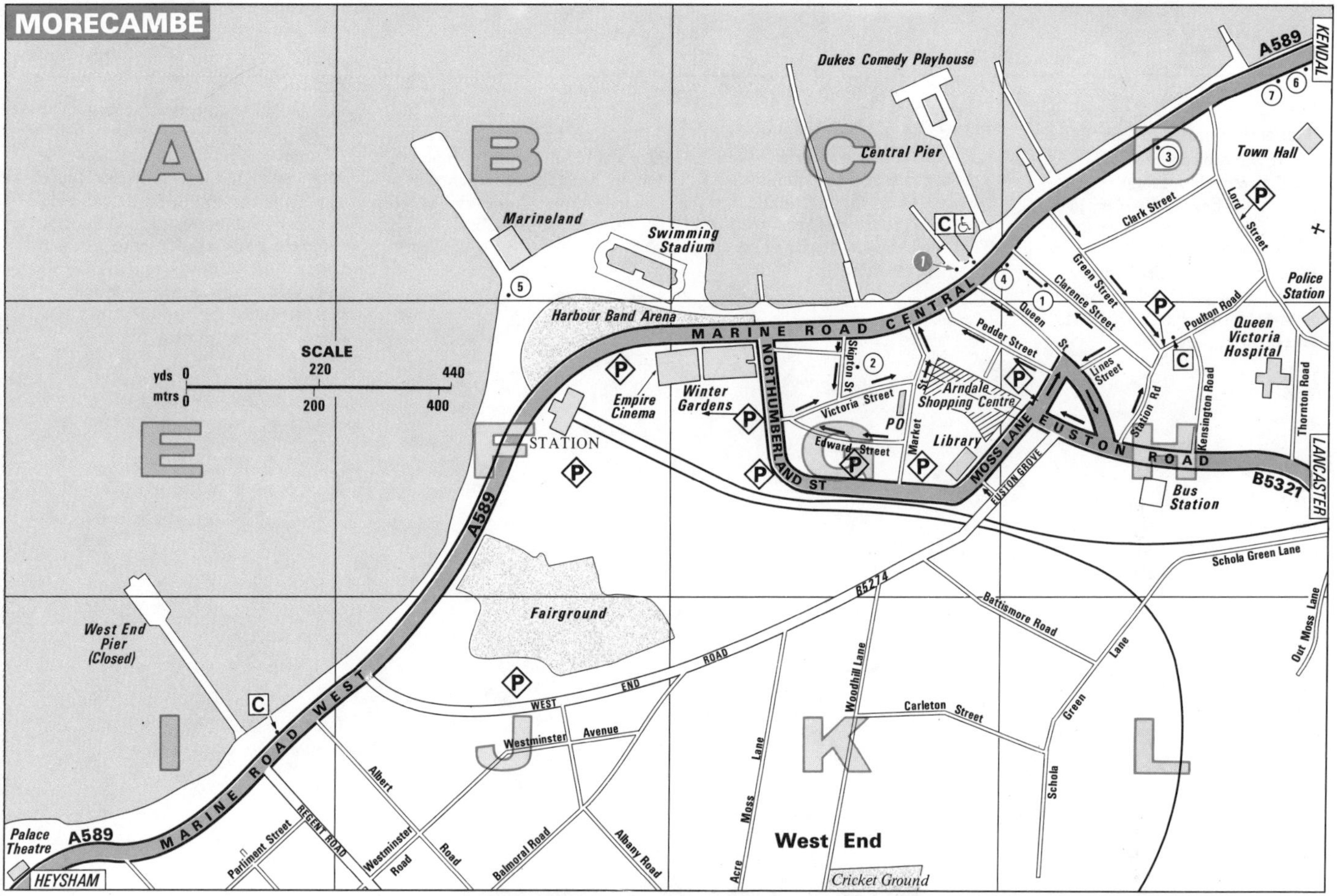

MORECAMBE

A B C D E F G H I J K L

A589 KENDAL
Dukes Comedy Playhouse
Central Pier
Town Hall
Marineland
Swimming Stadium
Clark Street
Lord Street
Green Street
Clarence Street
Queen St
Police Station
Harbour Band Arena
MARINE ROAD CENTRAL
Skipton St
Pedder Street
Poulton Road
Queen Victoria Hospital
SCALE
yds 0 220 440
mtrs 0 200 400
Empire Cinema
Winter Gardens
NORTHUMBERLAND ST
Victoria Street
Market St
Arndale Shopping Centre
Lines Street
Station Rd
Kensington Road
Thornton Road
PO
Edward Street
Library
MOSS LANE
EUSTON ROAD
LANCASTER
STATION
EUSTON GROVE
B5321
Bus Station
A589
Schola Green Lane
Fairground
B5274
Battismore Road
West End Pier (Closed)
Out Moss Lane
Green Lane
WEST END ROAD
Woodhill Lane
Carleton Street
Westminster Avenue
MARINE ROAD WEST
Albert Road
Moss Lane
Schola
Palace Theatre
A589
Parliament Street
REGENT ROAD
Westminster Road
Balmoral Road
Albany Road
Acre
West End
Cricket Ground
HEYSHAM

WEATHER CHART	Av hours of Sunshine in month	Hottest Av daily Temp °C
April	158	8
May	197	12
June	202	14
July	171	16
August	164	16
September	122	14

Shrimping

Gretna
The famous smithy of Gretna Green where runaway couples were married is still preserved although the ceremonies have taken place in the local registry office since 1940. Marriages were also solemnised in local inns. The border between England and Scotland is actually formed by the River Sark which enters the sea here.

Caerlaverock Castle
Founded in the late 13th century, this castle was besieged by Edward I in 1300 and subsequent assaults have reduced it to its present ruined condition. To the east lies a Wildfowl Trust sanctuary and some rather treacherous saltings.

Auchencairn
There are pebble beaches here which give way to sand at low-tide, when Hestan Island can be reached by a causeway from Almorness Point on the eastern side of the bay.

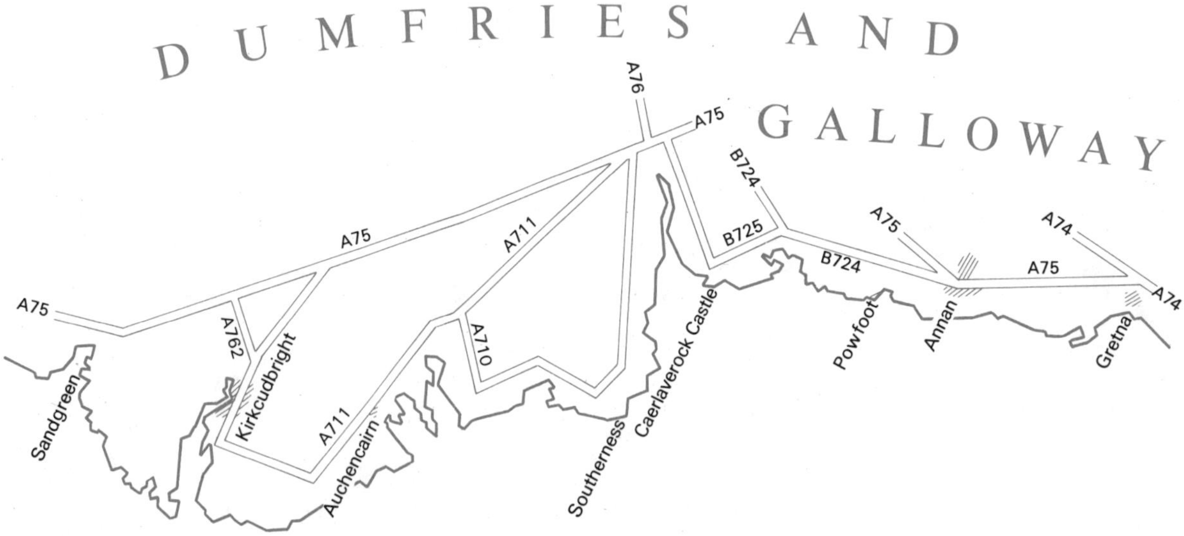

Annan
A Victorian town which is a popular boating centre and is still used by commercial fishermen. There is a sand and pebble beach.

Powfoot
The town was developed as a resort during the 18th century. The shingle beach gives way to sand at low-tide but swimming is dangerous due to strong currents.

Southerness
Safe, sandy beaches are to be found around Southerness Point. A holiday village lies along the western beach which is accessible on foot. Amusements are available.

Kirkcudbright
An ancient Royal Burgh and market town which stands at the mouth of the River Dee. The harbour is used by all kinds of pleasure craft and the town is a popular sailing centre. The western shore of the Dee estuary is dotted with sandy beaches and rocky coves. Boat trips are available. Kirkcudbright has many places of interest including Broughton House, an 18th-century building containing a collection of pictures by E A Hornel and the Stewartry Museum, devoted to local and natural history. The ruins of MacLellans Castle, a fortified manor house dating from 1582, overlook the harbour.

Sandgreen
A caravan park and holiday village has been established here on a wide sweep of safe sandy beach backed by dunes.

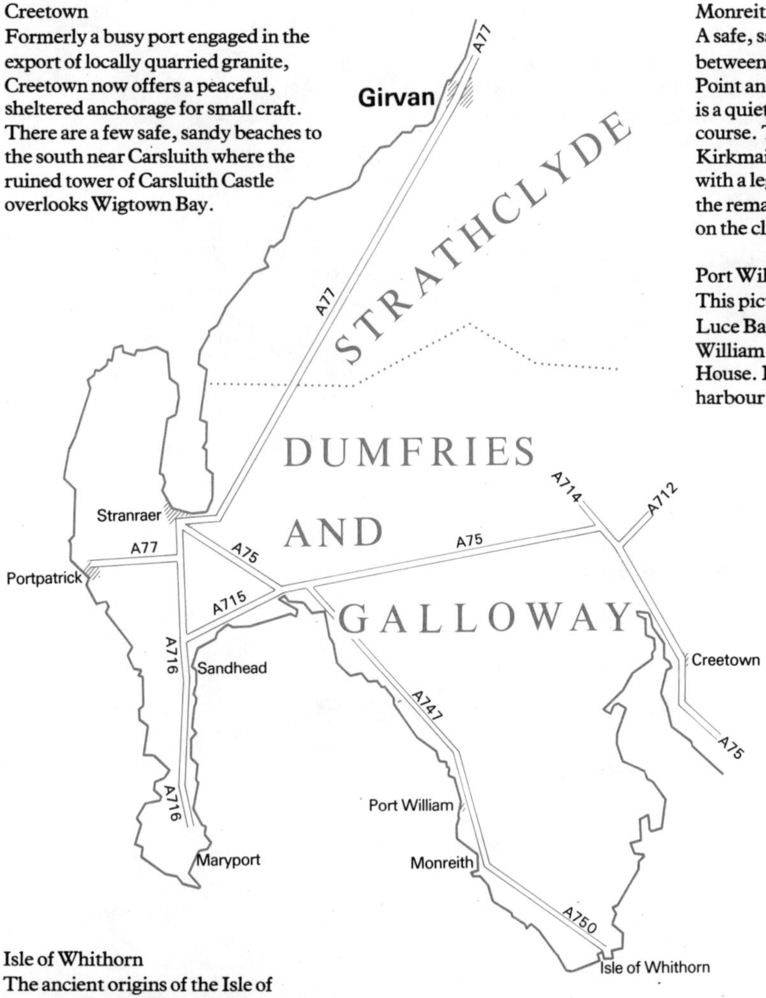

Creetown
Formerly a busy port engaged in the export of locally quarried granite, Creetown now offers a peaceful, sheltered anchorage for small craft. There are a few safe, sandy beaches to the south near Carsluith where the ruined tower of Carsluith Castle overlooks Wigtown Bay.

Isle of Whithorn
The ancient origins of the Isle of Whithorn are still apparent in the buildings which surround the harbour. Now no longer an island it has also lost a great deal of its seafaring trade, but the tradition is carried on by the many small craft that frequent the harbour. Back in the 4th century the son of a local chieftain left to study in Rome and upon his return brought Christianity to his homeland. He was St Ninian, who built what was thought to be the first Christian church in Britain. A 12th-century chapel dedicated to him stands near the harbour and St Ninian's cave lies to the west at the foot of the cliffs. There is a shingle foreshore at low-tide.

Monreith
A safe, sandy beach lies sheltered between the headlands of Barsalloch Point and the Point of Lag. Monreith is a quiet, secluded resort with a golf course. The nearby church of Kirkmaidens-in-Furnis is associated with a legendary Irish princess and the remains of an Iron Age Fort stand on the cliffs at Barsalloch Point.

Port William
This picturesque fishing village on Luce Bay was founded in 1770 by Sir William Maxwell of nearby Monreith House. From the haven of its safe harbour boats are available for hire and the village is a noted shark fishing centre. There is a sand and pebble beach. At nearby Mochrum village there is an earthwork mound, Druchtag Motehill, which is all that remains of a medieval castle.

Sandhead
Around the gentle curve of Sandhead Bay fine sands and safe bathing are to be found. To the north east on Torrs Warren, where Picts and Scots once fought a battle, the beach is under military control and is backed by a firing range. To the south, Ardwell House is open to the public, as is the Logan Botanic Garden, an annexe of the Royal Botanic Gardens in Edinburgh.

Maryport
Lying in the shelter of the Mull of Galloway, Maryport has a long stretch of level sand where swimming is safe.

Portpatrick
Close Irish connections over the years have helped to shape the character of Portpatrick, so named because it is believed to be the place where Ireland's Patron Saint left his native shores. This, too, was the port for the Ireland ferry service for many years until a safer haven was found at Stranraer. Now a pleasant holiday centre, its rocky coastline gives way to several sheltered sandy coves.

Stranraer
This busy port, an important Irish ferry terminal, is also a thriving centre for the surrounding area. Two sandy beaches provide safe bathing, although the sands are virtually covered at high tide, and next to the harbour is the Marine Lake for boating and bathing. There are good entertainment and sporting facilities in the town and lovely countryside is close at hand. Nearby Castle Kennedy Gardens are open to the public.

Girvan *see page 158*

GIRVAN

One of the leading coastal resorts in the south-west of Scotland, Girvan is sheltered by hills to the east and the islands of Argyll, Arran and Bute to the west across the Firth of Clyde. The coastline consists of rocky coves and cliffs interspersed with wide, sandy bays. Girvan spreads itself along just such a bay overlooked by the craggy head of Ailsa Craig, a 1,110-foot high rock some 10 miles off-shore lying halfway between Glasgow and Belfast, which has a varied history of invasion, shipwreck and smuggling. Today it is a nesting ground for sea birds and, until recently, provided the granite from which curling stones are made. Some 3 miles to the north-east of Girvan lies Killochan Castle, in the valley of the Water of Girvan, the impressive 16th-century stronghold of the Cathcarts of Carleton.

The resort has a mile of safe, sandy and gently-sloping beach backed by a promenade. Its harbour is the scene of various races and regattas throughout the summer and the harbour complex has a swimming pool, beach pavilion and boating lake. A sea angling and freshwater fishing centre, Girvan also has its own eighteen-hole golf course in addition to many parks and gardens. As a touring centre the town is ideally situated for day trips. The beautiful coast road running south to Ballantrae negotiates the dramatic cliffs of Kennedy's Pass.

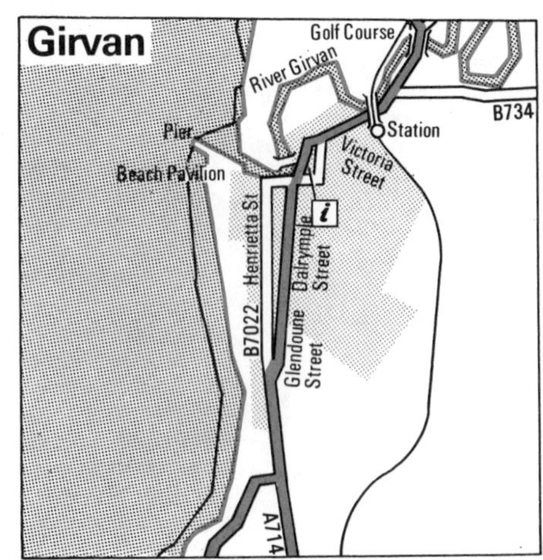

Recreation and Sports

Beach Pavilion – Children's entertainment, concerts, dances, organ recitals, variety performances, wrestling
Carrick Sailing Club Girvan ☎*3656*
Girvan Bowling Club Club House, The Avenue ☎*4292*
Girvan Golf Club House Golf Course Rd ☎*4272*
Girvan Swimming Baths Knockcushan St ☎*2056*
Knockcushan Gardens – Aviary
Morton Recreation Grounds – Tennis
Promenade and Sea Front – Boating lake, children's amusements, deck chair hire, putting

Cinema

The Vogue Club and Cinema, Dalrymple Street ☎*2101* (alternates between Bingo hall and cinema)

Tourist Information Office

Kyle and Carrick District Council Tourist Information Centre, Bridge St, Girvan ☎*2056*

Accommodation

The following establishments are recommended by the AA. Further information may be obtained from the Tourist Information Office.

★★	**Kings Arms** Dalrymple St ☎*3322*
★	**Ailsa Arms** Old St ☎*3172*
★	**Carrick Arms** Dalrymple St ☎*2261*
★	**Hamilton Arms** ☎*2182*
GH	**Barbara** 16 Louisa Dr, Sea Front ☎*2398*
GH	**Westcliffe Private Hotel** Louisa Dr ☎*2128*

Curling

Turnberry
A golfing centre with two championship standard courses. There is a sandy beach, backed by dunes and the northern portion of the beach is overlooked by the remains of Turnberry Castle where Robert the Bruce spent his childhood and may have been born. It was here that Bruce landed in 1307 on his way to his first victory over the English.

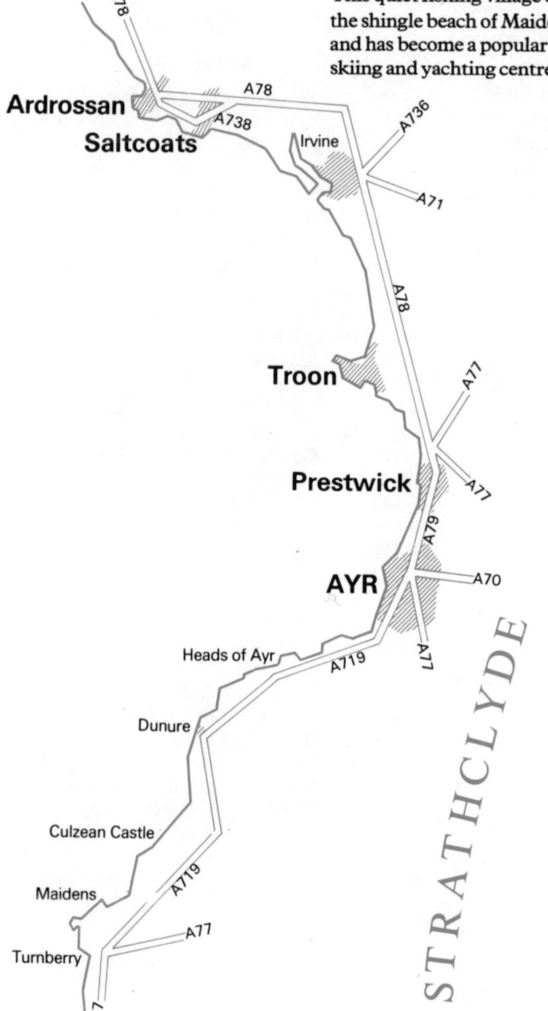

Maidens
This quiet fishing village overlooks the shingle beach of Maidenhead Bay and has become a popular water-skiing and yachting centre. A short distance inland lies Shanter Farm, the home of Tam O'Shanter, the hero of Burns' famous poem.

Culzean Castle
A late 18th-century fortress, designed by Robert Adam, which is surrounded by 500 acres of wooded parkland. The castle contains a fine collection of portraits and a guest flat which was presented to the late General Eisenhower who often stayed there when visiting Scotland. A country park, with nature trails and an exhibition centre, has been established in the grounds.

Dunure
The stone buildings of this old fishing village overlook a small harbour and a sandy beach with rocky outcrops lies at the foot of the steep cliffs. A ruined 15th-century castle, a former Kennedy stronghold, stands near the shore. The castle is best known for the roasting of Allan Stewart, the Commendator of Crossraguel Abbey, by Gilbert Kennedy, the 4th Earl of Cassillis, during a local feud in 1570.

Heads of Ayr
A high promontory overlooking Ayr Bay and providing fine views of the surrounding coastline. A holiday camp stands on the cliffs above a sandy beach.

AYR *see page 160*

Prestwick *see page 162*

Troon *see page 163*

Irvine
A Royal Burgh which has become a busy industrial port. Ardeer, to the north west, was the site chosen by Alfred Nobel, the famous Swedish chemist who founded the Nobel Prize, for the establishment of one of the largest explosives factories in the country. Irvine has associations with Robert Burns and contains several places of interest, including the remains of 14th-century Seagate Castle and the 120-foot Tower House. The area has recently been developed as a New Town and a unique innovation has been the creation of a Beach Park which incorporates safe sands, an artificial boating lake and copious amusement and recreational facilities.

Ardrossan/Saltcoats *see page 164*

Once the foremost port of Western Scotland, Ayr is now a busy market and maritime town combining its commercial activities with all the amenities of a first-class holiday resort. Fine sands provide safe bathing and pleasure boats run from the harbour, mingling with vessels of the fishing fleet and Irish cargo boats. The town abounds in parks and gardens which have won it several floral awards and The Low Green, adjoining the beach, provides ample space for sunbathing and games. Children's open-air entertainments are staged there during the summer. Paddling pools, a model railway, crazy-golf, trampolines and a well-equipped children's playground are also situated near the promenade. Ayr has an indoor swimming pool with a gymnasium and rest rooms and excellent sporting facilities including three golf courses. Outdoor events offer a fine variety of colourful spectacles including the West of Scotland Agricultural Show, Flower Shows, horse racing at Ayr Racecourse where the Scottish Grand National is held, the Belleisle Open Golf Championships, regattas, and Scottish League football. Ayr's greatest historical and literary connection is with the poet Robert Burns who was born at neighbouring Alloway in 1759. His birthplace is preserved as a museum as is Ayr's Tam O'Shanter Inn, the point from which the hero of Burn's famous poem *Tam O'Shanter* set out upon his memorable ride. The 13th-century Auld Brig across the River Ayr is also mentioned in Burn's works. Alloway's Land O'Burns Centre contains a wealth of information about the poet and his works and visitors may follow the Burns Heritage Trail around the surrounding area.

Other places of interest in Ayr include Loudon Hall, a late-15th-century building which is the oldest in the town and St John's Tower, incorporated in a 12th-century church. Further afield are Culzean Castle and Country Park, near Maidens, ruined Turnberry Castle, the alleged birthplace of Robert the Bruce and the 13th-century Crossraguel Abbey near Maybole.

Recreation and Sports

D	**Ayr Baths** South Beach Rd ☎ *69793*
C	**Ayr Ice Rink** 9 Limekiln Rd ☎ *63024* N off New Road
L	**Ayr Indoor Bowling Green** 54 Holmston Rd ☎ *69624* Off A70
	Ayr Racecourse ☎ *62340*
	Ayr United FC Somerset Park ☎ *63435* Scottish League
D	**Ayr Yacht Club** South Beach Rd ☎ *65442*
	Belleisle Golf Club ☎ *Alloway41258* S off A719
	Craigie Park – Bowls, pitch and putt, tennis
	Dalmilling Golf Club ☎ *63893* E off A77.
	Dam Park Stadium ☎ *64771*
D	**Esplanade** – Boating pool, childrens' playground, crazy-golf, miniature railway, paddling pool, tennis, trampolines
G	**Low Green** – Childrens' entertainment, putting
J	**Seafield** – Bowls, putting, tennis
	Seafield Golf Course N off A719

Cinemas

L	**Odeon** Burns Statue Sq ☎ *64049*
F	**Orient** Main St ☎ *63419*

Dancing

G	**Pavilion Ballroom** Esplanade ☎ *65489*

Theatres

F	**Civic Theatre** ☎ *63755* S off John St
H	**Gaiety Theatre** ☎ *64639*

Places of Interest

E(1)	**Academy** – Founded in the 13th century
F(2)	**Auld Brig**
I(3)	**Auld Kirk**
L(4)	**Burns Statue**
F(5)	**Carnegie Library**
H(6)	**Strathclyde Region Offices** – On the site of the old county prison
	Land O'Burns Centre Alloway ☎ *Alloway43502*
E(7)	**Loudon Hall**
H(8)	**McAdams' Monument** – Erected in 1936 in memory of the inventor of a roadmaking process
E(9)	**St Johns' Tower**
I(10)	**Tam O'Shanter Inn**
I(12)	**Wallace Tower**

Tourist Information

E(11)	**Town Hall and Information Bureau**
[i]H	**Tourist Information Centre** 30 Miller Rd ☎ *68077*

Accommodation

The establishments listed below are a selection of AA-recommended accommodation and restaurants located in the area covered by the Town Plan. Further information may be found in AA publications or obtained from the Tourist Information Centre.

1★★	**Ayrshire and Galloway** 1 Killoch Place ☎ *62626*
2★★	**Berkeley** Bains St ☎ *63658*
3✕	**Bumbles** Dalblair Arc ☎ *60993*
5☆☆☆	**Caledonian** Dalblair Rd ☎ *69331*
6✕	**Carle's** 27 Burns Statue Sq ☎ *62740*
7GH	**Clifton Hotel** 19 Miller Rd ☎ *64521*
8★★	**County** Wellington Sq ☎ *63368*
9GH	**Daviot House** 12 Queens Ter ☎ *63672*
10★	**Fort Lodge** 2 Citadel Place ☎ *65232*
11✕	**Fouters Bistro** 2A Academy St ☎ *61391*
12★★	**Gartferry** Racecourse Rd ☎ *62768*
13GH	**Inverlea** 42 Carrick Rd ☎ *61538*
14✕✕	**Kylestrone** Miller Rd ☎ *62474*
15★★	**Marine Court** Fairfield Rd ☎ *65261*
16★★★	**Savoy Park** Racecourse Rd ☎ *66112*
17★★★	**Station** Burns Statue Sq ☎ *63268*
18★	**Struan** 37 Carrick Rd ☎ *65679*
19GH	**Windsor** Alloway Place ☎ *64689*

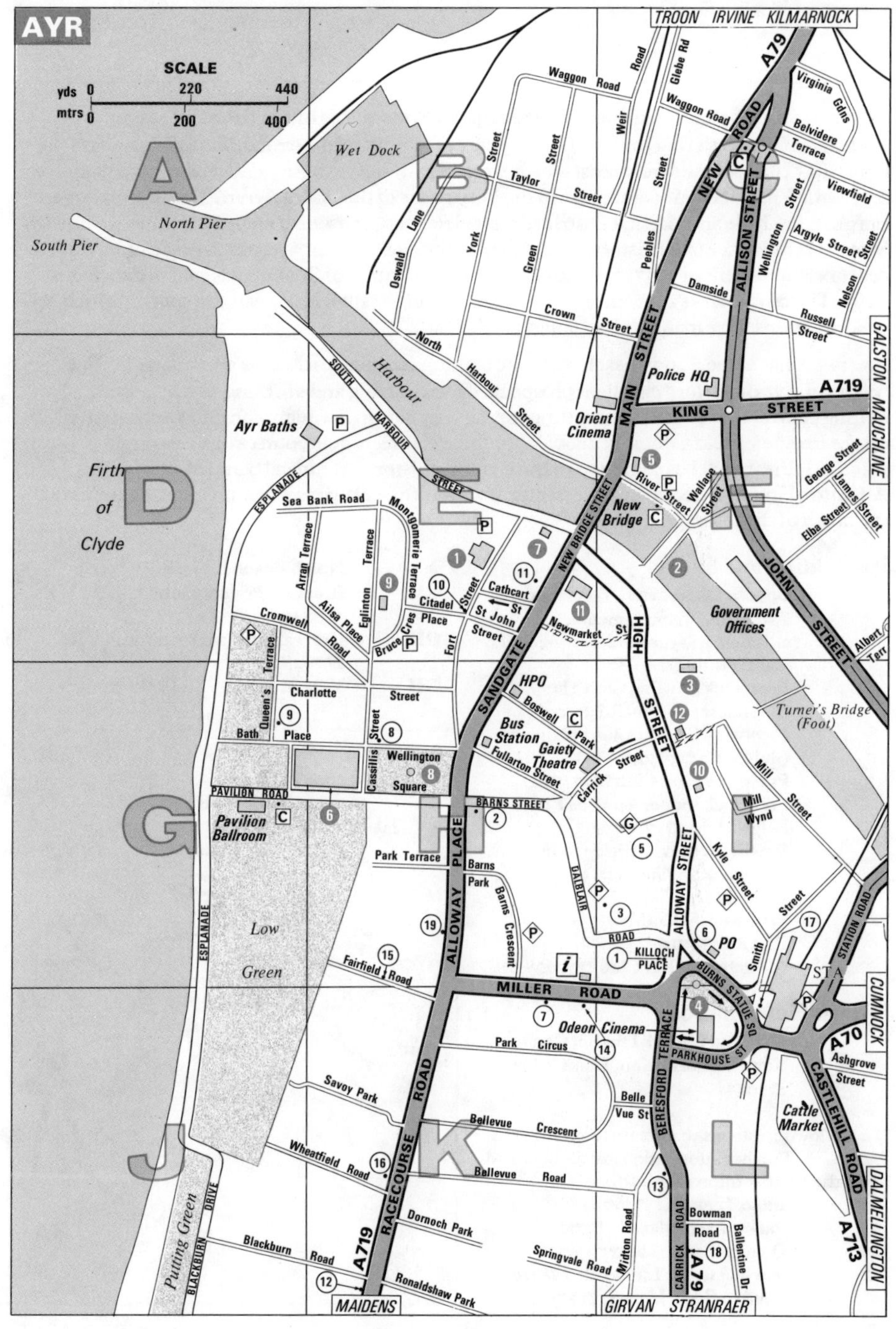
AYR
SCALE
yds 0 220 440
mtrs 0 200 400
TROON IRVINE KILMARNOCK
GALSTON MAUCHLINE
CUMNOCK
DALMELLINGTON
MAIDENS
GIRVAN STRANRAER
Wet Dock
North Pier
South Pier
Firth of Clyde
Harbour
Ayr Baths
Police HQ
Orient Cinema
New Bridge
Government Offices
Turner's Bridge (Foot)
HPO
Bus Station
Gaiety Theatre
Pavilion Ballroom
Low Green
Putting Green
Odeon Cinema
PO
STA
Cattle Market
KING STREET
MAIN STREET
NEW ROAD
ALLISON STREET
JOHN STREET
HIGH STREET
SANDGATE
NEW BRIDGE STREET
ALLOWAY PLACE
ALLOWAY STREET
RACECOURSE ROAD
MILLER ROAD
BERESFORD TERRACE
CARRICK ROAD
CASTLEHILL ROAD
STATION ROAD
ESPLANADE
BURNS STATUE SQ
PARKHOUSE ST
PAVILION ROAD
BARNS STREET
DALBLAIR ROAD
KILLOCH PLACE
A79
A719
A70
A713
Waggon Road
Weir Road
Glebe Rd
Virginia Gdns
Belvidere Terrace
Viewfield
Argyle Street
Wellington Street
Nelson Street
Damside
Russell Street
Taylor Street
York Street
Green Street
Peebles Street
Oswald Lane
Crown Street
North Harbour Street
South Harbour Street
George Street
James Street
Elba Street
River Street
Wallace Street
Albert Terr
Sea Bank Road
Arran Terrace
Eglinton Terrace
Montgomerie Terrace
Cathcart St
Citadel Place
St John Street
Fort Street
Newmarket St
Cromwell Road
Ailsa Place
Bruce Cres
Queen's Terrace
Charlotte Street
Bath Place
Cassillis Street
Wellington Square
Boswell Park
Fullarton Street
Carrick Street
Mill Street
Mill Wynd
Kyle Street
Smith Street
Park Terrace
Barns Park
Barns Crescent
Fairfield Road
Park Circus
Savoy Park
Belle Vue St
Bellevue Crescent
Bellevue Road
Wheatfield Road
Dornoch Park
Blackburn Road
Blackburn Drive
Ronaldshaw Park
Springvale Road
Midton Road
Bowman Road
Ballantine Dr
Ashgrove Street
A B C D E F G H I J K L

PRESTWICK

Well known as the site of an international airport, Prestwick is one of Scotland's most attractive resorts offering a relaxed atmosphere in uncluttered surroundings. Situated on the long, slow curve of the sandy coast which stretches from Ayr to Ardrossan, the town has views across the Firth of Clyde which take in the lofty peaks of the Isle of Arran. The second largest burgh in the Kyle and Carrick District, Prestwick is also the oldest recorded baronial burgh in Scotland. Evidence of its history is displayed in the ancient mercat cross dating from the 15th century, but rebuilt in 1777, and the nearby ruined Church of St Nicholas said to date from 1163. The cross marks the centre of the oldest part of Prestwick and was the spot on which proclamations were made and floggings carried out.

Prestwick has a fine, sandy beach with safe bathing facilities backed by an esplanade. The waters of Ayr Bay afford excellent prospects for sea angling and yachting. An important golfing centre, the town was the setting for the original Open Championship which took place on the Prestwick Old Course in 1860. With three eighteen-hole courses of a very high standard, Prestwick has some 400 years of golfing history. Medieval banquets are held at Adamton House, a Georgian-style mansion with 15th-century associations, some 2 miles to the north of the town.

Recreation and Sports

Boydfield Gardens – Band concerts
Esplanade – Amusement centre, children's playground, crazy-golf, go-karts, putting.
Prestwick Bowling Club The Clubhouse, Midton Rd ☎ *70085*
Prestwick Cricket Club St Ninians Clubhouse ☎ *77720*
Prestwick Golf Club ☎ *77404*
Prestwick Indoor Bowling Rink Bellevue Rd ☎ *77802*
Prestwick Park – Cricket, tennis
Prestwick Sailing Club 5 Esplanade ☎ *77686*
Prestwick St Cuthberts Golf Club East Rd ☎ *77101*
St Nicholas Golf Club ☎ *77608*

Tourist Information

Kyle and Carrick District Council Tourist Information, Links Rd ☎ *79234*

The following establishments are recommended by the AA. Further information may be obtained from the Tourist Information Office.

★★ **Links** Links Rd ☎ *77792*
★★ **Parkstone** Esplanade ☎ *77286*
★★ **Queens** Esplanade ☎ *70501*
★ **Auchen Coyle** Links Rd ☎ *78316*
★ **Golden Eagle** Main St ☎ *77566*
★ **North Beach** Links Rd ☎ *79069*
GH **Braemar Private Hotel** 113 Ayr Rd ☎ *78277*
GH **Kincraig Private Hotel** 39 Ayr Rd ☎ *79480*
GH **Villa Marina** 19 Links Rd ☎ *70396*

TROON

This quiet resort is situated in the centre of the Ayrshire coast with distant views across the Firth of Clyde to the Isle of Arran, and the bird sanctuary of Lady Isle some two miles off-shore. Originally a small, isolated fishing community, Troon sprang up around the curiously-shaped promontory that juts out into the Clyde estuary dividing Ayr Bay from Irvine Bay. The 4th Duke of Portland began the building of the harbour in the 18th century and the town has gradually developed, taking on the dual role of holiday resort and industrial centre. Old Troon, based on the original fishing village, is to be found around the harbour, but basically it is a twentieth-century town. A notable landmark is the distinctive dome of Marr College built in 1919 from money donated to the town by Charles Kerr Marr.

Troon has over two miles of soft, sandy beach extending both north and south of the busy harbour, popular with anglers. The beach slopes gently down towards the sea, and the south sands provide exceptionally good bathing. A well-known golfing resort, Troon has five courses including the Old Course and the Portland Course both owned by the Royal Troon Golf Club. During the season North Beach is the scene of various races and regattas organised by the Troon Sailing Club. Other recreational facilities, including the open-air swimming pool, are to be found alongside the two beaches with sub-aqua diving off-shore.

Recreation and Sports

Beach area – Bowls, crazy golf, putting, tennis, trampolines.
Concert Hall South Beach – Concerts, dances, disco every Friday, drama presentations.
Fullerton Woods – Picnic area
Royal Troon Golf Club Craigend Rd (Old Course and Portland Course) ☎*311555*
Troon Baths Titchfield Rd ☎*311431*
Troon Portland Bowling Club Beach Rd ☎*311045*
Troon Sailing Club Beach Rd ☎*311451*
Troon Tennis Club Bentinck Dr, Troon
Troon Municipal Golf Courses (Darley, Fullarton and Lochgreen) ☎*312464*

Tourist Information

Tourist Information Office
Municipal Buildings, South Beach
☎*315131*

Accommodation

The following establishments are recommended by the AA. Further information may be obtained from the Tourist Information Office.

★★★★ **Marine** ☎*314444*
★★★ **Sun Court** Crosbie Rd ☎*312727*
★★ **Ardnell** St Meddans St ☎*311611*
★★ **Craiglea** South Beach ☎*311366*
★★ **South Beach** South Beach Rd ☎*312033*
GH **Glenside** Bentinck Dr ☎*313677*
GH **Troon** 5 Bentinck Dr ☎*311177*

Restaurant

✕ **Lang Spoon** 42 West Portland St ☎*311797*

SALTCOATS & ARDROSSAN

The popular seaside resorts of Ardrossan and Saltcoats are closely linked in many ways. They have views across the Firth of Clyde which take in the Arran Hills, the island being easily reached by ferry. Both have long histories, the town and harbour of Ardrossan having been laid out by the 12th Earl of Eglington in 1805. Today, it is a busy commercial port from which ferry vessels operate to Arran, the Isle of Man and Northern Ireland. By contrast Saltcoats was once a fishing port and salt-making centre, but its picturesque harbour is now busy with pleasure craft and tourists. The towns have been carefully planned and Saltcoats has a fine shopping precinct popular with visitors. A feature of Saltcoats is the North Ayrshire Museum located in the ancient former Parish Church. The museum exhibits local historical items and early-19th-century interiors.

Ardrossan has extensive beaches with ample recreational facilities including sea fishing and boating and the harbour is a popular spot from which to watch the comings and goings of passing ships. Saltcoats has firm sandy beaches offering safe bathing and donkey rides. At low-tide twenty-six fossilised tree-trunks may be seen in the harbour. A promenade runs for about a mile along the sea front.

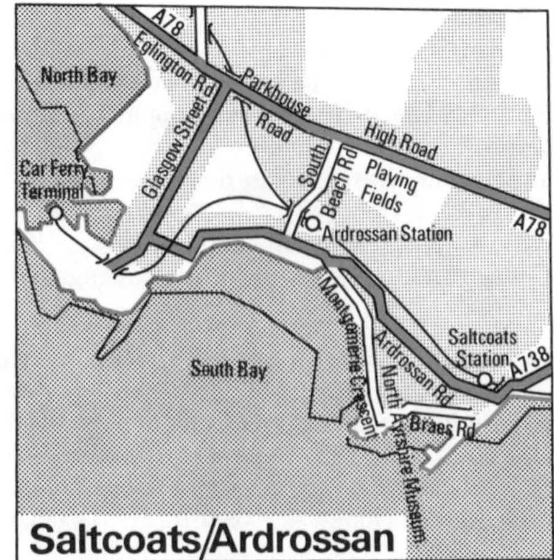

Recreation and Sports

Ardrossan Bowling Club Kilmeny Ter ☎*63805*
Ardrossan Indoor Bowling Club George St ☎*61059*
Saltcoats Bowling Club Springvale Pl, ☎*64874*
Saltcoats Promenade – Amusements, putting

Places of Interest

North Ayrshire Museum ☎*Saltcoats 64174*

Tourist Information

Town Clerks Office ☎*Saltcoats 64372*

Accommodation

The following establishments are recommended by the AA. Further information may be obtained from the Tourist Information Office.

★★ **Eglinton Arms** Princess St, Ardrossan ☎*65112*
★ **High Tide** Parkhouse Rd, Ardrossan ☎*61527*
GH **Ellwood House** 6 Arran Pl, Ardrossan ☎*Ayr 61130*

Fairlie
This one-time fishing village is now a small resort and residential area. It has a shingle beach and is a popular sailing centre, its waters sheltered by the island of Great Cumbrae two miles offshore. Steamer trips are available. A few miles to the south, Hunterston House and Castle are open to the public.

Largs *see page 166*

Skelmorlie
This village, which was developed as a health resort during the 19th century is now a residential area for Glasgow commuters. There is a pebble beach and fine views to the north and west across the Firth of Clyde.

Gourock
An industrial town which has become a holiday resort and touring centre. A long pebble beach lies below the town and there is an open-air swimming-pool.

Greenock
This busy dockyard town was the birthplace of James Watt of steam engine fame and has a museum devoted to his life.

Helensburgh
Created during the 18th century, the town of Helensburgh is set out in an orderly fashion of straight lines. It has, in the past, been the home of some of our great inventors – Henry Bell, who designed Europe's first passenger steamboat and John Logie Baird who pioneered the television. Today it is a popular holiday resort with a sand and shingle beach on the shores of Gare Loch.

Kilcreggan
The narrow pebble beach is overlooked by the small village and its eastern extremity is sheltered by Rosneath Point.

Holy Loch
There are pebble beaches here in wooded surroundings. American Polaris submarines can often be seen at anchor in the loch.

Dunoon *see page 167*

Port Bannatyne
The harbour accommodates a small fishing fleet and pleasure craft. There is a sand and shingle bay where boats are available for hire.

Rothesay *see page 168*

Ettrick Bay
Safe bathing is available here from a beach of reddish sand. Amusements are available.

Tighnabruaich
A sailing centre set amid fine wooded scenery. The beaches are mainly rocky.

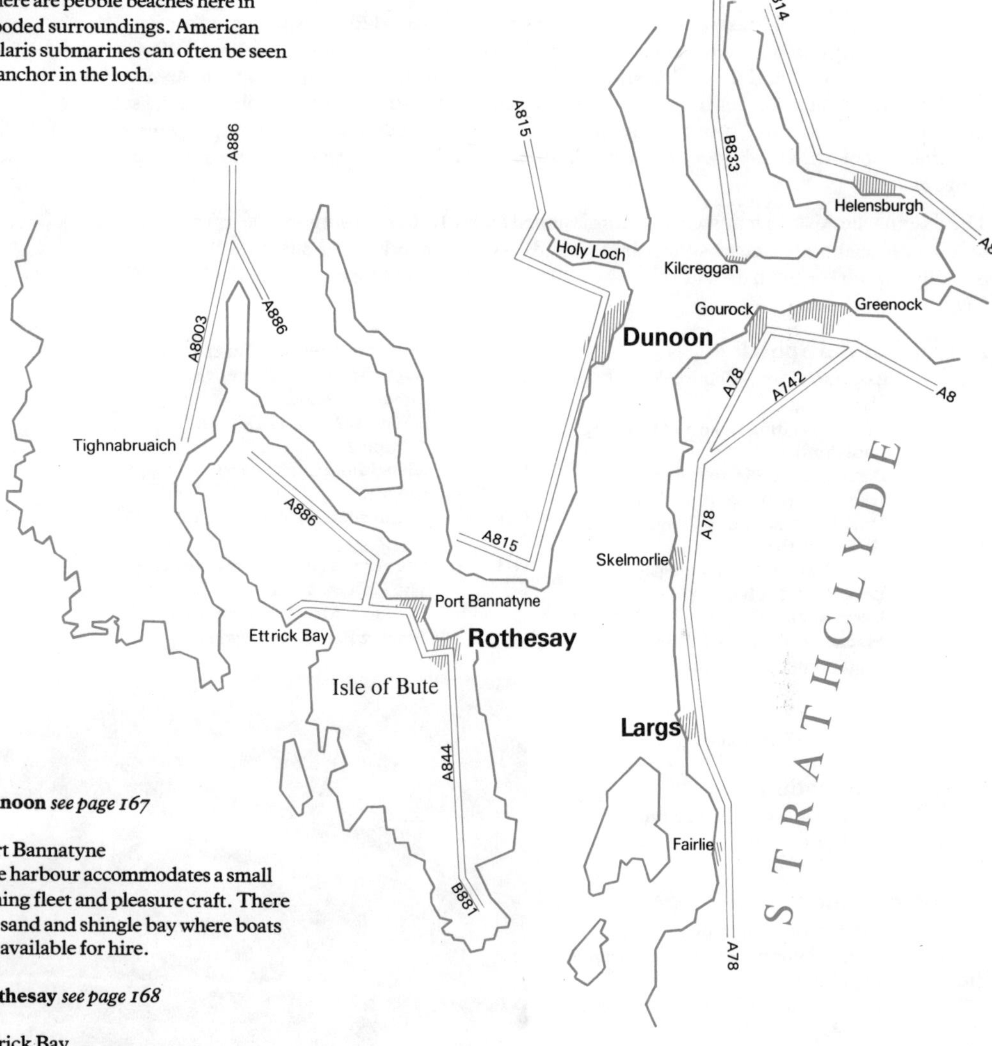

LARGS

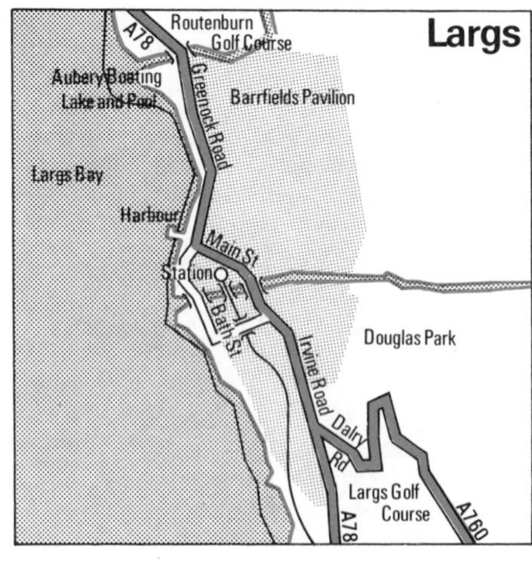

Largs was the scene of one of Scotland's most famous medieval battles when the Scots, led by King Alexander III, repulsed a Norwegian invasion in 1263 and finally put an end to centuries of coastal plundering. This event is commemorated by a memorial known as 'The Pencil' which stands on the shoreline near Bowen Craig.

Today this pleasant, old-fashioned town has become a popular holiday resort, noted for its bracing air. Largs' pebble and shingle beach, backed by a wide expanse of grassland, offers safe swimming for all and the shelter afforded by Great Cumbrae Island has made the area a favourite centre for sailing enthusiasts. A variety of pleasure cruises are available from the sea front and Largs has ample sporting facilities including two golf courses and a modern indoor swimming pool which incorporates a sauna bath. Several colourful regattas are held during the summer.

The Skelmorlie Aisle, a mausoleum commissioned by Sir Robert Montgomerie in 1636 and noted for its elaborate Italian-style paintings and carvings, stands in the old churchyard and the hills around the town provide pleasant walking country and fine views over the Firth of Clyde.

Recreation and Sports

Anderson Park – Children's playground
Aubery Boating Lake and Paddling Pool Promenade
Barrfields Pavilion – Indoor swimming pool, sports hall, sauna
Douglas Park – Bowls, tennis
Greenock Road – Putting
Largs Bowling Club Douglas St
Largs Golf Club ☎ *674681*
Largs Sailing Club John St ☎ *674782*
Mackerston Place – Putting
Routenburn Golf Course ☎ *673230*

Theatre

Barrfields Pavilion

Tourist Information

Information Centre The Promenade ☎ *673765*

Accommodation

The following establishments are recommended by the AA. Further information may be obtained from the Tourist Information Office.

★★★	**Marine and Curlinghall** Broomfields ☎ *674551*
★★	**Castle** Broomfields ☎ *673302*
★★	**Elderslie** Broomfields ☎ *672251*
★★	**Mackerston** ☎ *673264*
★★	**Queens** North Esplanade ☎ *673253*
★★	**St Helens** Greenock Rd ☎ *672328*
AP	**Haylie** 108 Irvine Rd ☎ *672572*
GH	**Aubery** 22 Aubery Cres ☎ *672330*
GH	**Douglas House** 42 Douglas St ☎ *672257*
GH	**Gleneldon Hotel** 2 Barr Cres ☎ *673381*
GH	**Holmesdale** 74 Moorburn Rd ☎ *674793*
GH	**Sunbury** 12 Aubery Cres ☎ *673086*
SC	**The Cottage** 2 Barr Cres. For bookings: Mrs E A Allen, Glen Eldon Hotel, 2 Barr Cres ☎ *673381*

Fishing in Largs

DUNOON

Dunoon has been a popular resort since a lone Glaswegian family arrived by hired wherry in 1779 to spend a holiday there. Since then many thousands of visitors have followed their example and the town has become the principal holiday centre of West Scotland.

Dunoon Pier, overlooked by Castle Gardens and Castle Hill with its ruined fortress and statue of Mary Campbell, the 'Highland Mary' of Robert Burns' poem, is, perhaps, the focal point of the town. Ferries and steamers serving the busy Firth of Clyde call here and a variety of pleasure trips are available. There are two safe, shingle beaches, West Bay, with its deep rocky pools, paddling and boating pool and Swing Park, being the most popular with children. Dunoon has good entertainment and sporting facilities and is the scene of a two-day Highland Gathering which takes place in Dunoon Stadium each year during late August. A weekly 'Visitors' Night Out' is organised in the spring and autumn by the local tourist authorities. There are many parks and gardens and the Cowal Peninsula with its Argyll National Forest Park, is an area of outstanding beauty. Kilmun Arboretum with a large collection of specially planted conifers and broadleaved trees lies a short distance away, overlooking picturesque Holy Loch, the American Polaris submarine base.

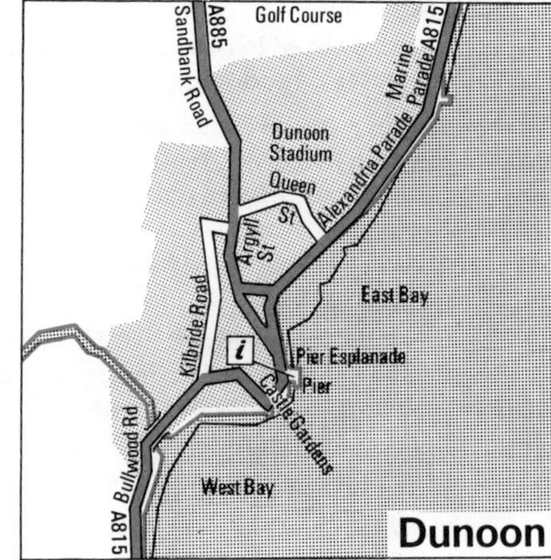

Recreation and Sports

Argyll Gardens Pier Esplanade – Bandshows, children's entertainment (July and Aug)
Bogleha Club Argyll St – Bowls
Castle Gardens – Adventure playground, putting, tennis
Castle Rocks West Bay – Crazy-golf
Cowal Golf Club Kirn ☎*2216*
Dunoon Stadium Argyll St ☎*2104* Athletics, football, highland games
Dunoon Swimming Pool Alexandra Prom, East Bay ☎*3735* – Indoor pool, Sauna
Hunters' Quay Marine Pde – Boats and dinghies for hire
Promenade West Bay – Putting
West Bay – Boats for hire, paddling and boating pool, Swing Park

Cinema

Studio 'A' 41 John St ☎*4545*

Theatre

Queens Hall ☎*2263*

Tourist Information

Dunoon Pier ☎*4374*
Tourist Information Centre Pier ☎*3785*

Accommodation

The following establishments are recommended by the AA. Further information may be obtained from the Tourist Information Office.

★★	**Argyll** ☎*2059*
★★	**McColl's** West Bay ☎*2764*
★★	**Queens** Marine Pde, Kirn ☎*4224*
★★	**Royal Marine** Sea Front, Hunters Quay, (2m N A815) ☎*3001*
★	**Caledonian** Argyll St ☎*2176*
GH	**Cedars Private Hotel** Alexandra Pde ☎*2425*
GH	**Claymore** West Bay ☎*2658*

Throwing the hammer at Highland Games

ROTHESAY

The principal town of the Isle of Bute, Rothesay was proclaimed a Royal Burgh in 1401 and its castle, the remains of which stand near the harbour, has been the scene of many a bloody encounter over the centuries.

Modern Rothesay lies on a wide, sweeping bay surrounded by peaceful wooded scenery, the modern pier with its ferry and steamer traffic contrasting with the Victorian buildings of the sea front. Safe, sandy beaches and an exceptionally mild climate have combined to make the town a thriving holiday resort and there are good sporting facilities. The Bute Highland Games are staged here during August.

The castle, built in a unique circular formation and surrounded by a deep moat, dates from the 13th century although much of the structure was destroyed by Cromwell in the 17th century. Rothesay contains The Bute Museum where prehistoric finds, natural history exhibits and models of Clyde steamers are displayed.

The 14th-century ruins of St Mary's Chapel, in the High Street, contain interesting early gravestones and a later one dedicated to Stephanie Hortense Bonaparte, Napoleon's niece.

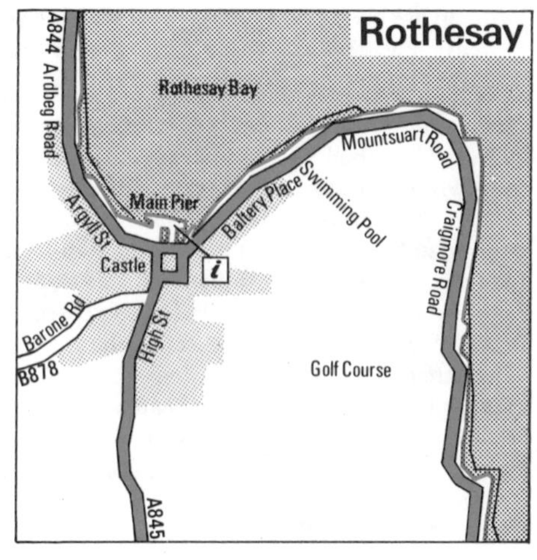

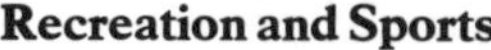

Recreation and Sports

Battery Place – Children's corner
Craigmore – Bowls, tennis
Esplanade Gardens – Putting
Isle of Bute Sailing Club West Bay
King George V Playing Fields – Highland Games
Meadows – Paddling pool, playground, tennis
Rothesay Golf Course ☎ *2244*
Rothesay Swimming Pool Mount Stuart Rd ☎ *3340* – Indoor pool
West Bay – Boating pool
West Promenade – Crazy-golf

Cabaret/Dancing

Pavilion Ballroom ☎ *3738*

Places of Interest

Bute Natural History Museum
Rothesay Castle

Tourist Information

Tourist Information Centre The Pier ☎ *2151*

Accommodation

The following establishments are recommended by the AA. Further information may be obtained from the Tourist Information Office.

★★★	**Glenburn** Glenburn Rd ☎ *2500*
★★	**Royal** Albert Pl ☎ *3044*
★★	**Victoria** Victoria St ☎ *3553*
GH	**Alva House Private Hotel** 24 Mount Stuart Rd ☎ *2328*
GH	**Battery Lodge Private Hotel** 25 Battery Pl ☎ *2169*
GH	**Morningside** Mount Pleasant Rd ☎ *3526*
GH	**St Fillans** 36 Mount Stuart Rd ☎ *2784*
SC	Mrs J McIntosh, **Beechwood Holiday Flats** 11 Bishop Ter ☎ *3999*

Relaxing in Rothesay

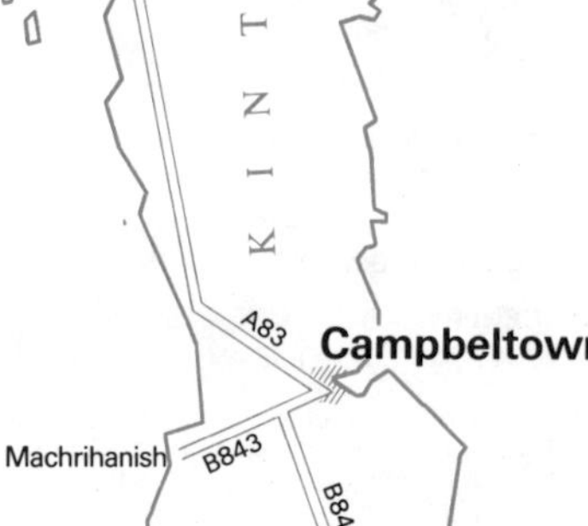

Lochgilphead
This holiday resort and boating centre is surrounded by farmlands. It has shingle beaches and steamer trips are available.

Ardrishaig
A former fishing village which is now a popular sailing centre. The embankment of the Crinan Canal runs through the village terminating in a rocky basin which forms a sheltered anchorage for yachts. Locks and a swing bridge separate the basin from the sometimes turbulent waters of Loch Fyne.

Tarbert
There are shingle beaches here and swimming is generally safe. Steep cliffs surround the harbour which is used by the local herring fleet and numerous pleasure craft and overlooked by the ruins of a 14th-century castle, the former stronghold of Robert the Bruce. Hills almost encircle the town with the massive Sliabh Gaoil rising to a height of 1,840 feet to the north-west.

Skipness
The remains of the 13th-century castle, which guarded the southern boundary of the lands of the Campbells, stands above a small village on a rocky bay. There are fine views of the northern coast of the Isle of Arran.

Carradale
Safe, sandy beaches lie before this village which was once a thriving fishing centre. There are several small rocky bays to the south, all completely unspoilt. The ruins of an ancient fort, apparently partially destroyed by fire, stands on Carradale Point. The Forestry Commission has extensive plantations to the north which can be visited on application.

Campbeltown *see page 170*

Southend
A holiday village backed by the wild, barren scenery of the Mull of Kintyre. Its sheltered, sandy beaches are safe for swimming under most conditions. A fine golf course stands upon the cliffs. Southend is generally held to be the landing place of St Columba on his first mission to Scotland and a flat rock, near the ruined chapel, is said to bear his footprints. It is possible to walk across the Mull to the lighthouse on the western shore, some four miles away, from which the coast of Ireland can be seen.

Machrihanish
Formerly a fishing village and important salt producing centre, Machrihanish has now become a popular holiday resort. Machrihanish Bay has a long sweep of sand, dotted with the odd rocky outcrop and backed by flat agricultural land. Swimming and surfing are both possible but care should be exercised at all times. There is a golf course on the cliffs at the southern end of the bay.

Tayinloan
This town has access to sheltered, shingle beaches. A passenger ferry runs from Tayinloan to Gigha Island, a fertile, rocky island supporting a number of dairy farms. There are sandy beaches on the east coast and Achamore House, near Ardminish the island's main town, has a unique garden, containing a multitude of azaleas and rhododendrons, which is open to the public.

CAMPBELTOWN

Towards the end of the Kintyre peninsula Campbeltown Loch cuts in on the east side forming a perfect natural harbour. At its mouth is Davaar Island and at its head lies Campbeltown, a cluster of predominantly grey buildings below the gentle slopes of the hills of Kintyre. Though seemingly remote, it is surprisingly accessible with regular bus and air services from Glasgow and occasional ferries from Clyde ports. Campbeltown is a busy market town and shopping centre for a wide area and its ancient origins are older than the Scottish nation itself. There were settlers here long before the Irish invaders landed on Kintyre and established their capital, Dalruadhain, where Campbeltown now stands. It emerged from a turbulent period of clan warfare under the protection of the Earl of Argyll, whose family name it took, to become a Royal Burgh of great prosperity. At the end of the 19th century a vast fleet of over 600 fishing boats operated from the harbour and the town boasted no less than 34 distilleries. There are only two distilleries today and visitors to the quay will see a somewhat depleted fishing fleet, but the harbour is still a lively place where herring boats are joined by dinghies, yachts, passenger steamers and the local lifeboat. On either side of the quay area there are safe, sandy beaches at Dalintober and Kilkerran. Above the town the 1,154ft Bengullion hides the mysterious Pipers Cave. On the island of Davaar is the remarkable rock painting of the crucifixion by Archibald MacKinnon.

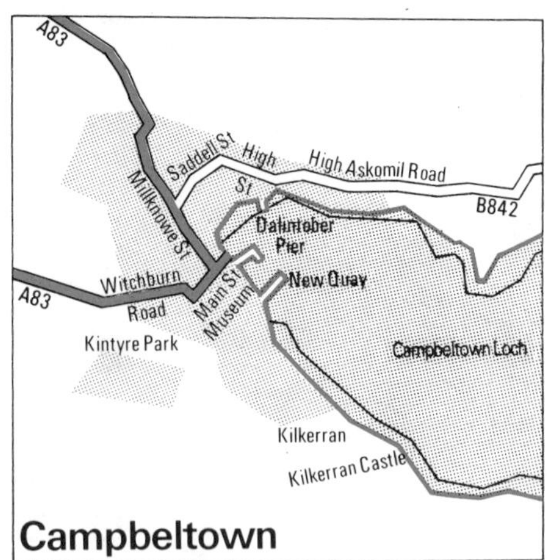

Recreation and Sports

Argyll Street – Bowls
Campbeltown Yacht Club Low Askomill Rd
Harbour – Sea angling trips
Kilkerran – Childrens paddling pool, putting, trampolines
Kintyre Park – Football
Kinloch Road Swimming Pool ☎ *3107*
Machrihanish Golf Club Machrihanish ☎ *Machrihanish213*
Millknowe – Bowls
St John Street – Tennis

Cinema

The Picture House ☎ *2264*

Dancing

Babettes 27 High Street, ☎ *3465*
Victoria Hall

Places of Interest

Carradale House Carradale ☎ *Carradale234*
Kilkerran Castle (remains), Kilkerran Road
Museum Hall Street ☎ *2097*

Tourist Information

Area Tourist Officer Mid Argyll, Kintyre and Islay Tourist Organisation ☎ *2056*

Accommodation

The following establishments are recommended by the AA. Further information may be obtained from the Tourist Information Office.

★★	**Ardshiel** Kilkerran Rd ☎ *2133*
GH	**Westbank** Dell Rd ☎ *2452*

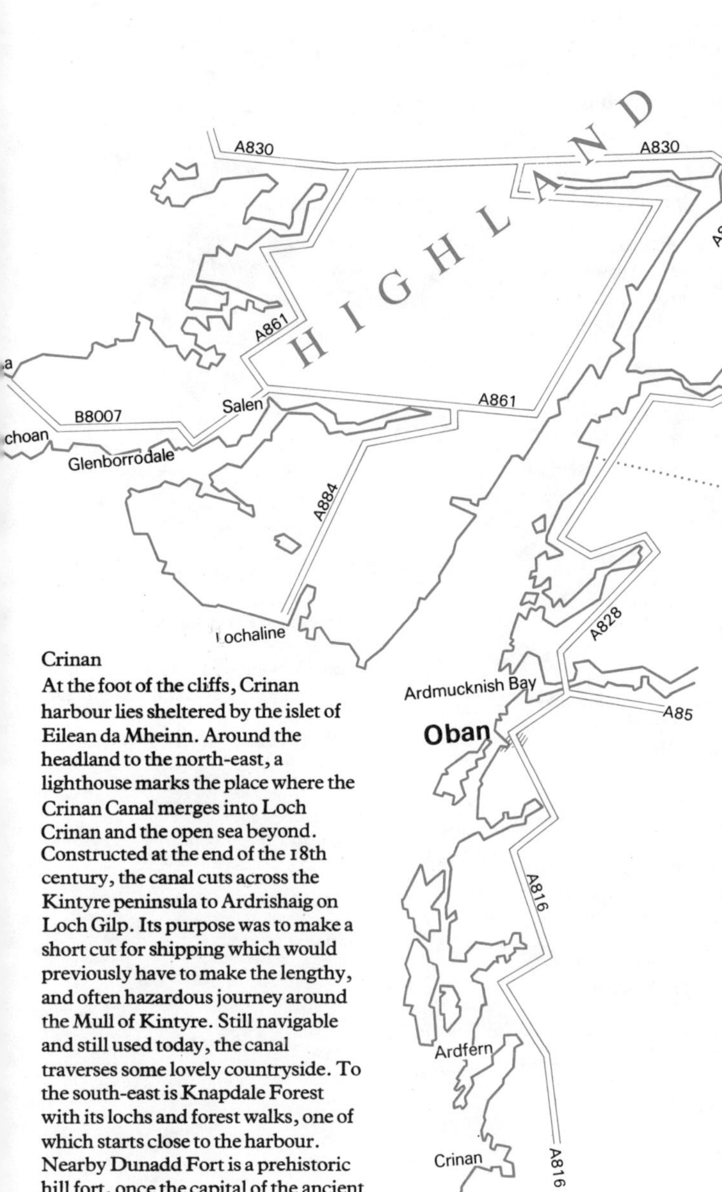

Crinan
At the foot of the cliffs, Crinan harbour lies sheltered by the islet of Eilean da Mheinn. Around the headland to the north-east, a lighthouse marks the place where the Crinan Canal merges into Loch Crinan and the open sea beyond. Constructed at the end of the 18th century, the canal cuts across the Kintyre peninsula to Ardrishaig on Loch Gilp. Its purpose was to make a short cut for shipping which would previously have to make the lengthy, and often hazardous journey around the Mull of Kintyre. Still navigable and still used today, the canal traverses some lovely countryside. To the south-east is Knapdale Forest with its lochs and forest walks, one of which starts close to the harbour. Nearby Dunadd Fort is a prehistoric hill fort, once the capital of the ancient Scots Kingdom of Dalriada.

Ardfern
There are safe, sandy beaches here along the banks of the sheltered Loch Craignish. The Craignish peninsula is rich in antiquities and just behind Ardfern village there is a Bronze Age grave known as Clach an t'Sagairt, or The Priest's Stone. The Lunga Wildlife Reserve here contains flora and fauna of the European region in a natural woodland setting. Towards the south of the peninsula is Craignish Castle.

Oban *see page 172*

Ardmucknish Bay
The flat sandy beaches around Ardmucknish Bay are backed by the level farmlands of the Benderloch peninsula. To the east lies an area of mountains and forests which is rich in ancient sites.

Lochaline
At the mouth of Loch Aline, on the headland overlooking the Isle of Mull, stands the village of Lochaline. The quay is a terminal for ferries to Oban and the Isle of Mull and there are some spectacular views. A sand mine here provides high quality sand for scientific instruments and optical glass. Across the Loch on the opposite headland, Ardtornish Castle was once the seat of the Lords of the Isles and featured in Sir Walter Scott's novel of that name.

Salen
With its beautiful wooded setting on the shore of Loch Sunart, Salen is a popular fishing and boating centre. There are several sandy bays to the south.

Glenborrodale
Glenborrodale Castle, a 19th-century fortress now converted into an hotel, stands beside the shore in the shelter of Risga Island, a breeding ground for seabirds. Seals may be seen on the rocks of neighbouring Glenmore Bay

Kilchoan
Safe, secluded beaches lie below this quiet village. A passenger ferry runs from Kilchoan to the Isle of Mull.

Sanna
A bay with dunes and fine, silvery sands. The surrounding countryside abounds in wildflowers and is a breeding ground for otters and badgers.

OBAN

Situated on Scotland's western seaboard, Oban has been described by some as being the capital of the Western Highlands; certainly it is the gateway to Mull and the islands of Iona and Staffa. The town lies on an almost land-locked bay at the foot of the hills of Lorne with the off-shore island of Kerrera sheltering it from the Atlantic winds. To the west, beyond Kerrera and its 16th-century castle, the mountains of Mull fill the skyline. Further north behind the Isle of Lismore the mountains of Morvern supply another dramatic backcloth. The town itself is no more than 200 years old and, in the mid 18th century, consisted only of a sparsely populated fishing community contrasting sharply with the busy harbour and town of today. In fact its development as a tourist centre only began in 1880 with the coming of the railways.

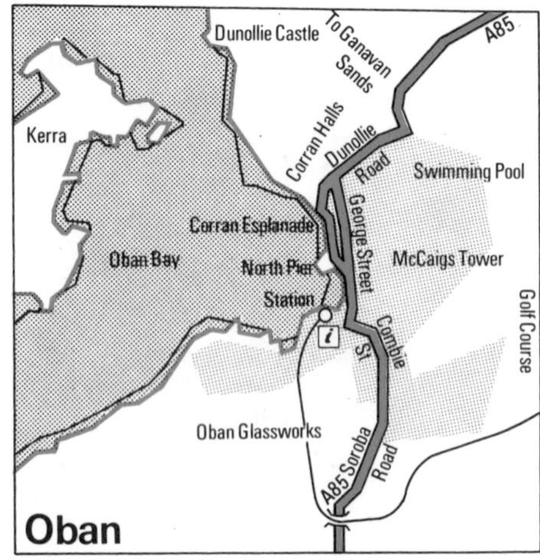

Oban has excellent shopping facilities and a crescent-shaped esplanade following the wide sweep of the bay. The town has no beach, but Ganavan Sands, two miles from the town centre, provide a wide expanse of beach, safe bathing and recreational facilities. A popular vantage point high above Oban is Pulpit Hill which offers fine views of the harbour and across the Firth of Lorne and the Sound of Mull.

A feature of the town is McCaig's Tower, a circular colosseum-like structure on Oban Hill overlooking the harbour. Planned as a museum to relieve local unemployment it was never finished and remains a familiar landmark with gardens within its walls. At the mouth of Oban Bay on a rocky promontory stands the ruin of 15th-century Dunollie Castle, principal seat of the Lords of Lorne. Near Dunbeg some 2½ miles to the north is Dunstaffnage Castle where Flora MacDonald was held prisoner in 1746.

Recreation and Sports

Corran Halls – Dancing, traditional Scottish entertainment
Dalraich Road – Bowls, tennis
Fishing – Information about fishing and permits are available from the tourist authorities
Ganavan Sands – Children's playground, sports centre, trampolines
Glencruitten Golf Club ☎*2868*
Oban Sailing Club The Secretary, Dungallan Park
Oban Swimming Pool Dalriach Rd ☎*4211* – Indoor pool, sauna

Cinema

Phoenix ☎*2444*

Places of Interest

McDonald's Mill Soroba Rd ☎3051 – Exhibitions of spinning and weaving
Museum and Library Corran Halls – Local history
Oban Glassworks Lochavullin ☎*3386*

Tourist Information

Oban and Mull Tourist Organisation
Boswell House, Argyll Sq ☎*3551*

Accommodation

The following establishments are recommended by the AA. Further information may be obtained from the Tourist Information Office.

★★★	**Alexandra** Corran Esplanade ☎*2381*
★★★	**Caledonian** Station Sq ☎*3133*
★★★	**Great Western** The Esplanade ☎*3101*
★★★	**Regent** Esplanade ☎*2341*
★★	**Columba** North Pier ☎*2183*
★★	**Lancaster** Corran Esplanade ☎*2587*
★★	**Marine** Esplanade ☎*2211*
★★	**Rowan Tree** George St ☎*2954*
★★	**West Bay** Corran Esplanade ☎*2067*
Ⓐ	**King's Knoll** Dunollie Rd ☎*2536*
Ⓐ	**Palace** George St ☎*2294*
GH	**Ardblair** Dalriach Rd ☎*2668*
GH	**Barriemore Private Hotel** Esplanade ☎*2197*
GH	**Corriemar Hotel** Corran Esplanade ☎*2476*
GH	**Crathie** Duncraggen Rd ☎*2619*
GH	**Glenburnie Private Hotel** Esplanade ☎*2089*
GH	**Heatherfield Private Hotel** Albert Rd ☎*2681*
GH	**Kenmore** Soraba Rd ☎*3592*
SC	Mr J Silverton, **The Cedars** Domollie Rd
SC	**Esplanade Court** Corran Esplanade ☎*2067*

Restaurant

✕✕	**Le Bistro** Breadalbane St ☎*3823*

Arisaig
The village lies on a wooded peninsula and has access to beaches of fine silver sands. The church tower is a local landmark and incorporates a clock dedicated to the Gaelic poet, Alasdair MacMhaigstir Alasdair who died at Culloden.

Back of Keppoch
There are safe sandy beaches here backed by dunes.

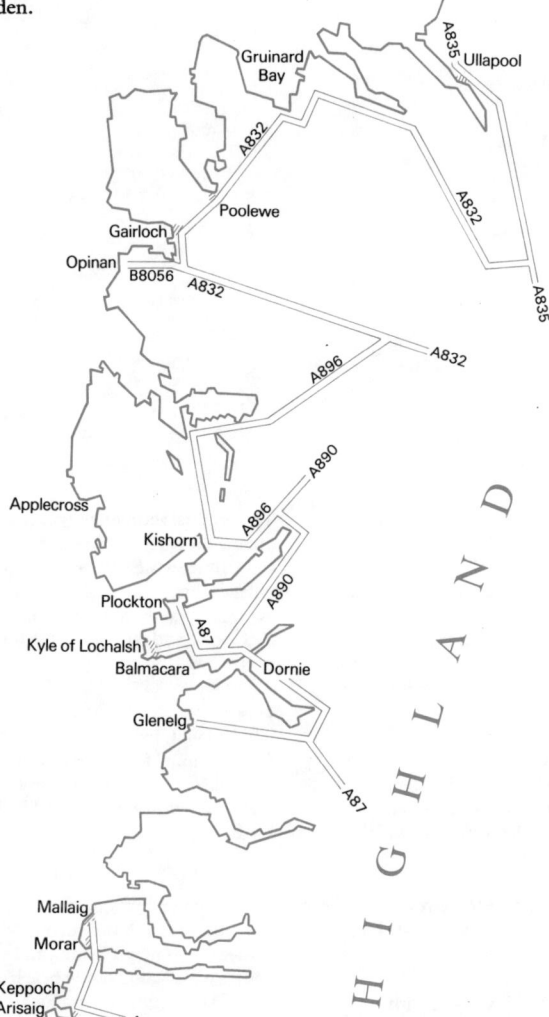

Morar
Fine beaches of white sand lie at the entrance to Loch Morar, the deepest loch in Britain, backed by the Falls of Morar which are now part of a hydro-electric scheme.

Mallaig
A busy fishing port where the Road to the Isles, which runs from Fort William, terminates. Car and passenger ferries run from the harbour to Skye and the neighbouring islands.

Glenelg
A rocky bay lies to the south of the village at the mouth of the River Glenmore.

Dornie
This attractive village stands at the meeting place of Loch Long and Loch Duich where a road bridge crosses Loch Long. Eilean Donnan Castle, a restored 13th-century fortress overlooks the village from a small island.

Balmacara
The cliff-top road provides fine views of Skye and Loch Alsh and the Balmacara Estate has many walks amongst fine scenery.

Kyle of Lochalsh
A fishing port from which a car ferry operates to Skye and steamers serve the Outer Hebrides.

Plockton
This fishing and crofting village has become a popular boating centre and a colourful regatta is held here every year.

Kishorn
A small village at the head of Loch Kishorn. Rassal Ashwood Nature Reserve covers the area immediately inland.

Applecross
A remote village accessible via the road over Bealach nam Ba, one of the highest mountain roads in Scotland. The road is not suitable for caravans. Sandy Applecross Bay lies at the foot of the cliffs.

Opinan
Reddish sands provide safe bathing but can only be reached on foot.

Gairloch
A harbour village in a picturesque setting with safe sandy beaches stretching away to the west. Boats are available for hire.

Poolewe
An attractive fishing village and touring centre with safe sand and shingle beaches to the north.

Gruinard Bay
There are sandy beaches here within a safe, sheltered bay.

Ullapool
This popular holiday resort stands on a peninsula which juts into Loch Broom. Swimming is safe and boat trips are available.

Achiltibuie
A village in a picturesque setting with a stony beach. Boat trips around the neighbouring islands are available.

Lochinver
This busy fishing village has a pebble beach and has become a popular angling centre.

Achmelvich
A small holiday centre on the northern shore of Loch Roe with a safe sandy beach.

Stoer
A crofting and fishing village with access to several small sandy beaches around Stoer Bay. There is a fine cliff-top walk to Point of Stoer, passing Stoer Lighthouse and the Old Man of Stoer, an unusual finger of rock.

Scourie
This small crofting community has established itself as a popular fishing resort. The harbour overlooks a rocky bay.

Cape Wrath
A wild, craggy headland, crowned by a lighthouse, Cape Wrath is the most northerly point of the Western Highlands. The cliffs to the south-east are the highest on the British mainland, rising to a height of over 900ft at Clo Mor. Access to the headland is by ferry across the Kyle of Durness and thence by mini-bus.

Balnakeil
A craft village has been established here which produces pottery, jewellery, sculpture and wood carvings. There is a long, sheltered sandy beach which provides safe bathing.

Durness
A sheep-farming village which stands on the cliffs above Sango Bay where a sandy beach provides safe bathing.

Melness
Fine beaches extend from Talmine to Tongue Bay providing safe bathing.

Bettyhill
A small holiday resort with wide, safe sandy beaches at nearby Torrisdale and Farr Bays.

Reay
The original settlement was engulfed during the early 18th century by the sand dunes which separate the present village from Sandside Bay. The bay contains a sandy beach with many rock pools and is crossed by a number of streams.

Scrabster
This popular fishing centre is also a ferry terminal for the Orkneys. It is set amid spectacular cliff scenery and is a favourite nesting ground for sea birds.

Thurso
The most northerly town on the British mainland, this former Viking settlement is now a fishing and sailing centre with a good sandy beach backed by large pebbles. Fishing trips are available and Thurso has ample amusement and sports facilities.

Dunnet Bay
High dunes overlook a wide expanse of firm sand where sand-yachting is a popular sport.

Dunnet Head
The most northerly road on the British mainland leads to a lighthouse 300ft above the sea. The headland is a famous viewpoint and, on a clear day, the eastern islands can be seen on the horizon.

Gills Bay
A sand and shingle beach with rocks and deep pools at low-tide where seals can frequently be seen.

John O'Groats
The Lands' End of the north where the 'Last House in Scotland', now converted into a gift shop, stands on the cliffs above a sand and shingle beach where swimming is safe inshore on an incoming tide.

Duncansby Head
Pounding seas have etched the rocks into an unusual collection of caves, arches and towers some of which rise to a height of almost 300ft. A steep path near the lighthouse leads to a mainly shingle foreshore. Small shells, known as 'Groatie Buckies' and believed to be lucky, may be found in the vicinity.

Noss Head
There are fine views from this headland which contains a lighthouse and two ruined castles dating from the 16th and 17th centuries. Footpaths lead to rocky coves below.

Wick
A royal burgh, Wick is a busy fishing centre with good amusement and sports facilities. The local glassworks is open to the public and the ruined tower of a 12th-century castle, known to sailors as 'The Old Man of Wick' stands on a high spit of land near the Brig O'Trams, a 300ft natural bridge.

Whaligoe
There is a small natural harbour here which can be reached by a long flight of man-made steps hewn from the steep cliff face.

Lybster
A picturesque fishing village set above a harbour filled with fishing boats.

Helmsdale
A busy lobster port where fishermen can be seen unloading and packing their live catch. There is a sandy beach where swimming is safe provided the mouth of the Strath of Kildonan is avoided.

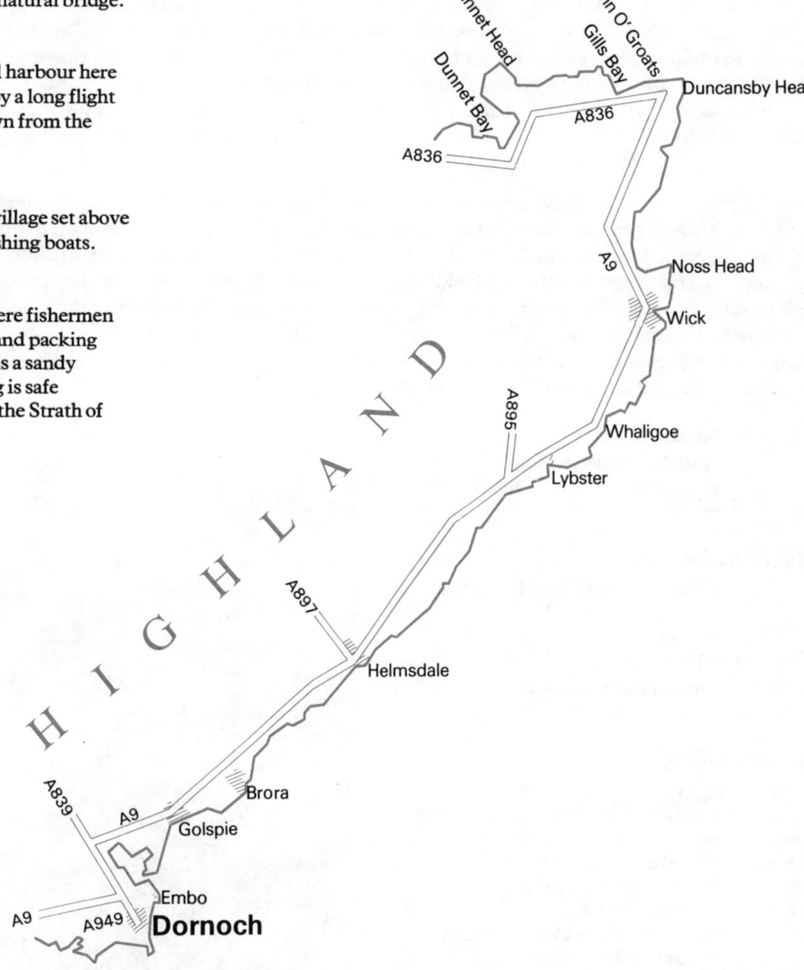

Brora
There is a safe, sandy beach here overlooked by a golf course designed by James Braid.

Golspie
This former fishing village is now a popular resort with a sandy beach dotted with outcrops of rock.

Embo
A fishing village with a distinct 19th-century appearance. The beach is sandy and rock pools are uncovered at low-tide on its southern extremity.

Dornoch *see page 176*

DORNOCH

Dornoch, a royal burgh, was the county town of old Sutherland and has historical associations stretching back to the founding of Dornoch Cathedral in 1224 by Gilbert, Archdeacon of Moray and Bishop of Caithness. Bishop Gilbert was killed by the Danes at the Battle of Embo near the town in 1248. A landmark for miles around, the cathedral was largely destroyed by fire in 1570 but restored in 1835, 1837, and 1924 after much neglect. As many as sixteen Earls of Sutherland are buried here. An effigy of Sir Richard of Moray stands in the nave. Bishop's Palace was ruined in 1570, and only the tower remains. This has been incorporated into an hotel.

Janet Horne, accused of turning her daughter into a pony, which was then shod by the Devil, was burnt in 1722. She has the doubtful distinction of having been the last women to be judicially executed in Scotland for witchcraft. The execution site is marked by a rough stone in a garden close by the golf course on the lower links. Dornoch possesses a world-renowned golf course, dating from 1616, one of the first three to be recorded in the history of the game. Extensive, clean sandy beaches lie to the north and south of Dornoch. The best sea-bathing area is situated immediately south of the rocks near the car park and the beach shelter. The shoreline has a gentle slope and bathing is safe.

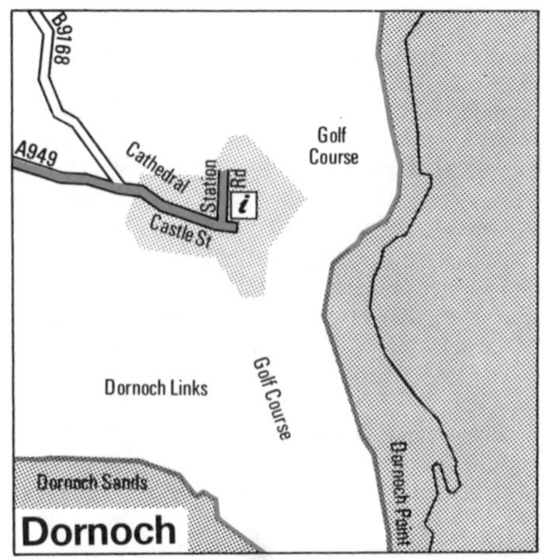

Recreation and Sports

Golf Road – Bowls, tennis
Royal Dornoch Golf Club Golf Rd ☎*381*

Places of Interest

Bishops Palace Castle Hotel, Castle St
Dornoch Cathedral

Tourist Information

Sutherland Tourist Organisation The Square ☎*400*

Accommodation

The following establishments are recommended by the AA. Further information may be obtained from the Tourist Information Office.

★★★	**Royal Golf** Castle St ☎*283*
★★	**Burghfield House** ☎*212*
★★	**Dornoch** ☎*351*
★★	**Dornoch Castle** Castle St ☎*216*
Inn	**Eagle** Castle St ☎*386*
SC	Mrs E M Grant, **Pitgrudy Farm Holidays** The Cabins, Pitgrudy Farm, Dornoch ☎*291*

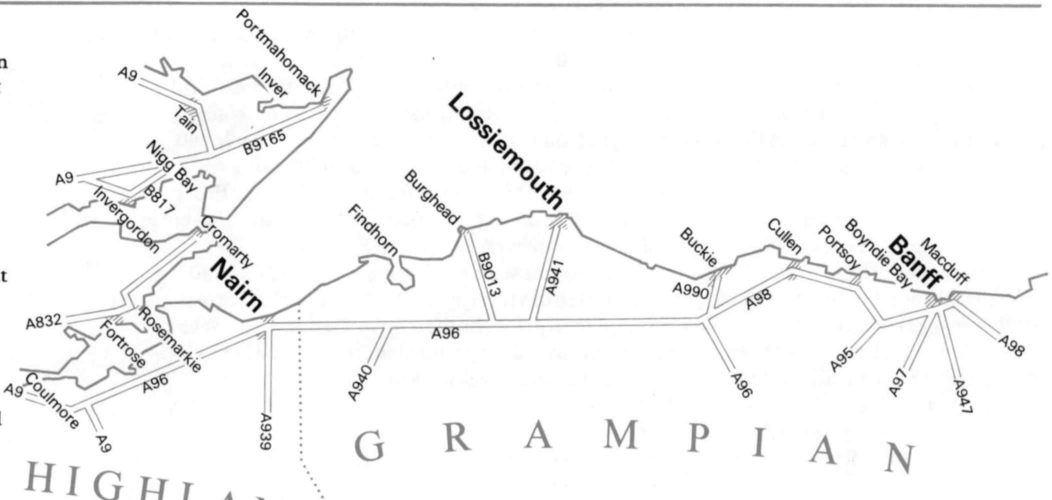

Tain
A royal burgh for over 900 years, Tain stands on sloping terrain overlooking a sandy beach dotted with patches of shingle and rock reached via a footbridge which crosses the River Tain. There is a fine golf course and amusements are available.

Inver
A sand and shingle beach is exposed at low-tide. To the west lies Morrich More, a sandy area of scrub and marshland.

Portmahomack
The sandy bay of this small resort and fishing village is sheltered from off-shore winds and provides safe bathing.

Nigg Bay
There are extensive sands here but deep channels make them hazardous for both the swimmer and the walker. Access is easiest from Barbaraville on the western shore.

Invergordon
An industrial harbour town which contained a Royal Naval dockyard during the first half of this century and is now used as a naval fueling station. There are sand and pebble beaches near the harbour where bathing is normally safe. Invergordon has an outdoor sea-water swimming pool and visits to the local distillery can be arranged.

Cromarty
An attractive, old-fashioned town with shingle-scattered sandy beaches. Bathing is safe except on the ebbing tide after heavy rain when there are strong currents in the Cromarty Firth. Boats are available for hire.

Rosemarkie
This small resort and yachting centre lies to the north of Chanony Point. It has a sandy beach, backed by shingle and the surrounding cliffs are nesting grounds for many species of birds.

Fortrose
This ancient royal burgh lies among wooded hills to the south of Chanony Point. Bathing is safe from the sandy beach, reached via a shingle bank. The remains of a 12th-century cathedral stand near the shore.

Coulmore
A caravan, camping and boating centre with a muddy shingle backed beach. Boats are available for hire and cruises operate to bird and seal sanctuaries.

Nairn *see page 178*

Findhorn
This pleasant village is the third to be founded on this site after severe sandstorms engulfed the first settlement in the 17th century and a flood destroyed the second in 1701. Modern Findhorn is a popular holiday and sailing centre and the sandy beaches to the north provide the safest swimming.

Burghead
There are safe, sandy beaches in Burghead Bay below a headland containing the remains of a Pictish fort and a 6th-century well.

Lossiemouth *see page 179*

Buckie
The largest fishing port on the Moray Firth, Buckie is set on a sloping hillside above a shingle, rock and sand shoreline where bathing is safest at half-tide. The harbour and fish market are open to the public and there are amusement and sports facilities.

Cullen
A Regency-style holiday resort with a safe, sandy beach where rock pools are formed at low-tide. Three high rocks, known as the 'Three Kings' stand on the shore and Logie Head, to the north, is a well-known viewpoint.

Portsoy
An attractive harbour town set amid rocky coastal scenery. Links Bay, to the east, has a safe, sandy beach. Portsoy is famous for its serpentine rock which is used by local craftsmen to make chessmen and curios. Portsoy rock was used in two chimney pieces in the Palace of Versailles.

Boyndie Bay
There is a long sandy beach here with recommended bathing areas marked by buoys.

Banff *see page 179*

Macduff
A busy fishing port and holiday resort. Sea bathing is safe from the rocks in calm weather and Macduff has one of the finest outdoor sea-water swimming pools in the country. Children's amusements are available and there is a large fish market near the harbour.

NAIRN

This ancient royal burgh, which received its charter during the 12th century, is now a pleasant residential area and resort. The town and harbour lie in a beautiful setting sheltered by mountains to the south and west. It enjoys a particularly dry sunny climate and the beautiful sandy beaches are safe for bathing although it is best to avoid the mouth of the River Nairn. There are rocks and pools on the western beach. Golf is well catered for with a nine-hole and two eighteen-hole courses and facilities for other sports include bowls, tennis, putting and trampolines. There are canoes, fishing dinghies and fishing tackle for hire on the East Beach together with facilities for snorkelling, diving, water ski-ing and pleasure trips. Annual events include the Open Tennis Tournament, Highland Games, Agricultural Show, Golf Championship and Open Bowls Tournaments. For the keen angler there is sea fishing and permits for local freshwater fishing are obtainable from the Sports Stores in the High Street. Entertainment is organised in the Community Centre (for children up to the age of fourteen years) during inclement weather. The Little Theatre stages performances by a number of local organisations during the summer. The Nairn Pipe Band gives performances with dance displays in the High Street on summer Saturdays with an extra performance on Wednesdays during July and August. Visitors are welcome at Nairn Ceramics (Pottery) in Viewfield, and Nairn has two museums. Outdoor draughts can be played on the seafront.

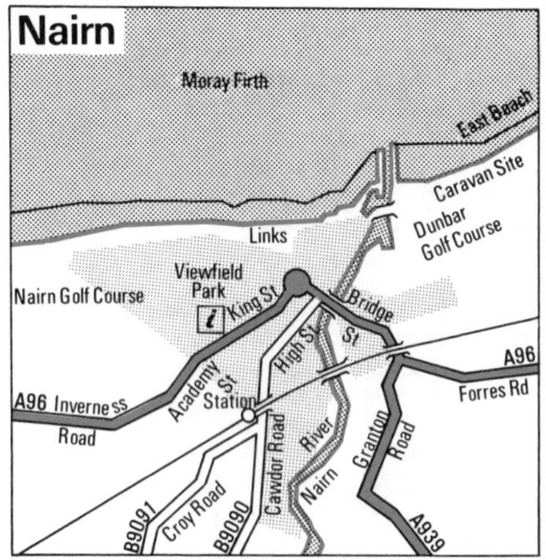

Recreation and Sports

Albert Street – Bowls, tennis
Caravan Site East Beach – Boat hire, canoes, crazy-golf, pleasure trips, water-skiing
Links Marine Rd – Paddling pool, play area, swings
Nairn Dunbar Golf Club ☎ *52741*
Nairn Golf Club ☎ *53208*
Nairn Newton Course (9 hole) ☎ *53208*
Riverside – Go-karts, trampolines
Viewfield Park – Bowls
West Links – Putting, table tennis

Cinema/Bingo

Regal Kings St ☎ *53287*

Places of Interest

Fisher Town Museum King St
Nairn Ceramics – Pottery
Nairn Museum Viewfield House

Tourist Information

Tourist Information Centre King St ☎ *52753*

Accommodation

The following establishments are recommended by the AA. Further information may be obtained from the Tourist Information Office.

★★★★	**Golf View** Seabank Rd ☎ *52301*
★★★★	**Newton** ☎ *53144*
★★★	**Royal Marine** ☎ *53381*
★★	**Alton Burn** Alton Burn Rd ☎ *53325*
★★	**Clifton** ☎ *53119*
AP	**Ross House** Seabank Rd ☎ *53731*
GH	**Dun-Craig** Glebe Road off Marine Rd ☎ *53345*
GH	**Glen Lyon Lodge** Waverley Rd ☎ *52780*
GH	**Greenlawns** 13 Seafield St ☎ *52738*
GH	**Lothian House Private Hotel** 10 Crescent Rd ☎ *53555*
GH	**Ramleh** ☎ *53551*
GH	**Sunnybrae** Marine Rd ☎ *52309*

Restaurant

✕	**Taste Bud** 44 Harbour St ☎ *52743*

LOSSIEMOUTH

This invigorating resort and fishing port, which has retained its 17th-century old town, stands at the mouth of the River Lossie and the Spynie Canal.

Lossiemouth was the home town of Ramsey MacDonald and a plaque may be seen outside No. 1 Gregory Place, the house where he was born.

The coastline around the harbour area tends to be rocky but there is an extensive sandy beach to the west and, to the east, a long sandy beach with sand dunes. Both beaches are safe for bathing and ideal playgrounds for the children.

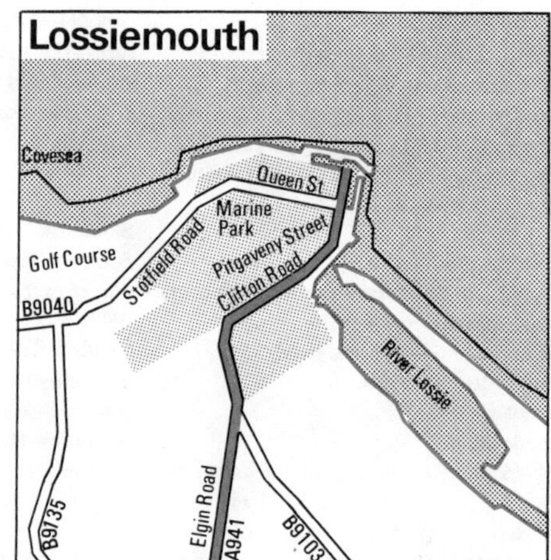

Recreation and Sports

Marine Park Bowls (not Sunday), putting, tennis
Moray Golf Club Stotfield Rd ☎ *2018*

Places of Interest

St Gerardine's Church
St James Church
Covesea Caves

Tourist Information

Elgin Information Centre
☎ *Elgin3388*

Accommodation

The following establishment is recommended by the AA. Further information may be obtained from the Tourist Information Office.

★★ **Stotfield** ☎ *2011*

BANFF

This ancient historical seaport and resort, with its steep terraced streets rising from the harbour, is situated on the west of Banff Bay into which flows the River Deveron. Spanning the river, is the old bridge with its seven arches built in 1772. The Bigger Fountain stands on the site of the former gallows where, in 1701, James Macpherson was said to have played his fiddle as he was led to his execution.

The ruins of the castle in Castle Street and the museum in High Street are both of historical interest. The Preservation Society have been busy here and many buildings of interest have been restored, including Duff House built in 1735, one of the best examples of Georgian Baroque architecture in Britain, which is now open to the public. There are facilities for bowls, fishing, golf, sailing and tennis. The swimming pool has restricted opening hours during school terms but there is an excellent open-air pool at Macduff, in the eastern corner of Banff Bay, in a beautiful rock setting. The coast north of the town is rocky and to the west Boyndie Bay, into which flows the Burn of Boyndie, is a mixture of sand and rocks. Swimming is safe in Banff Bay but it is advisable to keep away from the mouth of the river. The harbour, once a busy port, is now popular with the owners of pleasure craft and anglers.

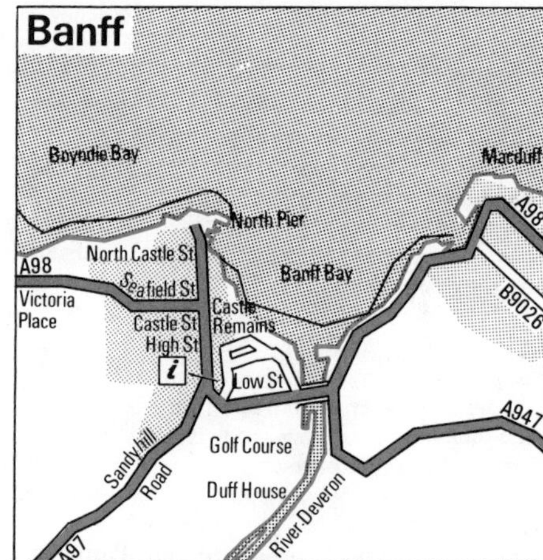

Recreation and Sports

Bridge Street – Tennis
Bellevue Road – Indoor pool (restricted opening during school terms)
Duff House Royal Golf Club ☎ *2278*
Seafield Street – Bowls

Places of Interest

Banff Castle Ruins
Banff Museum
Duff House

Tourist Information

Tourist Information Centre
Collie Lodge
St Mary's Car Park – ☎ *2419*

Accommodation

The following establishments are recommended by the AA. Further information may be obtained from the Tourist Information Office.

☆☆☆ **Banff Springs** Golden Knowes Rd ☎ *2881*
★ **Fife Lodge** Sandyhill Rd ☎ *2436*
GH **Carmelite House Private Hotel** Low St ☎ *2152*
GH **Ellerslie** 45 Low St ☎ *2545*

Pennan
A picturesque fishing village on a shingle bay backed by sheer red sandstone cliffs. Pennan Head, to the east, rises to a height of 350ft and is a nesting ground for guillemot, puffins and other seabirds.

New Aberdour
Access to the steep shingle beach is via a lane to the north of the village. There are many caves in the surrounding cliffs.

Rosehearty
This peaceful fishing village lies to the west of a rocky beach dotted with patches of sand amid rugged cliff scenery. Rosehearty has a modern open-air sea-water swimming pool and children's amusements are available.

Fraserburgh *see page 181*

St Combs
A former fishing village with a sand and shingle beach. The drinking and brawling of its fishermen earned St Combs an evil reputation during the 19th century. Many of its cottages, dating from that period, have been converted into holiday homes.

Strathbeg Bay
The port of Rattray once stood on this long desolate sweep of sand but silting and a violent 16th-century sandstorm virtually destroyed the town.

Rattray Head
A lighthouse overlooks a small bay of sand scattered with shingle and rocks. To the east a narrow stretch of sand extends for four miles, backed by high dunes.

Peterhead
Formerly an important whaling centre Peterhead is now a fishing port and a supply base for North Sea oil rigs. The beach, a mixture of rock, sand and shingle provides safe swimming if the mouth of the River Ugie is avoided, and Peterhead has many places of interest and good recreational facilities.

Sandford Bay
A sandy beach, hemmed in by rocks, where bathing is generally safe.

Cruden Bay
This small but popular family holiday resort has a long sandy beach, backed by dunes. Bram Stoker was a frequent visitor here and the ruins of Slains Castle which stand on the northern cliffs, are believed to have inspired his famous novel *Dracula*.

Sands of Forvie
There is a nature reserve here set among towering dunes. Sandy beaches are to be found to the south of Forvie Ness but they shelve steeply and fast currents make bathing dangerous.

Balmedie
A lane runs from this village in an attractive wooded setting to a fine expanse of beach which extends southwards for almost ten miles backed by dunes and grassy sandhills.

Aberdeen *see pages 182*

Nigg Bay
A sand and shingle beach overlooked by the Girdle Ness lighthouse.

Portlethen
There is a sheltered cove here with a shingle beach which provides a natural harbour for fishing boats and pleasure craft.

Muchalls
This 19th-century fishing village has a shingle beach backed by some spectacular rock formations. A 17th-century castle, reputed to be haunted, overlooks the shore. It contains an ancient tunnel once used by smugglers.

Cowie
A fishing hamlet with a sand and pebble beach. There are children's amusements close to the sands.

Stonehaven *see page 184*

Inverbervie
This small town stands on the bank of Bervie Water. There is a shingle beach giving way to rocks in the south. Inverbervie has good recreational facilities and is mainly concerned with the manufacture of flax and rayon.

St Cyrus
A long stretch of beach overlooked by a ruined medieval tower, the Kaim of Mathers. The northern sands are part of a nature reserve and are noted for the many species of wild flowers to be found there. The original town was destroyed by a storm in the late 18th century.

Montrose *see page 185*

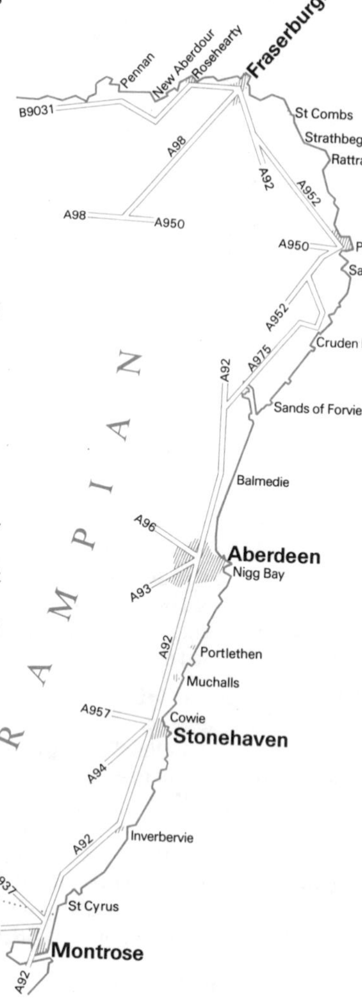

A popular holiday resort, situated on a rocky headland which has been one of Scotland's foremost fishing ports for the last 300 years. Fraserburgh offers the visitor an extensive stretch of clean, golden sand where bathing can be enjoyed in safety within the area marked by buoys. There are amusement and sports facilities within a short distance of the Esplanade. Other amenities include a skateboard arena, a golf course and a modern indoor swimming pool, although the latter is shared with a local school and is only available to the public on a full-time basis during July and August.

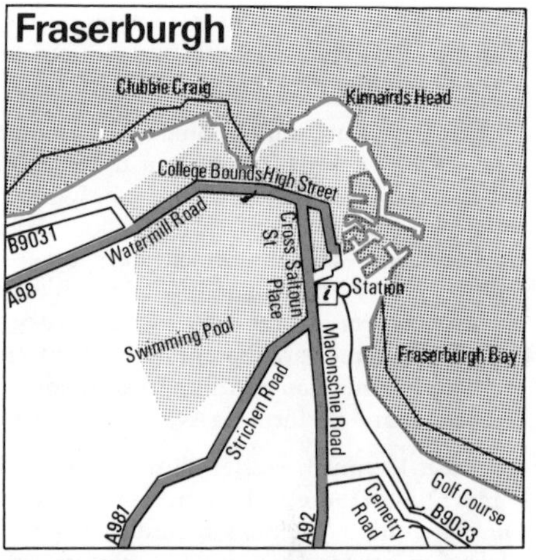

Fraserburgh has two lighthouses, one guarding the harbour entrance and the other standing on Kinnairds Head to the north. The Kinnairds Head lighthouse dates from the late 18th century and is built on the lower floors of a 16th-century castle tower. It may be visited by the public at weekends on application to the head lighthouse-keeper. The lifeboat station is open daily and a fish market is held in the harbour on most weekdays.

Recreation and Sports

Esplanade – Children's playground
Fraserburgh Golf Club Cemetery Rd ☎*2287*
Fraserburgh Swimming Pool Fraserburgh Academy, Alexandra Ter ☎*2627*
Links Sports Ground – Bowls, cricket, putting, table-tennis, tennis
Saltoun Place – Children's playground
Skatebowl Strichen Park Rd
West End Bowling Club junction Union Gv/Gallowhill Rd

Tourist Information

Tourist Information Centre 3 Saltoun Sq ☎*2315*

ABERDEEN

There has been a seaport here since the 13th century and Aberdeen's harbour is now crowded with merchant vessels, supply boats which service the North Sea oil rigs and the extensive fleet of trawlers which give the city its title of the third largest fishing port in Britain.

Despite these important trading connections Aberdeen offers the visitor two miles of safe, sandy beach backed by a wide expanse of grassland. Seaside amenities, including a fairground and an adventure playground are to be found little more than a mile from busy Union Street, the city's main thoroughfare, and children's games are organised on the nearby beach. Further facilities for amusement and sport are to be found in Aberdeen's many parks which have won several 'Britain in Bloom' trophies. The Cruickshank Botanic Garden has an extensive collection of shrubs, a water garden and a sunken heather garden. The city of Aberdeen offers a varied programme of entertainment including the Aberdeen Festival with Highland Games, music, drama, exhibitions and the annual International Festival of Youth Orchestras and Performing Arts, with troupes from all over the world taking part.

Aberdeen has much to offer the tourist in the shape of buildings of historical interest including James Dun's House; a children's museum containing Victorian toys; Provost Skene's House, one of the oldest dwellings in the city, now restored as a local museum; the 14th-century St Machar's Cathedral and the old fishermen's cottages at Footdee on the North Pier. An early morning visit to the Fish Market auctions is also a popular trip.

Recreation and Sports

ABC Bowl George St ☎*23001*
Aberdeen FC Pittodrie Park ☎*21428*–Scottish Premier Division
Balnagask Golf Course ☎*876407*
Beach Boulevard–Adventure playground, amusement arcade, funfair
Bon Accord Baths Justice Mill Ln ☎*27920*–Indoor pool
Duthie Park–Boating, bowls, playground, putting, swingball, table-tennis, tennis, trampolines
Hazelhead Academy Groats Rd ☎*30062*–Indoor pool
Hazelhead Golf Course ☎*35747*
Hazelhead Park–Maze, pets corner, putting, swingball, table-tennis
Ice Rink Spring Gdn ☎*28550*
Kincorth Academy Kincorth Circle ☎*872227*–Indoor pool
Links Golf Course ☎*52269*
Seaton Park–Adventure playground
Westburn Park–Bowls, paddling pools, playground, putting, swingball, table tennis, tennis, trampolines
Union Terrace Gardens–Dancing, outdoor draughts, swingball, trampolines

Cabaret/Dancing

Beach Ballroom Beach Front ☎*52337*
Big P Disco 24 Spital ☎*27875*
Crazy Daisy Disco 74 Commerce St ☎*20910*
Jay Jays Beach Front ☎*28396*
Ruffles 13 Diamond St ☎*29092*

Cinemas

ABC Shiprow ☎*51477*
Capitol 431 Union St ☎*23141*
Grand Central Picture House 286 George St ☎*22826*
Odeon Justice Mill Ln ☎*26050*
Queens 120 Union St ☎*23688*

Theatres

Aberdeen Arts Centre King St ☎*23456*
His Majestys ☎*28080*

Places of Interest

Aberdeen Art Gallery and Museum Schoolhill ☎*53517*
Cruickshank Botanic Gardens University of Aberdeen ☎*40241*
Gordon Highlanders Museum Viewfield Rd
James Dun's House 61 Schoolhill ☎*22234*
Kings College High St, Old Aberdeen
Provost Ross's House Shiprow
Provost Skene's House Guestrow ☎*50086*
St Machars Cathedral The Chanonry, Old Aberdeen

Tourist Information

Tourist Bureau St Nicholas House, Broad St ☎*23456*

Accommodation

The following establishments are recommended by the AA. Further information may be obtained from the Tourist Information Office.

★★★★ **Station** Guild St ☎*28214*
★★★ **Caledonian** Union Ter ☎*29233*
★★★ **Imperial** Stirling St ☎*29101*
★★★ **Marcliffe** Queens Ter ☎*51281*
☆☆☆ **Royal Darroch** Cults (3m SW A93) ☎*48811*
☆☆☆ **Sheraton Inn** Old Meldrum Rd, Bucksburn (3m N A947) ☎*Bucksburn3911*
★★ **Gloucester** Union St ☎*29095*
★★ **Lang Stracht** Lang Stracht ☎*38712*
★★ **Northern** Kittybrewster ☎*43342*
★ **Ferryhill House** Bon-Accord St ☎*50867*
GH **Broomfield Private Hotel** 15 Balmoral Pl ☎*28758*
GH **Carden Hotel** 44 Carden Pl ☎*26813*
GH **Crown Private Hotel** 10 Springbank Ter ☎*26842*
GH **Dunromin** 75 Constitution St ☎*56995*
GH **Glenmhor** 318 Great Western Rd ☎*27630*
GH **Klibreck** 410 Great Western Rd ☎*36115*
GH **Shieldaig House Hotel** 21 Albert St ☎*28067*
GH **Urray House** 429 Great Western Rd ☎*35204*
GH **Western** 193 Great Western Rd ☎*56919*
SC Mr J W Runcie, **Deeview Holiday Houses** 67 Prospect Ter ☎*25754*

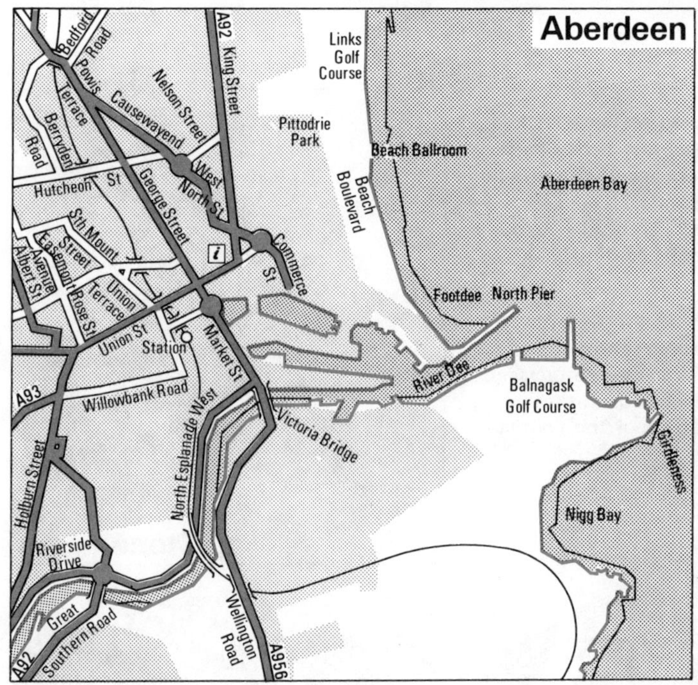

Restaurants

XXX **Fiddlers** 1 Portland St ☎ *52050*
XX **Chivas** 387 Union St ☎ *53135*
XX **Dickens** 347 Union St ☎ *20318*
XX **Gerrards** 50 Chapel St ☎ *571782*
X **Poldino's** 7 Little Belmont St ☎ *27777*

STONEHAVEN

One of the leading holiday resorts on the east coast of Scotland, Stonehaven lies between the mouths of two small rivers, the Cowie Water and Carron Water. The beach is mostly shingle, with a few small patches of sand, and is generally safe for swimming except near the mouths of the rivers. The pleasant fishing harbour is now mostly taken up with private craft, and sea fishing and coastal pleasure trips are available. Recreational facilities are concentrated at the north end of the promenade and include a heated open-air swimming pool, paddling pool, putting, tennis, bowling and trampolines, and amusement arcades.

Places of interest in and around Stonehaven include the Tolbooth Museum, a 16th-century storehouse and prison situated in the old part of the town around the harbour, Dunnottar Parish Church graveyard, south-west of the town, which contains the Covenanters Stone, and Dunnottar Castle, a late 14th- to 16th-century fortress situated on a rocky headland 1½ miles south-east, off the A92. Tours of the local distillery can also be arranged through the Tourist Information Centre.

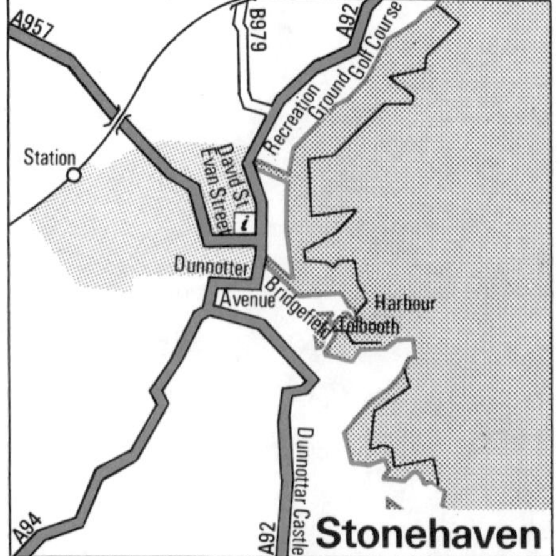

Recreation and Sports

Market Square – Outdoor draughts
Recreation Ground
Promenade – Amusements, bowls, paddling pool, putting, tennis, trampolines
Swimming Pool Promenade ☎*62134*
Open June – Sep
Stonehaven Golf Club ☎*62124* – NE off A92

Places of Interest

Stonehaven Tolbooth Museum
Harbour
Dunnottar Castle ☎*62173* – 1½m SE off A92

Tourist Information

Tourist Information Centre Market Sq (May – end of September) ☎*62806*

Accommodation

The following establishments are recommended by the AA. Further information may be obtained from the Tourist Information Office.

☆☆☆ **Commodore** Cowie Pk ☎*62936*
★★ **St Leonards** Bath St ☎*62044*

Peaceful harbour scene at Stonehaven

The Royal Burgh of Montrose is almost completely surrounded by water, lying between the sea and the two mile square Montrose Basin with the River South Esk flowing along its southern boundary. Montrose has been a port for many centuries and became a well-known spa during the 1800s. Since then it has continued to develop as a holiday resort and is now also an important maintenance centre for the North Sea oil-rigs.

Sandy beaches extend northward for several miles from the mouth of the South Esk, backed by sand dunes, and swimming is generally safe away from the river mouth. Lifeguards patrol the area between June and September. Most of Montrose's amusements and sports facilities are to be found in the promenade area and six fine golf courses lie to the north of the seafront. The Montrose Basin is the headquarters of the local sailing club and is a popular haunt of the less experienced sea angler.

The William Lamb Memorial Studio contains a collection of sculptures and etchings by this well-known artist and visitors to the Elephant Rock at Boddin Point, some two miles to the south, may be lucky enough to collect some semi-precious stones, such as agate, amethyst or onyx which are to be found among the pebbles at the foot of the cliffs.

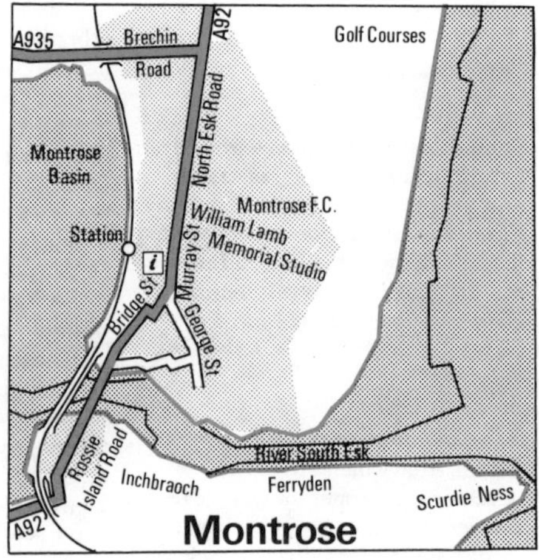

Recreation and Sports

Caledonia Golf Club Dorward Rd ☎*2313*
Dorward Place – Tennis
Melville Gardens – Bowls
Montrose Golf Courses Traill Drive ☎*2634*
Montrose FC Wellington St ☎*3200* – Scottish League
Montrose Mercantile Golf Club East Links ☎*2408*
Montrose Swimming Pool The Mall ☎*2026* – Indoor heated pool
Royal Albert Golf Club Dorward Rd ☎*2376*
Traill Drive – Amusements, boating lake, children's playground, pony rides, putting, sand-yachting, tennis, trampolines
Victoria Golf Club Links ☎*2157*
West End Park – Bowls

Places of Interest

William Lamb Memorial Studio High St

Tourist Information

Tourist Information Centre 212 High St ☎*2000*

Accommodation

The following establishments are recommended by the AA. Further information may be obtained from the Tourist Information Office.

★★★	**Links** Mid Links ☎*2288*
★★★	**Park** John St ☎*3415*
★	**Corner House** 134 High St ☎*3126*
GH	**Linksgate** 11 Dorward Rd ☎*2273*

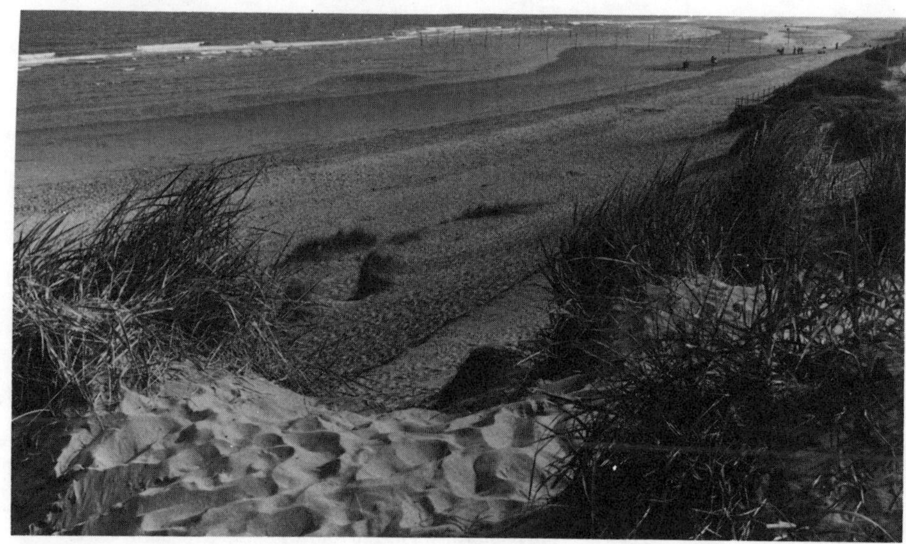

Scurdie Ness

Arbroath *See page 187*

Carnoustie *See page 188*

Monifieth
Extensive sands and dunes around the bay make this a popular resort, but much of the shore is used as a military firing range and is closed when the red flags are flying. There is a golf course, putting, crazy-golf, bowls, tennis, a children's paddling pool and playground.

Broughty Ferry
The harbour of the one-time fishing village, from which this resort developed, separates the shingle in the west from the sandy beach on the eastern side and bathing is safe close inshore. However, there are dangerous currents and deep channels where Dighty Water flows into the Firth. Places of interest open to the public include the 15th-century Broughty Castle, which now houses a museum, the Orchar Art Gallery and Claypotts Castle.

Tayport
Tayport's harbour is used by yachts and pleasure craft since its use as a port has diminished. The sand and shingle beach is popular with holidaymakers and safe for swimming. Nevertheless, about a mile to the east of the town there are dangerous quicksands which should be avoided.

St Andrews *See page 189*

Crail
This picture-book village is a popular resort and yet remains peaceful and unspoilt. Although the coastline is predominantly rocky, Roome Bay provides a good sandy beach with rock pools at low-tide.

Anstruther
Once the principal herring port in Scotland, but since the herring found other feeding grounds, the town has developed as a holiday resort. There is a sandy beach at Billow Ness and fishing and boat trips are available from the harbour. The award-winning Scottish Fisheries Museum is close to the harbour.

St Monance
This pretty fishing village has a long tradition of boat building. The nets and lobster pots around the harbour are an indication of the fishing industry which also thrives. Along this rugged stretch of coastline there are some fine views and the ruins of Newark Castle stand above the rocks to the south.

Elie/Earlsferry *see page 190*

Leven
Sandy beaches around Largo Bay are safe for swimming at all times and the town has good facilities for sports and entertainments. The golf course is immediately behind the beach, there is a fun fair on the promenade and the lovely Letham Glen is popular with those who prefer more peaceful surroundings.

Kirkcaldy
Excellent shopping facilities, industry, coal mines and seaport can all be found in Kirkcaldy as well as the sandy beach which attracts holidaymakers to the town. The ruined 15th-century Ravenscraig Castle stands on a rocky promontory to the east.

Kinghorn
A sandy beach below a cliff-top town. In 1286, King Alexander III was thrown from his horse over the cliffs and a monument on the Pettycur promontory marks the place of his death.

Burntisland
This town is a popular holiday resort with all the usual amenities and entertainments. A long stretch of sandy beach is almost a mile wide at low-tide and provides safe bathing.

Aberdour *see page 190*

ARBROATH

Once a small Pictish settlement, the Royal Burgh of Arbroath is now a popular holiday resort with all the usual amenities and attractions. The bustling harbour, where fishing boats unload their catch for the fish market, many destined to become the famous Arbroath 'Smokie', is a great centre of attraction for visitors and a popular annual event is the Angus Agricultural Show, held at Victoria Park each July. Important historical associations are centred mainly on the Abbey. Founded in 1178 by William the Lion in memory of Thomas à Becket, it stimulated the growth of the town and supported a considerable community. King Robert the Bruce held a specially convened Parliament here in 1320 as a result of which the Scottish Declaration of Independence was signed.

The Arbroath coastline displays tremendous variety, with sandy beaches on one side and spectacular cliffs on the other. The red sandstone rock has been carved by the relentless waves into strange shapes and mysterious caves. Both the cliff path and the boat trips from the harbour reveal these niches which hold relics of smuggling days and are the subject of many a cautionary legend.

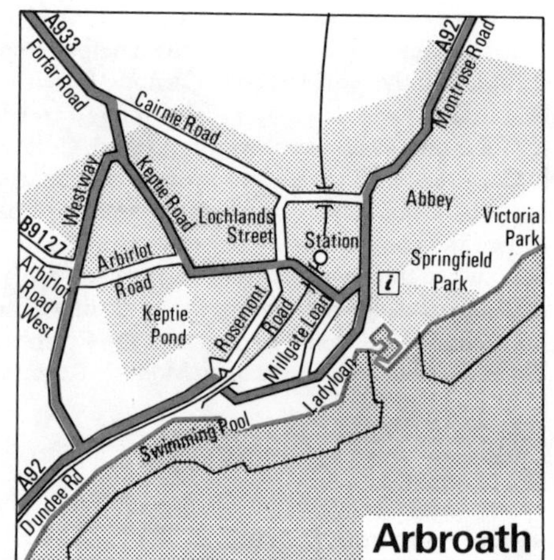

Recreation and Sports

Abbey Green – Bowls
Abroath Football Club Gayfield Pk ☎ *27157* – Scottish League
Arbroath Golf Club Elliot ☎ *72272*
Carinie Road Stadium – Indoor bowling
Cannon Common – Putting, tennis
Community Centre – Badminton, table tennis, wrestling
Inchcape Park – Crazy-golf, putting
Keptie Pond – Boats for hire
Lochlands – Bowls
Marketgate – Indoor swimming pool
Queens Drive – Indoor fun fair
Springfield Park – Paddling pool, pitch and putt, playground, putting
Victoria Park – Football, playground
West Links – Football, miniature railway, paddling pool, playground, pony rides, swimming pool, trampolines

Cinema

The Palace James St ☎ *73069*

Dancing

Marine Ballroom Hill Rd ☎ *73324*
Meadowbank Inn Montrose Rd ☎ *73979*
Seaforth Ballroom Dundee Rd ☎ *72232*

Theatre

Abbey Theatre Abbot St ☎ *76420*
Webster Memorial Theatre and Arts Centre High St

Places of Interest

Arbroath Abbey and The Abbots House
Art Gallery Hill Ter ☎ *72248*
Kellie Castle Arbroath (2 miles west)
St Vigeans Museum St Vigeans
Signal Tower Museum Ladyloan ☎ *75598*

Tourist Information

Angus District Council Information Centre 105 High St ☎ *72609*

Accommodation

The following establishments are recommended by the AA. Further information may be obtained from the Tourist Information Office.

★ **Towerbank** James St ☎ *75987*
GH **Davanna** 29 Market Gate ☎ *73933*
GH **Gladsheil** 38 Ogily Pl ☎ *73470*

CARNOUSTIE

The game of golf has a long and distinguished history in Carnoustie, spanning all of four centuries, and golfers from the town helped to pioneer the game and to spread its popularity throughout the world. Today Carnoustie, with two championship courses rated among the best in the world, is a major centre for golfers who come both to watch the champions and to try their own skill over the same ground. Golf widows and children are particularly fortunate in Carnoustie which offers one of the best beaches in the area, with five miles of sands and safe bathing. Every day during the high season a Beach Leader helps to entertain the children with games and competitions. The town also has an active Yacht Club which holds a regatta each July, when the town's annual Carnival takes place. To the east of the bay the sands give way to a stretch of rocky coastline in the midst of which is East Haven, a secluded hamlet with a tiny harbour. Inland from Carnoustie is the Crombie Reservoir, set amid lovely woodlands – a haven for wildlife. The nearby Monikie Reservoir offers good trout fishing.

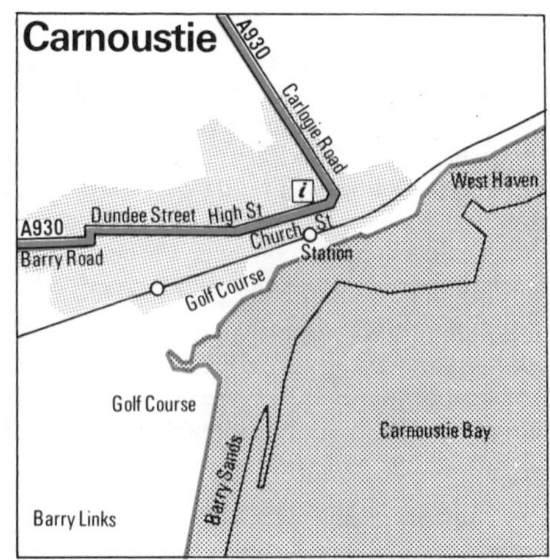

Recreation and Sports

Carnoustie Bowling Club Maule St ☎*53340*
Carnoustie Golf Club Links Pde ☎*52480*
Carnoustie Mercantile Golf Club Links Pde ☎*52525*
Carnoustie Yacht Club Links Pde ☎*52507*
Links Parade – Putting
Panmure Golf Club Barry ☎*53705*
Rest Gardens – Tennis
Tayside Street – Paddling pool

Dancing

Beach Hall ☎*53246*

Places of Interest

Affleck Castle Monikie

Tourist Information

Angus District Council Information Office 24 High St ☎*52258*

Accommodation

The following establishments are recommended by the AA. Further information may be obtained from the Tourist Information Office.

★★★ **Bruce** Links Pde ☎*52364*
★★ **Earlston** 24 Church St ☎*52352*
★★ **Glencoe** Links Pde ☎*53273*
★ **Station** ☎*52447*
Ⓖ **Carlogie House** ☎*53185*

ST ANDREWS

This ancient town, named after the patron saint of Scotland, once shared equal importance with Edinburgh. St Andrews was the ecclesiastical capital, its Cathedral, now in ruins, the largest in the country and the nearby ruined castle was the Archbishop's Palace. The town centre still preserves many historical buildings, among them the University, one of the oldest in Britain, whose students still wear the traditional red gowns.

The name of St Andrews is synonymous with golf and is known throughout the world as the home of the game. It was played here at least as early as the mid-15th century and it was in St Andrews that the Royal and Ancient Golf Club was formed in 1754 and gave its set of rules to the game. Now the undisputed mecca of all golfers, it is perhaps surprising that its four courses are available to all without the necessity of joining a club.

Where pilgrims once came for their Holy Days, visitors now flock for their holidays – not only the golfers but also the devotees of the seaside resort. Safe, sandy beaches stretch out on either side of the town, between them the harbour, two small beaches and an unusual tide-washed swimming pool. St Andrews has two main annual events – the Kate Kennedy Procession in April and the Lammas Market on the second Monday and Tuesday in August.

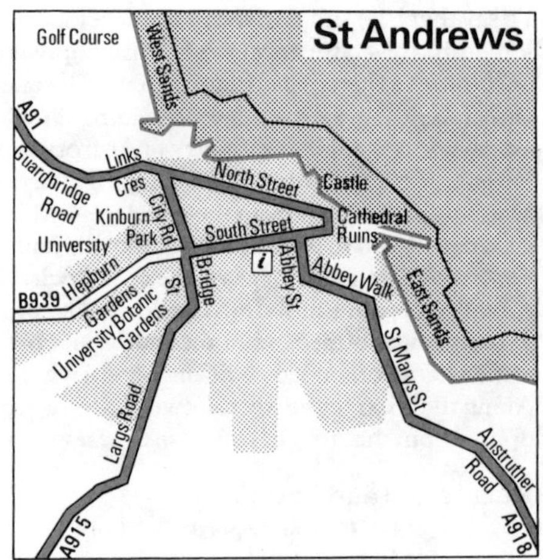

Recreation and Sports

Bruce Embankment – Putting
Cockshaugh Lade Braes – Children's playground
East Bents – Putting, shuffle boards, swings, trampolines
Kinburn Park – Aviary, bowls, children's playground, putting; tennis
Royal and Ancient Golf Club Club House ☎*2112*
St Andrews Angling Club The Hut, Cameron Reservoir ☎*Peat Inn 236*
St Andrews Bowling Club Kinnessburn Rd ☎*5201*
St Andrews Golf Club Links House ☎*3017*
St Andrews Golf Courses Golf Place ☎*5757*
St Andrews Ladies Putting Club West Sands ☎*5196*
St Andrews Sailing Club East Sands
Town Hall – Punch and Judy shows, table tennis

Cinema

Cinema House North St ☎*3164*
New Picture House North St ☎*3509*

Dancing

Cosmos Youth Centre Abbey Wk ☎*4140*
Town Hall

Theatre

Byre Theatre of St Andrews Abbey St ☎*2544*

Places of Interest

Castle Ruins
Folk Museum Ceres
Golf Museum D and W Auchterlonie, 4 Pilmur Links
Lochty Private Railway Lochty
Queen Mary's House South St
St Andrews Cathedral Priory Ruins and Museum ☎*2563*
University Botanical Gardens The Canongate ☎*3406*

Tourist Information

Information Centre Town Hall, South St ☎*2021*

Accommodation

The following establishments are recommended by the AA. Further information may be obtained from the Tourist Information Office.

★★★★	**Old Course** ☎*4371*
★★★★	**Rusacks Marine** ☎*4321*
★★★	**Rufflets** ☎*2594*
★★★	**St Andrew** 40 The Scores ☎*2611*
★★★	**Scores** ☎*2451*
★★	**Cross Keys** Market St ☎*2185*
★★	**Star** ☎*5701*
GH	**Beachway House** 4–6 Murray Pk ☎*3319*
GH	**Craigmore** 3 Murray Pk ☎*2142*
GH	**Nithsdale Hotel** Murray Pk ☎*3576*
GH	**Yorkston Hotel** 68–70 Argyle St ☎*2019*
SC	**Albany Park** St Mary's St. For bookings: The Bursar of Residences, College Gate, St Andrews ☎*4411*
SC	**Fife Park** Strathkinnes High Rd. For bookings: The Bursar of Residences, College Gate ☎*4411*

Restaurants

✕✕	**Grange Inn** ☎*2670*
✕	**Pepita's** 11 Crails Ln ☎*4084*

ELIE & EARLSFERRY

To say that Elie and Earlsferry has developed as a seaside resort would probably create something of a false impression. It *is* a popular place with holidaymakers, but it remains unspoilt and therein lies its attraction. The one main street follows the line of the bay, with narrow lanes at regular intervals leading down to the sandy beach where bathing is safe. Elie is a derivation of Ailie – or island – of Ardross which now forms part of the harbour. The name of Earlsferry confirms links with shipping, particularly the reputed journey from here of Macduff in his flight from the murderous Macbeth. Just along the coast is Macduff's Cave where he is said to have hidden before his journey across the Forth. Views from the South Beach take in the Isle of May, the Bass Rock, North Berwick Law and, on a clear day, so it is rumoured, even Edinburgh Castle. On the promontory of Elie Ness is the ruined Lady's Tower. It was built as a summer house and bathing hut for Lady Anstruther of Elie House, a somewhat petulant lady who once had a whole village removed because it spoilt her view! Along the coast to the west, Lower Largo is famous as the birthplace of Alexander Selkirk upon whom the story of *Robinson Crusoe* was based.

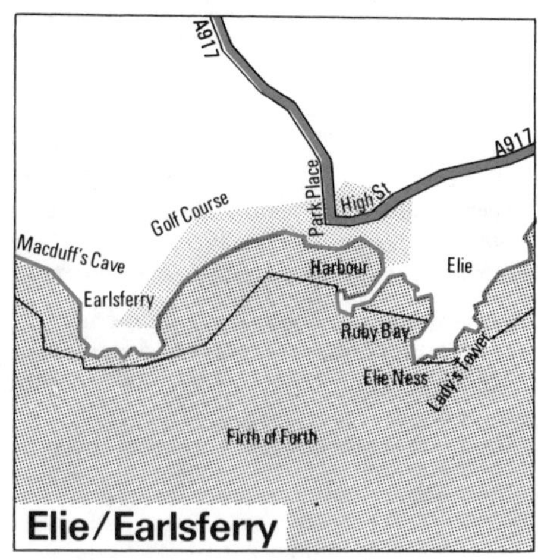

Recreation and Sports

Golf Club and Sports Club Golf House Club ☎ *301 and 327*

Places of Interest

Kellie Castle ☎ *Arncroach 271*
Scottish Fisheries Museum St Ayles, Anstruther ☎ *Anstruther 310628*

Accommodation

The following establishment is recommended by the AA. Further information may be obtained from the Tourist Information Office.

GH **Elms** Park Pl ☎ *404*

ABERDOUR

Where the Firth of Forth begins to open out towards the sea it begins to shed the mud and pollution that bedevils its upper reaches. Free from such ecological problems, Aberdour nestles in a section of the coastline indented with small bays between rocky promontories and enjoys great popularity as a holiday resort. Its safe beaches of sand, with the occasional patch of shingle, stretch out for a mile on either side of the town where buildings give way to attractive wooded slopes. Views across the Forth take in the islands of Inchcolm, Inchmickery and Inchkeith, the craggy outcrops of rock between them and the Oxcars lighthouse. Boat trips are operated from Aberdour to the island of Inchcolm where King Alexander was unintentionally landed during a storm in 1123. In gratitude for the hospitality he received from the resident hermit he founded a monastery on the island, of which substantial remains can be seen today. Aberdour itself is an historic town, its 12th-century church very highly regarded in terms of ecclesiastical architecture. There is also a castle – a mellow golden edifice still guarding the banks of the Dour after more then 600 years.

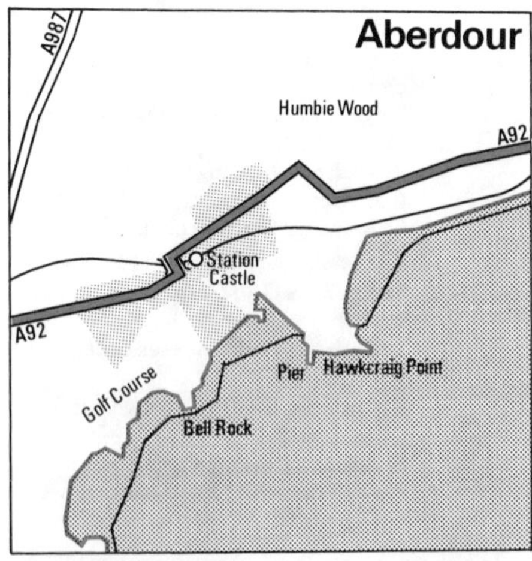

Recreation and Sports

Aberdour Golf Club Seaside Pl ☎ *860688/860256*
Aberdour Sailing School Hawkcraig Cottage ☎ *860204*
Burntisland – Children's playground, crazy-golf, fairground, paddling pool, putting, swimming pool, trampolines
Burntisland Golf House Club Dodhead Links, Burntisland ☎ *Burntisland 873247*
Shore Road – Bowls, putting, tennis

Places of Interest

Aberdour Castle
Inchcolm Abbey

Accommodation

The following establishment is recommended by the AA. Further information may be obtained from the Tourist Information Office.

★★ **Woodside** High St ☎ *328*

Cramond
A picturesque village with whitewashed houses surrounding an old harbour. There is a sandy beach and Cramond Island can be reached on foot at low-tide. Cramond has become a popular sailing centre and is a favourite retreat for residents of neighbouring Edinburgh.

Cockenzie and Port Seton
The western harbour, built by Robert Stevenson in 1835 to ship coal from the local mines, is now used mainly by pleasure craft. Port Seton is the base of the fishing fleet. There is a rocky, shingle beach and Port Seton has an open-air swimming pool and trampolines.

North Berwick *see page 192*

Dunbar *see page 193*

St Abbs
A pleasant little village lying in the shelter of the 483-ft St Abbs Head. There is a sandy beach with low-tide rock pools and boat trips are available.

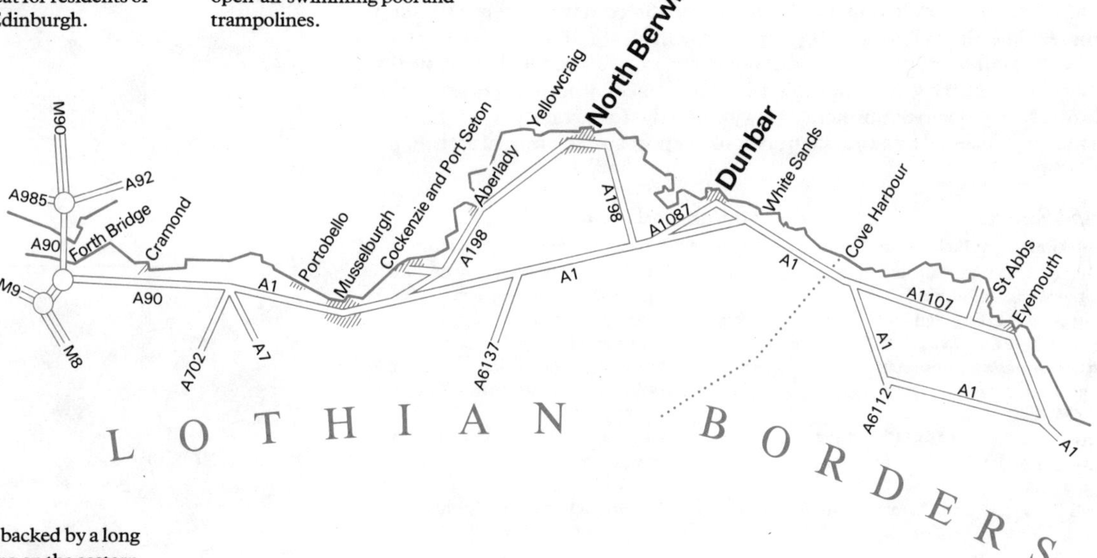

Portobello
A sandy beach, backed by a long promenade, lying on the eastern outskirts of Edinburgh. There are fine views over the Firth of Forth. Portobello has one of the largest open-air heated sea-water swimming pools in Europe with a capacity for about 3,000 swimmers and double that number of spectators.

Musselburgh
The largest town in the East Lothian District, Musselburgh stands on the banks of the River Esk amid pleasant wooded scenery. There is a shingle beach with outcrops of rock and patches of sand. Musselburgh has several interesting buildings, including a 16th-century Tolbooth, and good facilities for entertainment in the shape of a modern theatre complex.

Aberlady
This former fishing port overlooks Aberlady Bay which contains one of the first nature reserves to be established in Scotland containing many species of birds.

Yellowcraig
A natural coastal park has been established here around a sandy beach, backed by dunes and woodlands. One mile inland lies the village of Dirleton with a ruined 13th-century castle.

White Sands
Firm sands, backed by dunes, provide safe bathing. The surrounding rocks are noted for the fossils which may be collected and the area is a popular nesting ground for many species of seabirds.

Cove Harbour
A charming little harbour, below steep cliffs, used mainly by lobster boats. The bay contains sand and rock pools at low-tide and several caves once used by smugglers.

Eyemouth
This ancient port has a modern harbour which is the base for the local herring fleet. The sand and shingle beaches are dotted with rock pools and the area is popular with sub-aqua divers and canoeists.

NORTH BERWICK

An ancient royal burgh which was developed into a seaside and golfing resort during the 19th century. Firm, safe sands dotted with rock pools at low-tide lie beside the small harbour which is backed by red sandstone buildings, formerly used for storing grain, but now restored as flats. Quality Street, a tree-lined thoroughfare, leads inland from the harbour to The Lodge, originally the Laird's house, but now converted into modern flats within a landscaped public park by the National Trust for Scotland. Golfing facilities are exceptionally good. North Berwick has two local courses and many more are within easy reach including the world's oldest course at Muirfield. There is a cinema and shows are staged at the Harbour Pavilion during the summer. The North Berwick Museum deals with local and natural history and Tantallon Castle, the 14th-century stronghold of the Douglases, lies on the shore some three miles to the east overlooking Bass Rock, a 350-ft island inhabited by nesting gannets, puffins and other seabirds. North Berwick's principal viewpoint is the Law, a steep 600-ft hill which stands behind the town, capped by a 19th-century lookout post and an unusual arch made out of the jaw-bone of a whale.

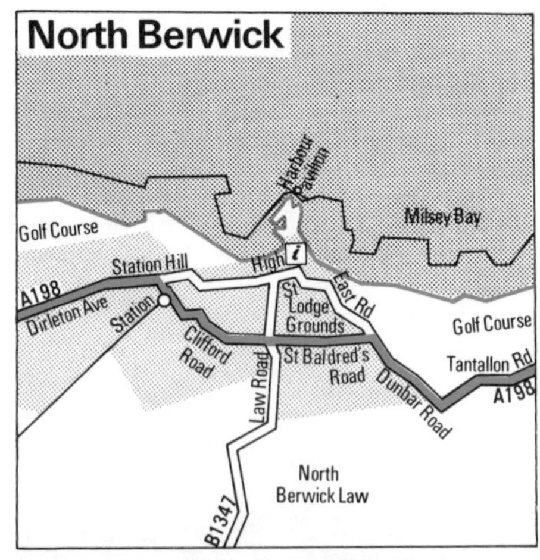

Recreation and Sports

Burgh Links East Bay – Model boating pool, pitch and putt, putting, tennis
Dunbar Road – Children's playground, putting, tennis
East Lothian Yacht Club ☎ *2698*
Lodge Grounds – Children's playground, crazy-golf, swing ball, trampolines
North Berwick East Golf Club ☎ *2221*
North Berwick RFC Dunbar Rd ☎ *3503*
North Berwick Sports Centre Grange Rd ☎ *3454* – Most indoor sports
North Berwick Swimming Pool ☎ *2083* – Outdoor heated pool (summer only)
North Berwick West Golf Club Beal Rd ☎ *2135*
West Bay – Putting

Cinema

Playhouse 81a High St ☎ *2422*

Theatre

Harbour Pavilion ☎ *2959*

Places of Interest

North Berwick Museum School Rd ☎ *3470*
Tantallon Castle – 3m E on A198

Tourist Information

Tourist Information Centre ☎ *2197*

Accommodation

The following establishments are recommended by the AA. Further information may be obtained from the Tourist Information Office.

★★★	**Marine** ☎ *2406*
★★	**Blenheim House** Westgate ☎ *2385*
★★	**Nether Abbey** Dirleton Ave ☎ *2802*
GH	**Belhaven Private Hotel** Westgate ☎ *2573*
GH	**Cragside** 16 Marine Pde ☎ *2879*
SC	**8 West Bay Road** For bookings: Mrs E M MacDonald, Blake Holt, Brownsea View Ave, Lilliput, Poole, Dorset ☎ *Canford Cliffs 707894*

Restaurant

✕	**Al Vagabondo** 35 High St ☎ *3434*

Dunbar has survived a violent history and its castle was the centre of fierce battles between the 14th century and 1650 when it was finally assaulted by Cromwell during the Battle of Dunbar and largely destroyed. Today the town is a popular holiday and golfing resort with safe, sandy beaches to the east and west of the harbour. Only the steep narrow streets of the old warehouse quarter and the 17th-century Town House in the High Street, Scotland's oldest civic building still to be in continuous use, recall the days when Dunbar was sustained by its fishing industry. There are good sporting facilities, including two golf courses, and family entertainment is provided at the Victoria Ballroom throughout the summer. Sand yachting takes place on Belhaven Beach and the Dunbar Veteran Vehicle Rally is held each August. The Myreton Motor Museum has a fine collection of vehicles and cycles dating back to the mid-19th century and an old horse mill, now incorporated in a garage forecourt, may be seen on the southern outskirts of the town.

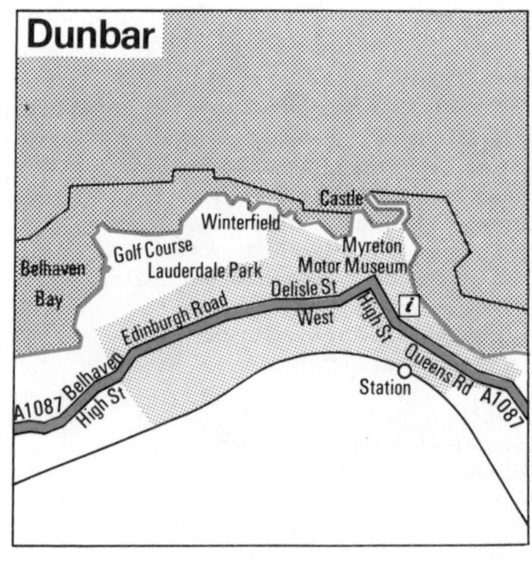

Recreation and Sports

Dunbar East Links Golf Club ☎*62317*
Dunbar RFC and Sports Club Winterfield, North Rd ☎*62454*
Dunbar Swimming Pool ☎*63333*–Heated outdoor pool
Dunbar Winterfield Golf Club ☎*62280*
East Beach–Amusements, funfair
Lauderdale Park–Boating, crazy-golf, trampolines
Winterfield–Putting, tennis

Theatre

Victoria Ballroom ☎*63434*

Places of Interest

Dunbar Castle
Myreton Motor Museum Castle Pk ☎*62365*

Tourist Information

Tourist Information Office ☎*63353*

Accommodation

The following establishments are recommended by the AA. Further information may be obtained from the Tourist Information Office.

★★	**Bayswell** ☎*62225*
★★	**Craig-en-Gelt** Marine Rd ☎*62287*
★★	**Goldenstones** Queens Rd ☎*62356*
GH	**Cruachan** East Links Rd ☎*63595*
GH	**Marine** 7 Marine Rd ☎*63315*
GH	**St Laurence** North Rd ☎*62527*
GH	**Springfield** Edinburgh Rd ☎*62502*
SC	Mr Henderson, **Pleasants** Dunbar ☎*63737*

Sand yachting

Berwick-upon-Tweed *see page 195*

Holy Island
Previously known as Lindisfarne, Holy Island has religious connections dating back to the 7th century when St Aiden founded the first English diocese. The island contains the ruins of an impressive 11th-century priory and is accessible via a causeway which is impassable at high tide. Extreme care should be taken to select the safest time to cross to the island.

Bamburgh
There is a fine beach here where swimming is safe. Bamburgh Castle, a red sandstone fortress, stands on a rocky outcrop above the shore. The Normans orginally built the castle on the site of a 6th-century fortification, but most of the present structure dates from the 18th or 19th century. Bamburgh village contains the Grace Darling Museum devoted to the life of the 18th-century herione who rescued shipwrecked sailors in an open boat.

Seahouses
A small, busy town and fishing port in a charming setting. Boat trips and amusements are available but swimming can be dangerous.

Beadnell
This holiday village overlooks a sheltered, sandy bay where safe swimming can be enjoyed. The harbour is used by crab and lobster fishermen and overlooked by some ruined 18th-century lime kilns now the property of the National Trust.

Newton Haven
A small, natural harbour and sandy beach lie in the shelter of an offshore reef.

Boulmer Haven
There are safe, sandy beaches here sheltered by a rocky reef and backed by low cliffs.

Alnmouth
This picturesque unspoilt resort lies on the River Aln estuary where safe sandy beaches are to be found. Bathers should, however, avoid the river mouth.

Amble
A former coal-exporting town now mainly concerned with the shipping of grain, Amble has become a popular holiday and sailing centre. There are firm, sandy beaches where bathing is safe during calm weather.

Newbiggin-by-the-Sea
There is a long sweep of sandy beach here backed by a promenade. Swimming is safe, provided the rocks at either end of the bay are avoided. Children's amusements and a paddling pool are available and the area is popular with water sports enthusiasts.

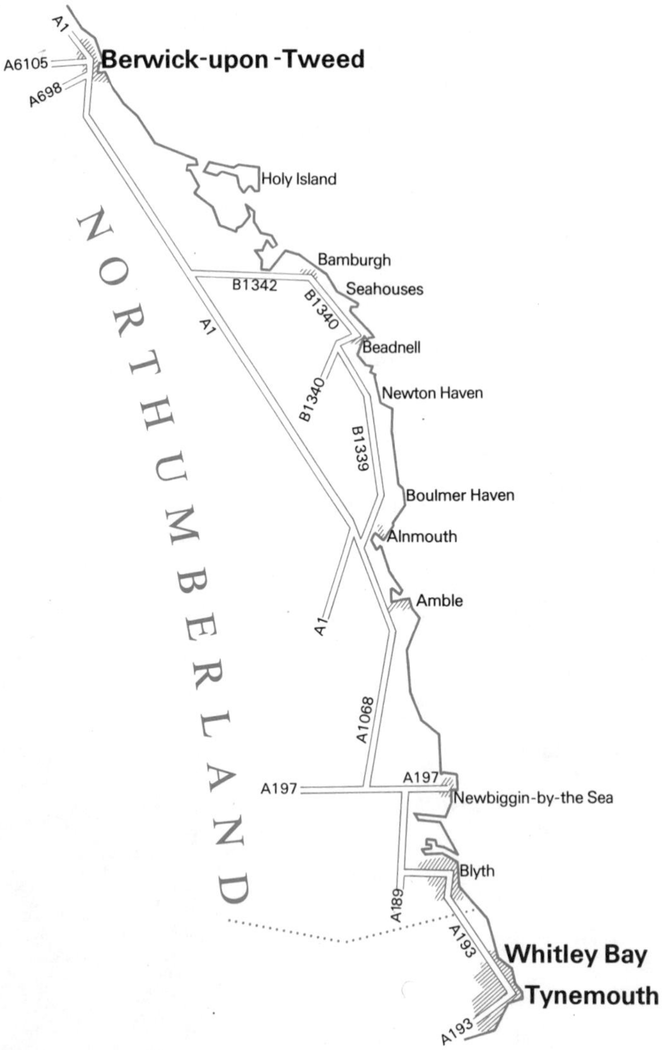

Blyth
A busy port chiefly concerned with the export of coal and ship breaking. Sandy beaches, backed by dunes, lie to the south of the harbour and Blyth has good shopping and entertainment facilities.

Whitley Bay *see page 196*

Tynemouth *see page 197*

BERWICK-UPON-TWEED

The most northerly town in England, Berwick-upon-Tweed was once one of Scotland's leading seaports and its strategic position made it the scene of many Border struggles between the 12th and the 17th centuries. During this period the town constantly changed hands and was captured or sacked on at least 14 occasions. As a result of this precarious existence it is now considered to be the best example of a fortified town in Europe and the defensive walls built during the 16th century, together with remnants of earlier structures, have been preserved in their original state.

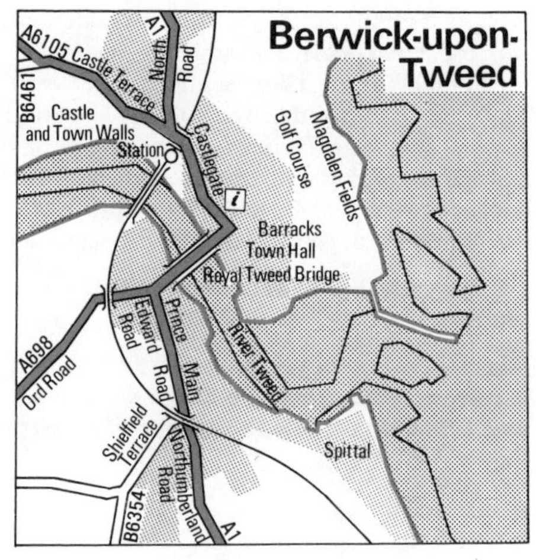

Modern Berwick is a salmon fishing port and holiday resort with sandy beaches. Although swimming is generally safe care should be taken at all times, especially where children are concerned, and particularly on Spittal beach on the southern bank of the River Tweed. Berwick has good amusement and sports facilities and is the scene of several ancient festivals including the May Fair and Tweedmouth Feast Week in July when the Salmon Queen is crowned. Little remains of the 12th-century castle but one of the town's three bridges, the Berwick Bridge with 15 arches, dates from the 17th century and the Barracks, designed by Vanburgh in 1717, which contains the King's Own Scottish Borderers Museum, and the Town Hall, dating from a similar period, are well worth a visit.

Berwick is an ideal centre for walking or touring. A favourite local walk is along the Elizabethan ramparts, which provide fine views of the town, and the Northumberland moors and the Cheviot Hills are a relatively short distance away.

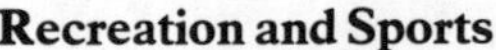

Recreation and Sports

Berwick Golf Club Goswick
☎ *Ancroft87256*
Berwick Rangers FC Shielfield Park
☎ *7424* – Scottish League
Berwick Sailing Club Spittal
Berwick Swimming Pool Sandgate
☎ *7895* – Heated indoor pool
Magdalene Fields – Bowls, children's playground, outdoor swimming pool, paddling pool, putting, trampolines
Pier Fields – Cricket, tennis
Shielfield Park ☎ *6806* – Speedway
Spittal Seafront – Amusements, bowls, children's paddling pool and playground, tennis

Cinema

Playhouse Sandgate ☎ *7769*

Places of Interest

Castle and Town Walls
Museum and Art Gallery Marygate
☎ *7320*
Museum of the King's Own Scottish Borderers The Barracks ☎ *7426*
Town Hall Marygate

Tourist Information

Tourist Information Centre
Castlegate Car Park ☎ *7187*

Accommodation

The following establishments are recommended by the AA. Further information may be obtained from the Tourist Information Office

★★★ **Turret House** Etal Rd ☎ *7344*
★★ **Castle** Castle Gate ☎ *6471*
★★ **Kings Arms** Hide Hill ☎ *7454*
★ **Queens Head** Sandgate ☎ *7852*
GH **Ravensholme** 34 Ravensdowne ☎ *7170*
SC **Dunrobin Holiday Flats** Main Street, Spittal. For bookings: Mr and Mrs A H Briggs Woodville Guest House, 139 Main St, Spittal, ☎ *6261*.

WHITLEY BAY

A popular family holiday resort and residential area, Whitley Bay has a fine long sandy beach with rocks and pools. Swimming is generally safe with lifeguards patrolling the beach during the summer, and red flags are flown when weather conditions render swimming dangerous. The rocks at the southern end of the town are ideal for angling and there are facilities for a variety of activities including ten-pin bowling and ice skating. Spanish City is a large amusement park with all the usual attractions of a fun fair. The indoor Leisure Pool complex has an unusual pool in which, by the touch of a button, waves are created. The pool is surrounded with palm trees, tropical plants and a beach area.

For those who like to wander around the shops there is the excellent Whitley Lodge shopping centre.

Just off-shore at the northern end of the town is St Mary's Island with a lighthouse and numerous old cottages. It is joined to the mainland by a pedestrian causeway which can be used at low-tide. To the south lies the picturesque fishing village and harbour of Cullercoats Bay.

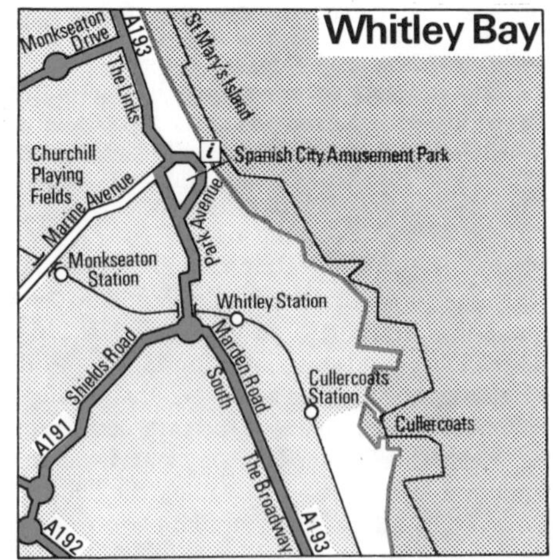

Recreation and Sports

Brierdene – Mini-golf
Churchill Playing Fields – Cycle track, play area
Crawford Park – Bowls, tennis
Hillheads Road – Ice Skating, ten pin bowling
Promenade – Mini-golf paddling pool, putting, swings, trampolines
Rockcliffe Park – Tennis, bowls
Souter Park – Bowls, tennis
Spanish City – Amusement Park
Victoria Park – Bowls, tennis
Whitley Bay Golf Club Claremont *Rd ☎520180*

Cinema

Classic Cauldwell Lane *☎525540*

Cinema/Theatre

Playhouse Marine Avenue *☎523505*

Tourist Information

Recreation and Amenities Dept Municipal Offices, Park Rd *☎523211*
Tourist Office Promenade *☎524494*

Accommodation

The following establishments are recommended by the AA. Further information may be obtained from the Tourist Office.

★★ **Holmedale** Park Av *☎523121*
★ **Newquay** South Pde *☎532211*
★ **Station** 168–170 Whitley Rd *☎22241*
GH **Croglin Hotel** 35–41 South Pde *☎523317*

Fun at the fair

Sandwiched between the Tyneside industrial conurbation and the lively resort of Whitley Bay, Tynemouth has chosen to contrast with its neighbours rather than compete with them. The unspoilt stretch of beach at Long Sands is aptly named and provides safe bathing with the added protection of lifeguard patrols and a safety warning system. At the southern end of the beach is a popular open-air swimming pool. Jutting out from the Tynemouth headland the North Pier, together with its counterpart on the southern side of the estuary, protects the access to the River Tyne and provides fine views over this busy waterway. Tynemouth has a history which stretches back to the building of Hadrian's great wall by the Romans, when supply ships would bring provisions to Tynemouth for distribution to the troops. In the 11th century the Priory was built on the headland and 500 years later it was joined by the castle. Both now stand in ruins overlooking the sea and the estuary, providing an impressive landmark for passing ships. Standing on grassy slopes not far from the end of Front Street, and looking characteristically out to sea, is the statue of Admiral Lord Collingwood, hero of Trafalgar, friend of Nelson and a most distinguished son of Northumberland.

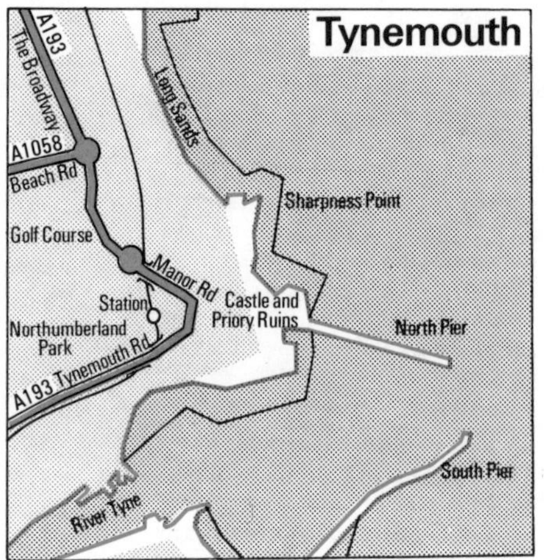

Recreation and Sports

Alexander Scott Park – Children's playground

Arnold Palmer Putting Course Plaza ☎ *North Shields 76576*

Northumberland Park – Bowls, Children's playground

Preston Avenue – Cricket, football

Sea Front – Open-air Swimming Pool

Smiths Park – Bowls, tennis

Tynemouth Golf Club Spital Dene ☎ *North Shields 76576*

Tynemouth Indoor Swimming Pool Preston Village

Tynemouth Park – Boating, bowls, tennis

Tynemouth Sailing Club Priors Haven ☎ *North Shields 72617*

Cinema

Crown Cinemas Russell St, ☎ *North Shields 72975*

Places of Interest

St Pauls Church Monastery and Old Hall, Church Bank, Jarrow ☎ *Jarrow 892106/897402*

Tynemouth Castle
Tynemouth Priory
Tynemouth Volunteer Life Brigade Watch House

Tourist Information

Tourist Information Centre Grand Parade, ☎ *North Shields 70251*

Accommodation

The following establishments are recommended by the AA. Further information may be obtained from the Tourist Information Office

★★★ **Grand** Grand Pde ☎ North Shields *72106*

★★ **Park** Grand Pde ☎ *North Shields 71406*

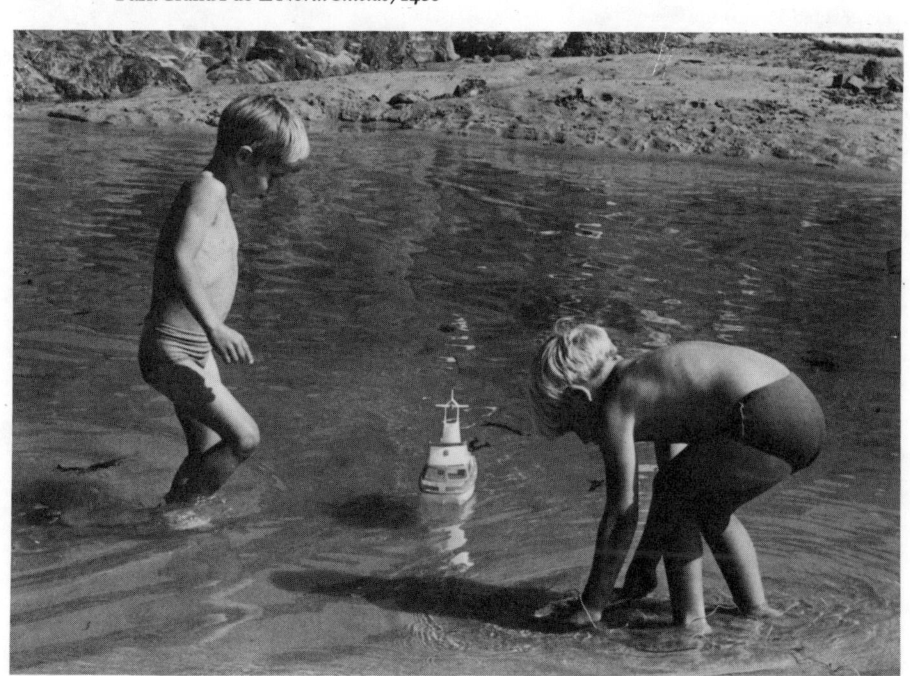

South Shields
On the eastern edge of the Tyneside industrial estate, South Shields too has its factories, warehouses and docks. In sharp contrast to this aspect of the town are its long, sandy beaches and sea front parks. The first lifeboat service in the world began here and a native of South Shields, William Wouldhave, invented the self-righting lifeboat which is on show in the Museum.

Sunderland
The largest town in the county of Durham, Sunderland is best known for its ship-building and coal mining activities, but it also has amenities for the holidaymaker. Beaches of sand, with outcrops of rock, stretch for almost two miles to the north of the Wear Estuary, backed by promenades and play areas. The town has facilities for every kind of sport and entertainment and at the North Dock there is a sailing centre. Places of interest include the Museum and Art Gallery, Hylton Castle, Washington Old Hall, Washington Wildfowl Trust, Monkwearmouth Station and Ryhope Engine House.

Seaham
A coal-mining town whose harbour was developed over the years for the shipping of coal. Unlike most mining areas, Seaham has a long sandy beach, extending northwards from the harbour, which is extremely popular with the neighbouring communities. There is a golf course, a sports centre and facilities for tennis, bowls, cricket and football as well as sea fishing from the beach and harbour walls.

Crimdon Park
This stretch of sandy beach, backed by dunes and heaths, is being developed as a recreation area by the local authority. There is a paddling pool, a playground and an amusement park and the two-mile-long beach is patrolled by lifeguards during the season.

Hartlepool and Seaton Carew
The ancient and modern town of Hartlepool has been a port for many centuries and prospered on the coal trade. Now, the docks handle other cargoes, and a large variety of industries exist in the town. There is still a small fishing fleet which provides for locally smoked kippers. The rocky headland and industrial dockland area give way to a long stretch of sands at the south of Hartlepool Bay where Seaton Carew provides resort amenities. There is a roller skating rink, paddling pool, obstacle golf, putting and amusements behind the beach. Further south is the new nuclear power station. Places of interest include the Gray Art Gallery and Museum and the Maritime Museum, both in Hartlepool.

Redcar *see page 199*

Saltburn *see page 200*

Runswick
Between the rocky headlands of Lingrow Knock and Kettle Ness lies Runswick Bay, traced along the shore by the Cleveland Way long distance footpath. The sand and shingle beach is backed by a very steep approach and a small village whose predecessor slipped into the sea in 1682. There is a lifeboat station and a launching ramp, but a permit must be obtained for its use.

Whitby *see page 201*

Redcar is a popular resort with miles of sands stretching as far as the Tees Estuary where the dunes are a haven for wild birds. The town's sandy beaches, backed by gardens and terraces of bay-fronted buildings, are patrolled by lifeguards and protected by the natural breakwaters of off-shore reefs which have helped to give Redcar its high safety record. The same reefs that shield bathers from the North Sea breakers were, in years gone by, a positive hazard to shipping, so much so that Redcar had one of the first lifeboats in existence, which is now preserved in the Zetland Museum. Redcar's attractions are by no means limited to the sand and sea. There is a vast range of evening entertainment including concerts, dances and discos. The mid-July Folk Festival is an important event in the local calendar and the carnival at the end of that month provides a week of pageantry and entertainment. Then, of course, there is the Sport of Kings with Redcar's own racecourse the venue for many important events.

Redcar
Coatham Enclosure
Coatham Road
Redcar Station
High St
Granville
Terrace
Locke Park
Park Ave
The Stray
A1085
Corporation Road
Coast Rd
Zetland Park
A1042
East Halt Station
Kirkleatham Lane
Race Course
Borough Park
Redcar Lane
A1042
A1040

Recreation and Sports

Borough Park–Bowls, putting, tennis
Coatham Enclosure–Boating lake, swimming baths, indoor amusement park and funfair
Locke Park–Boating, bowls, putting, tennis
Redcar Cricket Club ☎*3791*
Redcar Race Course ☎*4254/4068*
Redcar Rugby Club Green Ln ☎*2733*
The Stray–Paddling pool, putting
Zetland Park–Bowls, novelty-golf, tennis

Cinema

Regent, Newcomen Ter ☎*2094*

Theatre

Coatham Bowl Concert Hall ☎*744200*

Places of Interest

Captain Cook Museum Great Ayton
Ormesby Hall Ormesby
Zetland Museum King St ☎*71921*

Tourist Information

Tourist Information Centre Zetland Museum, King St ☎*71921*

Accommodation

The following establishments are recommended by the AA. Further information may be obtained from the Tourist Information Office.

☆☆☆ **Royal York** Coatham Rd ☎*6221*
★★ **Clarendon** High St ☎*4301*
★★ **Swan** High St ☎*3678*

SALTBURN

Just over a hundred years ago Saltburn was little more than a group of fishermen's cottages. Then industrialist Henry Pease came upon the picturesque scene, realised its potential and founded the Saltburn Improvement Company which created the town as it is today. The cottages are still here, cocooned amidst the Victorian development which gives Saltburn its atmosphere of dignity and charm. Steep cliffs separate the town from the beach below which can be reached by pathways or by the restored 19th-century cliff tramway which gives direct access to the pier. Five miles of sands stretch out along the coast where bathing is safe, except for a stretch between Saltburn and Marske, and outcrops of rock provide fascinating pools to explore at low-tide. Standing over 300-ft high, Huntcliff provides magnificent views and its footpath forms part of the Cleveland Way. Saltburn's gardens are a major attraction to visitors, particularly the Italian and Valley Gardens which embellish the glen of the Skelton Beck. Here a miniature railway runs through the woods, while a little further inland a 160-ft, eleven-span viaduct carries the 'real' railway over the beck. Nearby, Marske is a quiet coastal village and burial place of the father of Captain Cook.

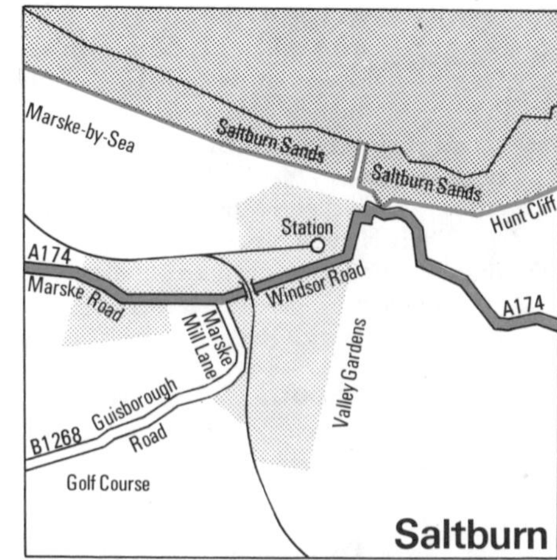

Recreation and Sports

Foreshore – Boats for hire, fishing, pony rides, roundabouts, swings.
Marske Cricket Club Windy Hill Ln, Marske ☎ *Redcar 4361*
Marske Lawn Tennis Club Playing Fields, off South Field Rd, Marske.
Saltburn-by-the-Sea Golf Club Hob Hill ☎ *2812*
Saltburn Cricket Bowls and Tennis Club, Marske Rd ☎ *2761*
Saltburn Leisure Centre – Most indoor sports, swimming pool, sauna and solarium
Valley Gardens – Miniature railway

Places of Interest

Chapel Beck Gallery Fountain St, Guisborough
Guisborough Priory
Skelton Castle Grounds
Upleatham Church

Tourist Information

Tourist Information Centre Zetland Museum, King St, Redcar ☎ *Redcar 71921*

Accommodation

The following establishments are recommended by the AA. Further information may be obtained from the Tourist Information Office.

★★ **Queen** Windsor Rd ☎ *3371*

Where the River Esk cuts through the cliffs to flow into the sea, Whitby stands on both sloping banks. Close to the river, particularly on the east side, are the picturesque buildings where seamen lived in days gone by. In Grape Lane stands the house where Captain Cook lived while he learned the art of seamanship on Whitby vessels, before embarking on his illustrious career in the Royal Navy. His monument stands on the West Cliff. Whitby is still a busy working port with cargoes arriving from across the North Sea and the town's boat-building tradition continues. There is also a growing traffic of yachts and high speed power boats which can often be seen off shore. While the east bank preserves something of Whitby's heritage, the west side of the town has developed to cater for the holidaymaker. Hotels line the streets behind the long stretch of Whitby Sands where bathing is safe. Dominating the whole scene are the ruins which were once the beautiful Abbey of St. Hilda. Many old customs are perpetuated in Whitby, among them the 'Blessing of the Waters', the 'Blessing of the Boats' and the 'Planting of the Penny Hedge' – all of which take place around the harbour. Other annual events include the Agricultural and Horse Show, the Floral and Horticulture Show and the Regatta – all in August.

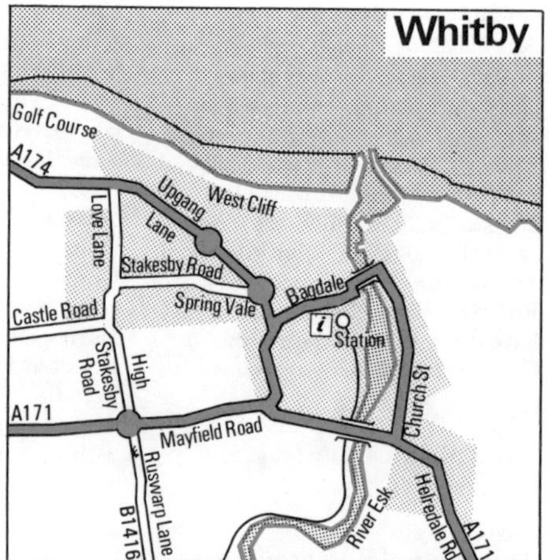

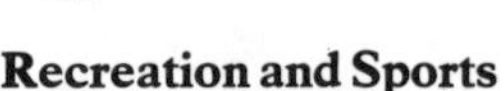

Recreation and Sports

Beach – Chalets for hire, donkey rides
Harbour – Boats for hire
Mulgrave Road – Open-air swimming pool
West Cliff – Archery, boating lake, bowling, crazy-golf, indoor swimming pool, mini-golf, miniature railway, paddling pool, putting, tennis
Whitby Albion Rangers FC Albion House, Silver St ☎*3821*
Whitby and District Rifle Club West Cliff Sports Ground ☎*3808*
Whitby Golf Club Low Straggleton ☎*2768*
Whitby Rugby Union Football Club White Leys Playing Fields ☎*2008*
Whitby Yacht Club Pier Rd ☎*3623*
Whitby Yacht Club Shore Racing Station ☎*2172*

Cinema

Empire Station Sq ☎*3194*

Dancing

Floral Pavilion West Cliff ☎*2124/2411*

Theatre

Spa Theatre West Cliff ☎*2124/2108*

Places of Interest

North Yorkshire Moors Railway Grosmont ☎*Pickering72508*
Pannett Art Gallery Pannett Pk ☎*2908*
RNLI Lifeboat Museum Pier Rd, Whitby
Whitby Abbey
Whitby Museum Pannett Pk ☎*2908*

Tourist Information

Tourist Information Centre New Quay Rd ☎*2674*

Accommodation

The following establishments are recommended by the AA. Further information may be obtained from the Tourist Information Office.

★★	**Royal** Westcliffe ☎*2234*
★	**Marvic** White Point Rd ☎*2400*
★	**Saxonville** Ladysmith Ave (off Argyle Rd) ☎*2631*
★	**White House** Upgang Ln, Westcliff ☎*2098*
ⓟ	**Beech** Sandsend (3m NW A174) ☎*Sandsend200*
GH	**Europa Private Hotel** 20 Hudson St ☎*2251*
GH	**Oxford Private Hotel** 1 Crescent Ter, West Cliff, N Prom ☎*2428*
GH	**Prospect of Whitby** 12 Esplanade ☎*3026*
GH	**Seacliffe Private Hotel** ☎*3139*
SC	Mrs J Griffiths **Regent House** 7 Royal Cres ☎*2103*

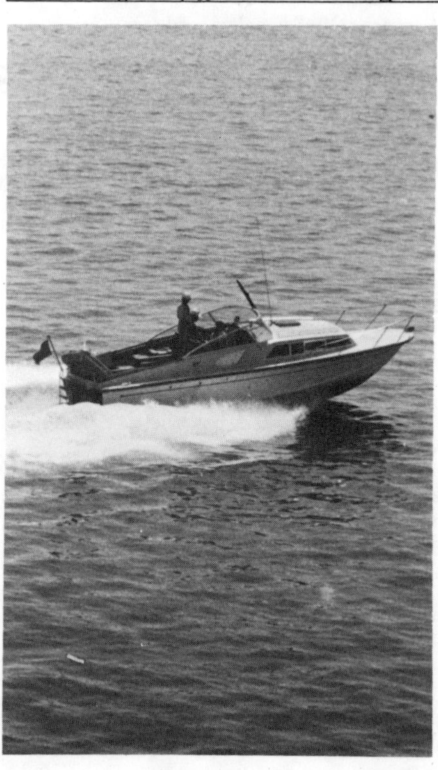

Robin Hood's Bay
An old fishing village clings precariously to the rocky slopes of the cliffs, the buildings connected by narrow passages and flights of steps. The rocky bay abounds in fossils and the southern cliffs are backed by Fylindales Moor which was the scene of much smuggling activity during the 18th century. The connections with Robin Hood are obscure, but he may have attempted to escape to the Continent from this neighbourhood.

SCARBOROUGH *see page 204*

Cayton Bay
There are level sands here, below towering cliffs. Swimming is safest on the incoming tide but there are ridges in the sand which can prove to be a hazard to children.

Filey *see page 203*

Bridlington *see page 206*

Barmston
A mainly sandy beach with scattered patches of shingle. There is an amusement arcade and a children's playground.

Skipsea
There is a narrow, sandy beach here, overlooked by a line of beach bungalows. The village contains the earthworks of a large Norman castle, once the stronghold of Drogo de Brevere and later demolished by Henry III in 1220.

Atwick Sands
The sandy shore here is safe for swimming except at low-tide. The inland area suffers regular erosion which can cause the beach access road to be closed at certain times.

Hornsea
A small resort with a sandy beach backed by an amusement area. Hornsea has the largest freshwater lake in the county covering almost 500 acres. It was formed by glacial deposits and is a refuge for herons, geese, swans and grebes. Boats are available for hire and a public footpath provides a pleasant two-mile walk around the lake's circumference. Hornsea Pottery is always an attraction to visitors and the complex, in addition to tours of the famous workshops, offers a leisure garden with an aviary, children's playground and a mini-zoo.

WEATHER CHART	Av hours of Sunshine in month	Hottest Av daily Temp °C
April	152	8
May	184	11
June	192	14
July	176	16
August	155	16
September	132	14

Withernsea
This small popular holiday resort has a sandy beach, with some shingle, banked between wooden groynes. Swimming is safe but care should be taken at low-tide. An inshore rescue boat operates during the summer. Withernsea is a popular boating centre and has an open-air swimming pool, a funfair, several amusement arcades and other recreational facilities.

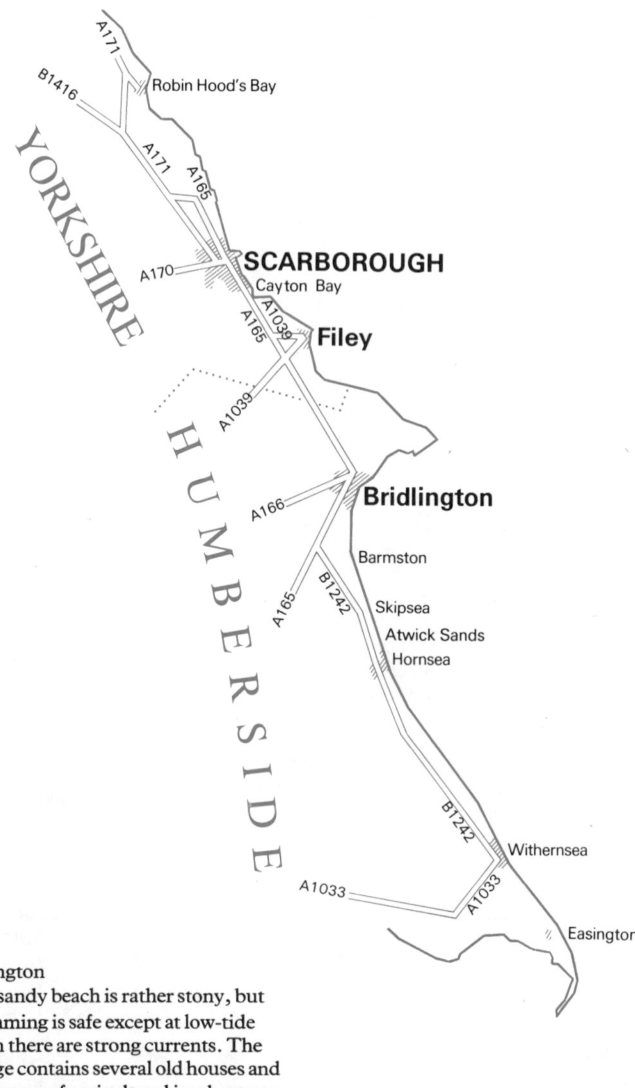

Easington
The sandy beach is rather stony, but swimming is safe except at low-tide when there are strong currents. The village contains several old houses and a museum of agricultural implements housed in a restored 14th-century tithe barn.

FILEY

Filey is a small, quiet resort which is ideally suited to family holidays. Its firm sands slope gently into the sea and stretch for six miles around the bay from the white cliffs of Flamborough Head in the south to the unique natural phenomenon of Filey Brigg in the north. This remarkable rocky reef stretches for a mile out to sea, forming a perfect natural breakwater to shelter Filey Sands. Evidence of Roman occupation has been excavated but in later years Filey sank into relative obscurity as a small fishing village. Then at the end of the 18th century, fashionable society came in search of the health-giving properties of the water and the climate and Filey developed as a holiday resort. Charlotte Brontë spoke very highly of the town and the house she visited is now the Brontë Café. Today the town retains an elegant charm, the beach area backed by colourful gardens and white-fronted hotels. In the bay yachts from the sailing club mingle with the fishing cobles which carry on their traditional industry, while land-locked sand yachts can sometimes be seen racing along the firm sands.

Filey
Country Park
A1039 Scarborough Road
Station
Muston Road
Filey Sands
Filey Bay
A165
Southdene
A165
Golf Course

Recreation and Sports

Clarence Drive – Football, cricket
Crescent Gardens – Putting
Country Park – Mini-golf, picnic area, putting
Filey Golf Club South Cliff ☎*Scarborough 513293*
Filey Sailing Club Coble Landing ☎*Scarborough 512529*
Glen Gardens Foreshore – Amusements, archery, children's playground, gadget-golf, golf-maze, motor boats, paddling pools, pony rides, putting
North Cliff – Mini-golf
South Cliff – Mini-golf
Southdene – Bowls, tennis

Cinema

Grand Union St ☎*Scarborough 512129*
Brig Station Ave ☎*Scarborough 513207*

Theatre

Sun Lounge The Crescent Gdns

Places of Interest

Filey Folk Museum Queen St

Tourist Information

Information Centre John St ☎*Scarborough 512204*

Accommodation

The following establishments are recommended by the AA. Further information may be obtained from the Tourist Information Office.

★★★ **White Lodge** The Crescent ☎*2268*

★★ **Hylands** The Crescent ☎*Scarborough 512091*

SC **18 Hope Street** For bookings: Mrs K Swann, Northcliffe Cottage, Filey ☎*Scarborough 513228*

SC **27 Hope Street** For bookings: Mr and Mrs K Swann, Northcliffe Cottage ☎*Scarborough 513228*

SC Mrs E Cutts, **Fern-lea Holiday Flat** 15 Rutland St ☎*Scarborough 512696*

SCARBOROUGH

Scarborough has been a popular seaside resort since the 18th century and it was here that the bathing machine made its first appearance. Today the town's equable climate, fine sands and landscaped cliff-top gardens attract many thousands of holidaymakers each year and it has also become one of the most important conference centres in the North of England.

North Bay and South Bay are separated by a headland, topped by an impressive Norman Castle which stands on the site of a Roman signal station. Both bays have sandy beaches but swimming is safest in sheltered South Bay as the northern shore is exposed to north-easterly gales which result in exceptionally heavy surf. Lifeguards and an inshore rescue boat patrol the sands during the summer months. There is an open-air swimming pool below South Cliff Gardens and another around the headland above North Bay where Northstead Manor Gardens contain Scarborough Zoo and Marineland, Yorkshire's largest Amusement Park, a miniature railway and an open-air theatre where 'It's a Knockout' contests are held. Scarborough's parks offer some unique features such as the twice-weekly naval battles re-enacted by model boats in Peasholm Park and the quarter-sized replica of the schooner 'Hispaniola' which operates on The Mere to the south-west of the town.

H	**AA Service Centre** (74) West Pier ☎*60344*

Recreation and Sports

B	**Alexandra Gardens** – Bowls
C/G	**Clarence Gardens** – Putting, tennis
O	**Esplanade** – Crazy-golf, maze
G	**Foreshore Road** – Amusement arcades
I	**Manor Road** – Bowls
B	**North Bay Swimming Pool** ☎*72744* – Open-air pool
A/B	**Peasholm Park** – Band concerts, boating, putting, tree-walk, water-skiing displays
B	**Scarborough Cricket Club** Cricket Ground ☎*65625* – County cricket
A	**Scarborough Swimming Pool** Ryndle Cres ☎*67137* – Indoor pool
P	**South Bay Swimming Pool** ☎*74446* – Open-air pool

Cabaret/Dancing

G	**Aquarius Night Club** Market St ☎*63425*
B	**The Corner** North Bay
K	**Golden Guinea** 7a Ramshill Rd ☎*73689*
K	**Minstrel Bar and Lounge** Futurist Buildings, Foreshore Rd ☎*62031*
K	**Ollies Club** 22 Huntriss Row ☎*73085*
K	**The Penthouse** 35a St Nicholas St ☎*63204*
O	**Spa Ocean Room** The Spa ☎*63937*
F	**Tiffanys Night Spot** Aberdeen Wk ☎*72506*
G	**Victorias** St Thomas St ☎*73049*

Cinemas

K	**Futurist** Foreshore Rd ☎*60644*
J	**Odeon** ☎*61725*
G	**Royal Opera House** ☎*69999*

Theatres

B	**Floral Hall** ☎*72185*
K	**Futurist Theatre** Foreshore Rd ☎*60644*
B	**Open-air Theatre** Northstead Manor Gdns
G	**Royal Opera House** ☎*69999*
O	**Spa Theatre** ☎*65068*
J	**Theatre in the Round** Westwood, Valley Bridge Pde ☎70541

Places of Interest

K(1)	**Art Gallery**
H(2)	**Castle**
O(3)	**Italian and Holbeck Gardens**
K(4)	**Londesborough Lodge Museum** The Crescent ☎*67326* – Local history
B(5)	**Northstead Manor Gardens** – Amusement park, miniature railway, open-air theatre
B(6)	**Planetarium**
K(7)	**Public Library**
K(8)	**Rotunda Museum** – Regional archaeology
B(5)	**Scarborough Zoo and Marineland** Northstead Manor Gardens ☎*64401*
H(9)	**Three Mariners**
K(10)	**Town Hall**
K(11)	**Wood End**

Tourist Information

K ℹ	**Information Centre** St Nicholas Cliff ☎*72261*

Accommodation

The establishments listed below are a selection of AA-recommended accommodation and restaurants located in the area covered by the Town Plan. Further information may be found in AA publications or obtained from the Information Centre.

1SC	**Adelaide House** St Martins Sq, Scarborough, N Yorks ☎*60928*
2SC	**16 Albion Road** For bookings: Mr D A Slack, 7 Lowdale Ave, Scarborough, N Yorks YO12 6JR ☎*65197*
3GH	**Burghcliffe Hotel** 28 Esplanade ☎*61524*
4★★	**Carlton** Belmont Rd ☎*60938*
5GH	**Church Hills Private Hotel** St Martins Ave ☎*63148*
6Inn	**Continental Lodge** 37 West St, South Cliff
7★★	**Crescent** The Crescent ☎*60929*
8★	**Dorchester** Filey Rd ☎*61668*
9★★	**Esplanade** Belmont Rd ☎*60382*
10SC	**Gables Holiday Flats** West Bank, Scarborough, N Yorks YO12 4DX ☎*61005*
11SC	Mrs G Wittering, **Grosvenor Road** South Cliff, Scarborough, N Yorks YO11 2LZ ☎*65566/66255*
12✕✕	**Lanterna Ristorante** 33 Queen St ☎*63616*
13GH	**Ridbech Private Hotel** 8 The Crescent ☎*61683*
14★★	**Southlands** West St ☎*61461*
15SC	Mrs G Wittering, **11 Valley Bridge Parade** Scarborough, N Yorks YO11 2PF ☎*65566/66255*
16SC	**15 Victoria Park** For bookings: Mr A A Squire, 54 Falsgrave Rd, Scarborough, N Yorks ☎*60542*
17GH	**Wave Crest Private Hotel** 34 Prince of Wales Ter, South Cliff ☎*73129*

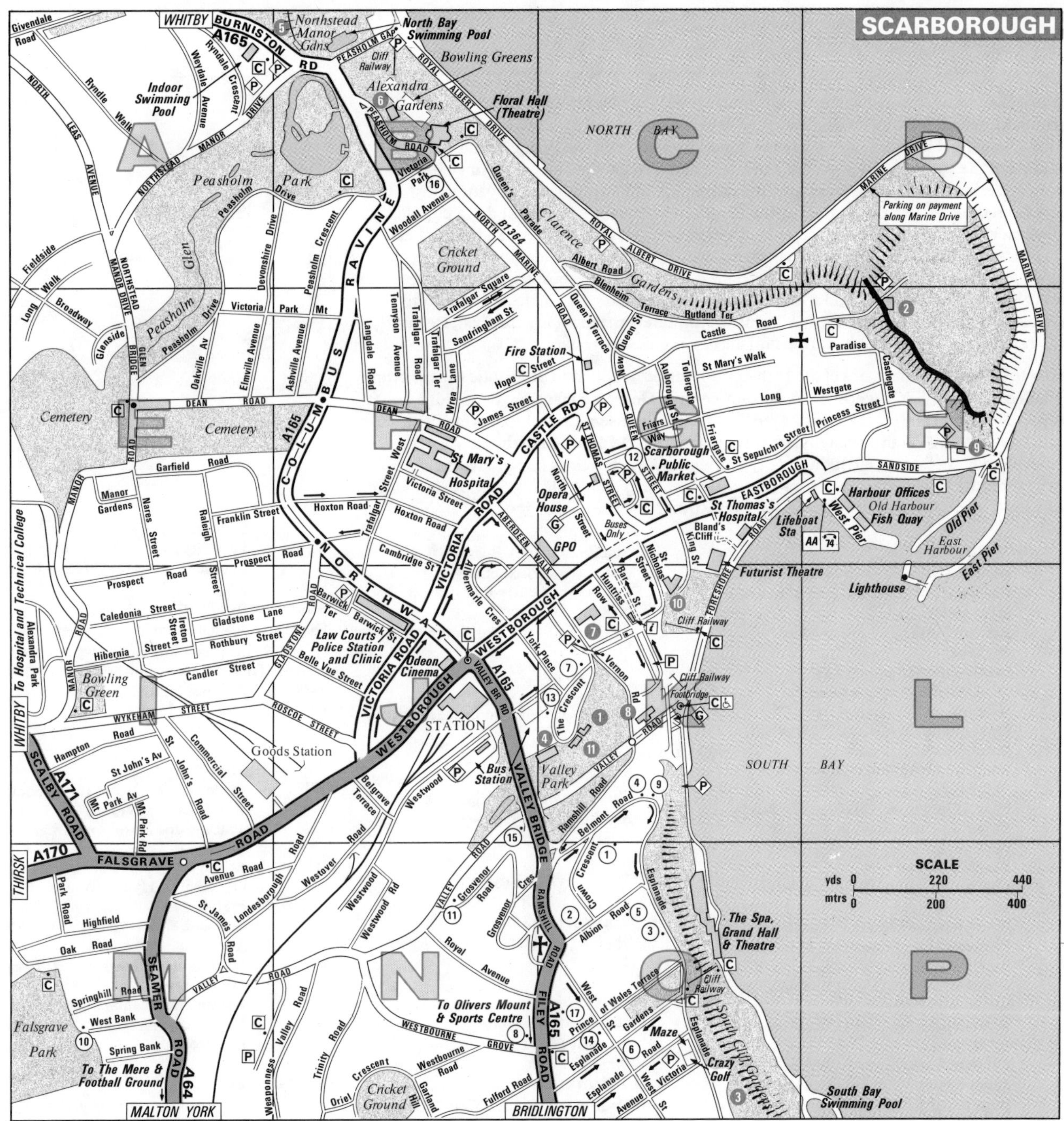
SCARBOROUGH
WHITBY
BURNISTON RD
A165
Northstead Manor Gdns
North Bay Swimming Pool
Cliff Railway
Bowling Greens
Alexandra Gardens
Floral Hall (Theatre)
NORTH BAY
Indoor Swimming Pool
Peasholm Park
Peasholm Glen
Cemetery
Cricket Ground
Parking on payment along Marine Drive
MARINE DRIVE
ROYAL ALBERT DRIVE
Fire Station
St Mary's Hospital
Scarborough Public Market
Opera House
GPO
St Thomas's Hospital
Harbour Offices
Old Harbour
Fish Quay
Lifeboat Sta
Old Pier
East Harbour
East Pier
Lighthouse
Futurist Theatre
Cliff Railway
Law Courts Police Station and Clinic
Odeon Cinema
STATION
Goods Station
Bus Station
Valley Park
SOUTH BAY
SCALE
yds 0 220 440
mtrs 0 200 400
The Spa, Grand Hall & Theatre
To Olivers Mount & Sports Centre
Maze
Crazy Golf
South Cliff Gardens
South Bay Swimming Pool
Falsgrave Park
To The Mere & Football Ground
To Hospital and Technical College
Bowling Green
WESTBOROUGH
FALSGRAVE ROAD
SCALBY ROAD
A171
A170
THIRSK
SEAMER ROAD
A64
MALTON YORK
BRIDLINGTON
FILEY ROAD
VALLEY BRIDGE
NORTHWAY
VICTORIA ROAD
COLUMBUS RAVINE
CASTLE RD
EASTBOROUGH
SANDSIDE
FORESHORE ROAD
Cricket Ground
A B C D E F G H I J K L M N O P

BRIDLINGTON

The most famous historical event in Bridlington's past took place in 1643 when Queen Henrietta Maria landed there in an attempt to bring arms and assistance to her husband, Charles I, causing the town to suffer a fierce bombardment from the Parliamentary fleet. By the middle of the 19th century, wealthy Yorkshire families had developed the town into a pleasant watering place but the coming of the railways in 1842 opened the way for many visitors from the industrial West Riding and Bridlington was soon established as a popular holiday resort. Today the harbour is filled with pleasure craft although a small fishing fleet is still in operation and the beaches which lie to the north and south provide fine sands, safe swimming, beach chalets, bathing tents and donkey rides. Various boat trips are available and there are ample entertainment and sporting facilities within the town including children's shows and a miniature circus at the Spa Theatre. Annual events include a carnival, Regatta Week and the East-Coast Run featuring vintage fire engines and buses.

The Bayle Gate, all that remains of the 12th-century priory, is open to the public as a museum and to the north-east lies Sewerby Hall, an 18th-century Georgian mansion, containing an art gallery and museum and set in extensive parkland where amusement and sports facilities and a zoo are to be found. A Walt Disney-type railway runs from Bridlington to the park gates. Flamborough Head, at the northern end of Bridlington Bay, provides impressive views from its 150ft summit. It is a favourite nesting ground for seabirds and the lighthouse overlooks the site of a sea battle between John Paul Jones and a Royal Naval vessel in 1779.

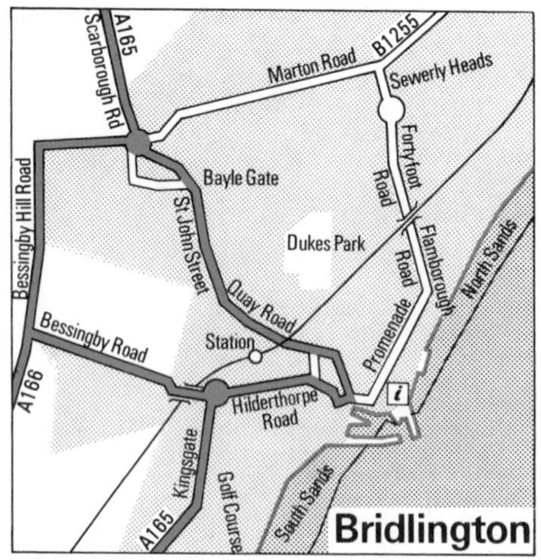

Recreation and Sports

Avenue Park – Bowls, putting, tennis
Beaconsfield Gardens – Bowls, model yachting lake
Bridlington Golf Club Belvedere ☎ *72092*
Bridlington Swimming Pool ☎ *78494* – Indoor pool, sauna, solarium
Dukes Park – Bowls, cricket, football, hockey, putting, tennis
Flamborough Head Golf Club ☎ *850333*
New Indoor Sports Hall Gypsey Rd ☎ *78077* – Badminton, golf, squash, table tennis
Northcliffe Pleasure Gardens – Children's amusements, pitch and putt
North Marine Gardens – Putting
Princess Mary Promenade – Model yachting lake
Royal Princes Parade – Children's amusements, crazy-golf
Royal Yorkshire Yacht Club Windsor Ct ☎ *72041*
Sewerby Park – Archery, bowls, children's amusements, pitch and putt, putting
Spa Promenade – Boating lake, children's amusements
South Marine Gardens – Bowls, putting
Yorkshire Yacht Club South Marine Dr ☎ *72016*

Cinema

Winter Gardens Promenade ☎ *73012*

Dancing

Barrons Studio Promenade ☎ *75885*
Central Ballroom Prince St ☎ *73826*
Spa Royal Hall ☎ *75885*

Theatres

Floral Pavilion Royal Princes Pde
3 B's Theatre Bar Promenade ☎ *72634*
Spa Royal Hall ☎ *75885*
Spa Theatre South Marine Drive ☎ *78258*

Places of Interest

Bayle Gate Museum
Sewerby Hall ☎ *73769*

Tourist Information

Tourist Information Centre Garrison St ☎ *73474* (Etr – Sep)
Publicity Department The Spa, South Marine Drive ☎ *78255* (Oct – Etr)

Accommodation

The following establishments are recommended by the AA. Further information may be obtained from the Tourist Information office.

★★★	**Expanse** North Marine Dr ☎ *75347*
★★	**Monarch** South Marine Dr ☎ *74447*
ⓐⓟ	**Ferns Farm** Main St, Carnaby (2m W A166) ☎ *78961*
GH	**Shirley Private Hotel** 47 – 48 South Marine Dr ☎ *72539*
GH	**Southdowne Hotel** South Marine Dr ☎ *73270*
SC	**22 Belgrave Road** For bookings: Mrs D Morgan, 4 Hymers Ave, Hull ☎ *Hull 41380*
SC	**Marsden Holiday Flats** 47 Blackburn Ave, Bridlington
SC	Mrs Ibbotson, **Southleigh** 41 Horsford Ave ☎ *72552*
SC	**7 Swanland Avenue** For bookings: Mrs C Botterill, 36 Tennyson Ave ☎ *72196*

Restaurant

✕ **Ye Olde Star Inn** Westgate ☎ *76039*

Grimsby

The name of Grimsby is synonymous with the fishing industry, and rightly so, for here is the largest fishing port in the world. It is possible to visit the docks with a permit from the Port Authority. With the prosperity of the fishing industry, other allied industries have grown up in the town, such as the manufacture of fish-meal fertilisers and quick-freezing plants. Grimsby is not just fish and factories though. It is an historic town with the oldest Royal Charter in England. Nevertheless, most of its buildings date back no more than a hundred years and a large amount of modern development exists. There are good sports facilities and the Doughty Museum has a collection of 18th- and 19th-century model ships among its exhibits.

Cleethorpes *see page 208*

Humberston Fitties

This modern resort has been developed to cater for the self-catering type of holiday with camping and caravan sites and chalet accommodation. Its vast expanse of sands, with a now obsolete sand fort, look out over the mouth of the Humber to Spurn Head across the estuary. Sailing here is increasing in popularity and there is a yacht club. There are good views of the shipping entering and leaving the Humber.

North Somercotes

The flat farmland around North Somercotes is riddled with dykes and drainage channels. A freshwater lake provides facilities for swimming, water-skiing and sailing, and the coastline here consists of marshes, dunes and extensive sand flats. It is inadvisable to venture too far across the sands because of the angle of the flooding tide. The seclusion and the nature of the coastline make this a haven for wildlife and seals can sometimes be seen on the sand banks offshore.

Mablethorpe *see page 209*

Sutton-on-Sea

This resort on the popular Lincolnshire coast has a level sandy beach, split up by numerous groynes. Swimming is safe and there are donkey rides along the beach. The promenade is backed by the Sutton Pleasure Gardens where there are facilities for putting, tennis and bowls. Launching facilities for small craft are provided both at Sutton and at nearby Sandilands where there is also a golf course.

Chapel St Leonards

The scattered village and holiday camp back a stretch of sandy beach, protected by groynes to the south and stretching northwards to Chapel Point. Bathing is safe and there are pony rides along the beach. An area of marshland has been transformed into a lake for boating and fishing.

Ingoldmells

This resort still manages to retain a little of its old village character although it has developed as a popular holiday resort over the years. One of the first holiday camps to be built was constructed here in 1936 and still offers accommodation and entertainment to visitors. The wide, sandy beaches are safe for bathing, and there are amusements at various points along the shore.

Skegness *see page 210*

CLEETHORPES

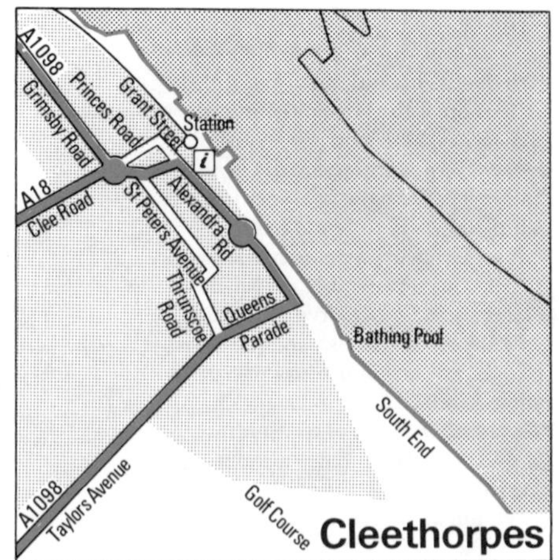

Situated on the South Humberside coast, Cleethorpes lies two miles to the south of Grimsby, although the two are virtually joined together by their respective suburbs. A popular resort, the town has fine views of shipping entering the mouth of the Humber bound for Grimsby, Hull and Immingham. Across the estuary some six miles away, the Yorkshire coast with Spurn Head and its distant lighthouse may be seen. About a hundred years ago Cleethorpes was little more than a fishing village, but today it has a sizeable population. Traditionally it is one of the Lincolnshire coastal resorts popular with the industrial towns of Yorkshire and the East Midlands.

Cleethorpes has three miles of wide, patrolled beach providing safe bathing and the largest open-air bathing pool in the country. The promenades and pier offer the usual entertainments of a seaside resort and the largest covered fairground on the east coast is to be found at North End. Other attractions include a boating lake set in parkland and the Lincolnshire Coast Light Railway, an historic narrow-gauge passenger-carrying railway.

Recreation and Sports

Beach – Children's amusements, donkey rides
Cleethorpes Bathing Pool ☎ *66111*
Cleethorpes Golf Club Humberston ☎ *Grimsby 812059*
Grimsby and Cleethorpes Yacht Club Kingsway ☎ *62951*
Haverstoe Park – Bowls, tennis
North End – Covered fairground
Sidney Park – Bowls, tennis
South End – Boating lake, mini-golf, miniature railway, paddling pools, putting, sand pits
Sussex Recreation Ground – Bowls

Cinema

ABC Grimsby Rd ☎ *61713*

Dancing

Winter Gardens and Memorial Hall

Theatre

Pier Pavilion ☎ *61022*

Place of Interest

Cleethorpes Zoo Kings Rd ☎ *Grimsby 813533*

Tourist Information

Information Centre Alexandra Rd ☎ *67472*

Accommodation

The following establishment is recommended by the AA. Further information may be obtained from the Tourist Information Office.

★★★ **Kingsway** ☎ *62836*

MABLETHORPE

A small holiday resort linked with Sutton-on-Sea, Mablethorpe offers invigorating sea breezes sweeping in from the east plus traditional seaside attractions. Its history is similar to many Lincolnshire townships in that its beginnings go back to medieval and even Roman times. Coastal erosion accounted for the medieval village long ago, but the little church of St Mary with its 13th-century nave, arcades and south doorway has survived the efforts of the encroaching sea. A feature of the church is the 14th-century tomb, above which hangs the broken helmet of a knight said to have been slain in a duel at nearby Earl's Bridge.

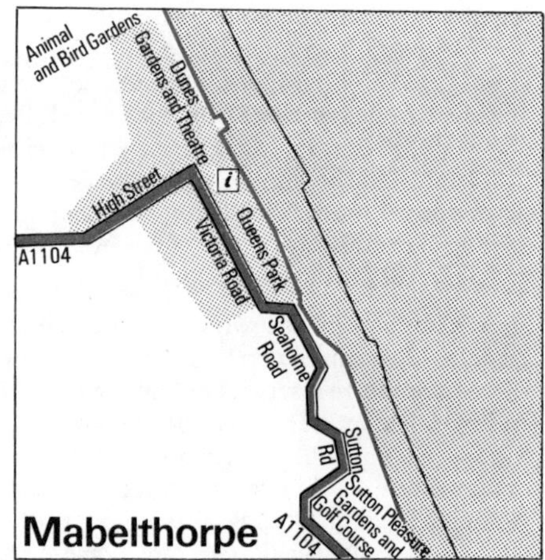

Mablethorpe has sand dunes and six miles of beach, consisting of firm, golden sand. The promenade is extensive, running for some four and a half miles along the front to Sandilands. Sea bathing is permitted but red flags are displayed when the conditions are considered unsafe. The beach is not patrolled but a lifeguard is available in the central area. Mablethorpe provides both sea and river angling and the 11-acre Queens Park behind the sea bank offers a wide range of recreational facilities.

Recreation and Sports

Central Promenade – Amusement park, beach huts for hire
Golden Sands Caravan Site – Swimming pool
Mablethorpe Chalet Park – Swimming pool
North Promenade – Beach huts for hire
Queens Park – Boating lake, bowls, children's paddling pool, crazy-golf, miniature railway, tennis, trampolines
Sandilands Golf Club Sutton-on-Sea ☎ *Sutton-on-Sea 41432*
South Promenade – Beach huts for hire
Sutton Pleasure Gardens – Bowls, children's paddling pool, crazy-golf, putting, tennis

Theatre

The Dunes North Promenade ☎ *2531*

Places of Interest

Animal and Bird Gardens North End Car Park

Tourist Information

Tourist Information Centre
Foreshore Office, Central Promenade
☎ *2496*

SKEGNESS

A popular holiday resort situated on the Lincolnshire coast well-known for its bracing winds. The flat coastal area consisting of buckthorne and sand-dunes, stretches from the mouth of the Humber to Gibraltar Point. Skegness lies in the district of East Lindsey and has traditional links with holidaymakers from the East Midlands. Early history records the Danish invasions of the late 8th century, Skegness having derived its name from 'Skeggi' a chieftain of the invaders. At the beginning of the 19th century Skegness was still very much a fishing village, a place where Alfred, Lord Tennyson spent much of his holiday time. It was only with the coming of the railways in 1875 that development began, following plans drawn up at the instigation of the Earl of Scarborough.

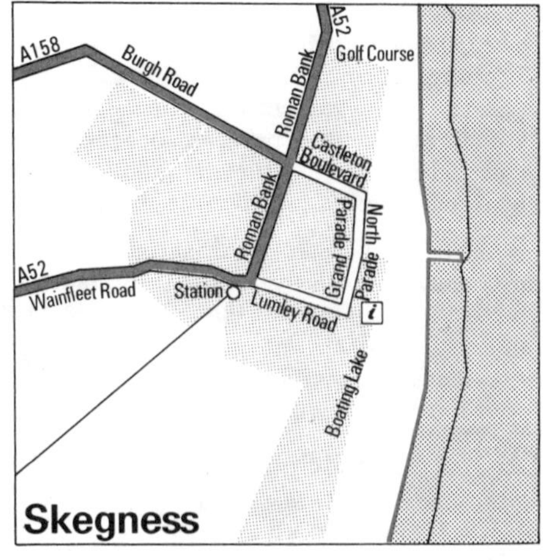

Skegness is a spacious town with wide, tree-lined streets and some 24 acres of seafront gardens. The firm, sandy beach stretches for some three and a half miles to Gibraltar Point, a 1,500-acre nature reserve. Sea bathing is permitted but should be attempted only from the area patrolled by lifeguards when the appropriate flag is flying. The pier was badly damaged in winter gales and, although plans are under consideration to effect repair and development, it is unlikely to be operational for some time. A wide range of recreational facilities are available including angling, boating, bowls, golf, putting and water-skiing. Other amenities and attractions include chalets for hire, horse-drawn landau rides and waterway trips through the foreshore gardens.

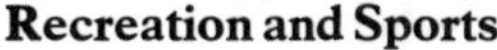

Recreation and Sports

Cricket Ground Richmond Dr – Squash, tennis
Grand Parade – Amusements, ballroom and restaurant, children's playground, mini-marina, yacht pond
North Parade – Amusements, bowls, children's pool, natureland, putting
North Shore Golf Club North Shore Rd ☎ *3298*
Peace Gardens Tower Esp – Sunday afternoon band concerts
Seacroft Golf Club Drummond Rd ☎ *3020*
Skegness Boating Club Club Secretary, 21 Prince Alfred Ave ☎ *4467*
Skegness Outdoor Swimming Pool Grand Pde ☎ *4467*
Skegness Outdoor Swimming Pool Grand Pde ☎ *66157*
Skegness Sailing Club Club Secretary, Club-house, Jackson Corner, Ingoldmells
Skegness Stadium Marsh Ln, Orby – Stock car racing
South Parade – Boating lake, bowls, crazy-golf, dolphinarium, kiddies' corner, model village

Cinemas

Marina Sea Ln, Ingoldmells ☎ *72651*
Tower Lumley Rd ☎ *3938*

Theatres

Arcadia Drummond Rd ☎ *3102*
Embassy Grand Pde ☎ *2263*
Festival Pavilion Tower Esp ☎ *2395*

Places of Interest

Gibraltar Point Nature Reserve ☎ *2677*
Skegness Church Farm Museum Church Rd
Skegness Natureland Marine Zoo North Pde, The Promenade

Tourist Information

Tourist Information Centre Tower Esp ☎ *4821*

Accommodation

The following establishments are recommended by the AA. Further information may be obtained from the Tourist Information Office.

★★ **County** North Pde ☎ *2461*
★★ **Crown** Drummond Rd ☎ *3084*
★★ **Links** Drummond Rd ☎ *3605*
GH **George Hotel** 98 South Pde ☎ *3391*
SC Mr and Mrs Jackson, **Links Cottages** Roman Bank ☎ *66202*
SC Mr and Mrs F Langton, **Merrie Meade Bungalows** Merrie Meade Drive, Drummond Rd ☎ *4368*

Skegness and Mablethorpe.
The seaside in the countryside.

Skegness and Mablethorpe have everything for happy family holidays. Miles of safe sandy beaches on Lincolnshire's golden coast . . . accommodation to suit every taste and purse from caravans and chalets to self-catering apartments, guest houses and hotels . . . entertainments of all kinds for young and old.

And if you want to get away from it all (but not too far away) the peace and quiet of the picturesque Lincolnshire Wolds are only a short drive away.

This year, make it Skegness or Mablethorpe.

For the best of both holiday worlds.

For more details of attractions and forthcoming events in Skegness and Mablethorpe, write to the Publicity Department, enclosing 25p P.O., East Lindsey District Council, Tedder Hall, Manby, Louth, Lincs. LN11 8UP.

**EAST LINDSEY
DISTRICT COUNCIL**

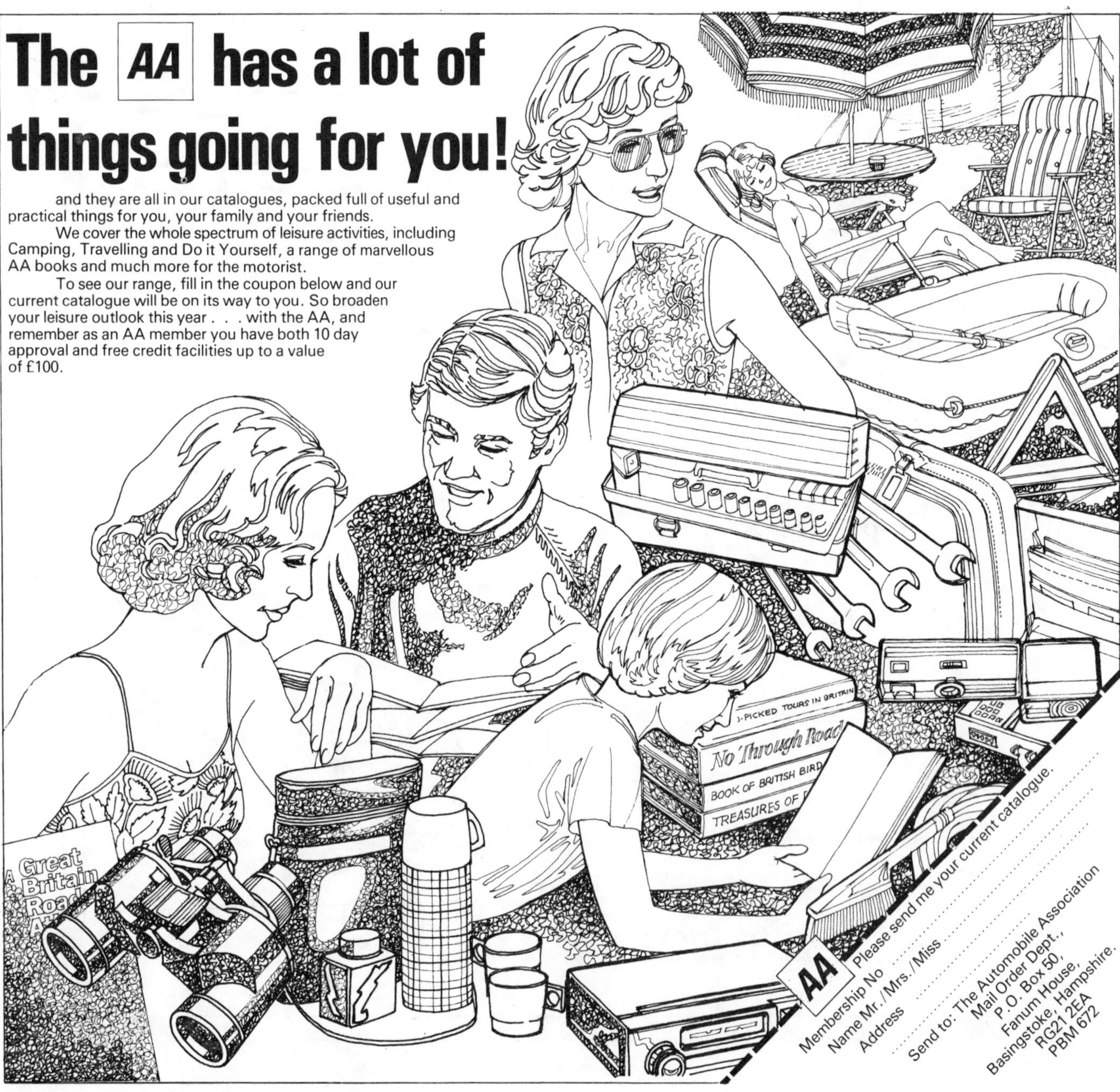
The AA has a lot of things going for you!
and they are all in our catalogues, packed full of useful and practical things for you, your family and your friends.
We cover the whole spectrum of leisure activities, including Camping, Travelling and Do it Yourself, a range of marvellous AA books and much more for the motorist.
To see our range, fill in the coupon below and our current catalogue will be on its way to you. So broaden your leisure outlook this year . . . with the AA, and remember as an AA member you have both 10 day approval and free credit facilities up to a value of £100.
No Through Road
BOOK OF BRITISH BIRD
TREASURES OF
Great Britain Road
AA Please send me your current catalogue.
Membership No
Name Mr./Mrs./Miss
Address
Send to: The Automobile Association
Mail Order Dept.,
P.O. Box 50,
Fanum House,
Basingstoke, Hampshire.
RG21 2EA
PBM 672

Heacham
There is a good stretch of shingle beach here, overlooking The Wash. Heacham is associated with Pocahontas, the Red Indian Princess who married John Rolfe of Heacham Hall in 1614. Nearby Caley Mill is devoted to the growing and distilling of lavender. Tours of the mill may be arranged on application.

Hunstanton *see page 214*

Holkham Gap
Holkham Meals, with sand dunes and pine trees, are a favourite spot for picnics and swimming is generally safe at high-tide. Inland lies Holkham Hall, a Palladian-style building dating from the mid-18th century, set in attractive grounds which also contain Holkham Pottery.

Cley-next-the-Sea
A former port, now almost one mile from the sea. The village has a fine windmill, dating from 1713, which is now a private dwelling. There is a nature reserve on the nearby marshes, owned by the Norfolk Naturalists Trust, devoted to the birds which the area attracts. A public path crosses the reserve leading to Cley Eye where there is a steep shingle beach. Swimming is dangerous due to strong currents.

West Runton
A pleasant village where the Caravan Club established its first site. The sandy beach, dotted with patches of pebbles, is safe for swimming during calm weather. Half a mile inland stands Beacon Hill, rising to over 300ft.

East Runton
There is a safe, sandy beach here, backed by low cliffs. Rocks are uncovered at low-tide on the western extremity.

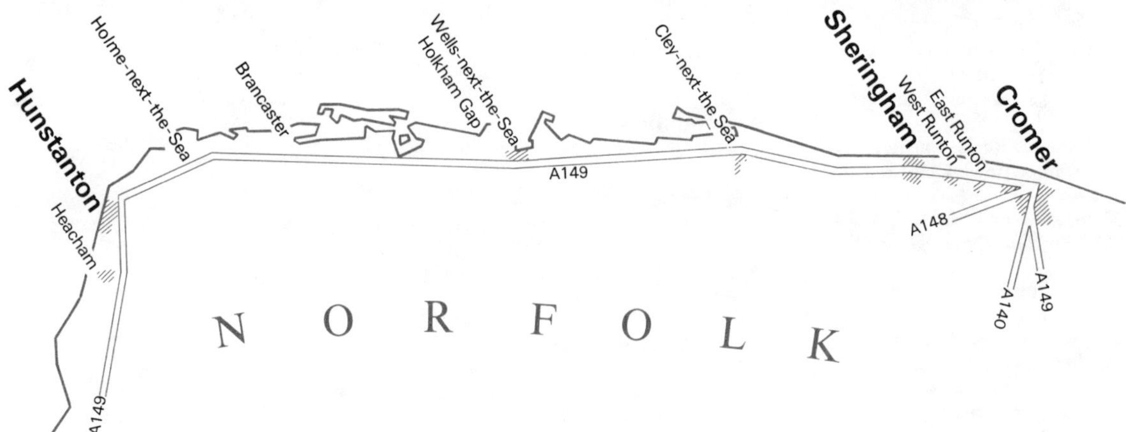

Holme-next-the-Sea
The village lies at the end of two ancient thoroughfares, the Peddars Way and the Icknield Way. North of Holme is Gore Point with a long, desolate, sandy beach and to the east lies a nature reserve, owned by the Norfolk Naturalists Trust, which contains many species of birds.

Brancaster
A former Roman naval base, Brancaster has a broad, sandy beach where swimming is safe close to the shore. There is an old-established golf course and boat trips run from Brancaster Harbour to the nearby nature reserves.

Wells-next-the-Sea
An interesting resort with many flint built houses lining its narrow streets. Wells is renowned for its cockles and whelks and has a pleasant pine-fringed beach. Bathing is safe but the mouth of the harbour should be avoided. Wells has a sailing club and a large boating lake, known as Abraham's Bosom, which was once a harbour. There are good amusement and recreational facilities here and Wells is a popular centre for fishing and water sports.

Sheringham *see page 215*

Cromer *see page 216*

HUNSTANTON

Extremely popular with holidaymakers, Hunstanton is the only east coast resort that faces west. It is on the coastline of the Wash, believed by treasure hunters to conceal the Crown Jewels of King John. In October 1215 he left King's Lynn en route for Newark Castle and sent his baggage train on a short cut. They were overtaken by the tide and everything, including his treasure, was lost. The long beach of Hunstanton is sandy, with occasional patches of shingle, and is backed by an unusual cliff formation of red carrstone topped with a layer of white chalk. The town provides all the usual amenities associated with a lively resort including a funfair and amusement arcades. Although not large, the town was well-planned in 1840 by the then Lord of the Manor whose intention it was to transform a small fishing village into the holiday resort that exists today. A cliff-top walk to the north passes the ruins of a chapel and a disused lighthouse on the point where St Edmund is said to have landed in the 9th century. Further along, the cliffs give way to quieter beaches backed by grassy dunes and a 400-acre nature reserve at Holme-next-the-Sea.

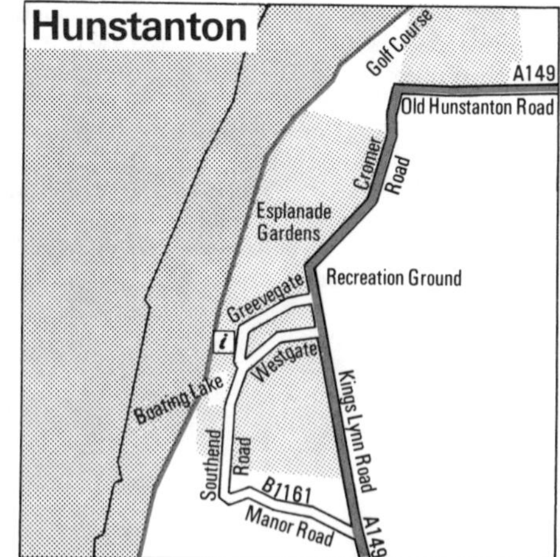

Recreations and Sports

Beach – Donkey and pony rides
Esplanade Gardens – Bowls, childrens playground, crazy-golf, putting
Golf Course Road – Pitch and putt
Hunstanton Bowls Club Cromer Rd ☎2488
Hunstanton and District Power Boat Club Clubhouse, South Beach ☎33464
Hunstanton Golf Club Golf Course Rd ☎2811
Recreation Ground – Bowls, children's playground, cricket, croquet, football, tennis
Southern Promenade – Amusements, boating lake, funfair

Places of Interest

Carmelite Friary Burnham Market ☎*Norwich 611122* ext *5224*
Creake Abbey North Creake
Holkham Hall Holkham ☎*Wells 227*
Norfolk Lavender Caley Mill, Heacham ☎*Heacham 70384*
Sandringham House and Grounds Sandringham ☎*King's Lynn 2675*
Wolferton Station Sandringham ☎*Dersingham 40674*

Tourist Information

Information Centre Le Strange Ter ☎*2610*

Accommodation

The following establishments are recommended by the AA. Further information may be obtained from the Tourist Information Office.

★★	**Le Strange Arms** Sea Front, Old Hunstanton ☎*2810*
★	**Lodge** Cromer Rd ☎*2896*
★	**Wash and Tope** ☎*2250*
GH	**Dolphin Private Hotel** 15 Cliff Terrace ☎*2583*
GH	**Driftwood Hotel** Lynn Rd ☎*2241*
GH	**Hurst** 14 Glebe Av ☎*2724*
GH	**Lincoln Lodge Private Hotel** Cliff Pde ☎*2948*
GH	**Norfolk Private Hotel** 32 Kings Lynn Rd ☎2383
GH	**Sutton House Hotel** 24 Northgate ☎*2552*
GH	**Tolcarne Private Hotel** 3 Boston Sq ☎*2359*
SC	**Grosvenor Bungalows Sandringham Bungalows and Manor Park** For Bookings: Hoseasons Ltd Sunshine Holidays, Sunway House, Lowestoft Suffolk. ☎*Lowestoft 62270*

As with so many coastal towns, fishing has played an essential part in Sheringham's history and economy. Then, with the advent of the railway in 1887, holidaymakers came to sample the bracing air and the town developed as a dignified resort. The fishermen's cottages and some quaint streets are still here, but for the most part the buildings are of the Victorian era. This is a quiet resort with no funfairs or amusement arcades; no loud music or bingo callers echoing along the promenade. There is a carnival though, which lasts for a week and takes place around the end of July and beginning of August, depending on a favourable tide. Sheringham's gently-sloping sands, protected by groynes, retain shallow pools at low-tide and sea bathing is safe.

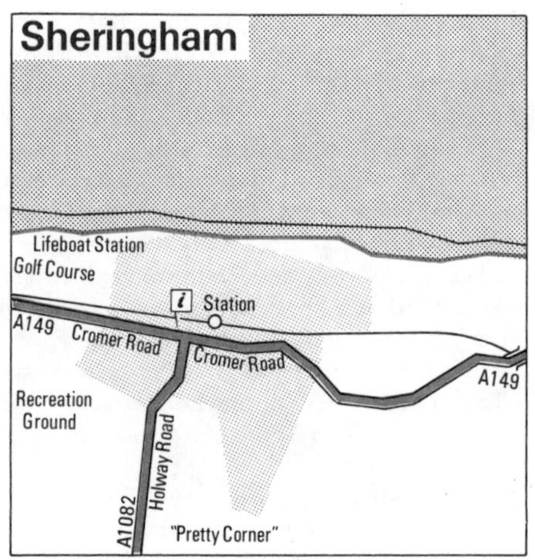

The area around Sheringham is particularly attractive with heaths and woodland and there are fine views from the popular 'Pretty Corner'. There are ancient dwelling sites too, from Roman and Saxon times and at nearby Aylmerton the 'Shrieking Pits' are said to be haunted. Along the coast to the west Weybourne Hope is popular with divers and fishermen, its exceptionally steep beach enabling boats to come close inshore.

Recreation and Sports

Promenade – Crazy-golf, model yacht pond, pony rides, putting
Recreation Ground – Bowls, cricket, football, tennis
Sheringham Golf Club Sweetbriar Ln ☎ *822038*

Theatre

Little Theatre Station Rd ☎ *822347*

Places of Interest

Baconsthorpe Castle
Guildhall Blakeney
Kelling Park Aviaries Weybourne Rd, Kelling ☎ *Holt 2235*
Lifeboat Museum Lifeboat Station
North Norfolk Railway Company Ltd Sheringham Station ☎ *822045*
Sheringham Hall Upper Sheringham ☎ *2074*
Walsingham Abbey Grounds Walsingham ☎ *Walsingham 259*

Tourist Information

Information Centre Station Rd ☎ *3610*

Accommodation

The following establishments are recommended by the AA. Further information may be obtained from the Tourist Information Office

★★ **Beaumaris** South St ☎ *822370*
★★ **Burlington** Esplanade ☎ *822224*
★★ **Southlands** South St ☎ *822679*
★ **Two Lifeboats** Promenade ☎ *822401*
GH **Beacon Hotel** Nelson Rd ☎ *822019*
GH **Beeston Hills Lodge** 64 Cliff Rd ☎ *822615*
GH **Crossways Hotel** 1 The Boulevard ☎ *823164*
GH **Melrose Hotel** 9 Holway Rd ☎ *823299*
SC **Long Plantation** Sheringwood. For bookings Mr J M Sharp, Pinewood, Sheringwood, Sheringham ☎ *823975*

Preparing for a dive

CROMER

A popular holiday resort, Cromer offers the bracing air characteristic of this part of the country and a stretch of sandy beach with safe bathing. The cliffs are a favourite haunt of fossil hunters as well as those who enjoy the magnificent views from the cliff top walks and gardens. The pier has twice been rebuilt, once after bomb damage and again shortly afterwards, following the violent storms of 1953. It is from the end of the pier that the famous Cromer Lifeboat is launched, whose crews have, over the years, earned a reputation for outstanding heroism. The present lifeboat, a modern vessel with all the advantages that technology has to offer, bears the name of Henry Blogg who served from 1909 to 1947 and received many awards for bravery. What was once a thriving fishing industry has now dwindled to around a dozen boats, but the Cromer crab remains a great delicacy and the fishermen's craft is still very much in evidence along the beach. The town, which clings to the hillside above the beach, embraces many architectural styles. Fishermen's cottages cluster together as a reminder of the old village and ornate Victorian hotels trace a later stage in the history of the town. The whole scene is dominated by the 160-ft tower of the 15th-century church.

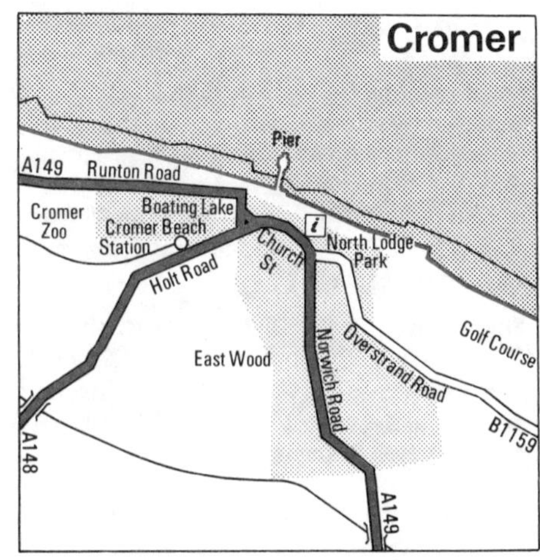

Recreation and Sports

Cromer Lawn Tennis Courts Association Norwich Rd ☎*3741*
Cromer and District Bowls Club Runton Rd ☎*2213*
Evington Lawns – Boating lake, crazy-golf
Fearn's Park – Bowls, childrens playground
The Marrams – Bowls, putting
The Meadow – Playground, pitch and putt
Mill Road – Football
North Lodge Park – Bowls, childrens corner, model village, model yachting, putting
Norwich Road – Tennis
Pier – Amusements, fishing
Royal Cromer Golf Club Overstrand Rd ☎*2219*
Suffield Park – Bowls, childrens playground

Cinema

Regal Hans Place ☎*2457*

Theatre

Pavilion Theatre Cromer Pier ☎*2495*

Dancing

Hotel de Paris ☎*3141*

Places of Interest

Blickling Hall Blickling
Cromer Museum
Cromer Zoo ☎*2947*
Felbrigg Hall Felbrigg
Stow Mill Mudesley ☎*Mudesley720298*
Wolterton Hall Wolterton ☎*Matlaske274*

Tourist Information

Information Centre North Lodge Park ☎*2479*

Accommodation

The following establishments are recommended by the AA. Further information may be obtained from the Tourist Information Office.

★★ **Colne House** ☎*2013*
★★ **Cliff House** Overstrand Rd ☎*2445*
★★ **Cliftonville** Runton Rd ☎*512543*
★ **West Parade** Sea Front ☎*2443*
GH **Chellow Dene** 23 Macdonald Rd ☎*3251*
GH **Grange Court** Cliff Av ☎*2419*
GH **Home Farm** ☎*2751*
GH **Westgate Lodge** 10 Macdonald Rd ☎*2840*
SC **41 and 110 King's Chalet Park** Overstrand Road For bookings: Mr J M Sharp, Pinewood, Sheringwood, Sheringham ☎*Sheringham 823975*

Mundesley
Although the largest of North Norfolk's coastal resorts, Mundesley is comparatively quiet and undeveloped. The safe, sandy beach is lined with beach huts and a sea wall, built to prevent the sea from further eroding this vulnerable stretch of coastline. The village itself is hidden from view behind the grassy slope of the cliffs. The poet, William Cowper, lived in Mundesley for five years in a fine Georgian house which now bears his name. There is a golf course and a bowling green in the town. To the south, near Bacton, is a North Sea gas terminus.

Happisburgh
The long stretch of sandy beach retains some deep pools at low-tide and care should be taken not to get cut off by the incoming tide. The village of Happisburgh, pronounced 'Hazeboro', is set back from the beach and is dominated by the 110-ft tower of its parish church. It is thought that the tower was built to serve as a beacon before the lighthouse was erected, to warn shipping of the treacherous Happisburgh Sands seven miles off shore. The sea bed is littered with the wrecks of vessels that have foundered on the sands and during stormy weather wreckage is still washed up on the beach.

Hemsby
The sandy beach, scattered with stones, is backed by grassy dunes beyond which lie the caravan parks and holiday camps which cater for the many visitors to this stretch of coastline. Swimming here is safe and there is also an open-air swimming pool, crazy-golf and amusements.

Caister-on-Sea
A quieter resort than neighbouring Great Yarmouth, Caister-on-Sea has a sandy beach which is generally safe for bathing. However, the sea bed does shelve steeply in places so care should be taken. At the time of its Roman origins Caister was at the mouth of an estuary which has since silted up completely. There are Roman remains which can be seen on the A1064. To the west of the town a major attraction to visitors are the ruins of Caister Castle, once the home of Shakespeare's Sir John Falstaff and the place where many of the *Paston Letters* were written. Additional attractions here are a 98-ft tower and a large collection of vintage motor vehicles in the motor museum.

WEATHER CHART	Av hours of Sunshine in month	Hottest Av daily Temp °C
April	170	8
May	211	11
June	211	14
July	202	16
August	186	16
September	150	15

GREAT YARMOUTH *see page 218*

Gorleston-on-Sea
Although officially a part of Great Yarmouth, Gorleston has an entirely different character and is quieter than its brash neighbour. Swimming from the sandy beach is generally safe, except for a section between the model yacht pond and the breakwater where warning notices are displayed. There is a regatta in August and facilities for many sports and entertainments.

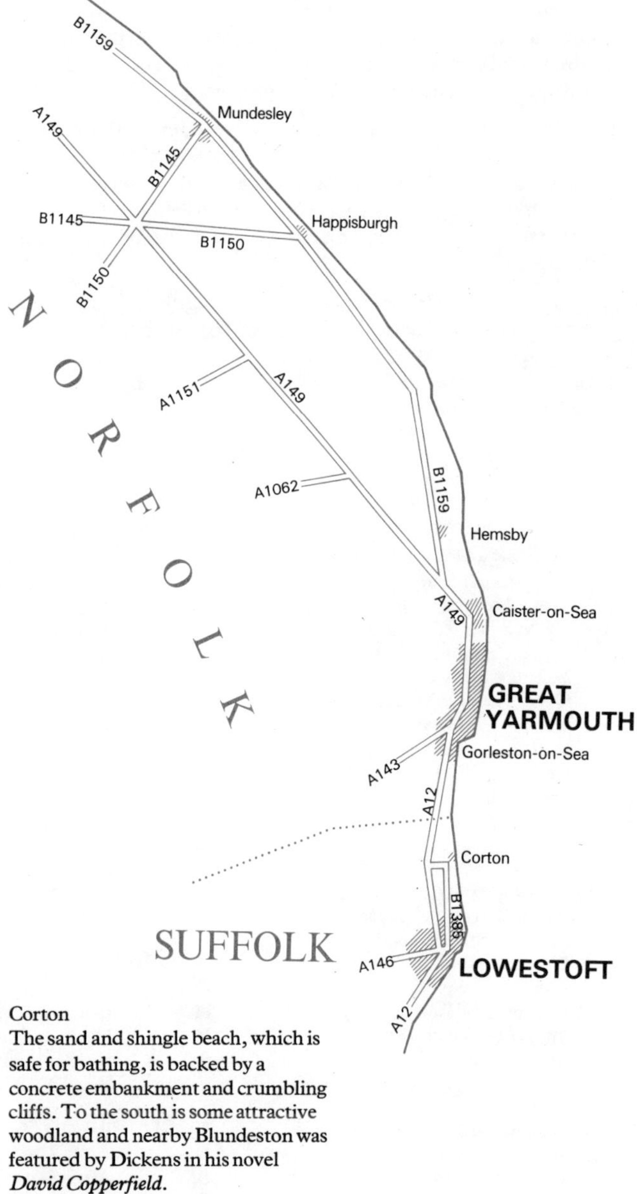

Corton
The sand and shingle beach, which is safe for bathing, is backed by a concrete embankment and crumbling cliffs. To the south is some attractive woodland and nearby Blundeston was featured by Dickens in his novel *David Copperfield.*

LOWESTOFT *see page 220*

GREAT YARMOUTH

This town was established on a sandbank in the River Yare estuary during the Saxon era and flourished as an important herring fishing centre between the 15th and 16th centuries. Today the harbour is used mainly by cargo ships and vessels servicing the North Sea gas and oil rigs and the town has become a thriving holiday resort.

The long, sandy beach, much of it untouched by the exceptionally gentle tide, provides safe bathing and beach huts and tents are available for hire. A Punch and Judy show gives regular performances on the sands and Marine Parade contains a wealth of attractions including the Pleasure Beach Amusement Park with one of the world's largest roller coasters. Regular race meetings are held at Great Yarmouth Racecourse and greyhound and stock car racing at Yarmouth Stadium.

Great Yarmouth has good shopping facilities – a number of large modern stores and a shopping precinct supplemented by one of the largest open-air market places in England, a scene of great activity on Wednesdays and Saturdays. There are many places of interest, notably the remains of the 14th-century town walls which originally had sixteen towers and ten gates. Conducted tours of these impressive fortifications take place weekly during the season.

Recreation and Sports

	Gorleston Golf Club Warren Rd, Gorleston ☎*61911*
	Great Yarmouth and Caister Golf Club Caister Rd ☎*720214*
	Great Yarmouth and Gorleston Sailing Club South Pier, Gorleston
	Great Yarmouth Racecourse North Denes – Horse racing N off Marine Pde
F	**Hall Quay** – Boat hire, pleasure cruises
H	**Joyland** Marine Pde – Children's amusement park
HLP	**Marine Parade** – Bowls, crazy-golf, donkey rides, putting
	North Dene Aerodrome North Dene Airfield ☎*56410* – Pleasure flights
D	**North Drive** – Boating lake, bowls, putting, tennis, Venetian Waterways
	Phoenix Indoor Swimming Pool Bradwell ☎64575
G	**Regent Bowl** Regent Rd ☎56830 – Ten pin bowling
P	**South Beach** – Bowls, boating lake, Pleasure Beach Amusement Park, putting
P	**Wellington Pier Gardens** – Roller skating
	Yarmouth Stadium Caister Rd ☎720343 – Greyhound racing, stock car racing

Cabaret/Dancing

G	**Chicago Club** Regent Rd
G	**Cleopatras Disco** Tower Building, Marine Pde
C	**The Garibaldi** St Nicholas Rd ☎*2662*
G	**Senator Disco** Marine Pde
G	**Tiffanys** Tower Centre, Marine Pde ☎*57018*
G	**Wheels** Apsley Rd ☎*58600*

Cinemas

F	**ABC** Regent Rd ☎*3191* (Except during summer season)
G	**Cinema 1 and 2** Marine Pde ☎*2043*
G	**Empire** Marine Pde (late night shows only) ☎*3147*
G	**Regent** Regent Rd ☎*2354*

Theatres

F	**ABC** Regent Rd ☎*3191* (Summer)
H	**Britannia Pier Theatre** ☎*2209*
K	**Hippodrome Circus** ☎*4172*
P	**Wellington Pier Theatre** ☎*2244*
K	**Windmill Theatre** ☎*3504*

Places of Interest

H	**Aqua Zoo** Grotto Castle, Marine Pde
B	**Anna Sewell's House**
F	**Elizabethan House Museum** South Quay ☎*55746*
B(1)	**Fishermen's Hospital**
F(2)	**Greyfriars Cloister**
K(4)	**Maritime Museum**
J(5)	**Merchant's House**
P	**Merivale Model Village**
B(7)	**North-West Tower**
J(8)	**Old Tolhouse Museum**
B(9)	**Priory Hall Refectory**
F(10)	**Town Hall**
J(11)	**Town Wall** remains and South-East Tower
G	**Wax Works Museum** Regent Rd ☎*4851*

Tourist Information

G [i]	**Tourist Information Centre** Marine Pde ☎*2195* (May – Sep)
F [i]	**Tourist Information Centre** Regent St ☎*4313*

Accommodation

The establishments listed below are a selection of AA-recommended accommodation and restaurants located in the area covered by the Town Plan. Further information may be found in AA publications or obtained from the Tourist Information Centre.

1SC	**94 Albion Road** For bookings: Mrs J Goodwin, 9 Beatty Rd, Great Yarmouth, Norfolk NR30 4BT ☎*55218*
2★	**Burlington** North Dr ☎*4568*
3★★★	**Carlton** Marine Pde South ☎*55234*
4GH	**Georgian House Private Hotel** 16 North Dr ☎*2623*
5✕✕	**Il Valentino** 85 North Quay ☎*4299*
6★★	**Imperial** North Dr ☎*2000*
7★	**Marine View** North Dr ☎*2879*
8GH	**Palm Court Hotel** ☎*4568*
9★★★	**Star** Hall Quay ☎*2294*

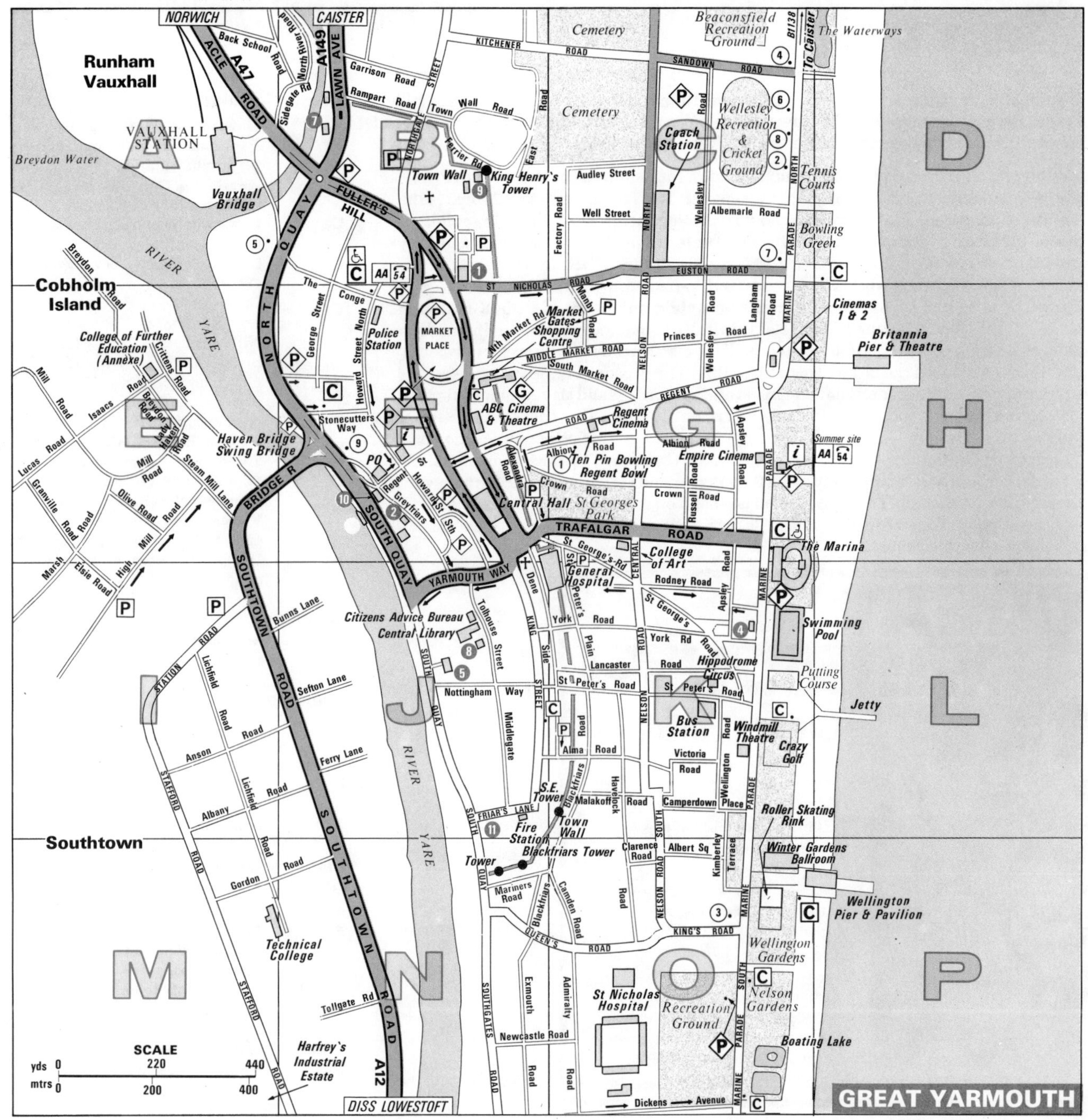
GREAT YARMOUTH
NORWICH
CAISTER
DISS LOWESTOFT
Runham Vauxhall
Cobholm Island
Southtown
VAUXHALL STATION
Breydon Water
Vauxhall Bridge
RIVER YARE
Haven Bridge Swing Bridge
College of Further Education (Annexe)
Town Wall
King Henry's Tower
Police Station
MARKET PLACE
Market Gates Shopping Centre
ABC Cinema & Theatre
Regent Cinema
Ten Pin Bowling Regent Bowl
Empire Cinema
Central Hall
St Georges Park
College of Art
General Hospital
Citizens Advice Bureau
Central Library
Hippodrome Circus
Bus Station
Windmill Theatre
Crazy Golf
Jetty
Putting Course
Swimming Pool
The Marina
Britannia Pier & Theatre
Cinemas 1 & 2
Coach Station
Wellesley Recreation & Cricket Ground
Beaconsfield Recreation Ground
Tennis Courts
Bowling Green
The Waterways
Cemetery
S.E. Tower
Fire Station
Blackfriars Tower
Roller Skating Rink
Winter Gardens Ballroom
Wellington Pier & Pavilion
Wellington Gardens
Nelson Gardens
Recreation Ground
Boating Lake
St Nicholas Hospital
Technical College
Harfrey's Industrial Estate
SCALE
yds 0 220 440
mtrs 0 200 400

LOWESTOFT

Lowestoft became an important fishing port around the middle of the 19th century and still possesses a large fleet of trawlers. The town's position on the coast at the head of Oulton Broad makes it an ideal holiday centre and it has gradually grown into a popular resort.

Lowestoft offers the visitor fine sands which are safest for swimming near the South Pier, where lifeguards are on patrol throughout the summer. Red flags are displayed when bathing is considered dangerous and the groynes should be avoided at all times. There is a children's corner on the beach by the South Pier with swing-boats, trampolines and a Punch and Judy Show and beach huts are available for hire. Quieter beaches are to be found to the south at Pakefield. The main beach is backed by a wide, traffic-free promenade. There are amusements on South Pier and Claremont Pier and a children's boating lake in Kensington Gardens, off the Upper Esplanade. Nicholas Everitt Park, overlooking Oulton Broad, has an outdoor swimming pool, a children's playground, a pets corner and facilities for bowls and tennis. Boats of all kinds can be hired here for touring The Broads. The Sparrows' Nest complex provides outdoor entertainment in its pleasant gardens and also contains a theatre which stages a Summer Show and the town's Maritime Museum. The Talk of the East on the South Pier provides shows, cabaret and dancing. Annual events include power-boat racing and a regatta on Oulton Broad and Lowestoft Hospital Carnival. There are regular guided tours of the harbour and fish market during the summer and at frequent intervals a trawler is open for public inspection. The Ness, a small headland on the northern shore, is England's most easterly point. A short distance inland lie the Scores, steep cobbled lanes which have survived from the 19th century.

Recreation and Sports

A **Denes Oval** – Putting, tennis
D(1) **Esplanade** – Boating lake, children's playground, putting
F **Kensington Gardens** – Boating lake, bowls, tennis, S on Kirkley Cliff
C **Lowestoft Swimming Pool** Water Ln – Indoor heated pool
C **Lowestoft Sports Centre** Water Ln ☎*69116*
Lowestoft Town FC Crown Meadow, Love Rd ☎*3818*
Nicholas Everitt Park Oulton Broad – Boating, bowls, children's playground, open-air swimming pool, pets corner, putting, tennis
E **Normanston Park** – Cricket, tennis
Rookery Park Golf Course ☎*4009*
F **South Cliff** – Putting, tennis
D **South Pier** – Amusements
B **Sparrows Nest Park** – Bowls
Waveney and Oulton Broad Yacht Club Nicholas Everitt Park ☎*65619*
F **Wellington Gardens** – Model yacht pond

Cinemas

D **Marina** ☎*4186*
D **Odeon** ☎*3946*

Dancing

D **South Pier** ☎*4793*

Theatres

D **The Talk of the East** (formerly South Pier Pavilion) ☎*4793*
A **Sparrows Nest Theatre** ☎*3318*

Places of Interest

D(2) **Archaeological Museum** The Prairie
A(3) **High Lighthouse**
B(4) **Lowestoft Ness**
A(5) **Maritime Museum** Bowling Green Cottage, Sparrows Nest Park
A(6) **Royal Naval Memorial**
B/D **The Scores**

Tourist Information

F [i] **Tourist Information Centre** Esplanade ☎*65989*

Accommodation

The establishments listed below are a selection of AA-recommended accommodation and restaurants located in the area covered by the Town Plan. Further information may be found in AA publications or obtained from the Tourist Information Centre .

1GH	**Cleveland House** 9 Cleveland Rd ☎*62827*
2✕	**Ffrench's** High St ☎*62403*
3GH	**Kingsleigh** 44 Marine Pde ☎*2513*
4GH	**Royal Crescent** 19A The Esplanade ☎*3952*
5★★★	**Victoria** Kirkley Cliff ☎*4433*
6GH	**Westview House Hotel** Lyndhurst Rd ☎*65774*

WEATHER CHART	Av hours of Sunshine in month	Hottest Av daily Temp °C
April	171	8
May	211	11
June	217	14
July	202	16
August	183	16
September	150	15

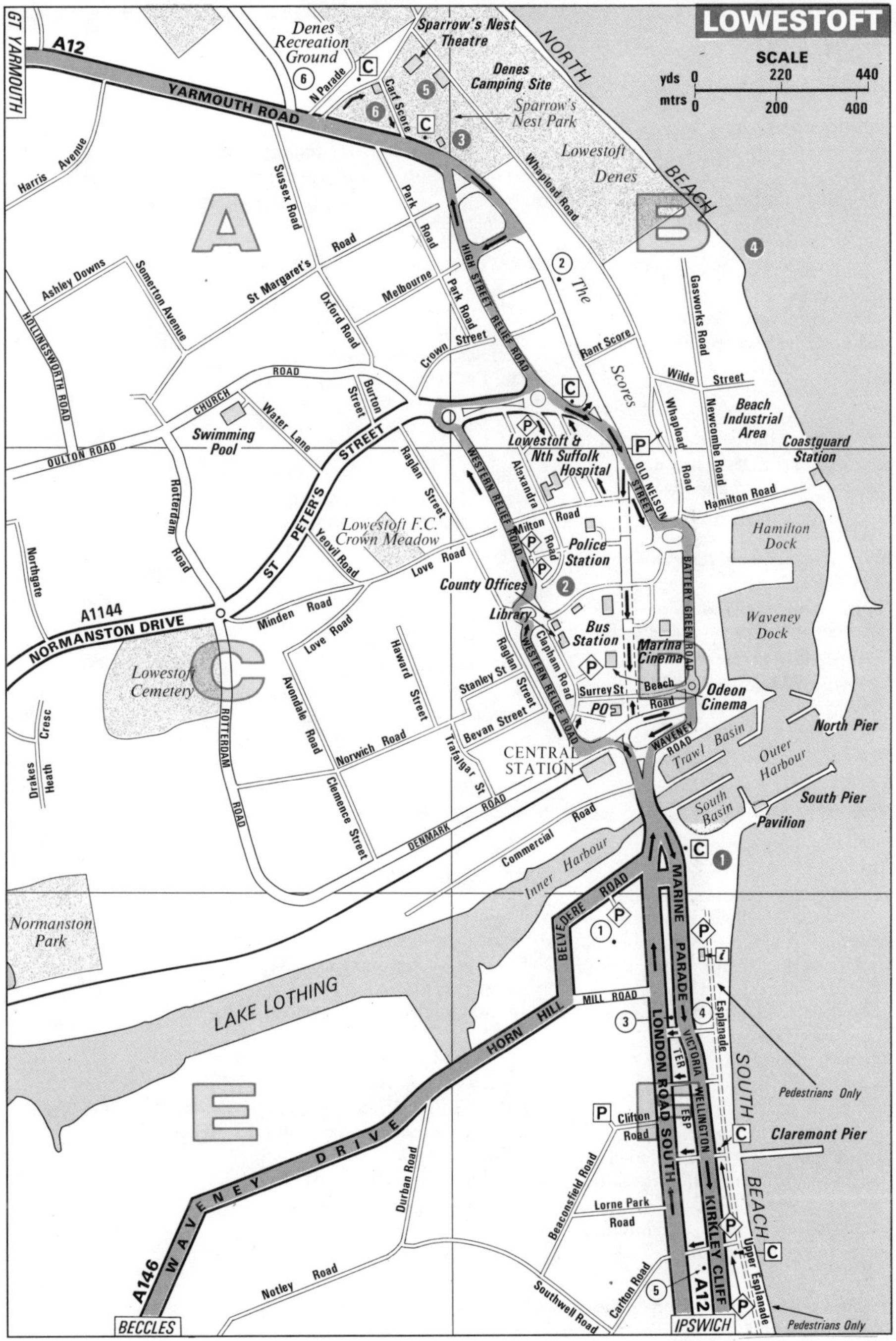

LOWESTOFT

SCALE

yds 0 220 440

mtrs 0 200 400

Southwold *see page 223*

Walberswick
Once an important fishing, trading and shipbuilding centre, Walberswick is now best known as a popular centre for artists and birdwatchers. There is a sandy beach and swimming is safe provided the mouth of the River Blyth is avoided.

Thorpeness
A resort developed around the beginning of this century in varied architectural styles. The shingle beach is safe for swimming.

Aldeburgh
This quiet, unspoilt resort is a popular yachting centre with a long shingle beach. Aldeburgh has several interesting buildings including the 16th-century Moot Hall. The Aldeburgh Festival, the largest music festival in Britain, now held at the new concert hall in nearby Snape, takes place each year.

Felixstowe *see page 224*

Harwich
An ancient port handling trading vessels from Northern Europe and Scandinavia in addition to passenger and car ferries. The town has much of historical interest, and a well-preserved treadmill is displayed on The Green. There are good recreational and entertainment facilities.

Dovercourt
This seaside resort was developed in the mid-18th century. It has a sandy beach, backed by lawns and gardens, an outdoor swimming pool and ample amusement and sporting facilities.

Frinton-on-Sea and **Walton on the Naze** *see page 225*

Holland-on-Sea
The residential area of Clacton with good sandy beaches which are usually quieter and less crowded than those of the resort proper.

CLACTON-ON-SEA *see page 226*

Jaywick Sands and Seawick Sands
This area abounds in holiday bungalows, chalets and caravan parks. The beaches are safe and sandy and there are good amusement and entertainment facilities.

Brightlingsea
A pleasant yachting centre with a sand and shingle beach. Swimming is dangerous due to strong currents.

West Mersea
This small island is connected to the mainland by a road bridge and is a popular residential and holiday centre. There is a shingle beach and the area is popular with boating enthusiasts.

Burnham-on-Crouch
A sailing centre which has been called the 'Cowes of the East Coast'.

SOUTHEND-ON-SEA *see page 228*

Leigh-on-Sea
Although now more or less engulfed by Southend, Leigh has retained the atmosphere of a quiet fishing village and cockle boats still operate there.

Canvey Island
Linked to the mainland by a bridge over Benfleet Creek, Canvey Island has been quite heavily industrialised over the last 50 years. Bathing is safe around high-tide on the sandy beaches and there are amusement facilities.

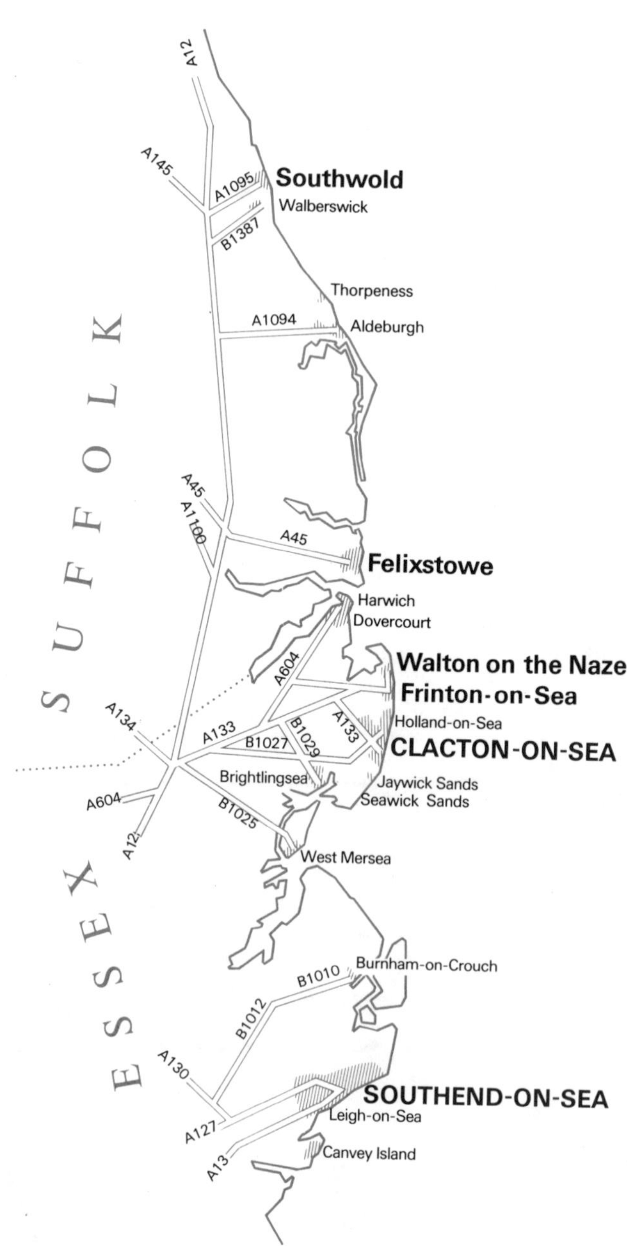

SOUTHWOLD

Surrounded by water and yet not an island, Southwold is bordered on the east by the sea and enclosed on the other sides by the River Blyth and Buss Creek. These in turn are surrounded by marshlands, the whole area within the 'Suffolk Coast and Heaths Area of Outstanding Natural Beauty'. The sand and shingle beach, where bathing is good, is backed by grassy slopes where patches of gorse add splashes of colour during the spring. There is a short pier towards the north end of the beach which is popular with anglers and the pier pavilion provides amusements, Southwold's one small concession to commercialism. At the southern end of the beach Gun Hill is named after the six ancient cannons which have defended the town since 1745. The beach at Southwold is by no means the only attraction to holidaymakers, who come also to enjoy the historic charm of the small town. Its quaint streets lined with historic houses remain largely unaltered and dotted among them are several greens where buildings were destroyed during the Great Fire of 1659 and never replaced. The whole scene is dominated by the great white tower of the lighthouse. The harbour, on the River Blyth estuary, is a yachting centre. A harbourside inn bears a record of the flood level in 1953 when the waters almost reached first-floor windows.

A1095
Boating Lakes
Station Road
Pier
Southwold Golf Course
Museum
High St
Town Hall
Common
Gun Hill
River Blyth
Southwold

Recreation and Sports

Common – Playing fields, tennis
Ferry Road – Model yacht pond
Hotson Road – Tennis
North Road – Boating lakes, model yacht pond, paddling pool, putting
Southwold Golf Club Club House, The Common ☎ *723234*
Southwold Sailing Centre ☎ *723683*

Theatre

Southwold Repertory Company St Edmunds Hall – end Jul to beginning Sep only

Places of Interest

Dunwich Museum St James St, Dunwich ☎ *Westleton218 or 276*
Heveningham Hall Heveningham ☎ *Ubbeston355*
Laxfield and District Museum The Guildhall, Laxfield ☎ *Ubbeston369 and 393*
Sailors' Reading Room East St
Southwold Museum St Bartholomew's Green
Suffolk Wildlife Park ☎ *Lowestoft740291*
Sutherland House High St

Tourist Information

Tourist Information Centre Town Hall ☎ *722366*

Accommodation

The following establishments are recommended by the AA. Further information may be obtained from the Tourist Information Office.

★★★	**Swan** ☎ *2186*
★★	**Crown** High St ☎ *2275*
★★	**Randolph** Wangford Rd, Reydon ☎ *723603*
★	**Pier Avenue** Pier Av ☎ *2632*
GH	**Craighurst Hotel** ☎ *3115*
GH	**Mount** North Pde ☎ *2292*

FELIXSTOWE

Developed as a seaside resort towards the end of the last century, Felixstowe became fashionable following a visit by the German Empress Augusta in 1891. Today it is a popular resort, predominantly modern with some examples of Edwardian architecture, having all the facilities associated with the great British seaside holiday. Its sand and shingle beach has very little tidal movement, ensuring safe swimming at all times, and overlooks the busy shipping lanes from Harwich. Behind the beach a traffic-free promenade and extensive gardens provide a pleasant backdrop, the colourful Spa Gardens being particularly attractive.

Although the town's history as a resort is comparatively short, there is much evidence of earlier activity. The site of a Roman settlement now lies buried beneath the waves and the 11th-century Priory of St Felix is thought to have stood on the site now occupied by the Church of Sts Peter and Paul. The 16th-century Landguard Fort was featured in one of Gainsborough's paintings before he gained universal recognition as an artist and the nearby Martello tower is a relic of the days when Napoleon was expected to attempt an invasion. Felixstowe has an annual carnival, festivals of folklore, drama, art and fishing and various major sporting events.

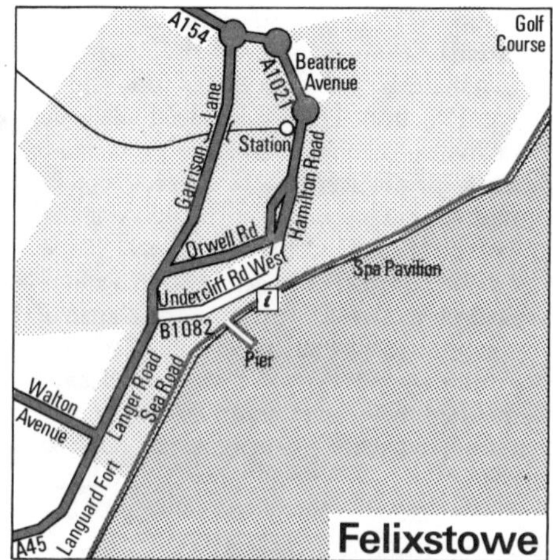

Recreation and Sports

Bath Road – Croquet, putting, tennis
Crescent Road – Bowls
Dellwood Avenue – Cricket
Felixstowe Bowls Club Crescent Rd ☎*3961*
Felixstowe Corinthians Cricket Club Coronation Ground, Mill Ln ☎*5284*
Felixstoweferry Sailing Club Club House, Felixstoweferry ☎*3785*
Felixstowe Golf Club Felixstoweferry ☎*3060, 6834 or 3975*
Felixstowe Lawn Tennis Club Bath Rd ☎*2940*
Felixstowe and Suffolk Bowling Club St Edmunds Rd ☎*2298*
Lancer Rd – Roller skating rink, skateboard bowl
Manor Road – Putting
Pier – Amusements, angling, bingo
St Edmunds Road – Bowls
Sea Road – Amusements, crazy-golf, mini-golf, miniature railway, model yacht pond, playground, putting

Cinema

Ladbrokes Lucky Seven Twin Cinema Crescent Rd ☎*2787*

Theatre

Pier Pavilion ☎*4680*
Spa Pavilion Promenade ☎*3303*

Tourist Information

Tourist Information Centre 91 Undercliff Rd West ☎*2126/2122*

Accommodation

The following establishments are recommended by the AA. Further information may be obtained from the Tourist Information Office.

★★★★	**Orwell Moat House** Hamilton Rd ☎*5511*
★★	**Cavendish** Sea Front ☎*2696*
★★	**North Sea** Sea Front ☎*2103*

WALTON ON THE NAZE & FRINTON-ON-SEA

These two towns, which stand side by side on the East Coast, were both developed into seaside resorts around the end of the 19th century. Both offer the visitor fine sandy beaches from which bathing is safe but Frinton-on-Sea is by far the more sedate of the two, having the distinction of being the only resort in the country which has no pubs. It is a town of broad, tree-lined avenues and sea-front gardens and lawns, particularly popular with anglers and golfers. Walton on the Naze, whilst retaining much of its neighbour's peaceful atmosphere, contrives to offer the visitor a selection of amusement and recreational facilities. There is a pleasure pier and ten-pin bowling and dancing are available. The Naze, a grassy area set upon low cliffs and crowned by an 18th–century tower, which was once a navigational aid, provides fine views of the busy shipping lanes around Felixstowe and Harwich. To the north-west lie Walton Backwaters, a wilderness of creeks and tidal saltings, a favourite habitat for many species of birds which provided the setting for Arthur Ransome's children's adventure story *Secret Water*.

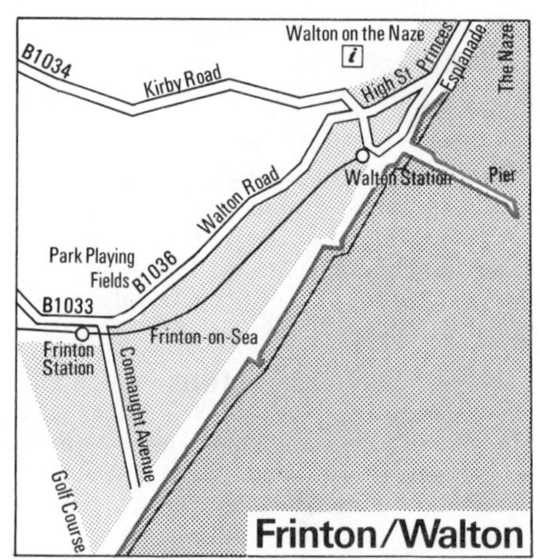

Recreation and Sports

Frinton-on-Sea Bowling Club Park Playing Fields

Frinton-on-Sea Golf Club ☎ *Frinton 4618*

Frinton Tennis Club Holland Rd ☎ *Frinton 4055* – Croquet, tennis

Kirby-le-Soken Bowling Club Halstead Rd, Kirby Cross, Frinton

Park Playing Fields Frinton – Cricket, football, putting, tennis

Parade Walton on the Naze – Boating lake, crazy-golf

Princes Esplanade Walton on the Naze – Putting

Walton and Frinton Yacht Club Mill Ln ☎ *Frinton 5526*

Walton Pier – Angling, funfair, miniature railway, ten-pin bowling

Dancing

The Blue Room Disco Albion Hotel, Walton on the Naze

Tourist Information

Information Bureau Mill Ln, Walton on the Naze ☎ *Frinton 5542*

Accommodation

The following establishments are recommended by the AA. Further information may be obtained from the Tourist Information Office.

★★★	**Frinton Lodge** The Esplanade ☎ *Frinton 4391*
★★★	**Grand** Esplanade ☎ *Frinton 4321*
★★	**Maplin** Esplanade ☎ *Frinton 3832*
★	**Linnets** Kirby Cross ☎ *Frinton 4910*
GH	**Forde** Queens Rd ☎ *Frinton 4758*
GH	**Uplands** 41 Hadleigh Rd ☎ *Frinton 4889*
GH	**Blenheim House Hotel** 39 Kirby Rd, Walton on the Naze ☎ *Frinton 5548*

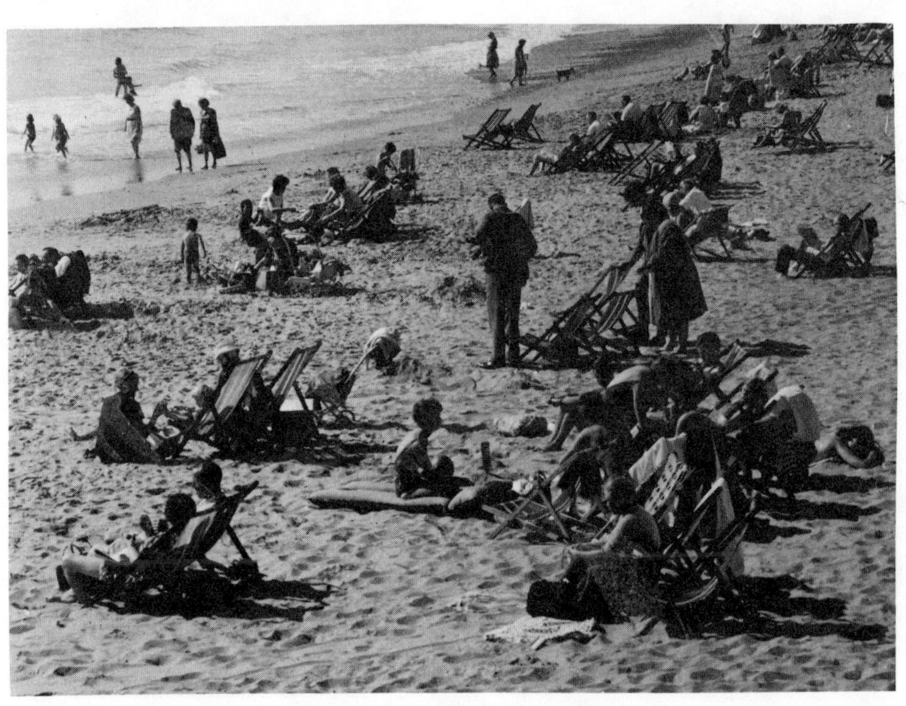

CLACTON-ON-SEA

Clacton has developed, over the last century, from a coastal agricultural village into a pleasant, well-planned holiday resort assisted by the natural assets of extensive sands and a mild, dry, healthy climate.

The gently-sloping sandy beach offers the visitor safe bathing although the groynes should be avoided as the depth of the water can vary considerably on either side. Lifeguards patrol the sands during the summer season. The pier contains a Dolphinarium and plentiful amusements, including some unusual fairground rides; it is also a favourite spot for anglers. There is a children's zoo on the seafront, situated in the grounds of a Martello tower. Facilities for archery, bowls, putting and tennis, together with a large indoor swimming pool are to be found in Vista Road Recreation Ground.

Despite the quiet, peaceful appearance which Clacton presents to the visitor, those requiring entertainment are well catered for. Shows, concerts, wrestling, children's entertainment and pre-general release films are all available in addition to facilities for bingo and dancing. Pleasure flights run from an airstrip near the large Butlin's Holiday Camp and boat trips are available from the beach. The outstanding feature of Clacton's summer is the Carnival, usually held in August, with processions, fireworks and competitions.

Clacton is a town of wide, tree-lined streets, well-kept lawns and attractive gardens. Its recent emergence has left it with virtually no areas of historical interest, although the church of St John the Baptist, in Great Clacton, is of Norman origin and still retains some of its 12th-century features.

Clacton is an ideal touring centre. St Osyth, a few miles to the north, has a fine 12th-century priory set amid lovely gardens, which is open to the public. Colchester, one of the oldest towns in England, with its Roman wall, huge Norman castle and nearby zoo is a bare sixteen miles away. The Constable Country villages of Dedham and Flatford, with its famous mill, are also within easy reach as are the attractive villages of Layer Breton and Layer Marney.

Recreation and Sports

E **Clacton Airfield** West Rd ☎*24671* – Pleasure flights NW off Marine Parade West

E **Clacton Bowling Club** Marine Pde West ☎*21482*

D **Clacton and District Indoor Bowls Club** Recreation Ground, Valley Rd ☎*22186* – Off B1027

A **Clacton Greyhound Stadium** Old Rd ☎*25323*

C **Clacton Indoor Swimming Pool** Vista Rd ☎*29647*

E **Clacton-on-Sea Golf Club** West Rd ☎*21919* – NW off Marine Pde West

F **Clacton Pier** – Angling, funfair

D **Clacton RUFC** Clubhouse, Valley Rd ☎*21602* – Off B1027

Clacton Sailing Club Holland Haven ☎*813027*

A **Clacton Town FC** Old Rd ☎*24415*

D **Happy Valley Bowling Club** Sladburys Ln – Off B1027

D **Happy Valley Sports Ground** – Pitch and putt, tennis – Off B1027

F **Pavilion Sundeck** – Amusements, crazy-golf

C **Vista Road Sports Ground** – Cricket, football, hockey, putting, tennis

Cinemas

B **Mecca Entertainments Centre** 129 Pier Av ☎*21188*

F **The Salon** (Formerly the **Odeon**) West Av ☎*21103*

Dancing

B(2) **Town Hall**

F **Westcliff Apartotel** Marine Pde West

Theatres

B(2) **Princes Theatre** Town Hall ☎*22958*

E **Westcliff Theatre** ☎*21479*

Places of Interest

E **Clacton Children's Zoo** Martello Tower, Marine Pde West ☎*28960*

F(1) **Dolphinarium** Clacton Pier ☎*20604*

St Osyth Priory St Osyth

Tourist Information

F[i] **Information Bureau** Marine Pde ☎*23400* (summer only)

B(2) **Amenities and Recreation Department** Town Hall ☎*25501*

Accommodation

The establishments listed below are a selection of AA-recommended accommodation located in the area covered by the Town Plan. Further information may be found in AA publications or obtained from Amenities and Recreation Department, Town Hall.

1Inn **Argyll Private Hotel** 8 Colne Rd ☎*233227*

2★★ **Royal** Marine Pde ☎*21215*

WEATHER CHART	Av hours of Sunshine in month	Hottest Av daily Temp °C
April	172	9
May	213	12
June	229	15
July	207	17
August	195	17
September	156	15

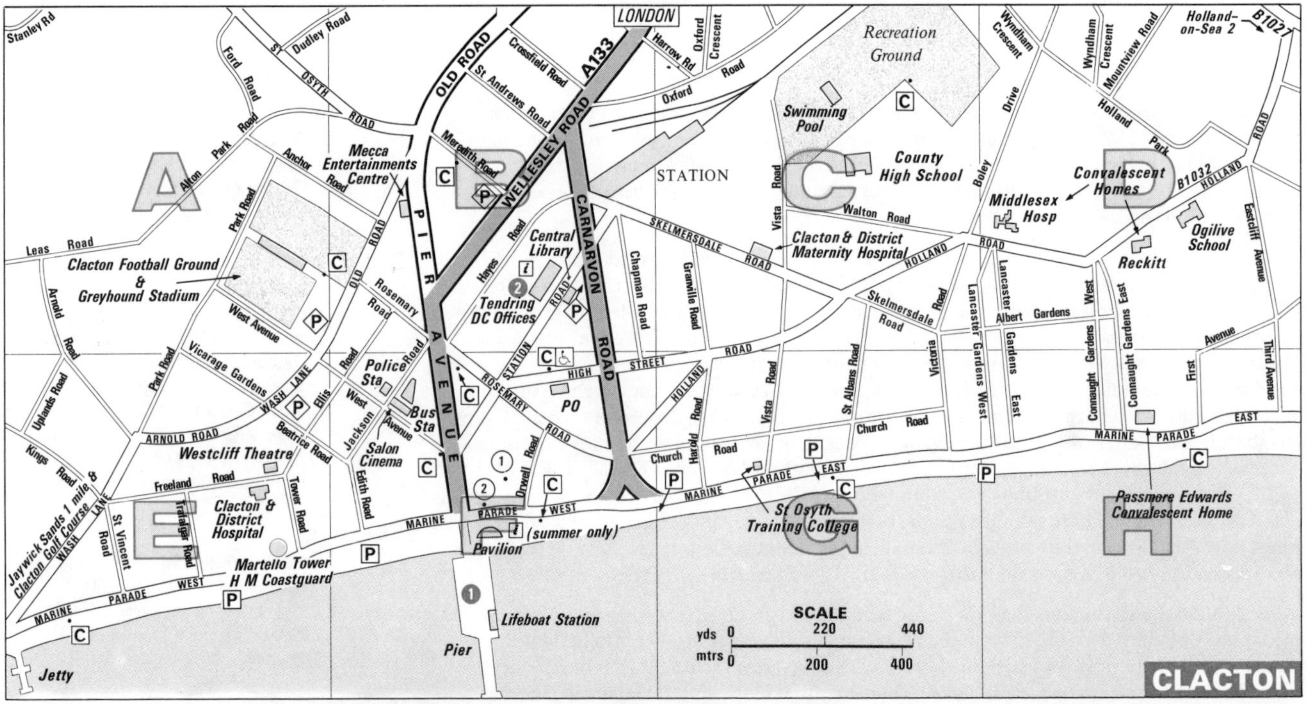

CLACTON
LONDON
A133
Holland-on-Sea 2
B1027
B1032
Recreation Ground
Swimming Pool
County High School
STATION
Mecca Entertainments Centre
Convalescent Homes
Middlesex Hosp
Ogilive School
Reckitt
Clacton & District Maternity Hospital
Central Library
Tendring DC Offices
Clacton Football Ground & Greyhound Stadium
Police Sta
Bus Sta
Salon Cinema
PO
Westcliff Theatre
Clacton & District Hospital
Martello Tower
H M Coastguard
Pavilion
(summer only)
Lifeboat Station
Pier
Jetty
St Osyth Training College
Passmore Edwards Convalescent Home
Jaywick Sands 1 mile & Clacton Golf Course
Stanley Rd
Dudley Road
Ford Road
St Osyth Road
Old Road
Crossfield Road
St Andrews Road
Wellesley Road
Carnarvon Road
Pier Avenue
Harrow Rd
Oxford Road
Oxford Crescent
Wyndham Crescent
Wyndham Crescent
Mountview Road
Holland Park
Holland Road
Alton Park Road
Anchor Road
Meredith Road
Park Road
Leas Road
Old Road
Rosemary Road
Hayes Road
Station Road
Skelmersdale Road
Walton Road
Vista Road
Boley Drive
Chapman Road
Granville Road
Lancaster Gardens West
Lancaster Gardens East
Albert Gardens
Connaught Gardens West
Connaught Gardens East
Eastcliff Avenue
First Avenue
Third Avenue
Arnold Road
West Avenue
Vicarage Gardens
Wash Lane
Ellis Road
West Avenue
Jackson Road
High Street
Holland Road
St Albans Road
Victoria Road
Uplands Road
Kings Road
Arnold Road
Beatrice Road
Edith Road
Orwell Road
Church Road
Harold Road
Freeland Road
Trafalgar Road
Tower Road
St Vincent Road
Marine Parade West
Marine Parade East
SCALE
yds 0 220 440
mtrs 0 200 400

SOUTHEND-ON-SEA

Southend began life as a Saxon settlement and became prominent as a holiday resort after Princess Charlotte of Wales stayed there during the first decade of the 19th century. Since then the town has become known as the 'Blackpool of the South Coast', its world-famous mile-long pier, colourful illuminations and jellied eel stalls attracting multitudes of visitors, particularly from the London area.

The beach is mainly sand and shingle but becomes muddy near the low-water mark, which can be as much as a mile from the shore. The most popular area of the sands is to the east of the pier at Thorpe Bay. The pier itself has a modern electric train running along its length and contains amusement arcades and a ten-pin bowling alley. Pleasure steamers run from the seaward end. A replica of Sir Francis Drake's *Golden Hind* stands at the pierhead near Peter Pan's Playground, a large funfair with a zoo and a pet's corner. On the promenade is the Kursaal Amusement Park with fairground rides and a banqueting hall and ballroom. Southend has a roller-skating and skateboard rink, located on the sea front, an indoor swimming pool and ample sports facilities. Pleasure flights operate from Southend Airport. The Cliffs Pavilion and Cliffs Bandstage provide family entertainment and the Palace Theatre presents plays of all kinds. Annual events include sailing regattas, bus rallies, Carnival Week in August, the Thames Barge Match and the Southend Festival in September. County cricket and league football are both played in the town and there is greyhound racing at Southend Stadium.

Southend offers the visitor excellent shopping facilities, so good, in fact, that many Continentals descend upon the town in search of bargains. A large market is held on the football ground on Thursdays and Saturdays. Places of interest include Prittlewell Priory, founded in 1110, now restored, 14th-century Southchurch Hall, and the Historic Aircraft Museum, near the Airport. Slightly further afield lie Rayleigh with its restored windmill and 11th-century castle remains, the ruined hill-top site of Hadleigh Castle, to which Catherine Parr was banished by Henry VIII, and the ancient market town of Rochford.

Recreation and Sports

J **Alexandra Road** – Bowls
Belfairs Golf Club Eastwood Rd North, Leigh-on-Sea ☎*520322*
I **Chalkwell Esplanade** – Bowls, putting – W on Western Pde
E **Chalkwell Park** – County cricket, tennis – W on London Rd
L **Eastern Esplanade** – Amusement arcades
G **Indoor Swimming Pool** Warrior Sq ☎*64445* – Heated pool, sauna, solarium
L **Kursaal Amusement Park**
K **Marine Parade** – Amusement arcades, boating lake, crazy-golf, roller skating and skateboard rink
K **Pavilion Lanes** ☎*63081* – Ten-pin bowling
K **Peter Pan's Playground** – Children's amusement park, go-karts, zoo
B **Priory Park** – Bowls, tennis – N off Victoria Ave
L **Southchurch Park** – Athletics, boating, bowls, tennis – NE off Beresford Rd
Southend Bowling Club Tunbridge Rd ☎*67073*
K **Southend Pier** – Amusements, electric railway, pleasure cruises
Southend-on-Sea Municipal Airport ☎*40201* – Pleasure flights
Southend-on-Sea Golf Club Eastwood Rd, Eastwood ☎*524836*
B **Southend Stadium** Grainger Rd ☎*68156* – Greyhound Racing – N off Milton St
B **Southend United FC** Roots Hall ☎*40707* – League Division III – NW off Victoria Ave
Thorpe Hall Golf Club Thorpe Hall Ave ☎*582050*
I **Westcliff Leisure Centre** Westcliff Pde ☎*353822*

Cinemas

J **ABC** Alexandra St ☎*44580*
A **Classic 1 and 2** London Rd ☎*42773*
F **Odeon 1 and 2** Elmer Approach ☎*44434*

Dancing

L **Kursaal Ballroom**
I **Cliffs Pavilion** Westcliff Pde ☎*351135* – W on Westcliff Pde
K **Quills** Marine Pde ☎*67305*
F **Scamps** Elmer Approach ☎*42882*
K **T.O.T.S.** Lucy Rd ☎*67921*
Zero 6 Aviation Way, Southend Airport ☎*546344*
B **Zhivagos** Victoria Circus ☎*611269*

Theatres

J **Cliffs Bandstand**
I **Cliffs Pavilion** Westcliff Pde ☎*351135* – W on Westcliff Pde
A **Palace Theatre** London Rd ☎*42564* – NW on London Rd

Places of Interest

I **Beecroft Art Gallery** Station Rd, Westcliff-on-Sea ☎*47418* – W off Westcliff Pde
K **Golden Hind** Marine Pde
Historic Aircraft Museum Aviation Way, Southend Airport
B **Prittlewell Priory Museum** Priory Pk – N off Victoria Av
L **Southchurch Hall** Southchurch Hall Cl
K **Waxworks Museum** Marine Pde

Tourist Information

J [i] **Information Bureau** Pier Hill ☎*44091*

Accommodation

The establishments listed below are a selection of AA-recommended accommodation in the area covered by the Town Plan.

1GH **Ferndown Hotel** 136 York Rd ☎*68614*
2GH **Gladstone** 40 Hartington Rd ☎*62776*
3GH **Terrace Hotel** 8 Royal Ter ☎*48143*
4GH **West Park Private Hotel** 11 Park Rd, Westcliff-on-Sea ☎*330729*

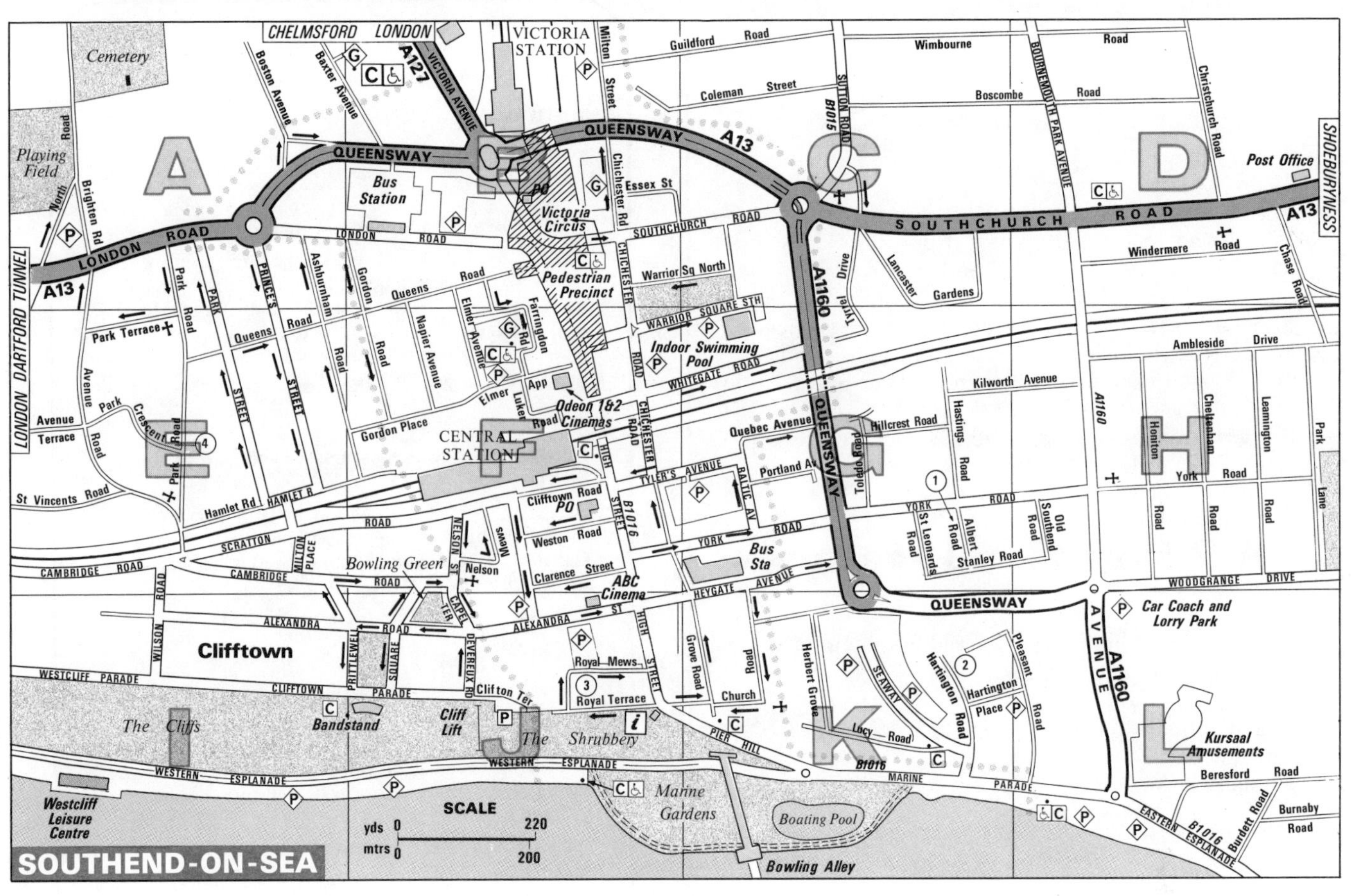

WEATHER CHART	Av hours of Sunshine in month	Hottest Av daily Temp °C
April	166	9
May	210	12
June	219	15
July	201	17
August	191	17
September	153	15

Other AA Guides to help you on your way . . .

Guesthouses, Farmhouses and Inns in Britain

Ref No. 55725. By the sea, on the farm or in the city. Low cost accommodation and modestly-priced meals in over 2,500 establishments, all AA-inspected for cleanliness, comfort, good food and hospitality. Over 50,000 copies sold last year.

Price £1.75 + 20p p&p (non-members £1.95)

Stately Homes, Museums, Castles and Gardens in Britain

Ref No. 55741. The ideal holiday book for day trips to all sorts of interesting places. Includes Abbeys, Art Galleries, Narrow Gauge Railways, Wildlife Parks, to name but a few.

Price £1.75 + 20p p&p (non-members £1.95)

Camping and Caravanning in Britain

Ref No. 55738. Comprehensive gazetteer of 1,000 sites in British Isles, inspected for quantity and quality of facilities. Feature on camping accessories and towing tips, plus country parks, nature trails and location atlas.

Price £1.75 + 20p p&p (non-members £1.95)

Hotels and Restaurants in Britain

Ref No. 55712. For business or pleasure, the definitive guide on where to eat, drink and stay. Over 5,000 AA-inspected hotels and restaurants plus town plans and location atlas.

Price £2.95 + 30p p&p (non-members £3.25)

Available to non-members from most good bookshops and to members from AA Service Centres or by post from AA Mail Order Dept, PO Box 50, Basingstoke, Hants, RG21 2EA.

INDEX

L

M

N

O

P

R

S

T

U

V

W

Y

Z